ISTANBUL

THE COLLECTED TRAVELER

ISTANBUL

THE COLLECTED TRAVELER

Collected by Barrie Kerper

An Inspired
Companion Guide

Vintage Departures
Vintage Books
A Division of Random House, Inc.
New York

A VINTAGE DEPARTURES ORIGINAL, SEPTEMBER 2009

Library of Congress Cataloging-in-Publication Data
Istanbul : an inspired companion guide / collected by Barrie Kerper.
      p.   cm.—(The collected traveler)
Includes bibliographical references.
ISBN 978–0-307–39059–2
1. Istanbul (Turkey)—Guidebooks.   2. Travelers' writings.   3. Istanbul (Turkey)—
Description and travel—Sources.   I. Kerper, Barrie.
DR718.I764 2009
914.961'8044—dc22
2009021982

Book design by Jo Anne Metsch

www.vintagebooks.com

Once again, to my mother, Phyllis,
who always believed my boxes of files
held something of value,
and to my father, Peter,
the most inspiring person in my life

CONTENTS

‿∞‿

CONTENTS   ix

The rich colors of the spectrum of Ottoman art, evocative of both a heavenly and an earthly Paradise, help to convey artistic messages that, while reflecting the religious and cultural complexities and subtleties of Ottoman civilization, at the same time speak to all of us in a clear and understandable artistic voice. The concept of "otherness," for all of the incredible suffering and destruction that it has caused when exploited in the political clashes of nations and cultures, is fortunately a very fragile one, whose hard and destructive edges erode very quickly once we familiarize ourselves with other cultures. The centuries-old artistic legacy of the Ottomans will always preserve the mystique of another time and another place, but their works of art still contain the power to move and fascinate us, whatever our culture, with the immediacy and freshness that enables all great art to overcome distance and years, cultures and beliefs. These artists and patrons were Ottomans of bygone ages, but they were also people just like us. What delighted, inspired, and moved them also delights, inspires, and moves us, putting interesting differences of time, space, culture, and language into their proper perspective against the enduring message of beautiful things.

—WALTER DENNY,
Iznik: The Artistry of Ottoman Ceramics

Istanbul may or may not be the world's most magnificent city, but it is certainly the most magnificently situated.

—STEPHEN KINZER,
*Crescent & Star: Turkey
Between Two Worlds*

It would be a dull visitor indeed who could not find, at certain times, in certain lights, a place in the city which did not whisper of "what is past, or passing, or to come." For Istanbul is still the Miklagard [Great City] of the Vikings, and still the Red Apple of the Turks. The handprint of the conqueror is still on its column, and the ruthless ambition of an empress is encapsulated in a mosaic. Yeats was right: many moments of greatness and decay reverberate across the modern city, built up by the voices of the living and the dead.

—JASON GOODWIN,
in the foreword to
Istanbul: Poetry of Place

INTRODUCTION

ೞ

Istanbul [is] like any great Imperial city a melting pot of
cultures, a homing ground for disparate peoples, a Tower
of Babel. Here Asia, the Transcaucasus, and the Balkans
meet, Tartary and Arabia converge, Black Sea and
Mediterranean types gather, Muslim, Christian, and Jew
pray, ancient and modern counterpoint.

—*Ateş Orga,*
Istanbul: Poetry of Place

THIS IS an exciting moment in history to visit Istanbul.
The United Nations has designated no fewer than nine
World Heritage sites in Turkey, and the European Union has chosen Istanbul to be a European Capital of Culture for 2010. If you
feel you may have an image of the city that is dusty and medieval,
you probably do, and it's outdated: an August 2005 cover story of
Newsweek proclaimed Istanbul "The Coolest City in the World";
Tyler Brûlé, founder of *Wallpaper*, was quoted in the May 2006
issue of *Australian Gourmet Traveller* saying that "Istanbul is the new
black. It's the new Barcelona and Turkey is now the emerging hot
spot for edgy food, cool design, and early adopters of premium
tourism that Spain was ten years ago"; Suzy Menkes, writing in
The International Herald Tribune in December 2006, noted that
"Istanbul, straddling East and West across the Bosphorus, is on the

cusp of change"; and three-Michelin-star chef Jean-Georges Von-gerichten opened an outpost of his Spice Market restaurant in Istanbul in 2008 in the swank new W Hotel. The *Wallpaper City Guide* to Istanbul enthuses that "some cities continue into the twenty-first century only as museum pieces or tourist traps—and in Istanbul, the impressively numerous sights and still more numerous carpet salesrooms fulfill both functions in one easily navigable crux—but Istanbul is a monster metropolis that never stands still (and that's not a coded reference to its seismic activity)."

On the other hand, those who think that modern Turkey has become too much like anywhere else are simply mistaken. Things *are* different in Turkey, as writer Anthony Weller noted in *European Travel & Life*: "Istanbul, which straddles the border between Europe and Asia, is schizophrenic; it cannot make up its many minds about anything. It is either the last noisy city in Europe or the first quiet town in Asia."

I admit that one of the reasons I initially wanted to visit Istanbul was due to my affection for that silly song, "Istanbul (Not Constantinople)," written by Jimmy Kennedy and Nat Simon and originally recorded by The Four Lads in 1953 for Columbia. (The fact that They Might Be Giants made it a hit again in 1990 was all the proof I needed that the song is catchy and endearing.) Some years later, I learned of an earlier song, "C-O-N-S-T-A-N-T-I-N-O-P-L-E," recorded by Paul Whiteman and Bing Crosby in 1928, which is even sillier. But I love them both, and for many years I couldn't imagine a more exotic city on earth.

Philip Mansel, in *Constantinople: City of the World's Desire*, relates that few people consistently used one name for the city.

Other names, spellings, epithets, and abbreviations have included Istanbul, Islambol, Stambul, Estambol, Kushta, Cons/ple, Gosdantnubolis, Tsarigrad, Rumiyya al-kubra, New Rome, New Jerusalem, the City of Pilgrimage, the City of Saints, the House of the Caliphate, the Throne of the Sultanate, the House of State, the Gate of Happiness, the Eye of the World, the Refuge of the Universe, Polis, and—simply—the City. It isn't difficult to find adjectives to describe Istanbul's beauty, uniqueness, and spirit.

Harder to describe are its inhabitants. You will surely find, as I did, repeatedly, that the Turks are among the kindest, friendliest, and most trustworthy people in the world. This is worth emphasizing, not only because just seeing the sights and not getting to know the people who created them leaves the visitor with half the insight and knowledge of a particular place, but because the Turks have been so misunderstood for so very long.

Nothing convinces like examples, so I will share a few: Godfrey Goodwin, in his autobiographical book *Life's Episodes: Discovering Ottoman Architecture*, relates a story about a time he and his wife were on a road somewhere in the middle of Turkey that was still meant for buffalo. The car jolted and died. He brought the car into a garage, and the next morning, he expected to be told that he would have to wait a day or two more for it to be fixed. "But not at all," he explains. "There was the car sparklingly polished and the tank filled. We were allowed to pay for the petrol but not for the two men who had worked all night on a wreck. 'Our road did the damage,' said the owner of the workshop. 'We had to put

it right.' Were all humanity like him, there would be no need of Paradise." My husband and I lost count of the times we left our bags at bus stations and shops for safekeeping, only to be told when we returned that no payment was necessary. And we remember well how a bus driver picked us up in Izmir and refused payment, saying only that we looked like we needed a ride so he was happy to give us one, and the guy who bought us coffee just because he wanted to talk to Americans and find out what we thought of Turkey. Lastly, Bill Penzey, founder of the excellent company Penzey's Spices (800 741 7787, penzeys.com, thirty-nine stores nationwide) related an experience he had in a taxi that he originally wrote about in his *Penzeys One* magazine:

> You can't be a good spice business without having really good bay leaves and really good oregano. We have found Turkey to be the best location for both of these, as well as Aleppo pepper. But this moment did not happen in the pepper fields or on the mountainous slopes outside of Izmir where the oregano and bay leaves grow. This moment happened in a taxi between Istanbul and Atatürk International Airport about a month after 9/11.
>
> . . . This ride started like so many—in silence. . . . The driver's English was not great, and my Turkish was non-existent, so communication was tough. He had studied to be an engineer in Germany and with my Wisconsin upbringing we were able to use a combination of a little English and a little German to get a conversation started. After a few minutes of small talk, he paused a moment and asked me where I was from. . . . Bad thoughts go through your head a month after 9/11 when someone who looks like he could be one of the terrorists' roommates from Frankfurt asks you where you are from. Still, I was not going to let my thoughts get the best of me, so I told him I was an American. I was watching his eyes in the rearview mirror and I saw a sadness come over him. . . . For him there was a deep sadness for the victims of the terrorists . . . for my driver

and many others I was surprised that they spoke of these deaths as though they were the deaths of their own family members. Their grief was immense, but coupled with their grief was anger. An anger that someone could have done this monstrous deed and then tried to say they did it for their religion. Over and over the driver said to me in English so I would not miss the point, that this was not Islam. . . .

Though this alone is a good story, it is not the moment that this tale is about . . . somewhere about three miles from the airport I must have been distracted by the taxi driver's words, thinking about what he had to say. While I was looking the other way, the driver reached over and turned off his meter and quickly restarted it. We got to the airport, I looked at the meter, and for what should have been a $16 fare, the meter read the Turkish equivalent of $1.85. . . . It is one thing to say you feel bad about what has happened; it is another thing to undercharge a random American by $15 to do something about it. Fifteen dollars is a lot of money in Turkey. We were standing there looking at each other and I was trying to figure out what to do. In the back of my mind was that old Harry Chapin song "Taxi." So I handed him the Turkish equivalent of $20 for a $1.85 fare and told him to keep the change. He tried to give me change; I would not take it. He shook my hand with more feeling than I had felt in a handshake in a long time. We walked away. Nothing in the world had really changed, but for the two of us it felt like it had. Turkey, it is a magical place.

Istanbul is an extraordinary city, filled with much that is old and plenty that is new. Asia Minor (or Anatolia, Greek for "east" or "the land of sunrise"), note Hugh and Nicole Pope in *Turkey Unveiled*, "is extraordinarily rich in ancient peoples. It bears some of the world's earliest traces of civilization. Like the architectural jumble of Istanbul, where buildings have been piling up on top of each other for millennia, the ethnic and historical origins of

Turkey's peoples are inextricably intertwined." The layers of history in Istanbul, combined with its vibrant pulse, ensure that to know the city well would take a lifetime. I hope that after reading this book, and traveling to Istanbul, you, too, will realize that, as Verity Campbell wrote in the *Lonely Planet Turkey* guide, "There simply is no other city like it."

ABOUT THIS BOOK

> A traveller without knowledge is a bird without wings.
>
> —SA'ADI, Persian poet,
> *Gulistan*

The Collected Traveler editions are meant to be companion volumes to guidebooks that go beyond the practical information that traditional guidebooks supply. Each individual volume is perfect to bring along, but each is also a sort of planning package—the books guide readers to many other sources, and they are sources of inspiration. James Pope-Hennessy, in his wonderful book *Aspects of Provence*, notes that "if one is to get the best value out of places visited, some skeletal knowledge of their history is necessary.... Sight-seeing is by no means the only object of a journey, but it is as unintelligent as it is lazy not to equip ourselves to understand the sights we see." Immerse yourself in a destination and you'll acquire a deeper understanding and appreciation of the place and the people who live there, and, not surprisingly, you'll have more fun.

This series promotes the strategy of staying longer within a smaller area so as to experience it more fully. Susan Allen Toth refers to this in one of her many wonderful books, *England as You Like It*, in which she subscribes to the "thumbprint theory of travel": spending at least a week in one spot no larger than her thumbprint covers on a large-scale map of England. She goes on to explain that excursions are encouraged, as long as they're about an hour's drive away.

I have discovered in my own travels that a week in one place, even a spot no bigger than my thumbprint, is rarely long enough to see and enjoy it all. For this reason, most of the books in *The Collected Traveler* series focus on either cities or regions, as opposed to entire countries. Though I did not plan to compile a book on all of Turkey, I am mindful that Turkey is a member of three communities: European, Mediterranean, and Asian. I have tried to reflect this wider world sense of community throughout the book.

The major portion of this book features a selection of articles and essays from various periodicals and recommended reading relevant to the theme of each section. The articles and books were chosen from my own files and home library, which I've maintained for over two decades. (I often feel I am the living embodiment of a comment that Samuel Johnson made in 1775, that "a man will turn over half a library to make one book.") The selected writings reflect the culture, politics, history, current social issues, religion, cuisine, and arts of the people you'll be visiting. They also represent the observations and opinions of a wide variety of novelists, travel writers, and journalists. These writers are typically authorities on Turkey or Istanbul, or both; they either live there (as permanent or part-time residents) or visit there often for business or pleasure. I'm very discriminating in seeking opinions and recommendations, and I am not interested in the remarks of unob-

servant wanderers. I am not implying that first-time visitors to Turkey have nothing noteworthy or interesting to share—they very often do, and are often very keen observers. Conversely, frequent travelers are very often jaded and apt to miss the finer details that make Turkey the exceptional place it is. I am interested in the opinions of people who want to *know* Istanbul, not just *see* it.

I've included numerous older articles because they were particularly well written, thought-provoking, or unique in some way, and because the authors' views stand as a valuable record of a certain time in history. Even after the passage of many years, you may share the emotions and opinions of the writer, and often you may realize that *plus ça change, plus c'est la même chose.* I have many, many more articles in my files than I was able to reprint here. Though there are a few pieces whose absence I very much regret, I believe the anthology you're holding is very comprehensive.

A word about the food and restaurant section, "The Turkish Table": I have great respect for restaurant reviewers, and though their work may seem glamorous—and it sometimes is—it is also very hard. It's an all-consuming, full-time job, and that is why I urge you to consult the very good cookbooks I recommend as well as guidebooks. Restaurant (and hotel) reviewers are, for the most part, professionals who have dined in hundreds of eating establishments (and spent hundreds of nights in hotels). They are far more capable of assessing the qualities and flaws of a place than I am. I don't always agree with every opinion of a reviewer, but I am far more inclined to defer to their opinion over someone who is unfamiliar with Turkish food in general, for example, or someone who doesn't dine out frequently enough to recognize what good restaurants have in common. My files are filled with restaurant reviews, and I could have included many more articles; but that would have been repetitive and ultimately beside the point. I have selected a few articles that give you a feel for eating out in Istanbul, alert you to some things to look for in selecting a truly worthwhile place versus a mediocre one, and highlight notable dishes from Turkey's surprisingly diverse cuisine.

The recommended reading for each section is one of the most important features of this book, and together they represent my favorite aspect of this series. (My annotations are, however, *much* shorter than I would prefer—did I mention that I love encyclopedias?—but they are still nothing less than enormously enthusiastic endorsements, and I encourage you to read as many of these as you can.) One reason I do not include many excerpts from books in my series is that I am not convinced an excerpt will always lead a reader to the book in question, and I think good books deserve to be read in their entirety. Art critic John Russell wrote an essay, in 1962, entitled "Pleasure in Reading," in which he stated, "Not for us today's selections, readers, digests, and anthologizings: only the Complete Edition will do." Years later, in 1986, he noted that "bibliographies make dull reading, some people say, but I have never found them so. They remind us, they prompt us, and they correct us. They double and treble as history, as biography, and as a freshet of surprises. They reveal the public self, the private self, and the buried self of the person commemorated. How should we not enjoy them, and be grateful to the devoted student who has done the compiling?" The section of a nonfiction book I always turn to first is the bibliography, as it is there that I learn something about the author who has done the compiling as well as about other notable books I know I will want to read.

Reading about travel in the days before transatlantic flights, I always marvel at the number of steamer trunks and the amount of baggage people were accustomed to taking. If I were traveling then, however, my trunks would be filled with books, not clothes. Although I travel light and seldom check bags, I have been known to fill an entire suitcase with books, secure in the knowledge that I could have them all with me for the duration of my trip. Each recommended reading section features titles I feel are the best available and most worth your time. I realize that "best" is subjective; readers will simply have to trust me that I have been extremely thorough in deciding which books to recommend. It disappoints me, however, that there are undoubtedly books with which I'm unfamiliar and that therefore do not appear here. I would be grateful to hear from you if a favorite of yours is missing. I have not hesitated to list out-of-print titles because some very excellent books are out of print (and deserve to be returned to print!), and because many of them can be easily found, through individuals who specialize in out-of-print books, booksellers, libraries, and online searches. I also believe the companion reading you bring along should be related in some way to where you're going, so these lists include fiction and poetry titles that feature characters or settings in Istanbul or Turkey or feature aspects of Turkey and the Turks.

Sprinkled throughout this book I have included the musings of a number of visitors to Istanbul—ranging from the best-selling writer Frances Mayes to noted chef Claudia Roden—briefly describing their most memorable sight or experience from their visits. I included some of my own family members in this group because, perhaps unusually, Istanbul has long been a favorite destination of ours.

An A to Z Miscellany appears at the end of the book. This is an alphabetical assemblage of information about words, phrases, foods, people, themes, and historical notes that are unique to Istanbul and Turkey. Will you learn of some nontouristy things to see and do? Yes. Will you also learn more about the better-known aspects of Istanbul? Yes. Topkapı Palace, the Blue Mosque, the Grand Bazaar, a sunset over the Bosphorus, a glass of *rakı*, a cup of *çay*, and making new friends at a *meyhane* are all equally representative of Istanbul. Seeing and doing them *all* is what makes for a memorable visit, and no one, by the way, should make you feel guilty for wanting to see some famous sites. They have become famous for a reason: they are really something to see, Topkapı and

Aya Sofya (Hagia Sophia) included. Canon number eighty-four in Bruce Northam's *Globetrotter Dogma* is "The good old days are now," in which he wisely reminds us that destinations are not ruined even though they may have been more "real" however many years ago. "'Tis a haughty condescension to insist that because a place has changed or lost its innocence that it's not worth visiting; change requalifies a destination. Your first time is your first time; virgin turf simply is. The moment you commit to a trip, there begins the search for adventure."

Ultimately, this is also the compendium of information that I wish I'd had between two covers years ago. I admit it isn't the "perfect" book; for that, I envision a waterproof jacket and pockets inside the front and back covers, pages and pages of accompanying maps, lots of blank pages for notes, a bookmark, mileage and size conversion charts . . . in other words, something so encyclopedic in both weight and size that no one would want to carry it, let alone read it. I envisioned such a large volume because I believe that to really get to know a place, to truly understand it in a nonsuperficial way, one must either live there or travel there again and again. It seems to me that it can take nothing short of a lifetime of studying and traveling to grasp Istanbul. I do not pretend to have completely grasped it now, many years later, nor do I pretend to have completely grasped the other destinations that are featured in *The Collected Traveler* series; but I am trying, by continuously reading, collecting, and traveling. And I presume readers like you are, too. That said, I am exceedingly happy with this edition, and I believe it will prove helpful in the anticipation of your upcoming journey, in the enjoyment of your trip while it's happening, and in the remembrance of it when you're back home.

Güle, güle! (Bon voyage, or "go with smiles!")

Turkey

When Turks meet friends in unexpected, remote locations they say, "The world is small." The saying has never been closer to the truth than at present times because, thanks to the advances in technology, the world is right in their sitting room every night. But while the Turks educate themselves as to the peculiarities of most nations, cultures, and lands, they still remain something of a mystery to the rest of the world, surrounded by a hazy cloud called the Orient. Turkish delight, carpets, towels, cigarettes, and coffee are all that most outsiders can associate with the country, yet beyond this parsimonious list one of the richest of cultures and the most welcoming of hosts lies, waiting to be discovered and appreciated.

—ARIN BAYRAKTAROĞLU,
Culture Shock! Turkey

In Turkey dreams come true, especially if they involve a glass of tea.

—TOM BROSNAHAN,
Turkey: Bright Sun, Strong Tea

It is customary to speak of westernization as having made Turkey two nations: one modern, the other primitive. But this suggests too neat a dichotomy. Most of the time, Turkey is modern *and* primitive. Simultaneously! Like the girl in the Moslem head scarf wearing a pair of designer glasses; or the old woman with a cordless phone sitting in a house so ancient, it seemed to be tottering.

—ERIC LAWLOR,
Looking for Osman

The Byzantine Empire
Rome of the East

MERLE SEVERY

ΩΩ

THE BYZANTINE civilization, centered on Constantinople, was a star that shone brightly during Europe's Dark Ages. The empire preserved the heritage of Greece and Rome and spread Christianity across a vast realm. After eleven centuries, it finally splintered, its many accomplishments falling in the shadow of the Italian Renaissance.

In this brilliantly detailed interpretive piece, Merle Severy takes an end-of-the-twentieth-century look at Byzantium's importance "as a buffer shielding medieval Europe from the empire-building Persians, Arabs, and Turks; as a bridge between ancient and modern times; as the creator and codifier of laws and religious, political, and social practices vibrant to this day." This essay, written in 1983, remains one of the most valued articles in my archive. It is one of the few pieces in which history is presented in a complete, wide-ranging circle.

As this piece originally appeared in *National Geographic*, it was naturally accompanied by some fantastic photographs and a beautiful, specially created map of the Byzantine world. I had wanted to include the map with this piece—it's made to look as if it were crafted into a mosaic—but as it was a foldout in the magazine, it would have been lost in a book of this size. Happily, the map was reproduced and enlarged and now hangs in the outer vestibule of Aya Sofya (Hagia Sophia), in Istanbul, just inside the main entrance.

MERLE SEVERY founded the National Geographic Society's book division and worked for the society for almost thirty-eight years. Another very good piece of his not included here, "The World of Süleyman the Magnificent," could be seen as a companion piece to this one, and I encourage readers to search for it (*National Geographic*, November 1987).

ON THE twenty-ninth of May in 1453—6,961 years after the creation of the world, by Byzantine reckoning; 1,123 years and 18 days after Constantine the Great dedicated his new Christian Rome on the Bosporus—Constantinople fell to the Turks. With it fell the heart of the Byzantine Empire that once ruled from the Caucasus to the Atlantic, from the Crimea to Sinai, from the Danube to the Sahara.

Yet 1453, a pivot on which ages turn, was a beginning as well. Just as the double-headed eagle, symbol of Byzantium and its spiritual heir, imperial Russia, looks both east and west, forward and backward in time, so Byzantine ways of government, laws, religious concepts, and ceremonial splendor continue to move our lives today.

Much of our classical heritage was transmitted by Byzantium. Its art affected medieval and modern art. Byzantines taught us how to set a large dome over a quadrangular space, gave us patterns of diplomacy and ceremony—even introduced forks. (An eleventh-century Byzantine princess brought these in marriage to a doge of Venice, shocking guests, just as her cousin, wed to a German emperor, scandalized his court by taking baths and wearing silk.)

"City of the world's desire," hub of the medieval universe, Constantinople bestrode a superbly defensible peninsula and sheltered harbor, the Golden Horn, at the crossroads of Europe and

Asia. Here in the legendary past Greek settlers named the place after their leader, Byzas. And Byzantium it also continued to be called, as well as the Eastern Roman Empire It ruled, until the Turks captured it in that fateful year, 1453, and later renamed it Istanbul.

To this day the city retains its fascination: the kaleidoscope of craft like water bugs on the Golden Horn, the cries of vendors in the labyrinthine covered bazaar, porters jackknifed under loads threading teeming alleys—the unpredictability of its life. Forget logic if you search a street address. Sit to sip tea by the seawall near Justinian's palace, and don't be surprised if a brown bear shags by with a gaggle of Gypsies.

Threading crowds of fervent Muslims boarding buses for the pilgrimage to Mecca, I entered Hagia Sophia, once the Church of the Holy Wisdom, Christendom's crowning glory. Fragmentary mosaics hint at the golden sheen that illumined the shrine. Light shafting through a corona of windows seems to levitate the giant ribbed dome. Let imagination fill the vast nave with worshipers, chanting clergy robed in brocade, incense swirling through a constellation of oil lamps toward that gilded dome suspended as if from heaven, and you will share Justinian's exultation. In 537 he beheld his masterwork complete: "Solomon, I have outdone thee!"

ɔɔɪɔɔɪɔɔɪ

Constantine and Justinian—these two emperors, both born in Serbia, set Byzantium on the path to greatness. Constantine's Christianization of the Roman Empire in the fourth century is one of history's mightiest revolutions. He chose a persecuted minority sect—an illegal, subversive intruder into the Roman state—and made it the cornerstone of a world-shaking power: Christendom.

His sainted mother, Helena, in her old age made a pilgrimage to the Holy Land. There, with a rapidity and assurance that can only strike wonder in the modern archaeologist, legend has it she unearthed the True Cross, the lance, and the crown of thorns and identified, under a temple of Aphrodite, the tomb of Christ. Over it her thrilled son ordered buildings to "surpass the most magnificent monuments any city possesses"—a decadelong labor now incorporated in Jerusalem's Church of the Holy Sepulchre.

Constantine himself presided over some 250 bishops assembled at Nicaea for the first of seven ecumenical, or universal, councils that forged the Orthodox faith. They formulated the familiar Nicene Creed ("I believe in one God, the Father Almighty, maker of heaven and earth . . ."). Those opposing the council's decrees were branded heretics.

Constantine gave Byzantium its spiritual focus. Justinian in the sixth century gave it its greatest temporal sway. Reconquering lands once Roman, he magnified his empire by founding or rebuilding cities, monasteries, and seven hundred fortifications. In the Balkans, the Levant, Italy, from the Euphrates to the Pillars of Hercules, I found impressive works. In Algeria, Tunisia, and Libya I strolled cities roofless to the North African sky. Triumphal arches, amphitheaters, baths, and grids of stone-paved streets lined with shops and town houses bespoke Roman origins. Justinian's fortresses and churches placed them in the Byzantine world. Some stand alone in an empty countryside.

In the Algerian-Tunisian frontier city of Tébessa (Byzantine Theveste), life pulses at the crossroads of a fertile belt of towns shielded from the Sahara by a crescent of the Atlas Mountains. Burnoosed men and veiled women, donkeys, and vehicles stream through a sculptured, porticoed Byzantine gate. Children clamber on Byzantine walls in whose shade old men sit and watch the passing parade, and women gossip.

But none of Justinian's cities matched the splendor of his Constantinople.

Medieval visitors from the rural West, where Rome had shrunk to a cow town, were struck dumb by this resplendent metropolis, home to half a million, its harbor crowded with vessels, its markets filled with silks, spices, furs, precious stones, perfumed woods, carved ivory, gold and silver, and enameled jewelry. "One could not believe there was so rich a city in all the world," reported the crusader Villehardouin.

The first Rome, on the Tiber, did not fall in 476, as schoolbooks often say; it withered away. No emperor died on its walls when it was sacked by Visigoths in 410, or by Vandals from Carthage in 455; emperors had long resided elsewhere. From the third century the course of empire had set eastward.

The Dark Ages are dark only if you look at Western Europe, for long centuries a backwater: decaying towns, isolated manors, scattered monasteries, squabbling robber barons. In the East blazed the light of Byzantium, studded with cities such as Thessalonica, Antioch, and Alexandria, more cosmopolitan than any Western society before the modern age.

While Charlemagne could barely scrawl his name and only clerics had clerical skills, many Byzantine emperors were scholars. Even laymen knew their Homer as they knew their Psalms. While men in the West for centuries tested guilt by ordeal—picking up a red-hot iron (you were innocent if you didn't burn your hand)—Justinian set scholars to compiling his famous Corpus Juris Civilis, the foundation of Roman law in continental Europe today. Via the Code Napoléon, Byzantine precepts were transmitted to Latin America, Quebec Province, and Louisiana, where they still hold sway.

Though the empire became officially Greek in speech soon after Justinian's day, people of the East still considered themselves Romans. (Westerners they called Latins or Franks, when they weren't calling them barbarians.) Their Emperor of the Romans was the legitimate heir of Augustus Caesar. Down to 1453 theirs was *the* Roman Empire. But it was the old pagan Roman world Christianized and turned upside down, the kingdom of heaven on earth.

ιϽϽϗϾϽϗϽϽϗ

Such was the Byzantine worldview: a God-centered realm, universal and eternal, with the emperor as God's vice-regent surrounded by an imperial entourage that reflected the heavenly hierarchy of angels, prophets, and apostles. One God, one world, one emperor. Outside this cosmos was only ignorance and war, a fury of barbarians. The emperor had a divine mandate to propagate the true faith and bring them under his dominion. Ceremony reinforced his role. His coronation procession moved through the Golden Gate along the Mese, the arcaded, shop-lined avenue leading through the Forum of Constantine and past the Hippodrome to the Augusteum, the main square with its gargantuan statue of Justinian on horseback gesturing eastward atop his pillar, and the Milion, the milestone where the routes of empire converged. Along the way a legitimate successor or victorious usurper transformed himself by a series of costume changes from a hero in gleaming armor to a robed personification of Christ. On Easter and at Christmas twelve courtiers symbolically gowned as the Apostles would accompany him in procession to worship in Hagia Sophia, the populace prostrating in adoration.

Ruling from his labyrinthine sacred palace, the emperor, crown and gown festooned with precious stones, invested his officials in silken robes and bestowed titles such as Excellency (used by ambassadors, governors, and Roman Catholic bishops today) and Magnificence (still used by rectors of German universities). Popes would adopt his tiara; England's monarchs, his orb and scepter; protocol officers, the order of precedence at imperial banquets.

The splendor of Byzantine ceremonial in rooms with doors of bronze and ceilings in gold and silver awed the foreigner, especially when a bit of mechanical wizardry was thrown in. Liudprand of Lombardy, on a diplomatic mission in 949, describes an imperial audience:

Golden lions guarding the throne "beat the ground with their tails and gave a dreadful roar with open mouth and quivering tongue." Bronze birds cried out from a gilded tree. "After I had three times made obeisance . . . with my face upon the ground, I lifted my head, and behold, the man whom just before I had seen sitting on a moderately elevated seat had now changed his raiment and was sitting at the level of the ceiling."

Beneath the glittering ritual we can perceive a prototype of today's bureaucratic state. A hierarchy of officials, including the custodian of the imperial inkstand, who readied the quill pen and red ink with which the emperor signed decrees, minutely supervised this "paradise of monopoly, privilege, and protectionism" that subordinated the individual's interest to the state's.

Constantinople organized its trades in tightly regulated guilds; controlled prices, wages, and rents; stockpiled wheat to offset poor harvests. Officials inspected shops; checked weights and measures, ledgers, quality of merchandise. Hoarders, smugglers, defrauders, counterfeiters, tax evaders faced severe punishment.

Unlike the West, trade or industry seldom bore a stigma. One empress distilled perfume in her palace bedroom. The emperor himself was the empire's leading merchant and manufacturer, with monopolies in minting, armaments, and Byzantium's renowned luxury articles. Justinian had founded its famed silk

industry with silkworm eggs smuggled into Constantinople. (Hitherto the empire had paid a pound of gold for a pound of Chinese silk.) Special brocades from imperial looms and other "prohibited articles" not for sale abroad made prestigious gifts for foreign princes.

Import, export, sales, purchase taxes, and shop rents swelled the imperial coffers (Basil II left 200,000 pounds of gold)—this at a time when the West more often bartered than bought. Nor were interest-bearing loans condemned as sinful; in the West they were, and this put moneylending into the scorned hands of Jews. Justinian set an 8 percent ceiling on interest—12 percent on maritime loans because of increased risk. (The borrower did not have to repay if ship or cargo was lost to storm or pirate.) Insurance and credit services were developed. Banking was closely audited. The gold solidus, the coin introduced by Constantine and later called bezant for Byzantium, held its value for seven centuries—history's most stable currency.

In the spirit "if any would not work, neither should he eat," the indigent were put to work in state bakeries and market gardens. "Idleness leads to crime," noted Emperor Leo III. And drunkenness to disorder and sedition—so taverns closed at eight.

God's state would protect the working girl: a fine of two pounds of gold for anyone who corrupted a woman employed in the imperial textile factories. Incest, homicide, privately making or selling purple cloth (reserved for royalty alone), or teaching shipbuilding to enemies might bring decapitation, impalement, hanging—or drowning in a sack with a hog, a cock, a viper, and an ape. The grocer who gave false measure lost his hand. Arsonists were burned.

The Byzantines came to favor mutilation as a humane substitute for the death penalty; the tongueless or slit-nosed sinner had time to repent. Class distinctions in law were abolished. Judges were paid salaries from the treasury instead of taking money from litigants, "for gifts and offerings blind the eyes of the wise."

"Men . . . should not shamelessly trample upon one another," observed Leo VI, the Wise Contractors had to replace faulty construction at their own cost. Housing codes forbade balconies less than ten feet from the facing house, storing noxious matter, or encroaching on a neighbor's light or sea view.

As solicitous for its subjects' welfare as it was in controlling their thoughts and deeds, the state provided much of the cradle-to-grave care expected by the Communist faithful today. Emperors and wealthy citizens vied in endowing hospitals, poorhouses, orphanages, homes for the blind or aged (where "the last days of man's earthly life might be peaceful, painless, and dignified"), homes for repentant prostitutes (some became saints), even a reformatory for fallen women aristocrats. Medical services included surgical and maternity wards, psychiatric clinics, and leprosariums. In contrast to the unwashed West, early Byzantium abounded in public baths. Street lighting made the nights safer.

A modern state in many ways. Passports were required for travel in frontier districts. Tourists can sympathize with Liudprand; he ran afoul of customs on his way out. From his baggage, officials confiscated prized cloths of purple silk.

⋊⋉⋊⋉⋊⋉

Sunrise burnished the gold of autumn leaves in the Balkan Mountains. A horse plowed a Bulgarian field where peasant women bent to their toil. My photographic colleague and I stopped our camper to capture the scene.

A police car pulled up. A policeman and a political official checked and recorded our documents. The official ordered us to strip our cameras. With no explanation, no heed to our anguished protests, he ground the cassettes under his heel, pulled out the film, and cast in the dirt our color record of the region's Byzantine churches.

The incident came as an unpleasant reminder that a harbinger of Eastern Europe's police states was Byzantium, suspicious of

foreigners and as chary about letting out information as it was
avid in gaining it.

State visitors were shown what officials wanted them to see. En
route to Constantinople a guard of honor kept them from deviat-
ing from the imperial post route. Assigned servants and inter-
preters learned as much as possible from the envoy's entourage.
Also, merchants were kept under surveillance. No alien might
trade or trespass beyond fairs held near the borders except in the
presence of an official. In the capital the prefect assigned them
separate compounds to curb spying—fur-clad Rus with drooping
mustaches; unkempt Bulgars belted with iron chains; Khazars and
Petchenegs from the steppes; merchants of Venice, Genoa, Pisa,
Amalfi, Lombardy, and Catalonia. If one overstayed his three-
month term, he was stripped of goods, whipped, and expelled.

How free was speech? How welcome criticism? One clue was
the name of the imperial council: Silentium. The historian Procopius extolled Justinian's military and building campaigns—on
the emperor's orders. He had to reserve his bitter personal opinions for a *Secret History*, "for neither could I elude the watchful-
ness of vast numbers of spies, nor escape a most cruel death, if I
were found out." Only at chariot races and other events in the
Hippodrome could the populace express discontent before the
emperor. Factions among the 60,000 spectators sometimes

exploded into riot. Justinian survived one attempted rebellion by drowning the Hippodrome in blood.

Behind the court's glittering facade lay perhaps "the most thoroughly base and despicable form that civilisation has yet assumed," fulminated a Victorian historian, William Lecky: "a monotonous story of the intrigues of priests, eunuchs, and women, of poisonings, of conspiracies, of uniform ingratitude, of perpetual fratricides."

Surrounded by would-be usurpers and assassins, no incompetent emperor remained God's vicar on earth very long. Of the eighty-eight emperors from Constantine I to XI, thirteen took to a monastery. Thirty others died violently—starved, poisoned, blinded, bludgeoned, strangled, stabbed, dismembered, decapitated. The skull of Nicephorus I ended up as a silver-lined goblet from which Khan Krum of the Bulgars toasted his boyars. The Empress Irene was so obsessed with retaining power that she had her son blinded and took his title of emperor. Even the sainted Constantine the Great had his eldest son slain and his wife suffocated in her bath.

Yet the empire, ringed with enemies, endured more than 1,100 years. Behind the silken glove of its diplomacy lay the mailed fist of its navy, sophisticated defenses, and small but highly trained army, based on a battering wedge of armored cavalry and mounted archers.

Proudly continuing Rome's iron discipline, the Byzantines now defended the empire as "champions and saviors of Christendom." On campaign they rose and slept to a round of prayers. Parading a most sacred relic—the Virgin's robe—around Constantinople's walls was credited with saving the "city guarded by God" from Rus attack in the ninth century. The Emperor Heraclius's ultimate triumph was not in crushing the millennial enemy, Persia, near Nineveh. Rather it was in recovering the True Cross looted by the Persians and returning it in person to Jerusalem in 630. What about that nasty reputation for duplicity and cowardice? The Byzantines weren't cowards. They neither romanticized war nor gloried in it as a sport. They studied it as a science and used it as a last resort if gold, flattery, and intrigue failed. Fire beacons and flag towers gave distant early warning. Ten centuries before Florence Nightingale set up field hospitals in the Crimean War, Byzantine medics got a bonus for each man they brought alive off the field of battle.

The fortified Crimea was the empire's listening post for the steppes, that invasion corridor for Huns, Slavs, Khazars, Magyar hordes "howling like wolves," and Bulgars born of that wild marriage of "wandering Scythian witches to the demons of the sands of Turkestan." Information also came from distant ports, naval patrols, envoys, merchants, spies, defectors. ("Never turn away freeman or slave, by day or night," counseled a tenth-century officer.) Collating this intelligence, the Bureau of Barbarians—Constantinople's CIA—analyzed strengths and weaknesses of each nation, calculated the price of each prince, determined when to unleash a pretender to spark rebellion.

If fight they must, Byzantines bet on brains over brawn. Military manuals stressed mobility, scouting, surprise. Immobilize an invader by capturing his baggage, food, and mounts while grazing. Scorch the earth, block the springs. Don't join an action unless strategy, numbers, and odds are in your favor. "God ever loves to help men in dangers which are necessary, not in those they choose for themselves," explained Justinian's famed general, Belisarius.

If things got desperate, the Byzantines unmasked their ultimate weapon: Greek fire. Volatile petroleum, preheated under pressure, was projected through a flamethrower, incinerating ships and crews. It even spread fire on the water, turning a foe's fleet into a raging inferno. This Byzantine A-bomb broke five years of naval assaults on Constantinople in the late seventh century and a year-long siege in the early eighth, changing history by stopping the Arabs at Europe's doorstep. And when, two centuries later, Rus flotillas swept into the Bosporus, Byzantines sent them reeling with "lightning from heaven," in the words of Prince Igor's defeated force.

I came to a place named Ohrid in today's Yugoslavia—a peaceful town, its red-tiled roofs shouldering down a peninsula to a Macedonian lake backed by the stern mountains of forbidden Albania. A fishermen's church stands on the promontory, high-cheekboned saints staring out of their halos with large black Byzantine eyes. Ohrid a thousand years ago was the capital of a Bulgarian empire whose Tsar Samuel had triumphed from the Black Sea to the Adriatic. But in Byzantine emperor Basil II, Samuel found his nemesis.

For decades their campaigns seesawed through the Balkans with ghastly carnage. Samuel, slippery as a Lake Ohrid eel, finally set a trap for Basil in a gorge along the upper Struma. Eluding it, Basil pinned Samuel's entire army there. Now he would teach the tsar a lesson in Byzantine revenge.

Descending at dusk from Samuel's citadel, which still crowns the peninsula at Ohrid, I joined the stream of parents, children, and lovers promenading in the main street. Dark eyes flashed, teasing in courtship; restless eyes scanned, recognized, questioned, eyes gazing boldly, eyes falling shyly.

A shudder shot through me when I

thought of another procession. Basil blinded the 15,000 prisoners, sparing one in a hundred to lead the macabre march home. Samuel watched in horror the return of his once proud army, eye sockets vacant, shuffling, stumbling, clutching one another, each hundred led by a one-eyed soldier. The sight killed him. And his empire too—swallowed by Byzantium. Basil the Bulgarslayer was one name Bulgarians would not forget.

Awesome magnificence and diplomatic cunning, military might, terror—more effective than these were Byzantium's missionaries. The Orthodox faith forged unity out of a diversity of nations. It brought the Slavs into the Byzantine universe.

The "apostles of the Slavs," ninth-century Cyril and Methodius of Thessalonica, invented an alphabet in which the newly converted Slavs first learned to write. Their script, and the Greek-based Cyrillic that soon supplanted it, conveyed Byzantine liturgy and learning to the Balkans, then to Russia, molding their thoughts, giving them brotherhood in faith and a Slavonic literary language, the Latin of the East.

"Civilizing the Slavs was Byzantium's most enduring gift to the world," Harvard professor Ihor Ševčenko told me. Among the consequences, Kievan Russia emerged from pagan isolation to join the European political and cultural community. Byzantium was Russia's gateway to Europe.

In Kiev, Professor Andrei Bielecki told me how Vladimir, prince in that Mother of Russian Cities, shopped about for a religion for his people. He sampled the Hebrew, Latin, and Islamic faiths. Fond of women, he favored the Muslim promise after death of fulfillment of carnal desires. But alas, no wine. "Drinking is the joy of the Rus," a chronicle has him say.

So he sent emissaries to Constantinople. Inspired by the resplendent liturgy in Hagia Sophia, they "knew not whether we were in heaven or on earth. For on earth there is no such splendor. . . . We only know that God dwells there among men."

Whereupon Vladimir had his people, on pain of the sword, baptized in the Dnieper.

Out of the wreckage of the Mongol empire, princes of Muscovy climbed to power, golden domes and crosses gleaming above the red-brick walls of their Kremlin. Cossacks, fur traders, missionaries spread across Siberia.

At Sitka, on snow-peaked Baranof Island in Alaska, the icons, incense, and chanting in onion-domed St. Michael's Cathedral serve as reminders that in the eighteenth century the faith of Byzantium came across the Bering Sea to its fourth continent: Russian America. Here I joined a Tlingit congregation worshiping with an Aleut priest—a ritual like that I had witnessed in Justinian's monastery of St. Catherine in Sinai.

"We change very little," Father Eugene Bourdukofsky said as he proudly showed me an icon, the Virgin of Sitka. "That is the essence of Orthodoxy, the true faith."

To change or not to change. Here was a key to understanding the chasm that divides the thought world of Byzantium—and eastern Europe—from the West. The West transformed itself through the Renaissance, Reformation, Enlightenment, and the rise of science into a dynamic society enshrining the individual and progress through free inquiry and experiment. The East, until the eighteenth century, remained essentially static. Byzantine thought sees its world not in process; it has arrived, its eternal order God-ordained.

The Byzantine mind transformed the classical Greek word *to innovate* into *to injure*. In a monarch, a penchant for innovation is disastrous, Procopius insisted, for where there is innovation, there is no security. In a subject, deviation is not only heresy but also a crime against the state. So threatening was change that ritual reforms in seventeenth-century Russia split the church. Old

moned the animals into the ark with such a resonant wooden plank and mallet, I had been told. Now it called the faithful into the spiritual ark, the church, to save them from the deluge of sin.

In Stavroniketa's church, under the brazen eagles of Byzantium agleam in chandelier coronas, I stood absorbed by the symphony of motion—monks bowing, prostrating themselves, making rounds to kiss the icons, lighting and snuffing candles, swinging the smoking censer, reading and singing antiphonally, raising voices in fervent prayer. The frescoed church itself mirrored the cosmos, martyrs and saints and angelic hosts rising in a scale of sanctity toward the symbolic vault of heaven where a stern Pantocrator, the almighty Christ, looks down disturbingly into the depth of one's soul.

To relax my limbs, I shifted position.

"*Hissssssssssssss!*"

I had clasped my hands improperly. As the hours wore on, if anyone made a false move or kissed an icon in the wrong order, a hiss signaled instant correction.

Back in our guest cell near dawn, my cellmate, an American anthropologist, whispered, "Reminds me of the military. The Benedictines in France are the infantry; the Franciscans in Italy, the air force, free and easy. These Orthodox monks are the marines—a crack outfit of shock troops under a tough master sergeant. No sloppiness here."

As I topped a shoulder of the 6,670-foot Holy Mountain, wincing at each sharp penitential stone in the steep path, I found monks building a wall. A decade earlier dilapidated Philotheou Monastery had seven graybeards. I counted ten times that many monks, beards as black as their robes.

Father Nikon, the young *archontaris*, or guestmaster, radiated inner peace and joy as he offered me the ritual brandy, coffee, gummy sweet *lokum*, and water, then showed me to a neat guest room near a flower-lined balcony over the courtyard. "People come to us troubled," Father Nikon said. "A day or two in the monastery brings peace, and they leave refreshed."

On Athos, even meals are a continuation of worship. A bell clangs in the courtyard. The monks file in, stand silently at long tables until the abbot blesses the food. After a communal prayer, all sit, and eat swiftly under the eyes of frescoed saints lining the refectory walls while a monk at the lectern reads from a saint's life. A bell tinkles. He returns the book to its niche, kneels to kiss the abbot's hand, receives his blessing. Then all file out silently. After Vespers, the monastery gates swing shut and everyone turns in, soon to rise for the night's round of prayers, for the first hour of the Byzantine day begins with sunset.

"Lord Jesus Christ, have mercy on me." Pinpoints of lamplight in the cells silhouette monks in ceaseless prayers of repentance. Four hours of solitary prayer before the call to four hours of communal prayer. Bread and tea, a snatch of sleep, and then silent prayer continues as the monk goes about his daytime tasks, in the kitchen, garden, at manual labor.

One moonlit night at Dionysiou Monastery a howling wind rattled the window of my cell. Dawn disclosed gray clouds beetling the brow of the Holy Mountain, and the face of the sea furrowed in anger. Below, waves slammed over the landing. No mail boat today. To get to Gregoriou, next monastery along the coast, meant going by foot.

"It's a very dangerous path," cautioned Father Euthymios as we set out together. The gangling New York–born Vietnam veteran was coming from the "desert," hermitages farther out on the peninsula, where he paints icons. "Part of it is along a causeway swept by the sea." Then came an afterthought of small comfort: "Darius lost his fleet here in such a storm." Three hundred of the Persian king's ships and 20,000 men dashed on the rocks of Athos in 491 BC.

Pausing on a crest, buffeted by a devil of a wind, Father

Euthymios said, "I always fear this next stretch. It's along a cliff with a straight drop to the sea. But with God's grace we will make it." We did. And next day we again tempted fate. The storm roared unabated. Winds clutched at us as we climbed and descended ravines, bone weary, wet through. Breakers roared as we leaped from rock to slippery rock at the base of sea cliffs. Too close.

If you must wait out an Athos storm, you will find no more dramatic haven than Simonopetra, high on a spur above the Aegean. It opens its dovecote of cells onto tiers of rickety balconies propped by aged beams. To walk along 108 feet over the sea in a storm is an act of faith. Clutching the splintery rail, stepping over a gap in the floor planks, I looked down mesmerized at walls of water battering walls of rock.

Next day Simonopetra no longer shook. The wind had lost its howl; the sea was flattening its crests. No more dodging waves. I had been lucky. Not so that boy who looked like my son. As he leaped across the rocks, a wave swept him away before his father's eyes. When the boats ran again, they found his body and brought it in from the sea.

ιοσιοσιοσι

The year 1071 was a bad one for the Byzantines, East and West. At Manzikert, in the highlands of eastern Turkey, the multinational Byzantine Army, riven by dissensions and desertions and for once sloppy in reconnaissance, was annihilated by the invading Seljuk Turks it had marched east to destroy. Anatolia, breadbasket and prime recruiting ground for Byzantium, subsequently was stripped forever from Christendom, opening the way to later Ottoman invasions of Europe.

In Bari, port city in southeastern Italy, I saw blood on the pavement. Assassins had gunned down a political opponent, and grieving partisans marched around the stain in bitter memorial. Nine centuries earlier blood had flowed in the streets of Byzantine Bari, sacked by the Normans after a three-year siege. Five years after the Battle of Hastings in England, the Normans had conquered southern Italy.

The year 1204 was even worse. On April 13 Fourth Crusaders en route to Jerusalem committed what historian Sir Steven Runciman called "the greatest crime in history"—the Christian sack of Constantinople. Burning, pillaging, raping, the crusaders looted what they didn't destroy to enrich Venice, Paris, Turin, and other Western centers with "every choicest thing found upon the earth." (They even brought back *two* heads of John the Baptist, so rich was Constantinople in relics.)

When, after fifty-seven years, a Byzantine emperor once again reigned in Constantinople, the Universal Empire was but a large head on a shrunken body. The Venetians and Genoese had a stranglehold on its trade. Franks still held territory. Trebizond ruled an independent empire on the Black Sea. Byzantine princes had set up their own power centers in Greece. Byzantium was soon pressed between the Ottoman Turks and the Serbs.

Crossing the Dardanelles, the Turks first settled in Europe at Gallipoli in 1354. A year later, with Serbian power at its peak, Stephen Dushan, who had proclaimed himself emperor of Serbs and Greeks, made his bid for Constantinople. Death robbed him of a chance to sit on Byzantium's throne, but the Serbs never forgot the common Balkan dream of conquering Constantinople. Nor will they ever forget the collision three decades later with the Turks.

༠༠༦༠༠༦༠༠༦

In the mists of morning rolling over brown-tilled earth at Kosovo in Yugoslavia, I peopled that "field of the blackbirds" with Turks and Serbs locked in battle. A physical defeat, it was yet a moral victory the Serbs celebrate to this day. Folk legend and epics extolling Serb bravery fed the fires of nationalism during the five centuries the Serbs suffered the Turkish yoke. Kosovo: June 28, 1389. How

Constantinople. Ancient Trebizond, where Xenophon's 10,000 Greek soldiers exulted to reach the Black Sea. Fabled Trebizond, where caravans brought riches of Persia and China, and monarchs sought the beauty of its Byzantine princesses. Noonday Trebizond, where phalanxes of schoolchildren in black smocks pour out onto cobbled streets teeming with colorfully garbed women and turbaned merchants hawking fish, hot chestnuts, and fruit.

Eight hundred feet over a foaming mountain stream I had climbed to a great monastery that seemed to cling to the towering rock wall by faith alone. Founded even before the age of Justinian, Soumela in the later Middle Ages was one of the richest monastic establishments in the East. I found it gutted, blackened by fire. Since 1923 no chant of Greek liturgy has sounded in that solitude, as it still does in the western mountains and valleys of Cyprus, where achingly empty Turkish villages tell of another more recent transfer of populations. These have lessened the danger from fifth columns but have done nothing to allay the hatred that has poisoned relations between Greek and Turk.

There on Cyprus I saw barbed wire and military checkpoints in the divided capital city of Nicosia, and white-painted UN tanks patrolling the advance lines of the Turkish Army, which had invaded in response to a Greek overthrow of the island republic. This 1974 coup brought to mind the *Megali Ithea*—the Great Idea—that fired the Greek imagination for generations: reconquest of Constantinople and the Byzantine Empire.

"For Greeks there is only one city. *The* City—Constantinople," the widow of a Greek Army officer told me in Thessalonica. "Even the Turkish name 'Istanbul' comes from the Greek *eis teen polis*—'in the city.' " Her sentiments echoed nineteenth-century patriots: "Our capital is Constantinople. Our national temple is Hagia Sophia, for nine hundred years the glory of Christendom. The Patriarch of Constantinople is our spiritual leader." In cherished legend a priest bearing the chalice, interrupted in the last liturgy in Hagia Sophia, will emerge to complete the service when the shrine is again Christian.

The Greek dream, however, collided with Balkan dreams of imperial glory. The sultan fanned endemic hatreds by classing all his Orthodox subjects—whether Serb or Bulgar, Greek or Albanian or Romanian—as the *Rum Milleti*, the Roman people, and putting them under the civil as well as ecclesiastical control of the Greek Patriarch of Constantinople. Patriarchs adopted the eagle symbol, ceremonies, dress, and functions of a Byzantine emperor and set their Greek bishops to hellenizing the proud Balkan peoples.

In the 1820s Greece rose against the Ottoman overlord; in 1830 it was the first Balkan nation to break free. But many more Greeks lived outside the new kingdom than in it. With *énosis*—union—with Greece the battle cry, the modern map of Greece was assembled piece by piece, escalating the hatred of her neighbors, who watched with cannibal eyes and devoured one another in two Balkan Wars.

Then Sarajevo . . . 1914. Today it is a market city tucked amid the stern Bosnian mountains of Yugoslavia, where minarets of nearly eighty mosques thrust like rockets above Orthodox and Catholic churches, and men in fezzes and women in veils and baggy trousers thread a booth-lined bazaar. Near this crossroad of cultures Emperor Theodosius the Great in 395 ran the line dividing the unwieldy Roman Empire administratively into East and West. Here, by the embanked Miljacka River, a pistol shot split the world when a Serbian student assassinated the heir to the Austro-Hungarian Empire, which had annexed lands once Serbian. Austria, backed by Germany, determined to crush Serbia. "Holy Russia" came to the aid of her Slavic Orthodox brother. And interlocking alliances swept Europe's nations into a war that claimed ten million lives.

Greece, entering that holocaust with the prospect of Turkish territory, at war's end occupied ancient Smyrna (today palm-shaded Izmir ringing its spacious Aegean harbor). Then, with defeated Turkey in revolt and the sultanate toppling, the Greeks saw their big chance. But their invasion deep into Asia Minor, hurled back, perished in the carnage of Smyrna and the mass exodus that ensued.

In Istanbul's Rum Patrikhanesi, a garden of peace amid the city's clamor and squalor, stands the eighteenth-century terra-cotta basilica of St. George and the modest residence and offices of the spiritual leader of the Orthodox faithful throughout the world. His All Holiness, Dimitrios, "by the Grace of God, Archbishop of Constantinople, New Rome, and Ecumenical Patriarch," rose from his desk and took my hand warmly in both of his.

The patriarch told me he sees as his role the promotion of understanding and harmony among "sister" Orthodox Churches. Many separated from Constantinople's fold when their nations broke free of the Turks.

More than 70 percent of the baptized Orthodox today dwell in Communist countries. Churches in exile abound. The national churches of Serbia, Bulgaria, Romania, and Russia are auto-cephalous (self-headed), with their own patriarchs. But the Ecumenical Patriarch is *primus inter pares*—first among equals—and his spiritual sway extends far beyond the confines of his church in Istanbul, which he heads as a Turkish citizen.

With a dwindling flock, stripped of the last vestige of civil authority, even forbidden to proselytize in his few Turkish parishes, why does he remain in a Muslim city? The Archbishop of Constantinople became head of the Byzantine Church because of his special position at the capital of the empire, he said. He is bound to this historic see.

On my way out I paused by the patriarchate's central gate, painted black and welded shut. Here a patriarch was hanged for treason when the War of Greek Independence broke out in 1821. As I stepped into the teeming streets where a priest is forbidden to wear his clerical garb, I thought back on the fallen glories of Byzantium's great church, still claiming universal dominion, still clinging in the City of Constantine.

God had punished the Greeks, Russians piously observed in 1453 when the Turks took Constantinople. For betraying their faith by submitting to Rome, He withdrew His protection, and their empire fell. Now Moscow moved from the periphery to the center of the Orthodox world, shining in the purity of her faith. "Two Romes have fallen. A third stands fast. A fourth there cannot be," ran the monkly prophecy.

Rising from medieval isolation in Russia's forested northern plains, Muscovy shook off the Mongol yoke that had crushed Kiev, overcame Novgorod and other fur-trading rivals, and pushed back Catholic Lithuanians and Poles. Ringed by enemies of her faith, xenophobic Moscow raised onion-domed churches and monasteries in forest clearings all the way to the inhospitable shores of the White Sea and fiercely clung to traditional rites.

Ivan the Great married Sophia Paleologos, niece of the last Byzantine emperor, and adopted the Byzantine double-headed

Riot broke out in Bethlehem's Church of the Nativity. Several
Orthodox monks were killed. Tsar Nicholas, accusing the Turkish police of complicity, reasserted his claim that he was protector
of the sultan's Orthodox Christian subjects, invaded Turkey's
Danubian provinces, ordered his ships to sea, and sank a Turkish
fleet in port. The specter of Russia cutting the England-to-India
lifeline soon brought Britain into the war, a war which ended seventeen months later with the fall of Sevastopol.

"Now it's Russian against Russian in Jerusalem," Uziely went
on. "The Soviets against the émigré Russians. They've been battling in Israeli courts for years. At stake are millions of dollars of
ecclesiastical properties in Israel."

In 1948 the new State of Israel, desperate for diplomatic recog-
nition, acceded to the Soviet demand that all Russian religious
holdings in Israel be turned over to its Orthodox Church in
Moscow—despite their belonging to the Russian Orthodox
Church Outside of Russia, now headquartered in New York
City. The crowning irony: after the Six Day War in 1967, the
Soviet Union severed relations with Israel.

ɩɔɔɪɔɔɪɔɔɔ

It is the eve of Easter in Jerusalem—Easter by the Orthodox calendar. From early morning, pilgrims have filled the Church of
the Holy Sepulchre for the ceremony of the holy fire, to me the
most exalting ritual of the Eastern churches.

Squeezed against a parapet amid that press of humanity, I watch
black-clad women kneel to spread oil on the Stone of Unction,
said to be the slab on which the body of Jesus was anointed, and
press their weeping faces against it.

The thump of maces and rhythmic clapping and chanting draw
my eyes to phalanxes of the faithful slowly moving around
Christ's tomb in the center of the rotunda. In the banners and
gleaming vestments I see Byzantium pass in review: skull-capped
Syrians, Armenians in pointed hoods, turbaned Copts of Alexan-

dria, Greek Orthodox in cylindrical hats and robes of gold and crimson and black.

Thrice circling the tomb in solemn procession, the Greek Orthodox Patriarch of Jerusalem pauses at its entry. He steps inside. The clamor in the rotunda fades to silence. The church is dark, the tension electric.

Suddenly I see a lighted taper thrust from the tomb—the holy fire, symbolizing Christ rising from the dead. Flames leap from taper to taper until the darkness is punctured by a thousand fiery holes. Tower bells thunder, shaking the very walls. Cries rise in a multitude of throats as the splintered churches of Byzantium coalesce into a single mass of believers celebrating the Resurrection.

"He is risen!" Through faith in this miracle, Byzantium lives.

"This is the most mysterious city on earth. I love the houses along the Bosphorus, the dervishes, Orhan Pamuk's *Istanbul*, the fortune-teller who told a truth, the raucous greetings of the rug merchants ("I can take your money!"), and the fantastic Topkapı complex that looks like an ideal liberal arts college. But most of all I love the strange call of the muezzin, especially when it splits the air between dark and dawn. The voice begins with a drone, a wobbly shriek, then works up to intensity. It's old, old, primitive—it sounds like something pulled up from a deep fissure. Sometimes it sounds like an otherworldly cry from beyond, sometimes like sawing through cellophane. When I wake up hearing that call, I always get a delicious flash, *I am somewhere very far from home.*"

—Frances Mayes, author of *A Year in the World: Journeys of a Passionate Traveller* (2007) and *Under the Tuscan Sun* (1997), among others

Turkish Delights

NORMAN KOTKER

ဣ

READERS OF my previous books know that I'm a huge fan of *Horizon*, now defunct, sadly. *Horizon* magazine was published in a beautiful hardcover format and featured outstanding articles, and would probably never survive if it were published today. (I have quite a collection now, my biggest cache obtained in a single swipe: my husband and I were house-hunting, and as we left one appointment, I noticed that the owners had thrown out a huge box of the magazines. It was raining and I couldn't bear to see those copies ruined, so to my husband's great embarrassment, I grabbed piles and piles of them and threw them into the backseat of the car. He still doesn't understand why they mean so much to me, but they are a prized possession.)

"Turkish Delights" was published in 1966, when an exhibit entitled Art Treasures of Turkey toured ten American cities. The exhibit was arranged by the Smithsonian Institution Traveling Exhibition Service after years of negotiations with the Turkish government. Many of the loans were from the Topkapı Palace and included works from the Late Stone Age and the Hittite, Greek, Roman, Byzantine, Seljuk Turkish, and Ottoman periods. A caption in the original *Horizon* piece referenced a companion book entitled *Treasures of Turkey*, by Swiss publisher Skira. I was curious to see if the book was still available, and a search on Abebooks .com revealed it was—and it's a gorgeous book: an oversize cloth-bound hardcover, 254 pages, with color and black-and-white inlay illustrations. Scholars from three nations, including Richard

Ettinghausen, an American authority on Turkish art, collaborated on the text. Like *Horizon*, it's the kind of book no one would dare to publish these days because it would be prohibitively expensive.

NORMAN KOTKER contributed a number of pieces to *Horizon* as well as to other newspapers and magazines, including *Military History Quarterly*. He was also the author of *The Earthly Jerusalem* (Scribner, 1969) and two other novels. He passed away in 1999.

IT IS against the law of Islam for anyone to paint a portrait. On the Day of Judgment, the prophet Mohammed is reported to have said, painters will be doomed to hell for their blasphemous attempts to compete with God by creating life. If the religious laws were practiced as much as they were preached, Moslem artists would never have represented any living thing. Yet the Moslems did develop splendid schools of portraiture and historical painting, for they have been no more noted for strict obedience to religious laws than members of other faiths have been. Over the centuries Islamic artists have painted pictures of dervishes, sultans, and saints, subjects from the Koran, the Bible, and Arab and Persian legends, and vignettes of everyday life, from women in childbirth to street sweepers at work. Palace walls were decorated with hunting scenes, or portraits of conquered kings, or dancing girls, and, in one case, even a representation of a Christian church, complete with praying monks. The Ottoman sultans of Turkey were in the forefront of Islamic society in their patronage of art, commissioning numerous portraits of themselves, their favorites, and their families. But this work was, often as not, done in secret, to keep the sultan's subjects from discovering that he was breaking the religious law. Despite the secrecy, the

Ottoman style of portraiture and miniature painting evolved into a distinctive and sophisticated art form, as splendid in its own way as Ottoman architecture, which is seen in so many beautiful mosques throughout Turkey and is usually considered the noblest accomplishment of Turkish art.

It was not until the eleventh century AD that the Turks themselves began migrating into the country. Their original home was in central Asia, where they were nomadic horsemen roaming the steppes. Even in that quarter of the world—seemingly so remote—the Turks were subject to the influence of the great centers of world civilization. Caravans made their way across the vast Asiatic plains, bringing Greek and Roman coins, silverwork and goldwork from Persia, and paintings and silks from China. At the same time, the Turks ranged widely over the steppes; remains of their own ancient art—showing these strong and varied foreign influences—are found throughout regions of Asiatic Russia, in Outer Mongolia and Afghanistan, and in the part of China that today is called Sinkiang, although it was formerly known as Eastern Turkestan.

By the end of the seventh century the Turkish tribesmen were in contact with the Arabs, whose armies had penetrated as far as the Turkish towns of Bukhara and Samarkand. The Arabs found the Turks to be formidable warriors, and soon the palace guard of the Arab caliphs at Baghdad was composed of Turkish mercenaries. From being the caliph's servants, they became his masters. By the ninth century the Seljuk Turks—tribesmen whose chieftains claimed descent from an ancestral hero named Seljuk—had made the caliph into a figurehead. In 1055 they took over most of the great Arab empire for themselves; a few years later, in 1071, they defeated the emperor of Byzantium at Manzikert in Asia Minor and began settling in that country. Shortly before the year 1300 a few hundred families of another Turkish tribe left their central Asiatic pastures near the river Oxus to settle in the domain of their Seljuk kin. Under their leader, Osman, they soon moved into western Asia Minor, and as the Seljuk empire broke into fragments, they extended their sway to gain control eventually over the entire region. Osman's descendants, the Osmanli or Ottoman sultans, continued to rule Asia Minor until the establishment of the Turkish republic in 1922.

One of the most famous of them, Mohammed II, captured Constantinople in 1453 and put an end to the diminished Byzantine empire. Once his capital was established there, he sent his armies off in all four directions. The swiftly moving Turkish horsemen returned victorious—and rich—and the sultans soon ruled an empire on three continents. Osman's descendants led glorious but dangerous lives. Whenever a new sultan ascended the bejeweled imperial throne, he had his brothers strangled to rid himself of rivals. Later, when the Turks became more civilized, the sultan's brothers—and often his sons—were merely imprisoned in cages, next to the royal harem, to keep them from mischief. But whenever one of them was lucky enough to reach the throne, he could style himself: "Sultan of the Sultans of East and West, fortunate lord of the domains of the Romans, Persians, and Arabs, Hero of creation . . . Sultan of the Mediterranean and the Black Sea, of the extolled Ka'aba and Medina the illustrious and Jerusalem the noble, of the throne of Egypt and the province of Yemen, Aden and San'a, of Baghdad and Basra and Lahsa and Ctesiphon, of the lands of Algiers and Azerbaijan, of the region of the Kipchaks and the lands of the Tartars, of Kurdistan and Luristan and all Rumelia, Anatolia and Karaman, of Wallachia and Moldavia and Hungary and many kingdoms and lands besides . . ." Turkish royal politics being what they were, it was a fortunate sultan who stayed on the throne long enough to memorize, or even recite, this formula.

The court artists who were called upon to depict so august and all-powerful a personage had a difficult task. They showed the sultan bigger than the people around him, his rich robes billowing out to fill an inordinately large share of the picture space. The painters, like almost everyone else who lived and worked in the Grand Seraglio, the enormous royal palace at Constantinople, were his slaves, about on a level with the servant who carried in the clock when the sultan wanted to know what time it was, or the man who bore an extra royal turban in public processions and bobbed it up and down to save the sultan the trouble of acknowledging the applause of the populace.

A number of the painters came from Persia, for the Turks then thought of that country as the home of art, much as Americans not long ago considered France. Persian miniatures, which earlier had been influenced by the art of Turkish central Asia, now influenced Ottoman art. Yet there were differences, many of them traceable to old Turkish traditions, inherited from the art of tribal days. The costumes depicted, the shape of mountains in landscape paintings, the postures of the sitters—who were usually shown seated with legs crossed, almost in the pose of Buddha—recalled the art of central Asia rather than that of Persia. The Persians used a wide range of delicate colors. The Turks employed fewer colors, but they were generally bolder. The Persians painted amorous scenes and gardens, or depicted the legendary exploits of ancient heroes. The Turks, more realistic, painted cities and soldiers, tradesmen and public festivals.

Persian influence on Turkish art was supplemented by Western influence. In the year 1479 Mohammed II asked the Venetian Senate to send him a qualified portrait painter. The Venetians exported Gentile Bellini, who provided the sultan with a number of portraits and with erotic pictures as well. Bellini soon left, terrified—as one story has it—when the sultan, who was dissatisfied with his picture of John the Baptist, decapitated a slave in his presence to show him what a severed head really looked like. But even after Bellini's departure from the Ottoman court, Western influences remained.

Evidently the sultans maintained high aesthetic standards. Indeed, their standards were so high that they required foreign ambassadors to dress in robes of silver or gold brocade—supplied from the palace storerooms—before they were welcomed into the royal presence. But it was not aesthetic considerations alone that formed the royal art collection. Greed was also an important factor, for the Ottoman rulers acquired art the same way they did provinces or women for the harem. They were particularly eager to possess ingenious and beautiful machines. Queen Elizabeth I of England sent Murad III a mechanical organ "16 foute hie" on which "did stande a holly bushe full of blackbirds and thrushis, which at the end of the musick did singe and shake their wynges." He loved it. During the sixteenth and seventeenth centuries the sultans were the most powerful potentates in the world, and the custom that rulers have always had—and still have—of sending gifts to each other rewarded them considerably. The English sent gilt plate and beautiful clocks, the French parcels of Lyons silk. From Russia came bales of fur. Aside from gifts, there was booty. When the Turks conquered Cairo in 1517, and on several occasions when they invaded the Persian capital of Tabriz, they seized immense quantities of Chinese porcelain, whose influence is evident in the fine Turkish ceramics that were made in the sixteenth and seventeenth centuries. Much of the Chinese ware is—perhaps understandably—of the variety known as celadon, which was supposed to detect poisoned food by making it bubble and seethe. In 1922, after the last sultan was overthrown, a great store of porcelain was discovered in the palace, still packed in the cases in which it had come centuries before.

After the eighteenth century Ottoman power declined. The boundaries of the empire receded, and native art traditions decayed and all but disappeared, since artists now preferred to imitate Western work. The Grand Seraglio in Constantinople sank into decrepitude, as the sultan moved his home and his harem to palaces built in debased Western style. Nowadays one can gain only a faint idea of the splendor that the Seraglio displayed in its heyday. The brightly colored tiles, with their tulip patterns, remain; but most of the painted paneling and silk hangings have been destroyed or are rotting away. No trace is left of the sultan's famous tulip garden. The gold paving of the floor of the royal reception chamber disappeared long ago. The sultan's great firework displays, with their dragons, castles, giants, and representations of Noah's ark, and the stately processions of soldiers and dignitaries in robes of satin and velvet and cloth of gold, can now be seen only in the miniatures which depict royal ceremonies and public festivals. The crumbling palace, the miniature paintings, and a fraction of the immense collection of royal treasures are all that survive of Osman's ancient dynasty.

My brother-in-law, Gordon, and his wife, Jennifer, who went to Turkey on their honeymoon, told me that though there are so many things they loved about Istanbul, they think most often about their food experiences there: "the sandwich of fried mussels at a shack near the Black Sea; the freshest yogurt in the world from a guy who boarded the commuter ferry; the amazing kebabs from street stands; the Turkish pizza outside one of the mosques; the *kokoreç* (offal) from a street vendor (he was sitting in the gutter by the Spice Market); and the martinis at the Çirağan Palace—not really food but what a setting!"

Peter Olson, former chairman and CEO of Random House, Inc., and Candice Olson, cofounder and former chief executive of iVillage.com, have a number of Istanbul memories that keep coming back to them. For Peter, these include "the call to prayer—it's so hauntingly evocative. I always felt a tug when I heard it and I miss it. It didn't make me feel like an alien; rather it felt like a welcome. Additionally, the image of the Galata Bridge always comes to mind, not just the physical bridge that's there now but the replacement bridges that have been built over the years and the bridge's part in the history of Istanbul. I will never forget my *hamam* experience, where, at the very end, the attendant literally cracked my back—it initially felt like he was going to break me in half—but immediately afterward I felt wonderful. Lastly, I have a two-part image of my sixteen-year-old son outside the Grand Bazaar, where he bought six pairs of socks for the equivalent of nine dollars. Then he tried to resell them, for eleven dollars, and he was offered a job by a nearby merchant!"

On Candice's short list are: "riding the subway, which makes you feel a part of the life of the city. (It's so easy to get around by subway!); eating dinner in Sultanahmet at a little sky-top restaurant with mediocre food but absolutely drop-dead views of the Blue Mosque minarets; taking the ferry from the coast back to the city—this wasn't a tourist ferry, but the one residents take to commute; the call to prayer. And the bookstores are spectacular!"

The Golden Age of Ottoman Art

ESIN ATIL

ʚʘɞ

THE AGE of Sultan Süleyman the Magnificent was an exhibit in every way equal to the magnificence of Süleyman himself. The show opened at the National Gallery of Art in Washington, D.C., in 1987 and went on to the Art Institute of Chicago and the Metropolitan Museum of Art. This excellent piece explores the prolific creativity of this time period and highlights the various types of artworks that were crafted.

ESIN ATIL is the former curator of the Freer Gallery of Art in Washington, D.C., and was guest curator responsible for assembling the 1987 exhibition The Age of Sultan Süleyman the Magnificent. She is also the author of more than a dozen books, including *Art of the Arab World* (Smithsonian, 1975), *Turkish Art* (Abrams, 1980), and *Süleymanname: The Illustrated History of Süleyman the Magnificent* (Abrams, 1986). This last was a stunning visual documentary record of the sultan's life. As J. Carter Brown, then the director of the National Gallery of Art in Washington, D.C., wrote in the foreword, "It is indeed fortunate that the illustrations in the *Süleymanname* are reproduced in facsimile, since the fragility and the uniqueness of the original manuscript have made it almost inaccessible for study."

OTTOMAN ART flowered magnificently in the sixteenth century. With unprecedented prolificacy, court artists created splendid examples of illuminated and illustrated manuscripts; objects fashioned of gold, silver, jade, rock crystal, ivory, and inlaid wood; ceremonial and functional arms and armor; brocaded satin and velvet kaftans and furnishings; flatwoven and pile rugs; and a variety of ceramic vessels and tiles. They formulated unique and indigenous styles, themes, and techniques that not only came to characterize the artistic vocabulary of the period, but which also had a lasting impact on Turkish art. The vestiges of that impact are still visible today.

This extraordinary burst of artistic energy took place during the reign of Sultan Süleyman I (1520–1566), a remarkable half century when the political and economic power of the Ottoman Empire reached its zenith. Süleyman—a brilliant statesman, acclaimed legislator, and benevolent patron of the arts—more than doubled the territories of his domain, personally leading a dozen military campaigns that extended its frontiers from Iran to Austria. His state occupied the crucial link between three continents and controlled western Asia, eastern Europe, and northern Africa, while dominating the surrounding seas. Istanbul, the capital, became one of the largest and wealthiest cities in the world, attracting flocks of diplomats, merchants, and artists, who came to reap its riches.

The Ottoman Empire was governed by a highly efficient centralized system, at whose core was Topkapı Palace, the administrative and educational seat of the state. Attached to the palace were diverse imperial societies of artists and craftsmen collectively called the *Ehl-i Hiref* (Community of the Talented). These societies included men whose backgrounds were as varied as the lands the sultan ruled, their talents ranging from calligraphy to bootmaking. The artists entered the imperial societies as apprentices and advanced to the rank of master, and the most outstanding finally rose to head their corps. They were assigned daily wages commensurate with their status, level of accomplishment, and range of responsibilities, and were paid four times a year. Their wages were carefully recorded in quarterly registers.

The registers preserved in the archives of Topkapı Palace reflect the scope of the Ehl-i Hiref. The earliest document, drawn up in 1526, lists forty societies with over six hundred members; by the seventeenth century the number of societies had increased and their membership had risen to some two thousand. In addition to the artists employed in the imperial societies, Istanbul, like all the major centers of the empire, had diverse guilds of artisans which supplied both domestic and foreign needs.

The Ehl-i Hiref attracted the most talented and promising artists; its members were the elite and were stylistically by far the most influential of the Empire's artists. Artists from Herat, Tabriz, Cairo, and Damascus worked alongside those hailing from Circassia, Georgia, Bosnia, and even from Austria and Hungary, collaborating with the local masters. They produced splendid works of art that represented a unique blend of Islamic, European, and Turkish traditions. And because the Empire was as centralized artistically as it was politically, the artistic themes and designs pro-

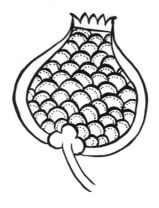

duced for the court soon spread to all corners of the sultan's lands and influenced the artists of neighboring countries as well. The heterogeneous nature of the imperial societies and the scrutinizing, personal patronage of the sultan fructified a cultural blossoming which affected all the arts.

Süleyman, known to Turks as Kanuni (Lawgiver) in honor of his numerous legislative acts, and as "The Magnificent" in Europe, in deference to his military conquests and the wealth of his court, was also a magnanimous patron. He himself was trained as a goldsmith, following the tradition of the Ottoman house that every sultan have a practical trade, and he wrote poetry under the pseudonym Muhibbi (Lover or Affectionate Friend), composing odes in Persian and Turkish.

The sultan personally inspected the works of the artists and rewarded them for outstanding performances. Palace documents pertaining to the list of gifts received by the artists during religious holidays record cash awards as well as kaftans made of luxurious fabrics. For instance, a document datable to 1535 indicates that Süleyman gave over 225,450 *akçes* (silver coins) plus 34 garments to some 150 court artists;

several masters received up to 3,000 *akçes*, a generous five months' salary for men making less than 20 *akçes* a day.

The most innovative artists belonged to the *nakkaşhane*, the imperial painting studio where hundreds of religious and secular manuscripts were produced. The primary duty of this society was to decorate the volumes commissioned for the sultan's libraries, that is, to illuminate and illustrate them. The *nakkaşhane* artists not only created original styles and themes that characterized the decorative vocabulary of the age; they also established the genre of historical painting that documented contemporary events and personages. They reinterpreted existing themes, experimented with new ideas, and formulated a synthesis which became unique to the Ottoman world. The styles and themes used in manuscript illumination quickly spread to the other imperial societies and were transmitted to a variety of other media, ranging from textiles and rugs to ceramic vessels and tiles.

One of the decorative styles that characterized the court arts of the age was called *saz*, an ancient Turkish word used to define an enchanted forest. It was originally applied to drawings which depicted such ferocious creatures as lions, dragons, *senmurvs* (phoenixlike birds), and *chilins* (four-legged creatures) in perpetual combat, engulfed by fantastic foliage bearing large composite blossoms and long feathery leaves. Also included in the repertoire were *peris* (fairies or angelic female figures). This imaginary world, inhabited by spirits which manifested themselves in flora and fauna, reflects a mystical approach with echoes of the shamanistic beliefs of Central Asia.

The originator of the *saz* style in Süleyman's court was Şahkulu. This artist, who was from Baghdad, first worked in Tabriz, was exiled to Amasya around 1501, then entered the *nakkaşhane* in 1520–1521. He became its head in 1545, a post which he retained until his death in 1555–1556. Şahkulu's drawings of placid *peris* and ferocious creatures in combat, and his studies of single blossoms and leaves, were incorporated into imperial albums. Their themes were employed by other imperial societies and applied to different materials.

One of the most spectacular representations of the *saz* themes appears on the *yatağan* (short sword) made for Süleyman in 1526–1527 by Ahmed Tekelü. This 66-centimeter (26-inch) ceremonial sword has an ivory hilt decorated with superimposed gold–inlaid *saz* scrolls, that is, scrolls bearing the same composite blossoms and long leaves found in the drawings. The upper portion of the blade shows the combat between a dragon and a *senmurv* in a fantastic landscape; the animals, cast separately of iron or steel and affixed to the blade, are gilded, and their eyes are set with rubies, enhancing their ferocity.

Intertwining scrolls with *saz* blossoms and leaves became a most popular decorative feature after the 1540s. They were applied to manuscript illuminations and bookbindings; jeweled objects made of gold, silver, rock crystal, and jade; and imperial arms and armor as well as textiles, rugs, and ceramics.

Carved in several superimposed layers, *saz* scrolls decorate a unique ivory hand mirror made in 1543–1544 for Süleyman by Gani. They also appear on a dazzling ceremonial kaftan worn by Süleyman's son Şehzade Bayezit (died 1561). Woven in polychrome silk and gold thread, the textile was designed almost like a painting, without a single repetition of the pattern.

Another decorative style that originated in the *nakkaşhane* was created by Kara Memi, who had studied with Şahkulu and became the head of the corps after his master's death. Kara Memi, who flourished between the 1540s and 1560s, was the promoter of the naturalistic style in which spring flowers, such as tulips, carnations, roses, and hyacinths, grew from clusters of leaves amidst blossoming fruit trees. This style was fully developed by the 1540s, as observed on the doublures, or linings, of a lacquered bookbinding used on a copy of the Hadis (in Arabic, *Hadith*, the collected sayings and actions of the Prophet Muhammad) made for Süleyman's favorite son, Şehzade Mehmet, who died in 1543. This binding re-creates a garden in perpetual bloom filled with spring flowers and trees.

Similar themes were used to decorate a splendid Koran transcribed in 1546–1547 by Ahmed Karahisari, the most innovative calligrapher of all time. Although the layout of the opening folios and the designs employed follow traditional schemes, the two pairs of ovals flanking the text depict branches bearing blossoms growing from leaves. This theme was called *bahar*, meaning "spring" as well as "a blossoming fruit tree," and was popularly used on diverse objects.

One of the favorite flowers in the Ottoman court was the tulip, which was cultivated in the gardens of the capital. This flower was introduced to Europe during Süleyman's reign by Baron Ogier Ghiselin de Busbecq, the Flemish-born Austrian ambassador to the court. Its name derived from *tülbent*—the Turkish word for the fine gauzelike fabric used to construct a turban—since its shape was thought to resemble the headdress worn by the Ottomans.

Three-petaled tulips and fan-shaped carnations became standardized and formulaic and were frequently combined, as on an embroidered wicker shield 64 centimeters (25 inches) across. Wicker, a strong and resilient material, is also lightweight, making it extremely desirable for both the Ottoman cavalry and infantry. These shields were constructed of withes wrapped with silk and metallic threads, then coiled and stitched together. The fronts were further reinforced with steel bosses and the backs padded and lined with velvet to cushion the elbow and protect the arm.

The naturalistic style was particularly favored by the potters of Iznik, a town which supplied the court with ceramic vessels and plates as well as tiles used on residential and religious architecture. The blossoming fruit tree was especially popular, and was used on tile panels decorating a number of buildings, including the mausoleum of Süleyman's beloved wife, Hürrem Sultan, who died in 1558. A similar version was used on a panel, constructed of forty-five square tiles, made in 1574–1575 for a chamber leading into the imperial baths in the Harem of Topkapı Palace.

In addition to *saz* scrolls and sprays of naturalistic flowers, the court artists employed such traditional designs as *rumis*, cloudbands, *çintemani* patterns, and spiraling vines. *Rumis* (split leaves) were generally used in scrolls, at times joined to create cartouches, as seen in the border of the tile panel from the Harem. Cloudbands, resembling twisted and knotted ribbons, were often combined with other elements. They appear in the spandrels of the tile as well as in the voids of a brocaded velvet cushion cover decorated with *çintemani* motifs. *Çintemani* referred to designs composed of clusters of triple balls and/or double wavy lines. Traced back to ancient Central Asian traditions, this pattern had talismanic as well as royal connotations, and is thought either to have derived from Buddhist symbols or to represent leopard spots and tiger stripes. The balls and wavy lines, used alone or together, were favored on satin and velvet textiles made for garments and furnishings, such as covers for cushions and bolsters or floor spreads.

The spiraling vine—thin branches bearing delicate blossoms and leaves—was first used on Süleyman's *tuğra*, the imperial monogram that contained his name and title. It was also applied to a group of ceramic vessels and plates painted in blue or blue and turquoise.

The artists fully exploited the decorative motifs created in the *nakkaşhane* and harmoniously combined them, as exemplified on the *tuğra* affixed to a *ferman* (edict) dated 1552. Here *saz* scrolls fill the large ovoid extension on the left, *rumis* and sprays of naturalistic flowers adorn the smaller ovoid, and cloudbands and blossoming fruit trees are placed in the voids between the vertical strokes at the top.

The same profusion of decorative elements appears in a most spectacular copy of the *Divan-i Muhibbi*, a collection of Süleyman's poems transcribed by Mehmed Şerif and illuminated in 1566 by Kara Memi. The margins of the folios have *saz* scrolls rendered in metallic gold and silver inks—the silver has now oxidized to gray—and the panels between the lines of text burst with brightly colored naturalistic flowers and trees.

Both stylized and naturalistic floral themes were skillfully combined by the other artists, including the potters and weavers. Ottoman textiles were greatly admired by the Europeans, who collected brocaded satins and velvets, some of which were fashioned into ecclesiastical garments or royal robes. Ottoman rugs were equally in demand, frequently used as wall hangings or table covers. One of the most celebrated sixteenth-century prayer rugs was preserved in the Schönbrunn Palace, the residence of the Austrian kings outside Vienna. Its field is densely packed with a variety of *saz* blossoms and leaves, intermingled with branches of blossoming fruit trees.

The decorative styles initiated in the *nakkaşhane* had a profound impact on the production of the other imperial societies of the Ehl-i Hiref, as well as on that of the artisan guilds. These styles constituted the artistic vocabulary of the age and were universally applied to both imperial and nonimperial arts throughout the Empire.

In addition to illuminating manuscripts and *tuğras*, the *nakkaşhane* artists illustrated scores of literary and historical works for the imperial libraries. These manuscripts were exclusively produced for the sultan's personal enjoyment. It was only when the imperial Ottoman collections became national museums, after the establishment of the Republic of Turkey in 1923, that these volumes were made public.

The *nakkaşhane* artists illustrated the texts of past authors as well as those dating from Süleyman's reign. But their greatest contribution was the representation of contemporary events and the creation of the most outstanding genre of court painting, that of

illustrated histories. This genre, which depicted the most important events of a sultan's reign, was fully established in the 1550s.

The two significant ingredients of illustrated histories—the
documentation of the settings and the portrayal of the personages—owed much to the efforts of two men who were not members of the *nakkaşhane* but belonged to the administration. The
most prolific among them was Nasuh (died about 1564), a court
official who accompanied the sultan on several campaigns and
recorded these events. Nasuh was a true Renaissance man: he was
a historian, calligrapher, painter, mathematician, swordsman, and
inventor of athletic games. He not only wrote about Süleyman's
campaigns but also transcribed and illustrated his own texts, carefully documenting the cities and ports conquered by the
Ottomans. One of his texts, entitled *Beyan-i Menazil-i Sefer-i
Irakeyn*, is devoted to the campaign to Iran and Iraq which took
place between 1534 and 1536. The first painting in this work
depicts Istanbul and represents in detail all the monuments of the
capital. Nasuh's topographic renditions are invaluable sources for
the re-creation of the city in the 1530s.

One of his colleagues was Haydar Reis (1492?–1572), a naval
captain who practiced the art of painting. He made portraits of
the sultan, his son Selim II, and other court officials, using the
pseudonym Nigari. His portrayal of Süleyman as an aging ruler

accompanied by two officials was made toward the end of the sultan's life and realistically depicts the physical condition of his subject. Nigari's paintings, executed from life, helped to promote the development of portraiture in the court.

Ottoman sultans were acutely conscious of their role in history and established the post of *şahnameci*, the official court biographer. During Süleyman's reign this post was held by Arifi, who was commissioned to write a five-volume history of the Ottoman dynasty. The fifth and last volume in the series is the *Süleymanname*, devoted to Süleyman's reign and completed in 1558.

Arifi chose the artists who illustrated this volume with great care. Most of the paintings were assigned to an anonymous master who devised the compositions for accession ceremonies, receptions of foreign dignitaries, sieges of fortresses, and battles in the field. He conjoined the topographic style seen in the works of Nasuh with Nigari's interest in portraiture, and depicted the events, the settings, and the participants with documentary realism. His paintings are exquisite works of art, as well as historical documents that re-create the age—whether they show the Battle of Mohács, Hungary's decisive defeat in 1526, a ceremonial event in the Throne Room during the 1539 circumcision festival of two princes, or an intimate meeting between the sultan and Barbaros Hayreddin Pasha, the grand admiral, in 1533.

The *Süleymanname* covers the sultan's life from his accession in 1520 to 1556, a decade before his death. The activities of his last years were recorded in two other manuscripts. The painter who illustrated them was Osman (active from the 1560s to the 1580s), a remarkably talented artist who followed the traditions initiated by the master of the *Süleymanname*.

One of these manuscripts was written by Ahmed Feridun Pasha, a famous statesman, and narrates the 1566 campaign to Szigetvár, Hungary. Süleyman was seventy-two years old at the time and in poor health, but he had insisted that he lead his own armies once again. He stopped en route to receive his vassal

Stephen Zápolya, the king of Hungary. The painting depicting this event portrays Süleyman as a majestic but tired and ailing monarch. An atmosphere of solemnity—even sadness—permeates the scene, almost as if the participants had a premonition that this was to be Süleyman's last campaign.

Arifi's *Süleymanname* was concluded by Lokman, the official court biographer who replaced him and wrote the *Tarih-i Sultan Süleyman*, ending his text with the death of the sultan. One of the paintings in this work, which was completed in 1579–1580, shows Süleyman's coffin being carried toward his grave, which is being dug next to the mausoleum of Hurrem Sultan, behind the Süleymaniye Mosque. This painting proves that although Süleyman's mausoleum had been designed at the time the Süleymaniye complex, comprising the mosque and some eighteen other buildings, was conceived between 1550 and 1557, it was not built until after his death.

Lokman and the following *şahnamecis* produced voluminous works illustrated by hundreds of paintings depicting the activities of the sultans in detail. But no Ottoman sultan was as celebrated as Süleyman, and none provided the artists with so many glorious subjects to represent.

The artists of Süleyman's *nakkaşhane* not only formulated the decorative style and themes that characterized the golden age of Ottoman art, but also re-created the life and achievements of their patron, enabling students and scholars to understand and appreciate a most remarkable man and the magnificent and fascinating age which he shaped.

A number of museums in the U.S. hold excellent Near East, Ottoman, Byzantine, or Islamic collections. Even if you missed the Süleyman or the Metropolitan Museum of Art's Byzantium: Faith and Power exhibits, the accompanying catalogs published for these exhibitions are the next best thing. And of course, visiting those museums whose related permanent collections are extensive is a great way to immerse yourself in Turkish history. Noteworthy museums to know about include:

- Art Institute of Chicago (312 443 3600 / artic.edu/aic)

- Dumbarton Oaks, Washington, D.C. (202 339 6409 / doaks.org), with a Byzantine collection that is one of the finest in the world; Dumbarton Oaks completed the restoration work on Kariye Camii (Chora Church) in Istanbul as well as at Aya Sofya.

- Freer Gallery of Art and Arthur M. Sackler Gallery, Washington, D.C. (202 633 4880 / asia.si.edu), with renowned Ancient Near Eastern Art, Arts of the Islamic World, and Biblical Manuscripts departments.

- Isabella Stewart Gardner Museum, Boston (617 566 1401 / gardnermuseum.org), with an Islamic arts collection that is small but varied.

- Los Angeles County Museum of Art (LACMA) (323 857 6000 / lacma.org), with an impressive Art of the Ancient Near East department.

- Metropolitan Museum of Art, New York (212 535 7710 / metmuseum.org), with a recently renovated Ancient Near Eastern gallery and one of the world's finest Islamic art collections. One of the most brilliant projects the museum created is its Timeline of Art History, accessible online. The Islamic section is an excellent resource for visitors to Turkey.

- Museum of Fine Arts, Boston (617 267 9300 / mfa.org), with an Arts of the Islamic World department.

- The Oriental Institute of University of Chicago (773 702 9514 / oi.uchicago.edu), dedicated to the study of the ancient Near East; most of its objects were found during archaeological excavations it sponsored.

- The Textile Museum, Washington, D.C. (202 677 0441 / textilemuseum.org), devoted exclusively to the handmade textile arts with a collection of more than seventeen thousand rugs and textiles dating from 3,000 BC to the present.

Additionally, see "A Global Guide to Islamic Art," January/February 2009 *Saudi Aramco World*, saudiaramcoworld .com; click on Indexes.

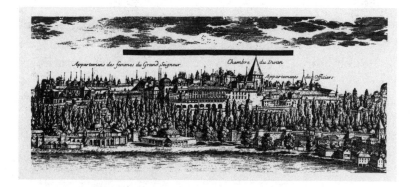

The Turkish Rose

FERGUS GARRETT

ﭏ

SURPRISINGLY PERHAPS, Turkey has more than twenty native species of rose, and in this piece the author details the ways in which this intoxicatingly beautiful flower so prominently figures in Turkish life.

FERGUS GARRETT is the head gardener at the Great Dixter House & Gardens in East Sussex, England. The manor house at Great Dixter—with one of the largest surviving timber-framed halls in the country—was built in the mid-1400s and, more recently, was the longtime home of famous British gardener Christopher Lloyd. Garrett is now at the helm of the gardens, which by all accounts have been deemed extraordinary.

IN ONE way or another, the rose is featured in many of the wonderful stories associated with love and romance in Turkish history, lore, and myth, relayed over the centuries by poets and historians. The rose is the essence of purity, sweetness, and femininity. An admiring lover will often affix the word *gül* (meaning "rose") to his sweetheart's name as a term of affection. He may describe her complexion as being as fair as a rose, or her skin as being soft as a rose petal. Dreaming of roses signifies an improvement in one's love life, health, and general well-being. Rose petals were stuffed into silken mattresses for the ultimate seductive experience. But love never comes without a price, and romance and tragedy often go hand in hand in Turkish lore. One old saying particularly comes to mind: "You cannot pluck roses without the fear of thorns, nor enjoy a fair wife without the danger of horns."

Along with the carnation and the tulip, the rose is an important flower in Turkish art and culture. Rose motifs are found on the garments of the sultans, on Iznik pottery, on carpets, and on copperware. Roses also feature prominently in Turkey's rich and varied cuisine. For centuries the rose's delightful scent has been captured by infusing petals in water, oil, honey, and sugar to flavor drinks, puddings, and sweets. The tradition lives on today, most notably in the rose flavoring of Turkish delight.

Turkey, rich in plants generally, has over twenty native species of rose. This includes *Rosa gallica*, the ancestor of many beautiful garden hybrids, as well as culinary roses such as the damasks that are so popular in Turkish kitchens. *Rosa gallica* was named by Linnaeus, who assumed that it had originated in Roman Gaul. In fact, the species stretches from Central to Southern Europe through to Iraq. It is found throughout Turkey in dry meadows and maquis, in dunes, and sometimes on pure sand. A low shrub growing up to three feet with stiff, upright, densely prickled stems, and dull, bluish-green leaves, *Rosa gallica* bears masses of strongly scented, deep-pink, solitary flowers followed by scarlet-orange hips. Naturally occurring hybrids of this rose are distributed throughout Europe and Western Asia.

Although *Rosa gallica* has a fainter scent than the damask roses, its petals possess the amazing virtue of retaining fragrance even after they wither. This means that they can be dried and made into scented powder, and then used in salves, oils, and rose-scented waters. Thought to possess many medicinal properties, rose potions are frequently referred to in ancient texts. Military doctors took *Rosa gallica* on campaigns, planting it whenever possible. With the ability to produce copious amounts of seed, sucker underground, and tolerate extremes of heat and cold in different habitats, the highly fertile *gallica* thrived in military outposts, monasteries, and gardens, spreading throughout the East and Europe. Selection and breeding gave rise to many variants. A highly fragrant, semi-double form of the species was selected and became the favored rose of apothecaries. This rose of legendary medicinal properties is known today as *Rosa gallica officinalis*, the Apothecary's Rose. Its quality was so superior that it initiated an entire industry dedicated to its medicinal and confectionary uses.

Rosa damascena, whose origin has been subject to much debate, is thought to be a hybrid of *R. gallica* and *R. phoenicia*. *R. phoenicia* is found in southern and western Turkey in scrubby, moist places. It is a stoutly prickled climbing shrub growing up to fifteen feet high, with white to pale-pink flowers borne on dense corymbs and possessed of a musky scent. Crossing this rose with *Rosa gallica* resulted in a very floriferous shrubby plant with an irresistibly rich scent. The pale-pink flowers borne in clusters carry a mixture of essential oils from both parents, giving them an unmistakable strong fragrance that lasts through processing. These qualities have made the summer-flowering damask rose *R. damascena*, also known as the Isparta Rose, world-renowned for the production of rose oil and rose water. A variant, *R. damascena* Trigintipetala, the "thirty-petaled" or Kazanlik rose, has the semi-double *Rosa gallica officinalis* as one of its parents. The resulting hybrid has such an abundance of petals, and such a delicious rich scent, that it has become the favored rose of growers in Turkey.

Rose oil, produced by steam-distilling freshly picked flowers, is called "attar" of roses, the name derived from an Arabic word meaning "fragrant." The distilling process is thought to have originated in Mogul India, where a means of separating the water and the essential oil was accidentally discovered at a banquet given by the Emperor Jahangir (1605–1627). His rose water–filled pools underwent a natural distillation in the heat of the sun, which left a thin film of oil floating on the surface that was found to have a lasting perfume. The Ottoman Turks developed the distillation process, and with the spread of their empire, which was to last for more than five hundred years, introduced it to many provinces. Today, Turkey and the once Ottoman-occupied Bulgaria are the most important producers of attar of roses. The two main centers of cultivation are in Kazanluk (from the Turkish *kazan*, meaning "still"), in Bulgaria, and the Isparta district of Turkey, in southwestern Anatolia.

Over 60 percent of the world's production of the highest-quality oil takes place in Turkey. Most of the roses are grown in small, family-owned farms. Picking starts at sunrise and is completed in the morning. The harvest is then rushed to the stills, and the distillation is done on the same day. The process involves passing steam over the petals and then condensing the steam into large bottles, which yields mainly fragrant rose water, but also a thin layer of rose oil. It takes more than four tons of flowers to produce a kilo of oil, which is worth literally its weight in gold. The first and second distillations are blended before being packed in wax-

sealed copper canisters and exported all over the world, including the famous perfumeries of Grasse, in southern France.

Go to any decent Turkish garden today and you'll see pink roses grown for the kitchen. More than likely, the species will be the Isparta Rose, *Rosa damascena*, or a close relative such as the Kazanlik, or possibly *Rosa centifolia*, the cabbage rose, known in Turkey as the *Okka gülü*. Whatever the species, it will be highly scented, and rich in essential oils. My mother swears by her Isparta roses tucked on either side of the main gate of our house in the coastal resort of Yalova, across the Sea of Marmara from Istanbul. The roses came with us from our last house in Istanbul, and probably from the house before that, cherished and preserved like a valuable piece of furniture. My great-grandmother used them, followed by my late grandmother, and now they are in the possession of my mother, who will then pass them on to me, and I on to my children. And, believe me, they are the real thing, for I have tasted the rose-petal jam that my mother lovingly produces from them year after year, following an old family recipe. This is a delicate breakfast jam to be eaten on fresh bread or toast.

Nebahat Hanim's Rose-Petal Jam

Ωℭ

1½ pounds (650 grams) fresh rose petals
9½ cups (1950 grams) superfine sugar
juice of 1 lemon
2½ cups (750 milliliters) fresh spring water
1 egg white

Wash the rose petals, and snip off and reserve their white bases. Alternately layer the petals and half of the sugar in a bowl, then pour the lemon juice over, reserving 2 teaspoons. Cover the bowl with a cloth and set aside.

Place the white tips of the rose petals into a separate bowl, boil the water, and pour 2½ cups boiling water on top. Cover with a damp cloth, and set aside. Let both bowls rest at cool room temperature for two days.

After two days, gently stir the sugar-and-rose-petal mixture. Cover again. Drain the liquid from the white petal tips into a saucepan. Add the remaining sugar and the egg white, and bring to a boil. Simmer, skimming off the froth, until you are left with a clear syrup.

Add the sugared rose petals and return to a simmer, again spooning off the froth. When the mixture starts to darken, add the remaining 2 teaspoons of lemon juice, then remove from heat. Let the jam cool for a few minutes, then put it into sterilized jars and seal.

This essay would not be complete without mentioning *aşure* (pronounced "ash ur ey"), a legendary sweet flavored with rose water and also known as Noah's Pudding. It contains a list of ingredients as long as your arm and looks like fruits and nuts preserved in aspic. Legend has it that Noah found himself running extremely short of supplies on the ark and ordered that all the remaining food be cooked together. The result turned out to be delicious. In Ottoman times the sweet was consumed in "*Aşure* month." Modern Turks still make and eat it, but unfortunately the dish is less popular in the kitchens of the young, as it's quite an effort to put together. My mother still makes it, and sends bowls of it to all the neighbors, who return the bowls full of figs, plums, or shortbread cakes. It's a tradition that I will carry on.

Aşure

ℒℴ

⅓ cup (50 grams) dried white beans
⅓ cup (50 grams) dried white lima beans
⅓ cup (50 grams) long-grain rice
⅔ cup (100 grams) wheat or bran flakes
1½ cups (450 milliliters) milk
1 cup plus 2 tablespoons (225 grams) sugar
⅔ cup (100 grams) chopped pitted dates
½ cup (75 grams) blanched whole almonds
½ cup rose water
seeds of 1 pomegranate
⅓ cup (50 grams) currants
⅔ cup (100 grams) raisins
⅓ cup (50 grams) chopped walnuts
3 tablespoons (25 grams) pine nuts
additional raisins, walnuts, and pomegranate seeds
  for garnish

Soak the dried white beans and dried white lima beans overnight. Boil them in separate saucepans until tender, about 1 hour. Drain them, and allow them to cool.

Boil the rice and wheat or bran flakes in separate saucepans in plenty of water, until they are tender. Strain them, reserving the water in which they were cooked. Chop coarsely.

Place a little more than one quart (1.2 liters) of the water used for cooking the rice and wheat in a saucepan. Add milk and sugar and bring to a boil, stirring until the sugar is fully dissolved. Boil until the mixture thickens enough to coat a spoon, then add all the other ingredients except garnishes.

Boil for 2 or 3 minutes more and remove from heat. Pour into individual cups and allow to cool.

Serve cold in individual cups decorated with raisins, walnut halves, and pomegranate seeds.

"Every trip is a journey, and a visit to Turkey can quickly come to seem epic. For one thing, there is your entire education spread out before you: Troy, the spot where Leander swam the Hellespont; Nicea (now Iznik), where the Catholic Church convened and produced its famous creed; Miletus, where Greek science and philosophy had their beginnings; Haghia Sofia, whose famous dome was the glory of Byzantine Christianity; and the Blue Mosque, whose equally famous dome and minarets were raised by Ottoman Mehmet II to celebrate Islam. Then there is Istanbul itself, an imperial city set on two continents on both sides of the Sea of Marmara, with a picture book castle, bazaars of all kinds—spice, fish, birds—and the Grand Bazaar with everything under the sun. A place where men in black pants run through the streets carrying slim cups of tea or coffee on brass trays swinging from a tripod of chains. In the midst of this bounty, I was lucky to have a cicerone who was himself magic. John Freely, sometimes joined by his wife, Dolores, old friends, kindly shepherded me and my nephew around the city sharing with us all kinds of historical and cultural facts.

"We stayed at a small, friendly establishment (which John Freely had suggested) at one end of the Hippodrome in the Sultanahmet neighborhood near Topkapı Palace and other delights. The Alzer is a simple hotel, but its location on the

Hippodrome—the oval that had been laid down by Constantine for horse-racing—gave it a wonderful advantage, which it exploited by providing a breakfast room, surrounded on three sides by windows, on its top floor, the sixth, just one floor up from our own rooms.

"We discovered this soon-to-be-our-favorite spot on the first evening when the desk clerk suggested we could go up there to watch the sunset. When we stepped into it we realized we were essentially eyeball-to-eyeball with the dome of the Blue Mosque, with the rosy, red-orange dome of the Haghia Sofia floating slightly off in the distance, and the Sea of Marmara and a gorgeous sky behind them. It was a sight of such exoticism and beauty at every hour we saw it that we never tired of it, and we ended up going there at every opportunity—to have breakfast, to write letters, just to absorb all the fascinating new things we had seen during the day. Grand buildings always inspire, but the special gift of the room at the top of the Alzer Hotel was that it gave us an intimacy, a special feeling of ownership, even love, for these two famous landmarks, epic in their importance to art, religion, and history."

—Ann Close, longtime senior editor at Alfred A. Knopf, and editor of John Freely's *Aladdin's Lamp: How Greek Science Came to Europe Through the Islamic World*

Million Must Quit Homes in Near East, Lausanne Decrees

EDWIN L. JAMES

ﾛﾛﾟ

THE 1923 population exchange between Greece and Turkey remains a major event in contemporary Turkish history, even now. Authorized by the Treaty of Lausanne, the exchange was the first of its kind in the twentieth century, involving nearly two million people.

In Greece the exchange is known as the Asia Minor Catastrophe, and it followed what could also be referred to as a catastrophe, the *Megali Idea* (Great Idea), the attempt to acquire land for a greater Greece—notably along the Aegean coast, up to Istanbul, and westward into Thrace. The Greeks felt this land was rightly theirs, and they were encouraged to embark on this folly by the British. After landing troops at Smyrna (present-day Izmir), the Greeks pressed onward until they met with the Turkish army, led by Kemal Pasha who later earned the title of Atatürk, Father of the Turks, in 1934. The Turks were the victors in this Greco-Turkish War (1919–1922), a surprising achievement, perhaps, after having sided with the defeated Central Powers in World War I. Few probably believed that the "sick man of Europe"—the phrase was coined by Tsar Nicholas I of Russia in 1844 to describe the Ottoman Empire—could succeed. Indeed, the Treaty of Sèvres, the 1920 peace treaty between the Ottoman Empire and the Allies (excluding Russia and the United States), virtually abolished Turkish sovereignty—and France, Italy, and Great Britain had secretly begun carving up the Ottoman Empire for themselves as early as 1915.

Turkish independence was thus extremely hard won, and once achieved, extremely hard to arrest. Atatürk and his followers understood that momentum was on their side, and they also believed that Anatolian Turkish nationalism was the only way forward for this new nation-state. Their determination for independence was so great that "it could trump the considerations of common sense or humanitarianism," according to reporter and author Bruce Clark. It is this goal—becoming a modern Turkish nation—and how it was attained that lies at the heart of this complex, controversial issue.

Turkey was not then and is not now ethnically or culturally homogeneous. Until the late 1800s, most Ottoman citizens weren't Muslim, let alone Turks; it was only after the Empire lost its European provinces that Turks became a majority, for the first time in centuries. The road to nationalism had no room for anyone who wasn't Turkish. As scholar Renée Hirschon notes in her excellent book *Crossing the Aegean*, the odds were not in favor of the survival of a multiethnic state after World War I: "The heritage of modern Turkey was said to lie in the true heartland of ethnic Turkishness, that is, inner Asia. The rich cultural history of Anatolia was glossed over. This suppression, which was necessary for the coherence of the energetically propagated official version of national history and identity, could not accommodate the lived experience of the existing population or the abundant physical evidence of a prior 'non-homogeneous' population." In fact, the government's stance on multiculturism has long been that anyone who lives in Turkey is a Turk, end of story. "Happy is he who calls himself a Turk," goes the slogan, and its translation has been that any other identity is unacceptable.

And so it was decided, in the Lausanne treaty, that the only criterion to distinguish a Turk from anyone else was religion. Therefore, a Greek-speaking Muslim who had lived his whole life in Greece and never set foot in Turkey was determined to be a Turk, and was forced to emigrate to Turkey. Likewise, Turkish-speaking Greeks, Armenians, Syrians, Russians, and others of the Greek Orthodox faith who had only ever lived in Turkey were determined to be Christian, and had to leave.

Ernest Hemingway was among the witnesses to the exchange. He was, at that time, a reporter for the *Toronto Daily Star* and on October 20, 1922, he filed the article "A Silent, Ghastly Procession," which began, "Adrianople [present day Edirne].—In a never-ending, staggering march, the Christian population of Eastern Thrace is jamming the roads toward Macedonia. The main column crossing the Maritza River at Adrianople is twenty miles long. Twenty miles of carts drawn by cows, bullocks and muddy-flanked water buffalo, with exhausted, staggering men, women and children, blankets over their heads, walking blindly along in the rain beside their worldly goods." And on November 14, his column "Refugees from Thrace" opened with these words: "In a comfortable train with the horror of the Thracian evacuation behind me, it is already beginning to seem unreal. That is the boon of our memories. I have described that evacuation in a cable to the *Star* from Adrianople. It does no good to go over it again. The evacuation still keeps up. No matter how long

it takes this letter to get to Toronto, as you read this in the *Star* you may be sure that the same ghastly, shambling procession of people being driven from their homes is filing in unbroken line along the muddy road to Macedonia. A quarter of a million people take a long time to move."

I had initially wanted to include here some personal chronicles from both a Greek and a Turk who had lived through the exchange. But in addition to it being a little difficult to find these of suitable length, I decided that I might be misrepresenting myself as a scholar or historian, which of course I'm not. Rather, I chose to feature a news story that recorded the event, which appeared on January 11, 1923, in *The New York Times*, and to include a brief bibliography of titles for readers who wish to learn more. I believe that historical events must be judged within the time frame in which they occurred, and though it is irrefutable that the exchange was traumatic and cruel on a humanitarian level, it did halt the warfare between Greece and Turkey and led to more stable societies. It also, for better or worse, has been seen as a comparable solution to situations and conflicts elsewhere in the world: the end of British colonial rule in the Indian subcontinent led to the formation of a separate Pakistan; British policy in the former Palestine forced population exchanges based on newly drawn borders (and Israel's borders continue to be in flux today); and more recently the breakup of Yugoslavia saw the separation of peoples in Bosnia and Kosovo.

EDWIN L. JAMES (1890–1951) was a cousin of Pulitzer Prize–winning columnist and journalist Russell Baker, and was a managing editor of *The New York Times*. He was eulogized at his well-attended funeral as a "trusted interpreter" of events.

LAUSANNE, Jan. 10—In the name of peace and justice 1,000,000 men, women and children are to be torn from their homes and forcibly taken to other lands. Such was the remarkable decision taken today by this remarkable Near East conference.

The statesman of the civilized nations and of Turkey this morning voted to exchange the Greek population of Turkey against the Turkish population of Greece. Excepted from the measure are the 200,000 Greeks in Constantinople, and in return the 300,000 Turks in Western Thrace, which belongs to Greece. By the terms of today's decision all other Greeks in Turkey and all other Turks in Greece must move. It is estimated that 600,000 Greeks in Turkey are affected and about 450,000 Turks in Macedonia and the rest of Greece.

Today's action is regretted by Allied diplomats, who admit its inhumanity, but defend it on the ground that it is the sole means of preventing a worse fate from overtaking the Greeks in Turkey. These same diplomats yesterday accepted the Turks' paper promises as being sufficient protection for the minorities in Turkey.

That there may be no misunderstanding, it must be made plain that this extraordinary step is due entirely and exclusively to the Turks' determination to expel the Greeks from their country. It was only after this determination became plain that the Greeks demanded that the Turks in Greece be expelled in order to make room for the Greeks who must leave Turkey, where their forefathers in many cases had lived for many centuries.

On the other hand, the Turks today agreed to let the Greek Patriarch remain in Constantinople on condition that he be shorn of all his secular powers and retain solely his religious jurisdiction. This concession is probably part of the price paid for yesterday's surrender of the Allies in the minorities controversy, just as the Turks' consent to leave the Greeks in Constantinople was given in return for the Greek promise to leave the Turks in Western Thrace, which, by the way, the Turks hope to eventually own.

It is to be remarked that the retention of the patriarchate in Constantinople and the permission given the Greeks to remain in that city represent two solutions favored by the Americans. It should also be pointed out that the dropping of the Armenian home project and the decision to exchange populations represent the rejection of two other measures advocated by the Americans. The net result does not indicate that the influence of the Americans is predominant in the settlements made here.

It is planned that the League of Nations shall supervise the exchange of populations, providing for transportation and seeing that the Turks on the one hand and the Greeks on the other obtain a fair settlement for the property they must leave behind them. While the time limit for the transfer was not fixed, it is generally believed that it will be placed at about six to eight months.

Strange as such a decision may seem—a decision under the terms of which Greeks may live in Constantinople and not in the suburbs, under which Turks may live in Western Thrace and not in Macedonia—everyone here seems to take it seriously. In effect the move seems to mean the actual exchange of a million persons or else formal permission to the Turks to persecute Greeks who remain in Turkey.

EXCHANGE OF POPULATION COMPULSORY

The Turks sought to have the exchange made non-compulsory or voluntary, which would mean that they would chase out the Greeks, whereas the Turks would not have to leave Greece unless they chose to do so. Ex-Premier Venizelos opposed this, demanding that if an exchange were decided upon it must be compulsory. The conference adopted his point of view.

In a speech at today's session Lord Curzon expressed the deepest regret at the necessity of deciding on an exchange of populations, but declared that a week's discussion showed that no other decision was possible. Admitting that he detested the solution and deplored it, he said that he thought there was nothing else to do. What he meant was that there was no way of preventing Turkey from ousting the Greeks unless the Allies were prepared to fight, and, like the Americans, the English are not ready to fight the Turks—for humanitarian ends.

In the account of today's events given by the spokesman of the Allies great emphasis is laid on "the Patriarchate Victory," which simply represents a Turkish concession for which an ample price has been paid.

The decision was well stage-managed. Senator Montagna, Chairman of the Committee on the Exchange of Populations, reported that an agreement had been reached, except that the Turks still demanded the expulsion of the Greek Patriarch as one of the conditions of allowing the Greeks to remain in Constantinople. Lord Curzon in an eloquent speech referred to the American pronouncement against the expulsion and said that the whole world would be aroused by such a step. He suggested that the proper solution might be to take away from the Patriarch all powers and confine his activities to religious matters, allowing him to remain on these terms. Camille Barrère, speaking for France, agreed to Lord Curzon's recommendation, and so did M. Venizelos. Ismet Pasha then read a statement renouncing the Turkish demand that the Patriarch be expelled and agreeing to his remaining as a purely religious leader. Of course, it had all been arranged beforehand.

CHANGE OF BRITISH POLICY TOWARD TURKS

The Allies' action of yesterday and today under Lord Curzon's leadership brings into relief the present British policy toward the Turks. After weeks of threatening them, the British seem now to have gone back to their traditional policy of buying them off

against the Russians. In the negotiations over capitulations and
Mosul the Turks are still demanding a high price, and on both
issues Lord Curzon has declared that he will not yield. But one
must wait and see. England is more likely to give way on the
capitulations issue than on that of Mosul and its oil.

But there seems little doubt that the British have shifted their
Lausanne policy, and it appears to be now a question of what
price the British will pay for a treaty with the Turks. England has
obtained a favorable solution of the Straits problem, whereas the
Turks have certainly won out on the minorities issue and their
determination to expel the Greeks. It seems likely that the capitulations settlement will be much nearer the Turkish than the
Allied demands. That leaves Mosul as the big issue before the
conference. The British realize that they will be criticized for giving in to the Turks on humanitarian issues, but their reply will
unquestionably be that they could not be expected to fight alone
for the humanitarian wishes of the world.

By the nature of their mission here the American delegates can
do little more than sit by and watch the wheel spin, rejoicing when
their numbers come up and remaining silent when their numbers
lose. The movements of the powers that be here have given the
Americans partial satisfaction in letting some warships through the
Straits, and denied them satisfaction in placing a League commission over the Straits. Americans may feel satisfaction because the
Greek Patriarch remains in Constantinople. Satisfaction was denied
them when the project of a national home for Armenians was dis-
carded. Americans will be pleased to know that the Greeks will be
left in Constantinople. They will be displeased at the decree for the
exchange of populations. One may wonder if the result would have
been much different had there been no American delegates here.

The belief that the conference will result in a treaty is much
stronger since the Allies' surrender of yesterday and today. It is
generally thought that the conference will run for several weeks
more or less, all depending on the Mosul issue.

Recommended Resources

Even the most cursory search on the topic of the Greek-Turkish population exchange reveals two books in particular: *Crossing the Aegean: An Appraisal of the 1923 Compulsory Population Exchange between Greece and Turkey*, edited by Renée Hirschon (Berghahn Books, 2003), noted above, and *Twice a Stranger: The Mass Expulsions That Forged Modern Greece and Turkey*, by Bruce Clark (Harvard, 2006).

In the first, Hirschon—also the author of *Heirs of the Greek Catastrophe* (Berghahn Books, 1998), a social anthropological study of Asia Minor refugees in Piraeus—presents the far-reaching ramifications of the population exchange in political, economic, demographic, social, and cultural spheres. In 1998, the seventy-fifth anniversary of the Lausanne Convention, Hirschon organized a four-day international conference on the consequences of the Convention. The chapters in *Crossing the Aegean* are the (slightly) revised papers given by the contributors, who hail from both sides of the Aegean Sea. Each chapter is worthy and, I think, quite unbiased. Hirschon refers to this book as a work in progress, and states that her own position "inclines towards ways of promoting coexistence and symbiosis rather than the enforced separation of diverse peoples." In the final chapter, Hirschon reveals the Turkish government's attempt to rename cities and towns as a way to erase from memory their previous associations. Similar-sounding Turkic names replaced Greek or Armenian names, and this became quite blatant in the nationalist attitude toward the sea: "In a country that is essentially a peninsula with a very long coastline, it is remarkable how minimal the population's relationship with the sea has been. The major reason is that the coast was regarded as the domain of the Greeks." Hirschon concludes that the result of this excising of the exchange from national history "has been a particularly schizophrenic existence for modern Turkey and especially for the identity of its inhabitants; the analysis is only now slowly getting under way."

Twice a Stranger is a less academic book, written by a journalist for *The Economist*. Bruce Clark is from Northern Ireland, so he himself is no stranger to this type of conflict. He emphasizes that the population exchange is a human story, and also a landmark in diplomatic history. Therefore he intersperses chapters about the lives of ordinary people with other chapters detailing the choices that politicians faced in 1923 and how those choices affected hundreds of thousands of Muslim and Christian families. "Whether we like it or not," Clark opines, "those of us who live in Europe or in places influenced by European ideas remain the children of Lausanne." This book is indeed well researched, but Clark should be especially commended for writing it in the first place as the legacy of Lausanne will soon be forgotten: anyone who still remembers the exchange will surely not be alive for much longer, given that the event occurred nearly ninety years ago. Clark traveled extensively throughout Greece and Turkey, and he aptly notes, "Quite apart from its wider implications for 20th century history, there is much about the contemporary state of Turkey and Greece which cannot be understood except in reference to Lausanne and the population exchange."

Among the numerous personal memoirs Clark shares in the book, I have selected two here that I feel are quite moving. The first is from a village schoolteacher in the Grevena region of Greece who was a child when his Muslim playmates were forced to leave:

> I was twelve years old. I remember seeing a crowd of people proceeding slowly and purposefully [from the outskirts of Grevena] towards Kozani, some on foot and some mounted. I saw the older ones dabbing their eyes with handkerchiefs, while the younger ones seemed to be marching in a more optimistic spirit, imagining the Utopian conditions of their new home-

land. There was a family friend of ours among them, and my heart went out to him. I felt an impulse to go up to him and say "May the hour be a good one for you," but something, I can't say what, held me back. I can still picture the heads of each one of them as they left. Some turned back and waved their red fezzes at the Christians who had gathered to see them off.

This second is from a man named Isa Erol, who was born in Greece and returned to his birthplace in 2003. Before leaving on this journey, he stated that he didn't miss his old home, saying, "Turkey is my homeland now." (Clark notes that most other Muslim survivors of the exchange would echo this sentiment, accurately so, since Turkey has provided for them for most of their lives.) However, when Erol returned from his village, he told a journalist that he felt differently:

I found the place where my house stood, but it wasn't there any more, there were just green fields. The new residents of the area—Greeks from Karaman in central Turkey—had built a new house just beside ours and they welcomed me in. I got very emotional when I stepped on the piece of land where I was born. My homeland is Turkey, but I wish the population exchange had not taken place, I wish we still lived there. After seeing my village, all my feelings had changed. Turkey is my homeland, but in these [Greek] places a good life could have been lived. But there is nothing that can be done about it any more.

In a review of this book, writer Theodore Dalrymple noted that "good fences make good, if not necessarily amicable, neighbors," and indeed Clark maintains that, on one level, the exchange can be viewed as a practical way of handling an immediate political and humanitarian crisis. With only Clark's final section of the book (bibliography and notes) in hand, an inquisitive reader would be well served for setting out on a fact-finding journey of his or her own.

Clark concludes that it is no longer possible for Greece and Turkey to "remain hermetically sealed and neatly divided from one another" in the twenty-first century simply because it's practically impossible for *anyone* to be hermetically sealed in a global economy; Europe is also much more multicultural today. He believes that the spiritual severance of the Byzantine-Ottoman world was never entirely complete, and that in it, and other, similar cases, "it is perhaps inevitable both that separation will be attempted; and also that it will never entirely succeed."

 околоолоо

A few other worthwhile related reads are

- *Farewell to Salonica*, by Leon Sciaky (Current Books, 1946). Like Thea Halo's book below, Sciaky's is a memoir, telling of his life in Salonica in the late 1800s and early 1900s. It's a portrait of Jewish life in Salonica and equally valuable for that fact as accounts like this aren't numerous. "Salonica became a Spanish city," writes Sciaky. "The Jews of Turkey, and especially of Salonica, retained their Spanish character, in their customs, in their cooking, in their social amenities, and in their pride and dignity." Sciaky reveals a childhood in which he felt secure and happy, but then recounts the changes that occurred as the Ottoman Empire fell apart and World War I began. Oddly, he doesn't say much about the population exchange, but he does portray well the tension that was created by it in the city.

- *Not Even My Name: A True Story*, by Thea Halo (Picador, 2000). Halo reveals the story of her mother, Sano, who at the age of ten was forced to leave her home with her family in 1920 on a death march to Syria. Halo's family and all the others from their remote village, south of the Black Sea, were Pontic Greeks. (*Pontus* is an ancient Greek word meaning "sea," *pontios* means "person of the sea," and the mountain range in the area is also known as Pontic.) Without doubt, Halo's is a harrowing, heartbreaking story, and it is nothing short of a miracle that Sano survived, and it's also quite amazing that she landed in New York at the age of fifteen with her new Assyrian husband—three times her age—and went on to raise ten children. There are many memorable passages in this book, among them this one: "I just wanted to go home. But there was no going home, and there never would be again. I had lost them all; everyone and everything I had ever loved. All I had left were my memories and two small scars on my leg. By the time I was ten years old, nothing else was left to me. Not even my name."

- *Salonica, City of Ghosts: Christians, Muslims and Jews, 1430–1950,* by Mark Mazower (Knopf, 2004). Mazower spent twenty years working on this project, and his book is a stellar achievement. The city that Mazower refers to as "an indexer's nightmare and a linguists' delight" (there are at least thirteen medieval spellings alone) is known by most people today as Thessaloniki. Salonica is the birthplace of Atatürk as well as Nâzım Hikmet, Turkey's best-known modern poet. By the time of the exchange, Jews made up a very large percentage of the population—as late as 1912 they were the largest ethnic group—and by July 1923, Mazower notes, there were still at least eighteen thousand Muslims (though by this time the city was predominantly Greek).

  By 1925, Mazower relates, the Salonica authorities, in an effort to erase any indication that there had ever been Muslims there, decided to demolish the city's minarets, which had defined its skyline for five centuries. He refers to the exchange as a turning point: "for like the departing Muslims, the Greek immigrants had been forced by the catastrophe that befell them to leave their own forebears behind. Since the dead who counted to them lay far away, often in unknown graves, why should they have attached importance to those who happened to be buried in their new places of settlement? . . . Feeling at home in Salonica meant turning it into an entirely new city, building settlements on the outskirts that had not even existed in Ottoman times."

• *Smyrna 1922: The Destruction of a City*, by Marjorie Housepian Dobkin (Harcourt Brace Jovanovich, 1966). The (long) subtitle of this book is *The first comprehensive account of the burning of the city and the expulsion of the Christians from Turkey in 1922*, and recounting this story, step by step, is exactly what Housepian, who is of Armenian descent, has done. Hers may be the only book to do so—or, at least, I haven't found another. Similar to *Twice a Stranger*, this reads quite like a novel.

Having researched official documents, letters, diaries, and news clippings and interviewed many eyewitnesses, Housepian reveals the events leading up to the burning of

Smyrna and its aftermath. In the process, she also reveals the economic motives behind the Western world's position and—surprise, surprise—the importance of oil in forming Near Eastern policy. (Remember the prescient quote, "He who owns the oil will own the world," written by French petroleum minister Henri Bérenger in a letter to Georges Clemenceau, December 12, 1919.)

Of all the personal narratives Housepian shares in the book, I am unable to forget one in particular, referring to the aftermath of the fire: "The family of Marika Tsakirides, intact, found it impossible to rejoice amid so much sorrow. 'Very few people were so lucky,' she says now. 'Almost everyone lost someone. "A mother lost a child; a child lost a mother." It has become—how do you say? A saying. A refrain. In Greek the words sound beautiful: *E Mana hani to pedi, ke to pedi ten Mana.* That is what happened in that time.'"

Housepian concludes by noting that "the brand of diplomacy that triumphed at Smyrna and Lausanne led to end products no less bizarre and even more costly in areas beyond Turkey. Yet the policy-makers of the 1920s, their agents, and their successors saw no portents of disaster in the discrepancy between what they had to gain and others had to lose." It seems to me that "to ponder the resolution of a minority problem in Turkey" nearly ninety years ago is more than a little relevant today.

The Kebab Conflict

MELINE TOUMANI

℘

IN ADDITION to the population exchange, the other two major controversial issues in Turkey today also involve people: the Armenians and the Kurds. To write a book on Istanbul and not mention them is equivalent to writing a book about a city in Germany and not mentioning the Holocaust, or writing a book about France and not mentioning the collaboration and resistance. So while I knew I had to present these subjects, I struggled with *how* I would deal with them. Again, because I am not a historian, I decided to provide a springboard for readers to jump off of and explore further if they wish.

"Since the 1920s, at least officially, no Armenians exist in Eastern Turkey. One may find an occasional village or valley which maintains traces of an Armenian past, but the passing tourist is unlikely to run into one." So states the current *Insight Guide to Turkey*. Most of the (very small) Armenian population in Turkey (about seventy thousand) is found in Istanbul. According to the group Armenians of Istanbul, there are ten Armenian churches in Istanbul, and there is the Armenian Patriarchate, which can be visited and is very interesting (Şarapnel Sokak 2, off Kennedy Caddesi in the Bazaar district). It's one of the smaller patriarchates in the Armenian church—there are only four: in Armenia, Lebanon, Istanbul, and Jerusalem—but it is greatly respected, and also unique: it marks the first time in history that a Muslim Sultan, namely, Mehmet the Conqueror, established a Christian center.

In their very good book *Turkey Unveiled*, Hugh and Nicole

Pope explain that "historians cannot say whether the gradual eviction of the great majority of Armenians, Greeks and other Christians between 1890 and 1923 was accidental or a premeditated attempt to make Anatolia into a 'Turkey for the Turks,' a phrase which is still the masthead motto of the nationalist newspaper *Hürriyet*. The Turks often say, with justification, that they were provoked, and Talaat's speech in 1918 [by Mehmed Talaat, minister of the interior] is as close as any senior Turkish official has come to an apology for the excesses. Armenian leaders, likewise, seldom admit to any fault." The Popes also discuss a book entitled *The Turkish National Identity and the Armenian Problem*, by Taner Akçam, who wrote the book as a political exile in Germany. In that book, Akçam explained that he preferred the Turkish word *kırım*, or "deliberate slaughter," to the modern word "genocide." "He also pointed to differences between the Turkish action and the genocide inflicted by Nazi Germany on the Jews. The Ottoman administration, for instance, had no ideology of racial purity, whatever the beliefs of the Young Turk leaders in the cabinet. He also pointed out that in Germany ordinary people have usually pleaded ignorance of the Jewish holocaust, while the state has admitted collective guilt. In Turkey, many older Turks know full well what happened to the Armenians and will privately admit it; it is the state which denies it."

Conversely, a character in Elif Shafak's *The Bastard of Istanbul*, Auntie Cevriye, represents another type of denial: "Twenty years in her career as a Turkish national history teacher, she was so accustomed to drawing an impermeable boundary between the past and the present, distinguishing the Ottoman Empire from the modern Turkish Republic, that she had actually heard the whole story as grim news from a distant country. The new state in Turkey had been established in 1923 and that was as far as the genesis of this regime could extend. Whatever might or might not have happened preceding this commencement date was the issue of another era—and another people."

The current state of affairs is that there are no formal diplomatic relations between Armenia and Turkey, and in 1993 Turkey
closed its borders with Armenia because of the Nagarno-
Karabakh War between Armenia and Azerbaijan, a Turkic nation
with close ties to Turkey. In 2007, Hrant Dink, editor-in-chief of
the newspaper *Agos*, advocate of Turkish-Armenian reconcilia-
tion, and one of Turkey's most prominent Armenians, was assassinated in Istanbul by a seventeen-year-old Turkish nationalist.
Dink's funeral was notable for the hundred thousand mourners
who marched in protest, chanting "We are all Armenians" and
"We are all Hrant Dink." Also in 2007, genocide declaration leg-
islation was introduced—but did not pass—in the U.S. Congress.
Turkey has proposed a joint commission of historians, open to
third parties, to study the facts and open up the archives on both
sides. Armenia agrees to this proposal in theory, but won't commit to it until Turkey admits to genocide first.

Though the following passage is from a novel, Louis de
Bernières's *Birds Without Wings*, it's worth keeping in mind: "It is
not possible to calculate how many Armenians died on the forced
marches. In 1915 the number was thought to be 300,000, a figure
which has been progressively increased ever since, thanks to the
efforts of angry propagandists. To argue about whether it was
300,000 or 2,000,000 is in a sense irrelevant and distasteful, however, since both numbers are great enough to be equally distress-
ing, and the suffering of individual victims in their trajectory
towards death is in both cases immeasurable."

∞∞∞∞∞

Most Armenian folktales and stories begin with a rather cryptic
phrase: *Djamangeen gar oo chagar*, or, "A long time ago there was
and there wasn't." Writer Peter Balakian refers to it as the
"Armenian invocation," and says it is "like the intrusive past,
which seemed to appear out of time, like lyric memory that had
been activated." Elif Shafak opens *The Bastard of Istanbul* with a

"preamble to a Turkish tale . . . and to an Armenian one": "Once there was; once there wasn't. / God's creatures were as plentiful as grains / And talking too much was a sin. . . ."

Storytelling is a revered Armenian tradition, and so is food. I was rather surprised to come across so many references to food while researching this book. Here are just a few passages I uncovered. From Peter Balakian, in *Black Dog of Fate*: "Food for us was a complex cultural emblem, an encoded script that embodied the long history and collective memory of our Near Eastern culture. I didn't know that eating also was a drama whose meaning was entwined in Armenia's bitter history." In chapter three of Shafak's *The Bastard of Istanbul* we are introduced to the Tchakhmakhchian clan: "Dikran Stamboulian gazed longingly at the food set out on the table, and reached for a jar of yogurt drink, Americanized with too many ice cubes. In multihued clay bowls of different sizes were many of his favorite dishes. . . . Though he was still fuming, his heart warmed at the sight of *hastırma* and entirely melted when he saw his favorite dish next to it: *burma*."

Food writer Paula Wolfert, writing for *Saveur* in 1998, related how she went to southeastern Turkey to learn about Turkish-Armenian cooking from her friend Ayfer Unsal, a renowned food writer in Turkey. "Ayfer may be Turkish," writes Wolfert, "but there could be no better way for me to learn Armenian cooking than through her. . . . She is deeply involved with a program that brings the children and grandchildren of exiled Armenians to Turkey, so that they can perhaps find common ground with contemporary Turks while visiting their ancestral land. Often, she entertains the visitors at her home, hoping that if we can cook and eat together, then maybe we can become friends. . . ."

And lastly, from *Black Dog of Fate*, Balakian says about his mother: "At certain moments her unacknowledged cultural past became an irrepressible force, a statement of things culinary, in the name of the kitchen, the inviolable sanctuary of a culture that had barely escaped extinction. In the kitchen, my mother really was saying: We are alive and well, things have order, the world has grace and style."

The piece below, which originally appeared in the April/May 2007 issue of the terrific magazine *Culture+Travel* (now published as an insert in *Art+Auction*), explores Armenian culinary specialties when they cross geographic boundaries. *Culture + Travel* is a beautifully produced magazine that has earned a reputation as an intelligent and gorgeous publication. Its top photographers and writers are known for truly getting under the skin of a place, as well as offering fresh takes on favorite places and lesser-known locales. Published by Louise Blouin Media, a subscription is complimentary: www.artinfo.com.

MELINE TOUMANI is an Armenian-American journalist and is working on a book, to be published by Random House, that delves into the conflict between modern-day Turks and the Armenian Diaspora. She has also written for *The New York Times*, *The Nation*, Salon.com, and *Mother Jones*, among others.

I JUST wanted to know what was ours. I was sitting at a long dinner table with my Armenian relatives in California, and I had raised a simple question that led to a full-scale argument. Among the vast spread of traditional Middle Eastern delights that we ate when we gathered together, was there a single dish that we could say was definitively *Armenian*?

"The most Armenian food is *khorovadz!*" declared my uncle. He'd used the Armenian word for kebab, or grilled meat. But that was too easy, I thought. Surely even cavemen had cooked meat on skewers, so the mere fact that we have a word for it in the Armenian language doesn't make it Armenian.

"I think the most Armenian dish is *choerek*," said my cousin. She was referring to a sweet buttery biscuit rolled into twists and sometimes cross shapes. It had to be Armenian, she argued, because we always eat it at Easter. Armenia was the world's first Christian nation, with an independent church, so she reasoned— sincerely if not convincingly—that an Easter dish had to stand apart from all the foods that were common with Muslim neighbors.

I raised the same question with Armenian friends in New York, where I live. Many waxed nostalgic for their grandmothers' *lahmajun*, a spicy pizza-like snack on paper-thin dough, spread with a fine puree of lamb, tomato, pepper, and onion, crisp at the edges but chewy in the middle. One young woman I know hosted parties with Armenian girlfriends where they rolled *dolma* and *yalanji*—varieties of stuffed grape leaves—for hours on end. Others spoke of *kufte*, a croquette of cracked wheat filled with ground meat, onions, raisins, and pine nuts. I recalled the festive Armenian gatherings of my childhood where we would cook a penny or a dime into the center of just one *kufte*, and whoever discovered it in their portion would have good luck. And wherever there was *kufte* there was sure to be *manti*, perhaps the ideal comfort food: a big bowl of tiny, crusty meat dumplings drizzled with yogurt and a peppery tomato sauce.

But my investigations also engendered a sense of futility. After all, the menu of any Middle Eastern restaurant—Turkish, Lebanese, Persian, Syrian, Georgian—listed nearly all the same dishes, and the partisans of those regions had just as many fond memories to bolster their claims.

When it comes to defining Armenian food, part of the problem is obvious: For much of their history, Armenians have been a people without a country. The Armenian Kingdom reached the height of its power in the first century BC, when it stretched from Syria to the present Azerbaijan. But centuries of conquest followed—Byzantine, Persian, Ottoman, and Russian—and Armenians adapted to survive. They maintained their unique language as well as their religion, in spite of being surrounded by Muslim neighbors. But by 1991, when the Soviet Union collapsed and the now-tiny Armenian Republic regained independence, more than half of the world's Armenians were scattered around the globe.

Many Armenians in the diaspora have roots in Turkey, as descendants of survivors of the 1915 genocide in which the Ottoman-Turkish government attempted to massacre or deport its Ottoman-Armenian population. These survivors often ended up in Lebanon or Syria. Later, many resettled in the United States. One of the largest Armenian communities grew in Watertown, Massachusetts, where Armenian grandmothers still round up orders for batches of *lahmajun* after church.

Charles Perry, an expert on Middle Eastern cuisine, believes that while names of dishes are no guarantee of origin, they are an important clue. The beloved *lahmajun*, for example, comes from the Arabic words *lahm* (meaning "meat"), *bi* ("with"), and *ajin* (meaning "dough"). He guesses that the dish was invented in Syria. *Kufte* comes from the Persian verb *kuftan*—to grind. *Dolma* is Turkish for "stuffed thing." And *choerek* comes from a Turkish word meaning "rounded," and besides, the Greeks and Georgians eat *choerek* at Easter, too.

Was it possible that a people with a unique language and faith, who had retained such a strong sense of identity over the centuries, nonetheless had no cuisine of its own?

Armed with these linguistics lessons, I paid a visit to Sevan Bakery in Flushing, Queens, an Armenian market run by Arthur Matevossian, a recent immigrant from Yerevan, Armenia. When I asked him why so many popular Armenian dishes had Turkish names, his smile disappeared. "I don't know, but there is no such thing as Turkish cuisine!" he shouted. Meanwhile, an elegantly dressed customer, Diane Piranian, making her regular weekly purchase of *manti*, told me that she was the granddaughter of General

Sebouh, a major figure in the Armenian revolutionary movement in Turkey. After surviving the massacres of 1915, he moved to the U.S. and opened a grocery store. "Whatever the Turks eat, they stole from us!" Piranian affirmed in a loud whisper. Ethnic pride (and a deeply troubled relationship with Turkey) notwithstanding, my compatriots were only partly wrong. In the fifteenth century, says Perry, when Mehmet the Conqueror won Constantinople, the city was nearly deserted. Mehmet ordered it repopulated, half by Turks and half by other peoples: Armenians, Jews, Greeks, and even some French and Italians. Soon, in the legendary kitchens of his Topkapı Palace, cooks of every nationality worked side by side, developing modern Turkish cuisine, and all the cultures of Constantinople added a few of their own ingredients.

But according to Perry, there is one dish that Turks always credit to Armenians, an appetizer called *topik*. He traces its provenance to the late Ottoman period in Constantinople, where lively pubs called *meyhanes* were the only places men could drink. Since Islam frowned on alcohol, *meyhanes* were often run by Armenians. They served elaborate spreads of *meze*, dishes designed to be "particularly good for cushioning the stomach so one could drink a lot." *Topik*, a chickpea puree layered with currants and pine nuts, fits the bill. At least Armenians got credit for one dish, even if it was basically a bar snack that neither I nor any of my Armenian friends in the U.S. had ever tasted.

On a recent trip to Turkey, I found myself far from Istanbul's *meyhanes*, spending a long day under the late-July sun of Southeastern Anatolia. I had been hiking with a team of researchers up steep hills and over slippery rocks, deciphering maps, trying to determine the origins of various architectural ruins. At each site, we looked around and debated: Had this been Armenian? Kurdish? Assyrian? The legacies of these once-thriving minority populations are unacknowledged by Turkish authorities, adding another layer of pathos to a poor and troubled part of the country.

So it was something of a relief to leave these sites behind at the end of the day and head into Van, the provincial capital, and search for a place to eat dinner. In the city center, among tea houses and tiny shops, I looked up and found myself in front of a restaurant whose gleaming glass window was painted in huge, bright yellow letters with one word: *Kebabistan.*

Could it be that simple? I was in the land of kebab, and—at least until the next day's work—that was all I really needed to know.

Recommended Resources

- Armenian Heritage Organization (AHO) (armenian heritage.com)

- Armenian Library and Museum of America (ALMA), Watertown, Massachusetts (617 926 2562 / almainc.org)

- Armenian National Institute (ANI), Washington, D.C. (202 383 9009 / armenian-genocide.org)

- Armenian Research Center, University of Michigan–Dearborn (313 593 5000 / umd.umich.edu/dept/armenian)

- *Black Dog of Fate: An American Son Uncovers His Armenian Past,* by Peter Balakian (BasicBooks, revised edition, 2009). This wonderful, beautifully written, and sometimes humorous memoir appears on nearly every recommended reading list for Armenian studies, and with good reason. As I've recounted above, the older members of the Balakian family strongly believed in the rituals of dining as primary expressions of cultural continuity. One day, shortly after moving from Teaneck to Tenafly, New Jersey, Peter asked his mother why they couldn't just have casseroles for dinner. "My mother said 'Casseroles?' and then snapped back, 'If the Americans want to eat that way, let them.' " Later, when he was bullied by two neighborhood boys, his mother said, " 'What do you expect if they eat casseroles and minute steaks? What kind of people are these?' "

Food aside, other Armenian quirks are lovingly revealed in this story of one family in suburban New Jersey in the late 1950s and '60s. Balakian's relationship with his grandmother Nafina is really the centerpiece of the story, and I was teary-eyed more than once when reading about her. It was in high school that Balakian discovered poetry, and he writes, "I've come to see poetry as the chain of language linking lands and events, people and places that make up our family story. Poetry has been a deep well of thought and feeling and language lushness that the Balakians have lived by." It might seem strange, but in the Balakian family Armenia, Turkey, death marches, massacres, and survival were not discussed, ever. Balakian's self-education began with the classic memoir *Ambassador Morgenthau's Story* (Doubleday, 1919), and he's been on a crash course ever since, devouring every book, oral history, and historical document he can get his hands on. As I only recently discovered, he edited a newly issued edition of *Ambassador Morgenthau's Story* (Wayne State, 2003). And happily, he continues to write poems. I particularly enjoyed *June-tree: New and Selected Poems, 1974–2000* (HarperPerennial, 2004), which includes his notable poems "The History of Armenia," "The Claim," and "The Oriental Rug."

• *The Burning Tigris: The Armenian Genocide and America's Response*, by Peter Balakian (HarperCollins, 2003). If you're interested in reading a single volume on the Armenian issue from the late 1800s to the present day that's both detailed enough and fast-paced, this is it. In addition to the

on this old conflict, and when I was searching through my files to find a piece that both outlined the history of the conflict and was fairly up-to-date, I found I didn't have one. So I turned to Christiane Bird's excellent book *A Thousand Sighs, A Thousand Revolts: Journeys in Kurdistan* (Ballantine, 2004) and decided that this was the right occasion to make an exception and feature a book excerpt. The excerpt below is from the first chapter of the book, "Through the Back Door."

CHRISTIANE BIRD is also the author of *Neither East nor West: One Woman's Journey Through the Islamic Republic of Iran* (Atria, 2001), among others.

THE KURDS are the largest ethnic group in the world without a state of their own. Probably numbering between 25 and 30 million, they live in an arc of land that stretches through Turkey, Syria, Iraq, Iran, and parts of the former Soviet Union, with the vast majority residing in the region where Turkey, Syria, Iraq, and Iran meet. About eight hundred thousand Kurds also live in Europe, with about five hundred thousand of those in Germany, while some twenty-five thousand Kurds live in the United States and at least six thousand in Canada.

Not a country, Kurdistan cannot be found on modern maps. The term was first used as a geographical expression by the Saljuq Turks in the twelfth century and came into common usage in the sixteenth century, when much of the Kurdish region fell under the control of the Ottoman and Safavid Empires. For the Kurds themselves, Kurdistan is both an actual and a mythical place—an isolated, half-hidden, mountainous homeland that has historically offered sanctuary from the treacherous outside world, and from treacherous fellow Kurds.

I became interested in the Kurds during a 1998 journey to Iran. While there, I traveled to Sanandaj, Iran's unofficial Kurdish capital, where I was immediately struck by how different the area seemed from the rest of the Islamic Republic—heartbreaking in its lonesome beauty, and defiant. Despite a large number of Revolutionary Guards on the streets, the men swaggered and women strode. These people are not cowed, I thought—no wonder they make the Islamic government nervous.

In Sanandaj, I stayed with a Kurdish family I had met on the bus, and attended a wedding held in a small pasture filled with about two hundred people in traditional dress. To one side were the city's ugly concrete buildings; to another, empty lots strewn with litter. But the people and their costumes, framed by the far-off Zagros Mountains, transcended the tawdry surroundings. Women in bright reds, pinks, greens, blues, and golds. Men in baggy pants, woven belts, and heavy turbans. Boys playing with hoops. Girls dreaming by a bonfire. Musicians on a mournful flute and enormous drum, followed by circling men dancing single file, one waving a handkerchief over his head.

After I returned home, I began reading more about the Kurds. Who are these people, and why don't we know more about them?

The Kurds are the fourth-largest ethnic group in the Middle East—after the Arabs, Turks, and Persians—accounting for perhaps 15 percent of its population. They occupy some of the region's most strategic and richest lands. Turkey's Kurdistan contains major coal deposits, as well as the headwaters of the Tigris and Euphrates Rivers—important irrigation sources for Syria, Iraq, and Turkey. Iraqi Kurdistan holds significant oil reserves, and Turkey's and Syria's Kurdistan, lesser ones. Much of Iraqi and Syrian Kurdistan also lies in the fertile valley of and adjoining northern Mesopotamia, one of the world's richest breadbaskets and most ancient lands.

The Iraqi Kurds, numbering about 5 million, constitute

between one-fourth and one-fifth of Iraq's population. Despite much repression, they have always been recognized by the state as a separate ethnic group. Iraqi Kurds have at times held important government and military positions, and between 1992 and 2003, ran their own semiautonomous, fledgling democracy in Iraq's so-called "northern no-fly zone." Post–Saddam Hussein, the Kurds are assuming a central role in the forging of a new Iraq.

Numbering 13 or 14 million, or one-half of all Kurds, Turkey's Kurds comprise at least 20 percent of their nation and boast a birthrate that is nearly double that of their compatriots—promising an even greater presence in the future. Turkey's Kurds have been brutally repressed both culturally and politically since the founding of the modern Turkish Republic in 1923. Turkey is now striving to join the European Union, however, and its acceptance therein will depend largely on an improvement in its human rights record toward the Kurds.

Numbering about 6.5 million, or 10 percent of Iran's population, Iranian Kurds ran their own semiautonomous state as early as the 1300s. Today, they have about twenty reform-minded representatives in Iran's Parliament, who, along with many others, are pushing for more liberalization in the Islamic Republic. Syrian Kurds, although numbering only about 1.4 million, constitute 9 percent of their country's sparse population, with the Syrian capital of Damascus home to an influential Kurdish community since the Middle Ages.

Exact population figures for the Kurds are unavailable because no reliable census has been conducted for decades. All of the countries in which they reside regard them as a political threat and downplay their existence. And without a nation-state of their own, the Kurds have been slow in letting their presence be known to the outside world.

This is changing. Thanks in part to recent political developments, of which the Iraq war of 2003 is only the latest, and in part to a growing diaspora, satellite communications, and the Internet, today's Kurds are both rapidly developing a national consciousness as a people, and overcoming the geographic and psychic isolation that has plagued them for centuries. And as they do so, questions of nationalism, multiculturalism, and a possible future redrawing of international boundaries arise.

The Kurds possess an ancient and romantic culture, which many Kurds trace back to the Medes, a people mentioned in the Bible and other early texts. Inhabitants of the Kurdish lands may have pioneered agriculture as early as 12,000 BC, while the first probable written mention of the Kurds appears in *Anabasis*, penned by Xenophon the Greek some twenty-four hundred years ago. In his account of a 401 BC battle, which pitted ten thousand Greek mercenaries against the Persian forces, he writes of the "Karduchoi"—probably Kurds: "The Greeks spent a happy night with plenty to eat. Talking about the struggle now past. For they passed through the country of the Karduchoi, fighting all the time and they had suffered worse things at the hands of the Karduchoi than all that the King of Persia and his general, Tissaphernes, could do to them."

The Arab armies arrived in Kurdistan in AD 637, bringing with them the new religion of Islam. At first, the Kurdish tribes put up a fierce resistance, but as the enormous might of the Arabs became clear to them, they gradually converted to Islam, nominally submitting to the new central power. However, in a pattern that has continued up into the modern era, the Kurds' first loyalty remained to their tribal leaders, who retained considerable local authority.

In the tenth century AD, the Kurds entered what some scholars call their "golden age." Kurds served as generals in the Islamic army, scholars and administrators in the Islamic court, and rulers of wealthy semiautonomous fiefdoms, which thrived on trade from the Silk Routes then passing through the area. The most famous Muslim warrior of all time, Salah al-Din, or Saladin, was a Kurd born in AD 1137 in Tikrit—also the hometown of Saddam Hussein, the infamous former president of Iraq. Of the Hadhabani tribe, Saladin reconquered Jerusalem from Richard the Lionhearted during the Crusades. He established the Ayyubid dynasty, which ruled in some form until the end of the fifteenth century. It is unlikely, however, that Saladin thought of his central identity as Kurdish; first and foremost, he was Muslim.

The vast majority of today's Kurds are also Muslim, with at least 75 percent belonging to the Sunni branch and 15 percent to the Shiite. Sunnis and Shiites are the two great factions of Islam, a schism based largely on the question of leadership succession. The Sunnis, who comprise about 90 percent of the world's 1.1 billion Muslims, believe that the Prophet Muhammad's successors should be chosen by consensus; the Shiites, who live mostly in Iran, believe that his successors should be his direct descendants. But whether Sunni or Shiite, most Kurds view themselves as moderate Muslims. The political side of Islam has also at times created tension between their Muslim and Kurdish identities. Some nationalist Kurds even say that Islam is detrimental to their people, as it subjugates the Kurdish cause to the larger Islamic goal of a united world community of believers. "Don't have any confidence in a holy man even if his turban should be straight from heaven," goes one Kurdish proverb.

The Kurdish region is religiously diverse, with many other Kurds belonging to one of three small religious groups—the Yezidis, Ahl-e Haqqs or Kakais, and Alevis—whose faiths combine pre-Islamic and Islamic beliefs; some scholars classify the Ahl-e Haqqs and Alevis as Muslim. Non-Kurdish Christian groups such as the Assyrians and Chaldeans (a Catholic branch of the Assyrians) also live in the area, as do evangelical Christians and a few Armenians, though most Armenians left the region following the Turks' massacres of their communities in the 1890s and

1915. A large Jewish Kurdish community once lived in Kurdistan, but departed the area after the founding of Israel.

The 1200s and 1300s brought disaster to the Kurdish lands. First came waves of Mongol invasions headed by Hulagu, grandson of Genghis Khan, destroying many Kurdish villages and major towns. Then came the invasions of the emperor Tamerlane and his son, who, after capturing Baghdad and Damascus, again sacked hundreds of Kurdish settlements.

But by the sixteenth century, the region was again flourishing. Under the reign of the Ottoman and Safavid Empires, which rose to power in Turkey and Persia respectively in the early 1500s, Kurdish princes ruled over emirates with such romantic-sounding names as Bahdinan, Bitlis, and Jazira bin Umar. Often only loosely controlled by their Turkish and Persian overlords, the princes had powerful militias—composed of nominally allied tribes—at their command, and courts filled with musicians, poets, scientists, and religious scholars. A complex social and political order was maintained, as the Kurdish princes, Kurdish tribes,

Ottomans, and Safavids successfully balanced power among them for about three hundred years.

With the passing decades, however, cracks appeared in the system. The importance of the Silk Routes declined, the rule of the empires became more oppressive, and quarrels among Kurdish princes and tribes turned into wars. Plagues devastated the region, and, by the mid–1800s, Kurdish high culture had again all but collapsed. Entire tribes were eviscerated or deported, and the Kurds' sedentary agricultural communities gave way to their more traditional nomadic lifestyle, already in existence for thousands of years. A chaotic tribal order, with an economy based on raiding, emerged. European travelers passing through Kurdistan in the nineteenth century wrote of meeting ruthless bandits and warring tribes, adding more fuel to the Kurds' by-then well-established reputation for ferocity. "It is better to fight than to sit idle"; "One crowded hour of glorious life is worth an age without a name," go two old Kurdish proverbs.

Many Kurds today downplay their tribal heritage, fearing that it portrays them as a primitive people. But to many outsiders, it is part of their distinction. There are dozens of tribes, and hundreds of subtribes, some of which date back centuries. In the past, many tribes had their own distinct dress, folktales, music, and social cus-

toms. Some were known for specific characteristics, such as red hair, broad builds, boorishness, or courage. Tribal affiliations united as well as divided people and, though much diminished in importance today, are still central to many Kurds' identity and to Kurdish politics. There are also many nontribal Kurds, living primarily in the cities and on the plains. The nomadic tribal lifestyle has all but disappeared. Only "seminomads" remain, living in villages in winter and in goat-hair tents in summer as they move their flocks between their lowland and mountain pastures.

After World War I and the collapse of the Ottoman Empire, the Kurds came close to achieving national independence. The 1920 Treaty of Sèvres recognized their political rights and left open to possibility the establishment of an autonomous Kurdistan. But the treaty was never ratified, and, three years later, with the rise of Turkey's Mustafa Kemal Atatürk, another treaty was negotiated. The 1923 Treaty of Lausanne recognized a new Turkish republic; paved the way for the new British Mandate of Iraq to acquire the oil-rich Kurdish province of Mosul; and made no mention of the Kurds, then in a state of political disarray, torn apart by tribal loyalties. Shortly thereafter, the Western powers finalized the modern international borders of Turkey, Syria, and Iraq—new countries carved out of the old Ottoman Empire—while reaffirming those of Iran, then known as Persia. In a few short strokes of the pen, Kurdistan—never more than a vaguely delineated land divided among many tribes—was literally erased from the map and the Kurds were parceled out among four nation-states.

Then a foreign concept to the Middle East, the nation-state is still an idea with which the entire region struggles. Many Kurds have never really accepted the West's imposed borders, which in some places severed tribes and even families in half. "A thousand sighs, a thousand tears, a thousand revolts, a thousand hopes," goes an old Kurdish poem about the Kurds' determination to be masters of their own lands. Meanwhile, the erstwhile nation-states, desperate to establish a national identity based on a unified culture, have marginalized and persecuted the Kurds.

Yet the Kurds have also been their own worst enemy. Their history is strewn with gut-wrenching tales of infighting, brutality, and betrayal. One recent definitive instance occurred in 1996, when the Iraqi Kurdish leader Massoud Barzani turned to Saddam Hussein—the Kurds' most lethal modern enemy—to help him defeat his rival Jalal Talabani, who had earlier solicited help from another traditional Kurdish enemy, the Iranian government. Saddam had been instrumental in manipulating the two leaders' actions, which occurred in the wake of a failed CIA-backed coup attempt to oust him from office, and the events enhanced his standing internationally while diminishing that of the Kurds.

Just what is it about the Kurds, I thought as I read about one revolt after another, that gives them their courage, determination, and cussedness? What is it that makes a people a people? And, conversely, why *haven't* the Kurds been able to establish their own state? How does a people evolve into a nation?

Some of the answers to these questions must lie in the mountains, I thought. Mountain people all over the world—Scotland, Appalachia, Afghanistan, Chechnya—are a notoriously independent, stubborn, rebellious, and proud lot. Isolated in their craggy fortresses, they are accustomed to taking care of themselves, and don't cotton well to being told what to do. There's a reason why one of the first great rebels of all time, the Greek god Prometheus, "guilty" of bringing fire to man against Zeus's wishes, was banished to a mountain in the Caucasus.

And some of the answers must lie in the extraordinary repression the Kurds have suffered—and survived; as the hackneyed saying goes, what doesn't kill you, makes you stronger. In the last two decades alone, the Kurds have endured multiple aerial bombings and lethal chemical attacks, the ruthless destruction of thousands of their villages, the assassination of their leaders, killings and kidnappings, torture and inhuman prison conditions, crippling economic conditions, the banning of their language and culture, and the deprivation of that most basic right of all: the right to call themselves "Kurds."

This last violation occurred in Turkey, one of the most democratic of Middle Eastern countries, between 1924 and 1991, during which time Kurds were declared to be "mountain Turks who have forgotten their language." Anyone who said otherwise risked arrest and torture. In contrast, modern Iran and Iraq, despite their repressive regimes, have never denied the Kurds their identity. Up until 1975, Saddam Hussein even made regular visits to Kurdistan, posing for the cameras in Kurdish dress, while Iran's Islamic government has always granted the Kurds some basic cultural—though not political—rights.

How do a people function after such a horrific history? How do they rebuild after attempted genocide? How does trauma shape and filter lives?

The Arabs have an old term for places such as Kurdistan—*hilad es-siba'*, meaning "land of lions"—i.e., land not controlled by central government. Once applied to the most inaccessible areas of the Middle East, including its mountains, deserts, and marshes, the term connotes regions inhabited by isolated peoples who listen more to their hearts and traditions than to "civilization." Some scholars even once posited a kind of division of labor "between the tame and the insolent, the domesticated and the independent" with the rebels keeping "the urban civilization of the Middle East refreshed and in motion." But in our age of telecommunications and cyberspace, urbanization and globalization, it's questionable how much longer such lands will exist—if indeed they still do. Once remote Kurdistan, for one, is now in the throes of rapid modernization, with the Internet, satellite dishes, and supermarkets making their arrival. How are the Kurds coping with jumping one hundred years in the space of a decade, maintaining a sense of self as their traditional world tips, whirls, and shudders around them?

I wanted to travel to Iraq to explore these questions. I wanted
to find out more about these mysterious, stubborn, seemingly
inextinguishable people called Kurds. And the world needs to
know more about them, too, I told my friends and editors—the
Kurds are important; they're central to the future of Iraq, Turkey,
Iran, and Syria, and hence to the whole Middle East.

Recommended Resources

- *Blood and Belief: The PKK and the Kurdish Fight for Independence,* by Aliza Marcus (NYU Press, 2007). Marcus
  reported on the Kurds for *The Boston Globe* and *The Christian Science Monitor* for eight years before writing this in-
  depth book, the first (in English) about the PKK. (She was
  also put on trial in Turkey for her reporting.) Marcus traces
  the beginnings of the PKK, in 1978, to the present day,
  including the capture of Abdullah Ocalan, the imprisoned
  leader of the PKK. Marcus was one of the first Western
  reporters to meet with PKK rebels and also cowrote with
  Andrew Apostolou, an analyst of Kurdish politics, a good
  piece for *The Boston Globe* entitled "Talking to Turkey's
  Kurds" (February 26, 2008) that lays out a reasonable plan
  for the U.S. to help Turkey end the conflict.

- Kurdish Heritage Foundation of America, Brooklyn, New
  York (718 783 7930 / kurdishlibrarymuseum.com)

- *Kurdistan: In the Shadow of History,* by Susan Meiselas (Random House, 1997; University of Chicago, 2008). This is
  the only illustrated book I know of about the Kurds, and
  it's beautiful. Photographer Meiselas first ventured into
  Iraq after the 1991 Gulf War and was so moved by her visit

that she decided to create a visual history of the Kurds. The book is filled with not only her photographs but also older images by journalists, colonial administrators, missionaries, anthropologists, etc., as well as letters, memoirs, maps, advertisements, and government reports, making it a kind of scrapbook—a format I particularly like.

- *The Kurds: A People in Search of Their Homeland*, by Kevin McKiernan (St. Martin's Press, 2006). War journalist McKiernan details the Kurds since 1975 and only in Turkey, Syria, and Iraq (not Iran). His extensive travels through the region—and his telling in the first person— combine to produce a memoir-documentary that reveals the diversity of the Kurds and the "secret horror" that is their history.

- "Minority Rules," by Meline Toumani (*The New York Times Magazine*, February 17, 2008). In this excellent article, Toumani visits Diyarbakir, in southeastern Turkey, and spends time with the former mayor, Abdullah Demirbas. She tells us that, according to a report by the pro-Kurdish Democratic Society Party, Demirbas had violated the ban on speaking or writing in Kurdish on several occasions. Toumani deftly wades through the complexities of the Kurdish–Turkish issue—this piece is very much worth accessing online.

- *A Modern History of the Kurds*, by David McDowall (I. B. Tauris, 2001, third revised edition). This impressive, scholarly work is for readers who really want the definitive volume. McDowall is a British specialist on Middle Eastern affairs and he presents a thorough history of the Kurds in Iran, Iraq, and Turkey from the nineteenth century to the present day.

• Washington Kurdish Institute, Washington, D.C. (202 484
0140 / kurd.org)

RECOMMENDED READING

At Home in Turkey, text by Berrin Torolsan, photos by Solvi dos
Santos (Thames & Hudson, 2008). A beautiful and substantive
volume by the winning duo of Torolsan—publishing director
of *Cornucopia: The Magazine for Connoisseurs of Turkey*—and dos
Santos—one of the world's best-known lifestyle photographers. Abodes all across Turkey are featured, a dozen of which
are in Istanbul, including the Kıbrıslı *yalı,* now home to Rahmi
M. Koç, Turkey's leading industrialist. Torolsan's unrivaled
knowledge of even the smallest details make this an inspiring,
must-have volume.

The Balkans: A Short History, by Mark Mazower (Modern Library,
2000). A volume in the Modern Library Chronicles series, this
is an excellent 188-page read complete with seven maps (from
1550 to 2000) and a thorough chronology (beginning with the
foundation of Constantinople).

A Byzantine Journey, by John Ash (Random House, 1995). In a
casual survey about Byzantium, Ash discovered that most people he spoke to were not at all clear on the subject. They didn't
know which territories became a part of the Empire, and most
didn't know that the Byzantines spoke Greek. "Such confusion," notes Ash, "was hardly shocking, but, given the enormous debt we owe the Byzantines, it was saddening." So he set

off on a Byzantine journey throughout Anatolia, and he created memorable and thought-provoking images.

Byzantium: The Early Centuries (1989), *Byzantium: The Apogee* (1992), *Byzantium: The Decline and Fall* (1995), and *A Short History of Byzantium* (1997), all by John Julius Norwich (published by Knopf in the U.S. and by Viking in the United Kingdom; paperbacks are also available). In his preface to *A Short History of Byzantium*, renowned historian Norwich wisely notes that the Byzantine Empire lasted for a total of 1,123 years and 18 days, "and if anyone thinks me foolhardy to have attempted to cover it in a single volume, I can say only that I agree." And I think *Short History* will appeal to most readers planning a trip to Istanbul (but I hope at least a few readers will be so fascinated by some period of the Empire's history that they will be inspired to pick up one of Norwich's individual volumes).

Crescent & Star: Turkey Between Two Worlds, Stephen Kinzer (Farrar, Straus & Giroux, 2001). Kinzer, a veteran foreign correspondent, was named the first bureau chief in Istanbul for *The New York Times* in 1996 (he is now based in Chicago). For this book, Kinzer has written ten chapters, and in between each is a minichapter of sorts referred to as a *meze*. Each *meze* is a more personal account of his life in Turkey, and taken with the other chapters makes for a winning combination.

The Crusades

It's impossible to fully grasp Istanbul's place in history without knowledge of the Crusades. First and foremost among resources is Steven Runciman's outstanding work, *A History of the Crusades*, originally published in three volumes in 1951, 1952, and 1954 by Cambridge University Press. Over the years it has also been published in paperback editions by Penguin and Cambridge, always in three individual editions (or at least, I've searched for a single-volume edition and cannot locate one). Sir Steven, who passed away in 2000, was perhaps uniquely qualified to write this: he was reading Latin and Greek by age five, and throughout his life he mastered an astonishing number of languages. So when he wrote about the Near East (and nearly all of his more than fifteen books relate to the Near East), he relied on accounts not only in Latin and Greek but also Arabic, Turkish, Persian, Hebrew, Armenian, Syriac, and Georgian. From 1942 to 1945 he was professor of Byzantine art and history at Istanbul University, where he began research on the Crusades. To say that *A History of the Crusades* is based on immense scholarship is an understatement.

According to his obituary in the *The Times of London*, Runciman did not portray the crusaders with sympathy. In his eyes, the crusaders destroyed the "real centre of medieval civilization and the last bastion of antiquity, Constantinople, and the Byzantine Empire." Even if you read only one volume in this trilogy, it will likely be an eye-opening and hugely interesting experience. (As an aside, if you get caught up in Runciman fever, Cambridge University Press published a wonderful tribute to him in 2006: *Byzantine Style, Religion and Civilization: In Honour of Sir Steven Runciman,*

featuring a collection of essays that was long planned by
British Byzantinists and includes a memoir of his life and a
full bibliography.)

The Crusades Through Arab Eyes, by Amin Maalouf
(Schocken, 1989), is revealed through an Arab lens. Interestingly, while the Arab view sees the Crusades as unprovoked
and brutal to the point of disbelief, it also proudly honors
Saladin, who was sultan of Egypt in 1175 and precipitated
the Third Crusade by his recovery of Jerusalem in 1187. Saladin was renowned for his knightly courtesy and made peace
with Richard I of England in 1192. He is a hero among the
Arabs for delivering the greatest defeat ever to a European
society.

I have written of Karen Armstrong in my previous books,
and her *Holy War: The Crusades and Their Impact on Today's
World* (Doubleday, 1991) is an excellent source. Armstrong,
one of our foremost commentators on religious affairs, is
also the author of the excellent *A History of God* (Knopf,
1993) and *Islam: A Short History* (Modern Library, 2000).
She has taught at the Leo Baeck College for the Study of
Judaism and the Training of Rabbis and Teachers and in
1999 was awarded a Muslim Public Affairs Council Media
Award. After writing *Holy War*, Armstrong explains she was
"so saddened by the conflict between the three Abraham
traditions that I decided to embark on the research for my
book *A History of God*. I wanted to demonstrate the strong
and positive ideals and visions that Jews, Christians, and
Muslims share in common. It is now over a millennium
since Pope Urban II called the First Crusade in 1095, but the
hatred and suspicion that this expedition unleashed still
reverberates, never more so than on September 11, 2001,
and during the terrible days that followed. It is tragic that

our holy wars continue, but for that very reason we must strive for mutual understanding and for what in these pages I have called 'triple vision.' " *Holy War* is a great single-volume work that appeals to both novices and know-it-alls.

Culture Smart! Turkey: A Quick Guide to Customs and Etiquette, by Charlotte McPherson (Kuperard, 2005), and *Culture Shock! Turkey: A Survival Guide to Customs and Etiquette*, by Arın Bayraktaroğlu (Marshall Cavendish, 2007, reprint version). I like these books and continue to use both. Since you may not find both at your favorite bookstore or library and therefore can't compare them on your own, just read the one you locate—but try hard to find at least *one* of these volumes, because they both go into much more depth than a guidebook.

Dreaming of East: Western Women and the Exotic Allure of the Orient, Barbara Hodgson (Greystone Books, 2005). Hodgson has been fascinated by the handful of Western European women who went to the eastern Ottoman Empire—Egypt, Palestine, Syria, Iraq, and Turkey—from 1717 to 1930. Countess Ida von Hahn-Hahn's comment from 1844 encapsulates what appealed to many: "From the world that *is*, I want to go to that which *was*. From the West of today to the Orient of yesterday." These women were seeking freedom in the East, and Hodgson found herself wondering how a region where women were typically secluded and restricted could possibly offer others a liberty denied to them in their own, more liberal countries.

A Fez of the Heart: Travels Around Turkey in Search of a Hat, by Jeremy Seal (Picador, 1995). In 1826, the turban was abolished in Turkey and replaced by the fez. In 1925, the fez was abolished (Atatürk regarded it as "symptomatic of a stubborn adherence among his people to discredited, obsolete, and reactionary values") and replaced by homburgs, panamas, bowlers, and flatcaps—Western hats, essentially. Eric Lawlor, in *Looking for Osman* (see page 114), notes that "Turkey has not been the same since the day in 1925 when Atatürk strolled through Kastamonu wearing not the fez decreed by tradition, but—of all things—a panama hat. The townspeople were dumbfounded. Perhaps they realized that history was being made, that by changing hats, Atatürk had altered Turkey forever." In *Portrait of a Turkish Family* (see page 120), Irfan Orga remembers this event: "What a consternation there was then and the state of the nation's nerves! Was Atatürk playing with them? Was he sitting in his chateau in Ankara devising new things to disturb and break their habits of centuries?" Seal confirms that headgear in Turkey "had a symbolic significance inconceivable in the West. In Turkey even today, you are largely identified by what you wear on your head." When Seal bought a fez in the Mediterranean town of Side, the shopkeeper told him, "I think you are not modern." Seal began to think about the fact that it's illegal for Turks to wear a fez, but not illegal for women to sunbathe topless on the beach, and he journeyed around Turkey to discover how the state of the fez had come to pass, how "this once grand hat, the hat of the greatest empire of the East, of the sultan and of Allah," had led to this humiliation.

Harem: The World Behind the Veil, by Alev Lytle Croutier (Abbeville, 1989). "I was born in a *konak* (old house), which once was the harem of a pasha." So opens this wonderful, beautifully illustrated book by Croutier, who indeed grew up in a house in Izmir with servants and odalisques. Her grandmother and grandmother's sister had been raised in a harem. "Since then, I have come to see that these were not ordinary stories. But for me, as a child, they were, for I had not yet

known any others," she says. Many of us may think of the
Grand Harem of Topkapı Palace as the only secluded enclave of
women, but in fact every well-off household of the Ottoman
Empire had a harem. And Croutier discovered that physical and
spiritual isolation of women, and polygamy, weren't unique to
Turkey. This is a thoroughly fascinating work, profusely illustrated with color and black-and-white photographs and reproductions of paintings.

Letters, by Mary Wortley Montagu (Everyman's Library, 1992).
Mary Wortley Montagu wrote to her sister that her letters
would one day be as valuable as those of Madame de Sévigné,
and indeed our knowledge of eighteenth-century Constantinople would be vastly lacking were it not for her prolific pen.
Of all the topics she wrote about in her Turkish embassy letters,
perhaps the most scandalous was her visit to a *hamam*, in 1717;
she was the first European woman on record ever to have done
so. There weren't many details of life in Constantinople that
escaped Montagu's eye—but the *hamam* was a feature of Ori-
entalism that, according to *Cornucopia Magazine*, "proved to be
imaginatively much more powerful than the truth. No matter
how much Lady Mary extolled the realities of the Ottoman
Empire, and how everyday life did not correspond to the preconceptions of the West, the romantic impulse was stronger
than the fact."

*Looking for Osman: One Man's Travels Through the Paradox of Modern
Turkey,* by Eric Lawlor (Vintage, 1993). Lawlor's new friend in
Istanbul, Selim, tells him, "Turkey is tired of being unique. We
want to raise our living standards. Exoticism! What a dumb
reason to go anywhere." Though Istanbul's distinctive character eluded Lawlor initially, a student who worked in the hotel
he was staying at gave him a tip: you have to look in the right
places, and for a start, try the Grand Bazaar. The bazaar was the

ticket, and it's fair to say that the rest of Turkey surprised and astonished him.

Lords of the Horizons: A History of the Ottoman Empire, by Jason Goodwin (Picador, 1998). "This book is about a people who do not exist," states Goodwin in his prologue. "The word 'Ottoman' does not describe a place. Nobody nowadays speaks their language. Only a few professors can begin to understand their poetry—'We have no classics,' snapped a Turkish poet in 1964 at a poetry symposium in Sofia, when asked to acquaint the group with examples of classical Ottoman verse." At 352 pages, this is also a great bring-along title, and it reads much like a novel. Each chapter head and section break features emblems of various Janissary regiments, which were taken from *Marsigli, Stato Militare dell'Impero Ottomano* (published at The Hague in 1732).

Great Reads for Kids

The Turks extend a warm welcome to children and include them in nearly every event or gathering—so bring them along! The way I see it, parents can make the decision never to go anywhere and deprive both children and adults of a priceless experience, or they can plan an itinerary with kids in mind and take off on a new journey. I haven't yet found a source exclusively devoted to traveling with kids in Turkey, but parents will find some useful tips and words of advice in guidebooks. Some good tips can also be gathered from Web sites: mylifeguard-forhealth.com and travelwithyourkids.com. And for a *really* ambitious account, read *One Year Off: Leaving It All Behind for a Round-the-World Journey with Our Children*, by David Elliott Cohen (Simon & Schuster, 1999). It's always a good idea to build excitement in advance of the trip by involving kids in the planning, showing them maps and books and talking about the things you'll see and do. Below are some recommended books for reading in advance or bringing along:

And to Think That We Thought That We'd Never Be Friends, by Mary Ann Hoberman and illustrated by Kevin Hawkes (Dragonfly, 2003). Nothing whatsoever to do with Turkey, but I love it for its underlying message of learning about other people and celebrating the world's diversity.

Cybele's Secret, by Juliet Marillier (Knopf, 2008). A companion volume to Marillier's *Wildwood Dancing*, this book takes place in Istanbul. For ages twelve and up.

Forgotten Fire, by Adam Bagdasarian (Laurel Leaf, 2002). Drawing from his great-uncle's real-life experiences—and definitely for older readers—Bagdasarian relates the story of a well-off Armenian family and the death and tragedy that befall them.

The Most Incredible, Outrageous, Packed-to-the-Gills, Bulging-at-the-Seams Sticker Book You've Ever Seen (Klutz Press, 1997). For ages four and up, and winner of a Parents' Choice Award, this is a lifesaver for those in-between moments in travel—at an airport, on a plane, in a hotel room, in a car. Klutz publishes many unique, fun activity packages that are also great for traveling, including *Road Trip Trivia*, *Kids Travel*, and *A Super-Sneaky, Double-Crossing, Up, Down, Round & Round Maze Book*; browse many more cool titles at klutz .com.

The Odyssey, by Adrian Mitchell and illustrated by Stuart Robertson (A Retelling for Young Readers, DK Classics,

2000). As much of the *Odyssey* takes place in present-day Turkey, this is a great, fully illustrated volume to bring along (and it's perfectly fine for adults, too).

People, by Peter Spier (Doubleday, 1988). Caldecott Medalist Spier created this wonderful picture book with a global view, depicting people in their habitats and cities on all four continents. Required reading for every American.

The Trojan Horse: How the Greeks Won the War, by Emily Little (Step-Into-Reading, Random House, 1988). For young kids who are reading chapter books.

Turkey (Grolier, 1997). This is a great volume in Grolier's *Fiesta!* series, celebrating special occasions in countries throughout the world. Though aimed at younger readers, each book is a good summary for older readers as well. The Birth of the Prophet, Kurban Bayramı, Iftar meal, Şeker Bayramı, and Aşure Günü are all featured in this edition, as well as a page on Atatürk—every year, on November 10, there is a moment of silence to honor the anniversary of his death.

What You Will See Inside a Mosque, by Aisha Karen Khan (Skylight Paths, 2003). Though Skylight published this for children—it follows *What You Will See Inside a Synagogue* (2002)—it's actually a book that is great for adults, too. (Plus, it's written by a fellow Hollins University alumna.)

Zeynep, the Seagull of Galata Tower, by Julia Townsend (Çitlembik, 2003). A tour of Istanbul in a picture book, available from Nettleberry, a great South Dakota–based distributor of books in Turkish and others about Turkey. Browse the Internet company's other books for kids at Nettleberry.com (see Miscellany, page 566).

In addition to books to read, a blank journal is great for kids of all ages, boys and girls. Let them pick out some colored pencils, pens, crayons, markers, or paints and they can begin creating a record of their trip on the first day. Encourage them to collect postcards, ticket stubs, receipts, stamps, and all kinds of paper ephemera to paste inside the journal. Give them a disposable camera and they can add their own photographs, too.

Lastly, it's worth mentioning a letter to the editor I read a few years ago in the travel section of *The New York Times*. The writer stated she felt that the author of a previously published essay underestimated the impact of a five-year-old child's first trip to Europe. She emphasized that twenty years after *her* first trip to Italy, she became an art student, earned her master's degree in art history, and worked as a museum curator. My personal experiences in traveling with children have taught me that one should never underestimate how much children will absorb and retain and what will inspire and enthuse them.

On Foot to the Golden Horn, by Jason Goodwin (Picador, 2003). Though Goodwin doesn't say so, it's hard not to think he wasn't inspired by two books about a similar trek, *A Time of Gifts: On Foot to Constantinople* (1977) and *Between the Woods and Water* (1986), both by Patrick Leigh Fermor (New York Review of Books in paperback and originally published by John Murray). Fermor's books are unsurpassed (Jan Morris refers to him as "the greatest of living travel writers" and calls these books in particular "an amazingly complex and subtle evocation of a place that is no more"), and Goodwin's is very good and insightful (he, too, has written about "a place that is no more," as when he set out in 1990, Poland, Hungary,

Czechoslovakia, Romania, and Bulgaria were just experiencing life without Soviet Communism).

Osman's Dream: The History of the Ottoman Empire, by Caroline Finkel (Basic Books, 2006). An outstanding work whose author successfully attempts to counter the oversimplified notion that "the Ottoman Empire rose, declined, and fell." Finkel notes that "the past is truly another country in Turkey, whose citizens have been deprived of easy access to the literary and historical works of previous eras by the change of alphabet in 1928 from Arabic script to the Roman alphabet familiar to most of the Western world." Her account extends to 1927 (most other books end in 1922), the year when Atatürk made his speech explaining how he was justified in ousting the empire and what his dreams were for a modern republic.

The first sultan, Osman, had a dream, too, and Finkel relates that he was sleeping in the house of a holy man named Edebali one night when he had it. The dream was beautiful, and when Osman awoke he told the story to Edebali, who said "Osman, my son, congratulations, for God has given the imperial office to you and your descendants and my daughter Malhun shall be your wife." Finkel notes that this dream was first communicated a century and a half after Osman's death, in about 1326, and that it "became one of the most resilient founding myths of the empire." Most uniquely in this book, Finkel shares as much as possible the vision the Ottomans had of themselves and their empire, a vision we have rarely been shown.

The Ottoman Centuries: The Rise and Fall of the Turkish Empire, by Lord Kinross (William Morrow, 1977). It has been said that just as Greece has her Lord Byron, so Turkey had her Lord Kinross—during World War II he was posted as intelligence officer to the Near East and later served as press counselor at the British embassy in Cairo. This posting enabled him to travel throughout the Levant, and repeated visits to Turkey deepened his interest in the country's history. *The Ottoman Centuries* had been the authoritative work on the subject for many years, and it's still relevant and I still recommend reading it.

A Peace to End All Peace: The Fall of the Ottoman Empire and the Creation of the Modern Middle East, by David Fromkin (Henry Holt, 1989). Fromkin takes the title of his excellent book from a comment by Archibald Wavell, an officer who served under Allenby in the Palestine campaign, about the treaties bringing World War I to an end: "After 'the war to end war' they seem to have been pretty successful in Paris at making a 'Peace to end Peace.' " This is that rare volume that is at once perhaps overly ambitious but very well done, complete in its scope, and fast-paced. For anyone wanting a single book that explains the history of the entire Near East situation, this is it.

Portrait of a Turkish Family, by Irfan Orga (Eland, London, 1993; Inman Press, 2008). I started this book somewhat hesitatingly, thinking it might be a little dull and insignificant, but it turned out to be one of the most moving books I've ever read. It stands apart, aside from its being an extraordinary story, because there isn't another one I know of that portrays daily life of regular Istanbul residents during the time Turkey became a republic. Upon its publication in America in 1950, the *New York Herald Tribune* hailed it as "one of the memorable books of 1950." I think it is one of the most memorable books of all time.

Sons of the Conquerors: The Rise of the Turkic World, by Hugh Pope (Overlook Duckworth, 2005). I was surprised to learn that, as Pope relates in his prologue, the Turks "constitute one of the world's ten largest linguistic families, numbering more than

140 million people scattered through more than 20 modern states in a great crescent across the Eurasian continents, starting at the Great Wall of China, through Central Asia, the Caucasus, Iran, Turkey, the Balkans, Europe and even a fledgling community in the United States. The Turkish spoken by its biggest and most developed member, Turkey, is widely spoken by significant ethnic minorities in European states like France, Britain, Austria, the Netherlands, Belgium, Russia and Romania. They are most prominent in Europe's most powerful state, Germany, where Turkish can be heard on every other street corner of the capital, Berlin." Pope traveled extensively through the lands of the Turkic-speaking peoples and argues that Turkic peoples can no longer be treated as marginal players; they are noteworthy peoples in their own right. An utterly fresh and fascinating book.

Tales from the Expat Harem: Foreign Women in Modern Turkey, edited by Anastasia M. Ashman and Jennifer Eaton Gökmen (Seal, 2006, fourth edition; the Turkish translation was published in 2005 in Istanbul, and with a foreword by Elif Shafak). "If there were ever a place," write this team of coeditors, "tailor-made to play host to wanderers, travelers, and those pursuing lives outside their original territory, surely Turkey is that place." The women's tales in this unique collection are funny, amazing, and sometimes heartbreaking. I shed a few tears while reading some of these narratives, but this is mainly an upbeat volume. These modern-day Scheherazades "wrestle urges to overly exoticize the unfamiliar and strive to balance self-preservation with the fresh expectations placed on them by Turkish culture."

A Traveller's History of Turkey, by Richard Stoneman (Interlink, 2006). I've been a longtime fan of this series. Each volume, authored by a different writer, presents a concise history of a place, in an entertaining style, without compromising any historical moments, all packed into a portable paperback.

Turkey: Bright Sun, Strong Tea, by Tom Brosnahan (Travel Info Exchange, 2005). Tom's memoir, which I referenced earlier, is a terrifically interesting and fun read. He tends to refer to it as good airplane and end-of-the-day reading, and it is, but I think that implies there isn't much substance in the book. Be assured that his personal story, though sometimes humorous, includes boatloads of tips and facts about Turkey and the Turks, and if you don't read this, well . . . you're truly missing something. The book is available online (go to either brightsunstrongtea .com or turkeytravelplanner.com) and in Turkey (notably at all the English-language bookstores in Istanbul).

Turkey Unveiled: A History of Modern Turkey, by Nicole and Hugh Pope (Overlook, 1998). The Popes are journalists, Nicole for *Le Monde* and Hugh for *The Wall Street Journal* (he was the bureau chief in Istanbul), so between them they are uniquely qualified to write about contemporary Turkey. Tom Brosnahan, in fact, says of Hugh that "we should all read just about anything Hugh Pope writes on Turkey. I do." Though this book was published almost a decade ago, it's still very much worth reading. The Popes learned that Turkey is not easily labeled: "European, Western, Eastern, Islamic, fascistic, anarchic, whatever. It has something of all these elements, of course. But Turkey is in a category all its own."

Turkish Delights, by Philippa Scott (Thames & Hudson, 2001). If this were just a book of pretty pictures, I would not love it so much, but the text is truly informative and interesting. Scott reminds us that "without the contributions and influence of the Ottoman Turks, life would be different and diminished. For centuries Western art and culture have been enriched and refined in many ways which today we take for granted. . . . All in all, this is a rich inheritance."

Turkish Reflections: A Biography of a Place, by Mary Lee Settle (Prentice Hall, 1991). Settle admits she knew next to nothing about Turkey when she first went there in 1972. "What I did not know then is that the country of Turkey has the worst and most ill-drawn public image of almost any country I know." Settle returned to Turkey in 1989, and she traveled all around the country, "to question and learn and give the Turks a chance, which they have had so seldom, to speak for themselves." Her journey, and the retelling, is warm, occasionally funny, and always significant.

The Turks Today, by Andrew Mango (Overlook, 2004). *The Washington Post Book World* said of *The Turks Today* that "Mango successfully peels modern Turkey to its core." The observation is dead-on: I think there is not any issue of modern Turkey that Mango shies away from in this excellent book. Mango—who was born in Istanbul into a family of Russian émigrés, speaks Turkish fluently, and worked for forty years at the BBC—is perhaps *the* man at the right time to write about a country that is not easily summed up. Mango covers events from the death of Atatürk in 1938 up to the current EU membership issue.

Turkish Chapters

Some other good books to read that feature Turkey, or Istanbul, or both in their chapters include:

Balkan Ghosts: A Journey Through History, by Robert D. Kaplan (St. Martin's, 1993). Part four, devoted to present-day Greece, features a very good chapter entitled "Farewell to Salonika."

Destinations, by Jan Morris (Oxford University, 1980). "City of Yok" is the chapter devoted to Istanbul in this collection of previously published *Rolling Stone* essays.

The Ends of the Earth: A Journey at the Dawn of the 21st Century, by Robert D. Kaplan (Random House, 1996). Part two of this book is entitled "Anatolia and the Caucasus," and at its beginning, Kaplan is in Istanbul standing on Seraglio Point, which T. S. Eliot referred to as "the still point of the turning world" in *Four Quartets*.

The Spirit of Mediterranean Places, by Michel Butor (Marlboro, 1986). The first part of this beautiful book is devoted to "Four Cities," one of which is Istanbul (which Butor refers to as an "Oriental Liverpool") and another Salonica.

Travels with a Tangerine: From Morocco to Turkey in the Footsteps of Islam's Greatest Traveler, by Tim Mackintosh-Smith (Random House, 2004). Islam's Greatest Traveler is Ibn Battutah, who, according to the author, spent half his lifetime on the road and traveled some 75,000 miles.

A Year in the World: Journeys of a Passionate Traveller, by Frances Mayes (Broadway, 2006). Before a cruise along Turkey's Lycian Coast, Mayes—renowned author of *Under the Tuscan Sun*—spends a few days in Istanbul, "the most multinational city, the quintessential crossroads of east and west, violent, poetic, melancholy, raucous, fleshy, austere, rapacious, sublime—this seems to me the most fascinating city on earth."

Additionally, these volumes on Mediterranean history all include much detail on Turkey and Istanbul:

The Inner Sea: The Mediterranean and Its People, by Robert Fox (Knopf, 1991). A fascinating work of reportage and travelogue by a journalist who is the Mediterranean correspondent for the *Daily Telegraph* in London.

The Mediterranean and the Mediterranean World in the Age of Philip II, by Fernand Braudel (HarperCollins, 1992). This (abridged) version of Braudel's acclaimed two-volume work (originally published in France in 1949) includes illustrations in black-and-white and color that weren't featured in previous editions.

The Mediterranean in History, edited by David Abulafia (Thames & Hudson, 2003). Profusely illustrated, with essays by an international team of scholars.

The Middle Sea: A History of the Mediterranean, by John Julius Norwich (Doubleday, 2006). Equally as interesting and unparalleled as his works on Byzantium and Venice.

On the Shores of the Mediterranean, by Eric Newby (Picador, 1985). While not as scholarly a tome as those above, Newby's is always rewarding and enlightening to read.

Guidebooks

It won't come as a surprise that I routinely consult a great number of guidebooks while I'm planning a trip. I don't bring all of them with me—I often take extensive notes from some books, especially if they are heavy, and incorporate them into my all-purpose journal (I also make photocopies of some pages and glue them into the journal). I pack a few guidebooks and a work or two of fiction, and on any given day of my trip, one or two of these goes into my everyday bag with my journal (the journal goes with me absolutely everywhere, every day). Not every edition in a guide-book series is written by the same author and therefore some volumes might not be quite as good as others; additionally, not every series publishes guides to every one of the world's destinations, which is why I don't always consult the same guidebooks for every trip.

For books on all of Turkey, I use the Frommer's, Lonely Planet, and Rough Guide series. I also very much like the lesser-known *101 Must-See Places in Turkey*, by Saffet Emre Tonguç and Faith Türkmenoğlu (Boyut, 2007). This is the number-one best-selling guidebook in Turkey, now available in English. Profusely illustrated with color photographs and packed with tips on where to stay, where to eat, how to travel, and what to do, I think this is an indispensable guide for readers traveling beyond Istanbul (though twenty-six pages are devoted to Istanbul). What's different about it, first, is that the two authors are Turkish and, in their own words, offer "a little bit of guidance, but not so much that you are drowning in it; a book that leaves room for your own discoveries; one that tells you something, but not everything; one that prompts you but doesn't force you." Additionally, the authors provide anecdotes, stories, and other recommendations throughout. Available through Nettleberry (see Miscellany, page 566).

Fiction

Ali and Nino: A Love Story, by Kurban Said (Overlook, 1999). This wonderful novel, which is at once a great love story and an epic tale of two cultures converging at the time of World War I and the Russian Revolution, is also cloaked in mystery. The book was originally published in Vienna in 1937, and if not discovered in a secondhand bookstore in postwar Berlin, it may never have seen an English translation and we would not have this splendid tale. Kurban Said is a pseudonym for Lev Nussimbaum, born in 1905 to a wealthy family in oil-rich

Baku, on the edge of the Caspian Sea. He escaped the Russian Revolution in a camel caravan and ended up in Germany, where he also wrote under the name Essad Bey.

If you become as curious as I did, track down "The Man From the East," by Tom Reiss (*The New Yorker*, October 4, 1999), in which Reiss and publisher Peter Mayer go to Vienna to meet with a lawyer, Heinz Barazon, who claims to know the true identity of Kurban Said. And read *The Orientalist: Solving the Mystery of a Strange and Dangerous Life*, also by Tom Reiss (Random House, 2005), which is the most up-to-date account we have of Said's life. More fascinating details may be found on this book's Web site, Theorientalist.info.

The Bastard of Istanbul, by Elif Shafak (Viking, 2007). Though Istanbul is in the title and is the main locale in the novel, this is really a bigger book about Turkish issues at large. It was the best-selling book of 2006 in Turkey, but Shafak was prosecuted by the Turkish government for "insulting Turkishness" under Article 301 of the Turkish criminal code. The charges were eventually dropped. Shafak's other novels are also worthy companion reading: *The Gaze* (Marion Boyars, 2006), which earned her the Union of Turkish Writers' Prize in 2000; *The Flea Palace* (Marion Boyars, 2007), a best-seller in Turkey; and *The Saint of Incipient Insanities* (Farrar, Straus & Giroux, 2004).

Birds Without Wings, Louis de Bernières (Knopf, 2004). An absolutely wonderful, moving, sweeping saga of history during the final years of the Ottoman Empire and World War I. One character who may be considered the main narrator is Iskander the Potter, who early on briefly sums up what is to come: "Much of what was done was simply in revenge for identical atrocities, but I tell you now that even if guilt were a coat of sable, and the ground were deep in snow, I would rather freeze than wear it."

The Black Book (2006) or any of Orhan Pamuk's other novels: *My Name Is Red* (2002), *The New Life* (1998), *Snow* (2004), and *The White Castle* (1998), all published in easy-to-pack paperbacks by Vintage. If forced to pick one favorite, I might say *My Name Is Red*—though it's hard not to immediately love *The New Life*, with its opening line, "I read a book one day and my whole life was changed." However, Maureen Freely, who translated *The Black Book* and *Snow*, has referred to *The Black Book* as "the cauldron from which [his other books] come." Based on her comment, I started with *The Black Book*, and later, after I'd read three more, I understood what she meant. In her "Translator's Afterword" in *The Black Book*, she talks about the difficulties of translating from Turkish to English. For starters, there is no verb *to be* in Turkish, nor is there a verb *to have*. "It's an agglutinative language, which means that root nouns in even the simplest sentences can carry five or six suffixes. ('Apparently, they were inside their houses' is a single word.)" For *Snow* and Pamuk's nonfiction book, *Istanbul*, Freely explains, "The author and I worked out a system whereby I worked straight to the end without consulting him. He then went over the finished draft, measuring his Turkish against my English and inserting his praises, curses, and exhortations in the margins. Only then did we sit down together and go through each manuscript, sentence by sentence, hour after hour, no matter how high the sun in the sky, or how hot." Before Pamuk's Nobel Prize acceptance speech, the introducer noted that "Orhan Pamuk has made his native city an indispensable literary territory, equal to Dostoyevsky's St. Petersburg, Joyce's Dublin, or Proust's Paris—a place where readers from all corners of the world can live another life, just as credible as their own."

No matter which one you pick up first, I don't think you'll be disappointed. Each is filled with memorable passages, such as this one, from *The Black Book*, when a character, Bedii Usta, brings the mannequins he's made to all the big stores in Istanbul, but is turned down by all of them.

For his mannequins did not look like the European models to which we were meant to aspire; they looked like us. "Consider the customer," one shopkeeper advised him. "He's not going to want a coat he sees worn by someone who looks like the swarthy, bowlegged mustachioed countrymen he sees ten thousand times a day in our city's streets. He wants a coat worn by a new beautiful creature from a distant unknown land, so he can convince himself that he, too, can change, become someone new, just by putting on this coat." One window dresser who was well versed in this game was good enough to confess, after admiring Bedii Usta's mastery, that he thought it a great shame he could not earn his keep by using "these real Turks, these real fellow citizens" in his shop windows; the reason, he said, was that Turks no longer wanted to be Turks, they wanted to be something else altogether. This was why they'd gone along with the "dress revolution," shaved their beards, reformed their language and their alphabet. Another, less garrulous, shopkeeper explained that his customers didn't buy dresses but dreams.

The Burnt Pages (Random House, 1991), *Disbelief* (Carcanet, 1987), *Parthian Stations* (Carcanet, 2007), and *To the City* (Talisman House, 2004), all books of poetry, all with Turkish themes, by John Ash.

The Delights of Turkey, by Edouard Roditi (New Directions, 1972). This collection of twenty stories—some with Istanbul as backdrop and some based on popular Turkish folklore—is unique and is a fine traveling companion in the spirit of *A Thousand and One Nights*.

Nâzım Hikmet poems and novels, notably *Beyond the Walls: Selected Poems* (Anvil, 2004), *Human Landscapes from My Country: An Epic Novel in Verse* (Persea, 2008), and *Poems of Nâzım Hikmet* (Persea, 1994). Like Atatürk, Hikmet was born in Salonica. Though he embraced Communism and became an enemy of the Turkish state, he was always revered by the Turkish people but was imprisoned numerous times, and was awarded the International Peace Prize by the World Peace Council in 1951. The latter part of his life was spent in exile in Moscow, where he died in 1963. Hikmet authored many works, including plays, but many are hard to find. The three I highlight here are favorites of mine *and* are fairly readily available.

The Janissary Tree (2006), *The Snake Stone* (2007), and *The Bellini Card* (2009), all by Jason Goodwin (Farrar, Straus & Giroux), compose an Edgar Award–winning Ottoman Empire mystery series, whose main character, Yashim, is a eunuch.

"I loved standing in the Aya Sofya and thinking about the fact that 1,400 years ago, when they were building this incredible structure, it was still the Dark Ages in Western Europe. My husband, Jerry Webman, and I were lucky to be in Istanbul in the winter because we will always have this magical image of how the city looked covered in snow during the once-in-a-decade snowstorm. Jerry really loved drinking *rakı* throughout our meals, and I really loved Dhoku Kilim in the Grand Bazaar: Hasan was so helpful and Dhoku's rugs were the only modern *kilim* designs I saw in Istanbul. We bought a large one for the living room at our beach house and it arrived in days, safe and sound. And it would be careless of me not to mention my good friend (and my brother's Yale roommate thirty years ago), Resit Ergener, who holds a PhD in economics and is a university instructor, an author, and a tour guide with an encyclopedic knowledge of Istanbul. He's been a guide since 1985 and takes incredible pride and joy in introducing visitors to Turkey." (Resit may be reached by telephone at +90 533 269 4393 or by e-mail at regener@ superonline.com or toturkey@dreamtours.com.)

—Susan Ginsburg, literary agent, Writers House

Memed, My Hawk, by Yashar Kemal (Collins and Harvill, 1961). This is a beautifully crafted novel that will keep you up late at night, anxious to see what will unfold. The word "swashbuckling" doesn't exactly apply, but the story is by turns breathlessly exciting, violent, tender, wonderful, and true in the way that it evokes southern Turkey in the early years of the twentieth century.

Rise the Euphrates, by Carol Edgarian (Random House, 1994). Edgarian's novel tells of an Armenian woman who escapes the 1915 tragedy and later pins her hopes and dreams on her conflicted American granddaughter.

Seraglio, by Janet Wallach (Nan A. Talese, 2003). Wallach began this book as a biography of Aimée Dubuca de Rivery, the subject of a chapter in *The Wilder Shores of Love* as well as in *The Palace of Tears* (both in the Istanbul section)—but ended up writing it as a historical novel. She maintains that, once she started her research on Aimée, it became clear that very little conclusive information exists about her. Yet she concedes that many people believe Aimée's story to be true—I am one of them, as it seems there are enough coincidences for it to be so.

The Towers of Trebizond, by Rose Macauley (Carroll & Graf, 1956).
   I love making lists of books with great opening lines, and the
   one from this book has long been a favorite: " 'Take my camel,
   dear,' said my aunt Dot, as she climbed down from this animal
   on her return from High Mass." Macauley creates characters
   much like those in a Barbara Pym novel, which is to say they're
   quirky or eccentric, and utterly lovable. The characters in this
   story travel to a number of destinations within Turkey, including Istanbul.

INTERVIEW

Tom Brosnahan

Tom Brosnahan is the reason I wanted to go to Turkey in the first place. I met him in the 1980s, when I worked for the original Banana Republic. Readers who remember the catalogs and stores know that in those days it was a much more interesting company than it is now—founders Mel and Patricia Ziegler had a vision for a company that sold not only clothes good for traveling the globe but also books, and not only guidebooks but tomes on all sorts of related subjects that curious travelers would want to read. Not every retail store had space for books, but a few in New York did, and I arranged for Tom to appear at two of them. He had written Turkey on $5 a Day *and* How to Beat the High Cost of Travel *for Frommer's and had for a number of years been the author of* Lonely Planet Turkey. *Tom wrote the very first* Lonely Planet Turkey *guide, and went on to update it for more than twenty years; he also authored the Lonely Planet Turkish phrase book and is the author of more than forty other guidebooks with over four million copies in print worldwide in more than ten languages; in 2005 he wrote* Bright Sun, Strong Tea, *a memoir of his life in Turkey. I had already had a growing curiosity about Turkey, as I mentioned in the introduction, but when the director of the Turkish tourist office came to Tom's book signing, and complimentary trays of baklava (with pistachios, which I'd never tried before) suddenly appeared, I realized I was in the presence of a "somebody" and I knew I would be en route to Turkey.*

To my mind, nobody knows more about contemporary Turkey than Tom. He is not a scholar of antiquities, literature, medieval society, or Islamic history (though he knows an awful lot about those subjects), but he really knows, and is greatly respected by, the Turkish people. He first

A: I wrote my first guidebook, *Turkey on $5 a Day* (Frommer's), while I was still in the Peace Corps. It was a Peace Corps project, and one of Peace Corps Turkey's most successful ones. After a few months in Turkey I realized that Americans knew virtually nothing about the country, and most of what they thought they knew was wrong. They thought Turkey still had a sultan with harems, and that Turks were Arabs, and their country a sandy desert. They thought it was a dictatorship and about to "go Communist," none of which was true. American tourists—the bulk of the world's travelers at that time—happily went to Greece and Israel, but passed right over Turkey. I thought this was a pity because Turkey had so much to offer. I hoped that a guidebook in a major series would help to convince people to explore this marvelous country. I calculated that *Turkey on $5 a Day* helped several hundred thousand travelers discover Turkey. My later Lonely Planet guide has now sold well over a half million copies in several languages and has become the all-time best-selling guide to the destination.

Q: What was it about guidebook writing that made you decide to quit and begin a life as a Web site master?

A: Guidebook authorship was extraordinarily rewarding. To see your work in print, to receive letters from travelers saying it has helped them to explore a new and different place, to meet travelers on the road who thank you for your help—it's a wonderful feeling. But it's also very demanding work, physically, emotionally, and financially. In the 1980s and 1990s I made a good living at it, but by the late 1990s the industry was changing. The work was ever more demanding, there was ever more competition for readers, legal exposure was rising and compensation falling. When the Internet came along, it was a no-brainer: a medium through which I could publish my work immediately, worldwide, forever, for very little cost! I experimented with online delivery of travel information in the mid–1990s, and moved all my efforts to the Web early in the new millennium. I taught myself HTML, how to develop Web sites in Dreamweaver, and other necessary skills so that I could be an online publisher as well as a writer and photographer.

Q: What are some of the most commonly asked questions about Turkey and Istanbul that you receive?

A: The variety of questions is unbelievable, from "How can I ship two hundred tons of steel to Turkey?" to "Are there pigeon-fanciers in Cappadocia?" But in my private consultations with travelers, they mostly want me to help make their itineraries fit together and work right in the limited time they have for travel. So the prime question is always "How do I see all the top sights in the shortest possible time?"

Q: What are some tips or suggestions that you would give to first-time visitors?

A: Most importantly (for any traveler anywhere): "Dump your preconceptions." As Aldous Huxley said, "To travel is to discover that everyone is wrong about other countries." You will find out for yourself, and you won't understand unless you let it tell you what it is, rather than you telling it what it should be.

Q: What are some of your favorite things to see and do in Istanbul?

A: I've always loved cruising on the traditional Istanbul ferryboats. Often I'd just board any boat and ride it to wherever it was going, then ride it back, sitting on the upper stern deck in the open air with a glass of fresh, hot, strong Turkish tea in my hand. Since the construction of the Bosphorus bridges and the advent of fast catamaran "sea bus" ferries, the old traditional ferries have been disappearing. They used to be the main traffic in the Bosphorus, making a real light show at night as their powerful spotlights swept the sea lanes looking to avoid fishing skiffs. Now they are fewer, but just as pleasurable. One thing about Istanbul hasn't changed and never will: the joy of dining with friends, Turkish-style. Gather a group of six to ten, allow at least five hours, order at least three dozen *mezes* (hors d'oeuvres) and bottles of wine and *rakı,* linger over them for two hours, then order the main course (serious consultations with the waiter), then dessert, then Turkish coffee, then a pousse-café liqueur, then go home to bed, regretful that it's over.

Q: Since you started your Web site, where do you most prefer to go in Turkey?

A: Istanbul, first and foremost Istanbul, always Istanbul! I can't think of a place in Turkey I wouldn't like to visit, but nowadays, with the seacoasts booming with tourism, I find myself drawn to many nontouristy places: the farming towns of the Aegean hinterland, the Black Sea coast, the East. It's a nostalgic trip, in a way. These less-developed places retain some of the innocence and courtly welcome that I found everywhere during my first years in Turkey. There's still plenty to see and do off the beaten track: natural wonders like beautiful lakes and mysterious caves, rolling vistas and craggy mountains, and everywhere—*everywhere!*—the impressive remains of the past: Hittite, Hellenic, Hellenistic, Roman, Byzantine, Selçuk, Ottoman. And the food's always wonderful, no matter where you are in Turkey.

Istanbul

I am listening to Istanbul, intent, my eyes closed . . .

—ORHAN VELI KANIK, *Turkish poet, 1914–50*

For much of human history it has been the greatest city on earth.

—*A Hedonist's Guide to Istanbul*

To arrive in Constantinople on a fine morning, believe me, *that's an unforgettable moment in one's life.*

—ALEV LYTI F CROUTIER,
The Palace of Tears

Istanbul is a hodgepodge of ten million lives. It is an open book of ten million scrambled stories. Istanbul is waking up from its perturbed sleep, ready for the chaos of the rush hour. From now on there are too many prayers to answer, too many profanities to note, and too many sinners, as well as too many innocents, to keep an eye on. Already it is morning in Istanbul.

—ELIF SHAFAK,
The Bastard of Istanbul

Evliya records in the *Seyahatname.*" Evliya Efendi appears throughout the book, and Freely enjoys having him at his side as he attempts to evoke the spirit of the Istanbul he has known over the years. Naturally, some of the characters and scenes portrayed here exist no longer. "Nevertheless," says Freely, "I have made no attempt to update the sketches, for they and the photos by Sedat Pakay are a picture of the city we knew and loved in years past, the old Stamboul of our memories." I urge readers who are even remotely interested in reading about the Istanbul of the recent past to track down this very special book.

JOHN FREELY teaches physics at Bosphorus University in Istanbul (formerly Robert College, the oldest American college outside the U.S.), and is the author of more than forty books, including *Strolling Through Istanbul* (with Hilary Sumner-Boyd, Redhouse, 1972), *Istanbul: The Imperial City* (Penguin, 1998), *The Western Shores of Turkey: Discovering the Aegean and Mediterranean Coasts* (Tauris Parke, 2004), *Strolling Through Athens* (Tauris Parke, 2004), *Strolling Through Venice* (Penguin, 1994), several editions of the Blue Guide to Istanbul, and, most recently, *Aladdin's Lamp: How Greek Science Came to Europe Through the Islamic World* (Knopf, 2009). In 2001, the John Freely Fellowship was established by the Joukowsky Family Foundation and the American Research Institute in Turkey (ARIT). In 2008, the first volume of works by five Freely fellows was published: *Studies on Istanbul and Beyond: The Freely Papers.* In the foreword, Nina Joukowsky Köprülü writes that the book "is a celebration of John Freely's lifelong passion for and curiosity about Istanbul." Dr. Robert Ousterhout, professor in the Department of the History of Art at the University of Pennsylvania, "whose dedication to Istanbul is matched only by that of Freely himself," relates in the introduction that "in July

2006, Freely celebrated his eightieth birthday surrounded by family, friends, colleagues, and devoted admirers. The gala, an all-day event, was hosted by Boğaziçi University, an institution with which Freely has been associated throughout much of his career, but more importantly, the event took place in a city that has become almost synonymous with his name. Freely has introduced Istanbul to countless readers— serious travelers, armchair adventurers, and scholars alike. In fact, it is hard to speak of Istanbul without mentioning John Freely, for many of us first saw the city through his eyes or first imagined the city through his words."

IT IS said that on a certain day in June the crazy tilt of the buildings allows the sun briefly into this alley. Between solstices it gets its light secondhand; from slime-silvered cobbles and from shining marble tabletops awash with beer. Osman Efendi passed by here an age ago and his delight in what he saw was such that the alley has been named for him. The Street of Osman Efendi Passed By leads from the flower market to the fish bazaar by way of an arcade lined with *meyhanes*, or curbside taverns, and is therefore a museum of Stamboul smells. It is more often called the Çiçek Pasajı, the Passage of Flowers.

The *meyhanes* of the Passage are the favorite haunts of the *Akşamcılar*, the Evening Drinkers, who can be seen there daily draining giant glasses of beer called Argentines. The Evening Drinkers, who on occasion have been known to drink in the afternoon and in the morning too, usually sit at long marble tables inside these *meyhanes*. In good weather they move out into the alley itself, taking their meals from the tops of beer barrels. Some prefer the Church, a spacious tavern hung with rococo chandeliers, but I prefer the Senate because the talk is best there. The Senate is in session throughout the day, but more important affairs are discussed in the evening, after the sun has set and steel shutters come crashing down in the shops around town. This nocturnal congress is illuminated by colored lights, protected by pendant talismans, and presided over by a bored and omniscient cashier.

The *meyhane* kitchens perch on the upper floors of the taverns. Swarthy, unshaven cooks lean out from smoke-spewing windows and gossip with their friends across the alley, commenting on the deformities of the strollers, whistling at passing girls, now and then disappearing into their cavelike kitchens when waiters rush out into the Passage shouting up orders from the taverns below. I sometimes amuse myself by walking quickly through the Passage, calling out the names of all my favorite dishes, and then sitting quietly at a beer barrel while waiters run about looking for the gentlemen who ordered the stuffed mussels, the grilled mullet, the shish kebab, the fried brains. Once accusing fingers were pointed at me and I was forced to eat it all, and did so with plea-sure.

The Turkish meal is a long and unhurried ceremony; a proces-sion of delicacies carried by platoons of staggering waiters; irri-gated with *rakı*, that soul-satisfying, intellect-deadening, national anise drink; and, above all, accompanied by talk. The talk is con-tinuous, loud and passionate; emphasized and punctuated by ritual hand gestures; illustrated by dramatic facial expressions; all pro-nouncements requiring exclamations of agreement, disagree-ment, astonishment or disbelief; all tipsy speeches applauded with roars of laughter and an exchange of rough embraces and bristly kisses; followed by a glass-clinking toast and a bellowed order for more food and drink. Exhausted waiters in unlaced shoes shuffle to the table with yet another tray of "Belly-Split-Open," a sweet plate of "The Lady's Navel," a savory dish of "The Imam Fainted," a girth-expanding mound of *zerde pilav*, that favorite dish of eunuchs and Janissaries, and one more round of *rakı*. And when they have had their fill of food, these stout men sing to one another soft and quavering Turkish love songs. Late at night, as they sway together at their long tables, the *Akşamcılar* resemble apostles at a drunken sacrament.

Istanbul is best seen from a seat by a tavern window in the Passage of Flowers, froth-crowned Argentine in hand. The city is at heart nothing more than the sum of its citizens, and most of these will eventually stroll by your window or sit next to you, drinking an Argentine themselves. You will get to know the Stamboullus in this way, and later you can visit them in the monuments they inhabit. This is the Levantine approach to sightseeing, a distinct improvement on the *Guide Bleu*.

The Stamboullus pass by with their hands clasped behind their backs, fingering worry beads. Their faces are seamed, furrowed, wrinkled, weathered and warted; their hooded eyes rheumy, bloodshot and jaundiced; their hooked and hairy-nostriled noses dripping beads of snot; their hat brims turned down and their collars up; their long, black, shroudlike overcoats skimming the muddy pavement; walking with the lurching, stumbling gait produced by a lifetime on cobblestones. They stroll through the Passage slowly, staring into the taverns without apparent interest, turning their massive bodies rather than their immobile heads, occasionally crashing into one another and rebounding impassively, then continuing on their aimless way. The hours pass as I review this drab parade, and gray afternoon changes imperceptibly into gray-blue evening. For there are no clocks in town and the light in the Passage is too diffuse to give the hour. The weather is known from the shine on the cobbles and the season from the dress of the strollers.

But I know that twilight has ended when I see the night people of Stamboul beginning to make their appearance in the Passage. There are itinerant peddlers: sellers of hepatitic shellfish, uncrackable nuts, timeless wristwatches, secondhand shoes with the backs folded down for easy removal in mosques, worn overcoats still warm from their last owners, horoscopes for the unlucky and zodiacal lapel pins for the star-crossed and supersti-

tious. There are wandering mendicants: beggars deaf, dumb,
blind, legless, armless, or with thickets of twisted limbs; along
with widows, orphans, veterans and abandoned patriarchs. There
are Gypsies: leading bears, playing fiddles, beating tambourines,
pounding drums, dancing, singing, begging, pimping and pilfer-
ing, their dark eyes always alert for the possibilities of plunder. A
drunken painter sells landscapes of an arcadia which can be
reached only after a long trip on cheap wine. A hairy peasant sells
chances on gaunt chickens which are always won by another hairy
peasant who is undoubtedly his brother. A purple-eyed prostitute
offers to measure our blood pressure, which does not rise at the
sight of her elephantine charms. A prick-eared dwarf limps by
using a tree branch for a cane, striking out at the tormenting
Gypsy-boys who pluck at his rags. A hunchbacked crone stops for
a thimbleful of beer and hands a passionate love note to Ali, the
handsome young barman. . . . One evening, while we were
drinking by candlelight during a power failure, a swift ancient
came running through the Passage and sold a whole carton of cigarette lighters; he assured us that they had been just recently stolen
by him. At the sound of police whistles from the fish bazaar we
put out our candles to assist the old thief in his escape. Then,
upon the arrival of the blundering police, we flicked our lighters
on and off to illuminate the comic chase as in a silent movie,
while the Passage echoed with cheers and derisive laughter.

When the evening is at its height our joy is momentarily withered by the appearance of a cigarette-seller with unfocused and
uncoordinated eyes, one orb apparently fixed on hell and the
other on paradise. We quickly buy his cigarettes so that he will
leave, after which we touch our amulets to ward off the evil eye
before resuming our conversations.

And although he has been standing in the doorway for hours,
we do not notice until late in the evening the bankrupt belt-seller,
Mad Ahmet. Swathed to the eyes in a black muffler, he peers
through his matted tangles of hair and beard and stands dreaming

in a hashish cloud while his belts are stolen by Gypsies. He buys the belts back later at a loss, but being demented he is not aware of the unfair exchange and so is not disturbed. The more cynical of the *Akşamcılar* say that he is a police spy.

Each evening new and eccentric characters appear upon the scene. An acrobat stands on his head in the center of the Passage. He walks upon his hands along the tops of beer barrels to my window. His earrings dangle beside his swarthy, upside-down face and I notice that he has a purple star tattooed on his forehead. I attempt to engage him in conversation but he silently takes my coin and leaves, walking along the Passage on his hands, hardly noticed by the strollers. A young man seated across the table lifts his Argentine to me and smiles. He has a darkly handsome face and the chest and shoulders of a young Apollo. He finishes his beer and bids me good evening, after which he climbs down from his stool and disappears. A moment afterward I see him in the alley as he turns and waves back to me, a bisected demigod striding on his stumps over the cobbles of the Passage.

As the evenings go by, I watch for the unpredictable transits of Arnaut Mehmet, the Albanian flower-peddler. At times he is not seen for many months and I am told in the taverns that he is dead.

Others who know him better say that he is wandering in the
lower depths of Istanbul and that we will see him again when he
has run his course. For this bum has the unerring sense of season
of a migratory bird, and resurrects each spring along with the
flowers he sells, like a drunken phoenix. We know that he is back
when we hear his familiar shout—"Rose! Rose!"—as he staggers
into the Passage from the fish market, swinging his bouquets
about him to clear a path through the throng. Totally and unre-
deemably drunk, his forehead deeply creased from an axe blow,
bloodshot eyes burning in his grimy face, nose busted, teeth shat-
tered and lips swollen from his violent encounters in the under-
world, gray-haired chest showing through the torn shirt and
tattered suit which have been stained by every foul alley in Istanbul, ragged trousers held up by a piece of frayed rope and the seat
ripped out as if by a mad dog, pant legs ripped and flapping in the
breeze, black toes protruding from the shards of shoes which he
must have fought for with an alley cat, his body caked with dirt
and stinking like a leprous rat, he has, nonetheless, a certain dignity about him. Standing now before my window, the Albanian
offers me a rose from his bouquet and bows from the waist when
I present him a double *rakı* in return. He downs the *rakı* in one
gulp, smacks his lips appreciatively, and then smashes the empty
glass on his head before continuing along the Passage. He now
feels fit to resume his flower-peddling and approaches lady shoppers with a charming but incoherent speech and what he believes
to be his most patrician manner. But when they see and smell this
drunken, reeking apparition the ladies invariably flee, while the
Albanian stumbles through the crowd in angry pursuit, hurling
his roses after them, bellowing in what I imagine must be Mon-
tenegrin. When the ladies make good their escape to the safety of
the main street, the Albanian, now roseless, shrugs his shoulders
and staggers sadly back through the Passage. Stopping once again
before my window, he bows to me and his ruined face brightens
in an angelic smile. I buy him another double *rakı*, which he

quaffs with the same ceremonial shattering as before. Then he bows again, twirls his cap around on his scarred head, and staggers off down the Passage shouting—"Rose! Rose!"—that unconquerable spirit. The Albanian is always followed in his wanderings by two furtive and stumbling figures, even more ruinous than he, who steal his roses from him, picking them up after he has thrown them all over the Passage in his wild career. And there are others, I am sure, who depend on these two in turn, living off them in some dark corner of this fantastic town.

After the Albanian has gone, a wandering minstrel enters the Passage through the fish-market gate. He strums a few chords on his *saz* and is then called to play for a group of old friends sitting together at a beer barrel. The minstrel sits with them and plays while the old men sing plaintive Anatolian ballads centuries old. When the old men have finished their songs and toasted one another with one last *rakı*, the minstrel bids them goodnight and sings a traditional parting song. Then he leaves too, and I hear the echo of his voice as he wanders off to play in the *meyhanes* of the fish bazaar, still singing of unrequited love.

And as I sit alone by the tavern window I recall the words which Evliya Efendi wrote so long ago, speaking of the wandering minstrels of his time: "These players are possessed of the particular skill to evoke by their tones the remembrance of absent friends and distant countries, so that their hearers grow melancholy." And Evliya's words evoke for me the memory of the dear friends who once sat with me in the Passage, most of them now far away and some of them gone forever, and so I grow melancholy too. Then I think of Evliya himself, who for so long has been my unseen companion in my strolls through Stamboul, and I wonder what he would say if he could see his beloved town today, so changed but so much the same, and then I lift a last glass in his memory.

Thus the evenings pass and the years go by in the Passage of Flowers, a little alleyway in Stamboul.

My favorite Turkish restaurant in New York City is Peri Ela (1361 Lexington Avenue, 212 410 4300), which serves a lentil soup to swoon over, delicious warm bread studded with black sesame seeds, and superior *sigara boregi*, among other very tasty dishes. Owners Silay Ciner, a native of Istanbul, and his American wife, Jill, wanted to open a place that didn't fit the stereotypical Turkish mold; starting with the name (which are the middle names of their two daughters), they've created an inviting restaurant of contemporary sophistication: dark wood paneling, a pressed tin ceiling, and bold artwork by California artist Andrzej Michael Karwacki. As Silay (pronounced Sly) says, "Peri Ela resembles hundreds of restaurants in Istanbul."

As he is known as the "Turkish ambassador of the neighborhood," responsible for dozens of his diners going to Turkey, I asked him for an Istanbul recommendation, and he told me about Bağdat Avenue, on the Asian side of the city, that is "one of the most iconic streets of Istanbul even though it is rarely mentioned in guidebooks." I regret that I didn't know about it, but as the French say, *il faut toujours garder une perle pour la prochaine fois* (it's necessary to always save a pearl for the next time).

Bağdat Avenue lies between Bostancı and Kızıltoprak and is about three and a half miles long. It was named in 1638 after the city was recaptured of by Sultan Murad IV, likely because it was the road connecting Istanbul to important trade routes, Baghdad being one of them. For centuries the neighborhoods surrounding the avenue have been wealthy, and many mansions here have magnificent views of the coast. Until about thirty years ago, affluent families from the European side would still spend the summer months here in their houses in

Fenerbahçe. This part of Istanbul has always been family and elderly friendly, and has never been as trendy as Etiler or Nişantaşi. The avenue is most vibrant on weekends, especially in summer with locals and visitors from other neighborhoods, and is a promenade street where you find elegant international and Turkish retailers and many mom-and-pop stores. Bağdat Avenue is also where Starbucks opened its first Istanbul outpost, and it didn't take long for a second one to appear a few blocks down. It's always fun to spend a Saturday afternoon here, immersed in the hustle and bustle of the avenue. Later you can have your five-o'clock tea at elegant Divan Pastanesi, knowing you are right in the heart of a very special place for the people of Istanbul.

Gönül Paksoy

One of my favorite, and one of the most distinctive, shops in Nişantaşı is that of designer Gönül Paksoy (Atiye Sokak 1/3, Teşvikiye / +90 212 236 0209 / closed Sunday). Paksoy, who has a background in chemical engineering and went on to earn a PhD from the Department of Sciences at Yildiz University, creates stunning one-of-a-kind articles of clothing as well as jewelry, scarves, and shoes. Her shop—open by appointment only—is a rather spare, minimalist space, yet quite warm and lovely. What you'll find there are women's-wear pieces (and some ties, sweaters, and bags for men) that harmoniously combine old fabrics with new—which sounds like stuff you've seen before, except you haven't: positively no one is doing what Paksoy is doing. She takes gorgeous Ottoman textiles and reworks them into something classic and contemporary at the same time. Paksoy uses natural fabrics and dyes and works not only with cotton, silk, and linen but also velvet. (She's also written eight lengthy books, which might explain why she sleeps only four or five hours a night and works seven days a week.) All the clothing items are loosely fitted, a bit like Eileen Fisher styles, and are in what she refers to as "Gönül Paksoy's Colors," which are mostly subtle shades (she herself likes beige, brown, and gray, but purple is a popular Ottoman color, so it turns up a lot in the fabrics she buys). She isn't afraid to dye old fabrics herself, and she takes a museum approach to each piece.

Paksoy reportedly wears only her own creations, and she describes herself not as a fashion designer but as someone who endeavors to create functional works of art. Her jewelry collection is particularly appealing—necklaces feature amulets, old tassels, needle lace, or antique beads—and is designed to complement her garments. "Timeless simplicity" is how she describes her work, and in an interview with We Are the Turks Web site, she noted that Turkish culture is so inspiring she never has a problem finding new ideas: "The simplicity of dervish costumes is the source of the same simplicity in my designs. This is a simplicity which few people seek, perhaps because it is so hard to attain." Paksoy's pieces range from about $5,000 to $12,000. Note that her brother, Doğan Paksoy, owns the nearby Teşvikiye Art Gallery (Abdi Ipekci Caddesi 21 / +90 212 241 0458), featuring Ottoman landscape painters; in 2007 he was director of the Art Bosphorus fair.

Miniskirts Meet Minarets in the New Istanbul

ANNETTE GROSSBONGARDT

∞

HERE'S A good piece featuring conversations with a few of Istanbul's elites—and illustrating how urban planners are constantly challenged to keep this rapidly growing metropolis functioning.

ANNETTE GROSSBONGARDT, based in Istanbul, reports for *Der Spiegel*, a weekly German magazine founded in 1947, with a circulation of over a million a week. This piece appeared in *Spiegel Online International*, the magazine's English-language Internet edition.

KAGAN GÜRSEL'S daily commute to work is one of the highlights of his day. The forty-seven-year-old Istanbul entrepreneur doesn't have to worry about the stress of driving, nor is he forced to breathe the exhaust fumes with which millions of cars stuck in Istanbul's never-ending traffic jams pollute the city's air. Gürsel, who runs a hotel chain, goes to work on a boat, crossing the Bosporus twice a day.

The "Esma Sultan," an old yellow and white pilot boat named after a proud daughter of a sultan, chugs steadily through the waves of the Bosporus. Along the way it passes giant container ships, oil tankers from Kazakhstan and a gleaming white cruise liner. "The Bosporus is different every day," enthuses Gürsel. On blue summer days the sea is as smooth as silk, on stormy days the wind and rain turn the water an ominous steel gray, and in freezing temperatures the water is the color of turquoise.

Thirty-two kilometers (20 miles) long and, at its narrowest point, only 660 meters wide (2,165 feet), the Bosporus is Istanbul's lifeline. Literature Nobel Prize winner Orhan Pamuk feels the city draws its strength from the Bosporus. "If the city speaks of defeat, destruction, deprivation, melancholy and poverty, the Bosporus sings of life, pleasure and happiness," he writes in his 2003 memoir *Istanbul*, a love letter to the city of his birth.

Istanbul's more affluent citizens live directly on the shore or pay a $1,000 premium for an apartment with a view of the Bosporus. Gürsel lives with his wife Merve, an interior designer and former show jumper, in one of Istanbul's most beautiful buildings: an old wooden Ottoman palace on the water in the Asian part of the city.

When Gürsel gets off the boat he has only a few steps to go before reaching the front door of his house and, behind it, a sweeping, curved staircase under a magnificent chandelier. The palatial rooms of his 450-square-meter (4,800-square-foot) house are filled with the splendors of the Ottoman era, when the Turks were still ruled by sultans and controlled the Middle East, the Balkans, North Africa, and the Crimean Peninsula, as well as Asia Minor. Built in 1860, Gürsel's villa was once the home of a princess from Egypt, an Ottoman province at the time.

The new elite is rediscovering old Istanbul's beauty and its historic legacy. In the past, the old wooden houses were neglected and sometimes even demolished or burned down to make room for streets or profitable but soulless concrete apartment blocks. Pamuk talks of a "frenzy to turn Istanbul into a pale, poor second class imitation of a Western city." In those days, the young republic wanted nothing to do with the dilapidated luxury of its Ottoman ancestors.

The Marmara hotel on Taksim Square, which Gürsel, as his

father's heir, runs, is one of those much-maligned buildings from the 1970s. But the popular and well-managed property is one of the top addresses in the area. The hotel advertises its "Turkish hospitality and European style," and targets mainly business-people, who are now coming to Istanbul in greater numbers. The booming Turkish economy is attracting foreign investors, and Istanbul is the engine of that boom; the city is responsible for more than one-fifth of Turkey's gross domestic product.

From the Marmara, it's only a short walk to the restaurants and bars of Beyoğlu, a district where a "little Europe" developed in the nineteenth century, complete with hotels, banks, theaters, and apartments for diplomats and businesspeople. Beyoğlu boasts rooftop bars with an excellent view of the Istanbul skyline, palaces, and magnificent mosques between the Sea of Marmara and the Golden Horn. The pulse and energy of this young coun-try, where more than half of the population is under twenty-five, is palpable here.

Every few hours the call of the muezzin cuts through the sound of the techno music, an aural reminder of Istanbul's position as the gateway between East and West. Especially because of its glitzy nightlife, Istanbul is celebrated as the "hip city on the Horn," and as a metropolis between "minarets and miniskirts." *Newsweek* even went so far as to call Istanbul "the coolest city in the world."

Of course, only part of this vibrating megacity, with its esti-mated population of fourteen million, is this cool and beautiful. Istanbul's districts are as big as entire cities elsewhere, and there are neighborhoods which even people who have lived here their whole lives have never seen.

THE EXPLODING CITY

The city hasn't grown—it has exploded, overrun by a surge of poor immigrants from Anatolia in eastern Turkey and the Black Sea region. Migrant workers have built makeshift houses known as *gecekondus*, illegal but tolerated, on Istanbul's fringes and interspersed throughout the city. These shantytowns cover the city like carpets.

The city has granted amnesty to many *gecekondus* and has even upgraded some of them, while neighborhoods in Istanbul's historic downtown were allowed to fall into disrepair. Istanbul's poor live in neighborhoods like Dolapdere or Tarlabasi, only ten minutes from Beyoğlu: Kurds, Roma, and refugees from Iraq, Asia, and West Africa live here, eking out a living as day laborers, pickpockets, drug dealers, or male prostitutes.

These crowded slums, bleak satellite cities, don't fit into the picture of a shimmering Istanbul, which has previously served as the capital of three different empires.

In some neighborhoods, where lemons are still sold from horse-drawn carts, where the men sit in blackened tearooms, and the women lay out sheepskins to dry on the asphalt, Istanbul seems less of a big city than a collection of Anatolian villages dotted with old palaces, voluminous mosques, and glass office towers.

Istanbul is probably the most Western city in the Islamic world. But those who take the trouble to go to the the Faith neighborhood to pay a visit to the tomb of the conqueror Mehmet II, who brought down Byzantium in 1453, turned churches into mosques, and transformed the Christian Constantinople into the Islamic

TOPKAPI—ISTANBUL

T O P K A P I

Istanbul, will also discover the city's deeply Islamic side. Here the women wear black, full-length veils, and many men are bearded and wear religious caps and collarless shirts. One small section consisting of a few streets is populated almost entirely by members of a fourteenth-century Islamic order and has no televisions or alcohol.

But it is not just the tension between religion and the secular republic, between miniskirts and minarets, which characterizes Istanbul. The visible social inequality that plagues Turkey is more readily apparent. Wealth is ostentatiously displayed in the form of expensive cars, yachts, and elite clubs like the Reina, which is designed to resemble the deck of a cruise ship. At the other end of the social scale is an entire caste of servants who work as chauffeurs, housekeepers, and cooks, carrying groceries from the market and hand-washing the Range Rovers and Jaguars of the rich every day, even in the cold and rain.

Nevertheless, those who employ servants create jobs, though badly paid, and there are possibilities for the poor to become upwardly mobile. Istanbul has a gold-rush feel to it, a place where Anatolian cotton porters and scrap dealers can become millionaires, like Haci Ömer Sabanci, whose family-owned holding company is now Turkey's second-largest corporation, or media mogul Aydin Dogan, one of *Forbes*'s 500 richest people in the world.

Those with the ambition to climb the social ladder work as street vendors, selling sesame rings known as *simit* for twelve to fourteen hours a day from three-legged stools which are wrapped in rags to make them less painful to carry on a shoulder. The fortunate ones can bring home twenty lira, about eleven euros, a day. Other workers spend their days hauling bales of material to textile factories or rinsing greasy plates in fish restaurants.

Sinasi Yalçin sits in a jogging suit in front of a steaming glass of tea in the small courtyard of the Culture and Solidarity Club of Istanbul's Karanfilköy district. Already retired at the age of fifty-five, he is one of the lucky ones who managed to make his own fortune.

The son of a mine worker left his home town of Sivas in Anatolia at the age of seventeen to try his luck in the big city. He traveled a day and a half by train to Istanbul, his belongings packed into a single suitcase. He had little education apart from a few years spent at the village school. But he was ambitious, and he knew that he needed an education before he could have any kind of future.

At first he slept in parks and scraped by, working as a cleaner and waiter. Then he made a deal with a Jewish orthopedist, getting room and board in return for waxing the floors in the doctor's office at night. He attended school during the day and, after six years, at the age of twenty-three, he finally finished high school.

"Istanbul is a tough city," says Yalçin. "It saps your strength and tries to swallow you up—but it also gives you a chance." It was a chance that he seized with both hands—after studying engineering and applied mathematics, Yalçin landed a good job with the city's electric utility.

Karanfilköy is another illegal migrant settlement that managed to escape the city's wrecking ball ten years ago. Beets and bitter Black Sea cabbage grow in the gardens of the Culture and Solidarity Club, which is fighting to have Karanfilköy and its 537 houses legalized.

Yalçin himself lives in a two-story house, the walls lined with pale yellow imitation wood paneling, and lovingly tends his garden. The constant drone of traffic from a nearby six-lane highway doesn't bother him. "I feel at home here, this is my Istanbul," he says.

"YOU CAN MAKE SOMETHING OF YOURSELF HERE"

Former residents of Istanbul who return to the city are amazed at how quickly it has changed. After living in Germany or elsewhere, they are now rediscovering their own country.

Defne Koryürek, thirty-eight, and her husband spent five years in New York, where they ran a small restaurant. When she returned nine years ago Koryürek found surprising similarities between the Big Apple and Istanbul. "Both cities are dynamic and full of energy," she says. "You can make something of yourself here. It's up to you whether you want to be part of the whole, and whether you are willing to learn."

Koryürek has tried many things. She studied history and cinematography, and worked as a TV producer until she discovered her love of cooking. When she returned to Istanbul, she brought back recipes for pancakes, quiches, and eggs Benedict from New York. She now runs Dükkan, an exclusive butcher's shop specializing in dry-aged beef. Juicy, dark cuts of beef dry in a climate-controlled glass cabinet. A label on each cut identifies how many days it's been drying.

As Koryürek fills sausage skins with meat, the door of the shop opens and a hotel chef walks in. He bends over the meat counter and selects the best pieces. Dükkan has become a supplier to Istanbul's five-star restaurants, including the Hilton, the Four Seasons, the Çırağan Palace Kempinski, and Les Ottomans, a luxury hotel on the banks of the Bosporus that is bringing the flair of the Ottoman era back to life.

"In this city, you never know what the future will bring, and you have no guarantee of anything," says Koryürek. "Business is going great, but then suddenly the customers stop coming and you have no idea why." Unlike businessmen in the West, says Koryürek, one cannot plan for the long term in Istanbul. "Our customers think in the short term. They're always hungry for the new."

Koryürek and her partner, Emre Mermer, thirty-eight, an economist and the son of a cattle farmer, don't even have an official permit for their exclusive shop, which lies in the middle of Küçük Armutlu, a poor *gecekondu* settlement adjacent to the highway. They chose the spot because the rent was affordable. When they tried to register the company, officials at the city planning office told them the buildings weren't registered—and so it was impossible to register a business there. Nevertheless, the authorities tolerate Dükkan, and business is booming. That's just the way it goes in Istanbul.

Istanbul is proof that chaos can be productive, but it has also brought the city to the brink of disaster. The daily traffic crisis was declared a national problem long ago. Tens of thousands of houses could collapse when the next earthquake, which has already been predicted, strikes the city.

Hüseyin Kaptan has been hired to save Istanbul. An architecture professor, Kaptan had already retired and moved to the country when the city's mayor begged him to help. The last master plan for the city is already twenty-six years old, and development spun out of control long ago. Now Kaptan's task is to come up with an urban vision for the next thirty years.

Plans, blueprints, and sketches are stacked on a large table in the middle of his office. The problems are so gargantuan and construction is continuing at such a rapid pace, says Kaptan, that he feels as if he were "in a tsunami." At seventy-one, he had hoped to quietly live out his days as a farmer.

The city wants Kaptan to put a stop to its growth. "We could open the doors tomorrow for a million new jobs, but we couldn't cope with it," he says. If development continues at the current pace, says Kaptan, Istanbul's population could easily swell to between twenty and twenty-five million in the next twenty years. Prime Minister Recep Tayyip Erdoğan recently called for a limit not just on the number of cars in Istanbul, but also on the number of new residents.

Planners want to cap Istanbul's population at sixteen million. To do so, they plan to divert migration into the nearby region along the Sea of Marmara. They also plan to upgrade Istanbul's Asian districts, currently home to hundreds of thousands of people who commute to jobs in office buildings on the European side. Kaptan's idea is to transform Istanbul's economy from low-wage manufacturing to high-value service industries. Thirty-two percent of the city's work force now works in industrial production. If Kaptan and his team have their way, that number will be cut in half in the next two decades. To achieve that goal, entire districts are slated for demolition.

A part of Turkey's textile industry is located in Zeytinburnu, which with its three hundred thousand inhabitants is practically a small city itself. Workers cut, sew, iron, and pack garments in more than fifteen thousand workshops in Zeytinburnu's basements and courtyards. The area's former leather tanneries, with their polluting waste water, have already been moved to Istanbul's eastern outskirts. Drawings of the new Zeytinburnu are spread out on Kaptan's desk: light-filled apartment buildings reminiscent of modernist Bauhaus designs, complete with shopping centers, playgrounds, and parks.

Many mistakes were made in the past decades. Buildings were not designed to be earthquake-proof. The old section of Istanbul—the historic peninsula where the Hagia Sophia, the Blue Mosque, and the Grand Bazaar are located—was neglected and is now sorely in need of repair and renovation. Politicians have placed too much emphasis on the automobile as the primary means of transportation, and Istanbul has only a very small and underdeveloped subway system. They also allowed the metropolis to sprawl into the city's water catchment area and forests to the north and east—a development Kaptan calls "criminal."

STUCK BETWEEN REMEMBERING AND AMNESIA

Now, in the search for a better quality of life and living conditions, something downtown Istanbul can no longer offer, many of the city's affluent residents are being lured out toward the Black Sea, where luxury gated communities are springing up like independent planets.

Göktürk, located about twenty-five kilometers (sixteen miles)

as the crow flies from downtown Istanbul, has turned in the space
of a decade from a village into a satellite city for between six thousand and eight thousand Istanbulites. Here life is green and pleasant and the bustle of Istanbul seems far away. For several thousand
dollars, residents can join the exclusive Kemer Golf and Country
Club, complete with golf courses, a manmade lake, stables, a music
school, tennis courts, gyms, and even an outdoor survival camp.

This is something that more and more Istanbulites can afford,
and not just the established upper class. The recent economic
boom has produced a new middle class who are intent on showing off their newfound affluence. To serve this new market, international fashion and luxury goods retailers, including Vakko,
Harvey Nichols, Ferragamo, Fendi, and Louis Vuitton, are coming to Istanbul.

Istanbul's traditional shopping street, İstiklâl Caddesi, is lined
with colorful little banners that read: "Istanbul, European Capital
of Culture 2010." According to the European jury, the city's
application for the one-year honorary title was especially "progressive and innovative." Istanbul hopes to make 2010 a magical year
for the city, complete with dazzling events for tourists, European
creative artists, street theater, floating platforms on the Bosporus,
and a trip back in time through seven thousand years of history.
Dilapidated historical monuments are now being restored, including those from the city's Christian and pre-Christian eras.

"We see the title as an opportunity to recapture the lost, old
Istanbul," says Nuri Çolakoğlu, the chairman of the 2010 initia-
tive. "We want to show how deep the cultural roots we share with
Europe are."

Author Elif Shafak called Istanbul the "stepchild of the modern, secular Turkish republic." With its multicultural heritage,
especially of Greeks and Armenians, Christians, Muslims, and
Jews, it resisted the young republic's myth that all were equal and
members of a homogeneous family of proud Turks. Nevertheless,
says Shafak, Istanbul still doesn't know exactly where it belongs.

"It swings back and forth between cosmopolitanism and nationalism, between remembering and amnesia"—a city on two continents, between Europe and Asia.

፧ටිඝටිඝටිඝ

It is now evening in Kagan Gürsel's wooden palace on the
Bosporus. The veranda offers a view of the bridge across the
Bosporus, on which drivers heading west are greeted by a sign
that reads: "Welcome to Europe." There is also a view of the
fortress of Rumeli Hisarı, from which Mehmet the Conqueror
launched his attack on Istanbul in 1453.

Gürsel, the hotelier, studied in the United States and always
wanted his country to be part of Europe. But now he is disap
pointed. "Why should I run after someone who doesn't want
me?" he asks irritably.

Just as the Gürsels are making themselves comfortable in the
library, where they like to pore over thick volumes on Ottoman
history, their house is suddenly plunged into darkness. The power
is out once again, another feature of life in Istanbul. And, like
most residents, the Gürsels have candles at the ready.

Five minutes later, the bridge and the fortress are brightly lit up
once again. Ships glide by on the Bosporus like giant shadows.
The beauty of the Bosporus turns satiny black at night, and Kagan
Gürsel says that he would not want to live anywhere else but in
the center of Istanbul.

—*Translated from the German by Christopher Sultan*

Celebration Istanbul

JOHN ASH

∞

NOT LONG ago I bought a used book at a garage sale, *A Muezzin from the Tower of Darkness Cries: Travels in Turkey*, by R. P. Lister, published in England. The title borrows from Omar Al-Khayyam's *Rubaiyat*, and the book is rather dated. A few passages, though, stand out, like this one, about the author's approach to Istanbul: "It had been bright blue weather all through the Mediterranean; now it was overcast and somber, and a drop or two of rain fell. The great city rose out of the water and loomed, where in other kinds of weather it sparkles, or shimmers. In all climatic circumstances it is magnificent." The piece below, by John Ash, devoted to the mood, the food, and the style of Istanbul, exemplifies the city's sparkle, shimmer, and magnificence.

JOHN ASH is a poet and writer who moved to Istanbul in 1996 and now teaches at Kadir Has University. In addition to his collections of poetry—including *The Burnt Pages* (Random House, 1991), *Disbelief* (Carcanet, 1987), *Parthian Stations* (Carcanet, 2007), and *To the City* (Talisman House, 2004)—he is the author of *A Byzantine Journey* (Random House, 1995) and *Turkey: The Other Guide: Western and Southern Anatolia* (Milet Publishing, 2001), which has somewhat of a cult following and has been described as going "beyond any guide ever written on Turkey." In a profile of Ash in *The Economist*, Hugh Pope referred to him as the "leading light in a new 'Istanbul School' of English-speaking poets taking their inspiration from the city." Ash has also written for *The New Yorker, The Paris Review, The Washington Post,* and *The New York Times,* where this piece originally appeared.

No one knows just how many people live in Istanbul, since migrants arrive daily, but everyone agrees that the figure must be at least twelve million. It dwarfs most Western European cities, and is probably older than any of them. At its back lie the lowlands of Thrace, on which Istanbul closes its gates. Instead it looks east to the hills and mountains of Asia, whose snows gleam invitingly on winter days.

THE MOOD

Istanbul is a city absorbed in constant contemplation of an enigma, so much so that sometimes it doesn't know itself. Is it Oriental or Occidental, secular or Muslim, ugly or beautiful, rich or poor? Here the arrogant certainty of New York or London is lacking. Its inhabitants regard their city with an appealing ambiguity and perplexity, yet it surely has as much to offer as any other on earth. The skyline of the old city still takes the breath away (and one notes with gratitude that no modern structures have been allowed to challenge the supremacy of Hagia Sophia and the Mosque of Süleyman). The Bosporus is still an azure ribbon or rope twisting between wooded hills, villas and palaces.

It is true, of course, that this busy strait is crossed by two suspension bridges, but the assertion that Istanbul is "a bridge between East and West" is likely to provoke tired smiles or theatrical yawns among natives of the place. Since it ceased to be the capital of great empires (as it was from the early fourth century to the early twentieth century), since its grandiose embassies were reduced to consulates and the ambassadors suddenly found themselves marooned in the provincial boredom of Ankara, Istanbul has been very much a city on the edge.

But if Istanbul is on the edge, what is it on the edge of? The answer is both obvious and riddled with paradox. What the Austrian poet Ingeborg Bachmann said of Vienna (twice besieged by the Turks, who thereby inadvertently introduced coffee and percussion music to Central Europe) is surely a hundred times more true of Istanbul: "The breath of Asia is beyond." But here we enter a territory that has been mythologized almost out of recognition. By Asia (I am excluding the Far East) we mean emptiness—dead civilizations, mud-built villages, thin poplars, elusive crossing points of vast migrations and invasions; and, more specifically, we mean central Anatolia, where no middle-class citizen of Istanbul would be caught dead. So Istanbul continually confronts what it is not: emptiness, migration, impermanence. It follows that its mood is at once deeply rooted in its imperial past, and the sheltering presence of its architectural heritage, and at the same time as volatile and fickle as the winds that blow through it. (In "Istanbul, the Imperial City," John Freely identifies no fewer than twenty-seven such winds or storms, each with its distinctive name, ranging from the Storm of Roasting Walnuts to the Storm of Mating Rams.)

In Istanbul you must orient yourself in time as much as in space. A brief stroll can take you from the nineteenth century through the sixteenth to the sixth (though not necessarily in that order). It is a deeply layered city where you should walk carefully and respectfully, since you can never know what lies beneath your shoes. Just recently, for example, while wandering in streets behind the Blue Mosque, I stumbled on the enormous vaulted substructures of a Byzantine palace directly under an expensive carpet store. Maps will give you the broad outlines of the city, but the mystery, as usual, is in the details, and the street I live on goes unmarked. Even the name of my neighborhood furrows the brows of taxi drivers. I have to tell them it is "near the Galata Tower," and this is how you should find your way about, steering yourself according to monuments, and glimpses of what the sixth-century poet and historian Procopius referred to as the city's "garland of waters."

Your excursion might take you to the deeply religious quarter of Eyüp, where huge flocks of pigeons swirl above the domes of octagonal tombs, or the teeming concrete underpasses of Eminönü, where you could find yourself buying something you never knew you needed, or you could take a leisurely ferry to the Princes' Islands, where plane trees shade the cool streets, and the only vehicles are horse-drawn phaetons. The oleanders of the islands are a promise, but one we don't keep often enough. Because of them we never feel hemmed in. Because of them, the door to the balcony is always ajar, and the view is limitless.

THE FOOD

In Turkey idleness is not a sin, indeed it is an essential element of *keyif*, a word my dictionary translates somewhat inadequately as "pleasure or delight." An extraordinary amount of time is spent sipping tea and playing backgammon in cafés, or loitering in restaurants over the prodigious variety of appetizers known as *meze*, the point being to extend *keyif* for as long as humanly possible, or at least until the waiters start to yawn and talk among themselves.

Although there are complex subcategories, most Turkish restaurants fall under two headings—*lokantas* and *meyhanes*. The former are essentially lunch places serving good, plain food to workers. Alcohol is rarely available, and menus are for the uninitiated. You simply walk up to the steam tables where the food is displayed, and pick whatever you like the look of. There will be succulent soups (recommended for colds, flu, or hangovers), stewed meats and vegetables (okra, spinach, chard, eggplant), and fresh green beans and white beans in tomato sauce. And your choice will be on your table almost before you've had time to sit down.

While it is true that you can find any kind of cuisine you might desire in Istanbul, from Korean to Iberian, served in settings that range from the rudimentary to the drop-dead elegant, if you want to understand the soul of the city a long evening in a *meyhane* is obligatory. In discussing *meyhanes* we aren't just talking about food, but about the exuberant expression of an entire way of life. *Meyhanes*, which serve alcohol, tend to come in clusters, and in Kumkapı and Beyoğlu there are whole streets of them, all vying with polite desperation for your custom. Weaving your way between gesticulating waiters and itinerant musicians, your party (which should ideally consist of at least six people) will soon find a table, and you should immediately order *rakıs* all round. *Rakı* is the legendary, Turkish anise potation that destroyed the liver of the great Kemal Atatürk. Since it also indirectly caused the death of Orhan Veli—the greatest poet of *meyhane* culture, who once wrote "I should have been/A fish at the bottom/Of a bottle of booze"—it should be treated with deep respect. As soon as your drinks have arrived, a waiter will swoop toward you balancing an enormous, round tray heavy with *meze*. This is why you will need at least six people, to appreciate the full panoply of flavors, from *lakerda* (pickled fish with red onions) through roasted, sweet red peppers to *semizotu* (purslane in a yogurt and garlic dressing).

As the evening progresses your main course—often seafood, such as shrimp baked in a casserole or whiting, battered and fried and served with arugula—may come to seem less and less important, and you should postpone ordering it until the last minute, since its arrival signals the beginning of the end of *keyif*. Toward the end of the evening in a *meyhane*, any number of things may happen, but, despite the amount of *rakı* consumed, drunken boorishness is very rare. Musicians are usually within earshot, so perhaps a group of women (out on the town without their menfolk) will rise to their feet, urged on by the shrill squealing of a *zurna* (a kind of elongated clarinet) and the clatter of a hand-drum and indulge in some impromptu belly dancing. And yes, it is quite likely that they will dance on the chairs and the tables, but they will do so with a surprising decorousness. It is even more likely that an entire table will burst suddenly into song, and will soon be joined by neighboring tables exchanging deftly harmonized verses. The song will be infinitely melancholy, but one should not conclude from this that Istanbul is a city of depressives. Their native wisdom urges the Turks to embrace sadness as an inevitable concomitant of living. At such moments, everyone in a *meyhane* is at one with the spirit of Orhan Veli as he sat by the Bosporus overcome, for no particular reason, with an "indescribable sadness," and sang his song to the city he called "my lover, my fever."

THE STYLE

When we think of Turkish style we think of Iznik ceramics, *kilims*, carpets and *hamams*, but we are living in the past, which is not where most Turks want to be. Good quality *kilims* are still being produced, but it is mostly foreigners who buy them, and rugs can't tell us much about the style of contemporary Istanbul.

A style only becomes identifiable when it becomes self-aware, and something to aspire to. All it takes is a few cafés and bars where like-minded people can sit and talk and listen to the same music, and feel that they are—well—*onto something*, even if they aren't sure precisely what it is. In the last five or six years all of these factors have come together in a small, central district of Istanbul, which, for purposes of simplicity, I will call the Tünel. This name, which derives from the fact that the district is home to the world's shortest subway line, covers many diverse quarters with difficult names. It forms part of the Ottoman European quarter of Pera-Galata, and stands on a steep hill overlooking the Golden Horn and the old city. For decades it suffered from decline and neglect as the original, polyglot population, consisting mostly of Greeks and Jews, began to drift away, and was replaced by poor, rural migrants. It was no longer a place where the middle class wanted to live. As a result, it entered the '90s with the vast majority of its splendid Beaux-Arts and Art Nouveau apartment buildings intact, at which point it began to benefit from the growing cultural maturity of republican Turkey, a maturity that involved a certain disenchantment with modernity. One fin de siècle was joined to another. Why live in a banal box miles from the city's historic center when you could rent or buy an authentic late-Ottoman apartment with stuccoed ceilings and the projecting window bays known as *cumbas*, whose origins can be traced back to Byzantine times?

The pioneers of this movement, which is both a return and an advance, were artists, intellectuals (some of whom had never left), and foreigners—the usual suspects, you might say. Small art galleries soon opened, and groups of young artists took to staging exhibits in derelict buildings. Cafés and bars sprang up overnight, ranging from the funky and friendly Babehane to the ultrastylish, and expensive, New Pera, with its spectacular roof terrace. The seal was set by the opening, just off vine-shaded Sofyali Street, of a fashionable club called Babylon.

Although impeccably cool, Babylon is not just a place where you go to see and be seen, it is home to some very serious and sophisticated music making. Indeed, the whole neighborhood seems to be gripped by melomania. Galip Dede Street, which begins with a Mevlevi dervish lodge, is otherwise given over to stores selling ouds, zithers, synthesizers, and sound systems. In cafés and bars you will hear jazz classics (especially early Miles Davis and Chet Baker), acid jazz, hip-hop, house, rai, trip-hop, techno, in fact just about anything other than the groaning behemoths of white, Western, male rock.

The new generation of British-Asian musicians—Nitin Sawhney and Talvin Singh, for example—are also increasingly popular.

This gives us a clue to what is going on here. Istanbul has an enormously rich and diverse musical tradition, and it is also a city that has long taken a passionate interest in jazz. A hybrid was perhaps inevitable. After all, improvisation and a certain soulful melancholy are common to both traditions. So we find Burhan Ocal's Istanbul Oriental Ensemble collaborating with black musicians from New York and Philadelphia, or Brooklyn Funk Essentials blending seamlessly with a (mostly) traditional Gypsy band called Layco Tayfa. These musicians, along with many others, have recently been heard at Babylon. The groove runs deep, and Istanbul is fulfilling its ancient role as a cultural meeting place with a new—or recovered—sense of confidence and flair.

> *The News in Istanbul*
> Watching the news in Istanbul
> I understand nothing;
> But the weather forecast
> is easier.
>
> Temperatures and winds in different towns,
> Names from all the centuries,
> From all the human layers,
> Of which the Turks are top.
>
> Mostly, if I know them,
> It is in their old forms:
> Sinope and Trebizond and Ephesus,
> Kars and Van and Erzerum.
> Greece on the west,
> Armenia on the east.
>
> And Constantinople straddling
> the two continents.
>
> But it is Istanbul now.
>
> —MICHAEL E. STONE

MICHAEL E. STONE is a professor of Armenian Studies and Gail
Levin de Nur Professor of Religious Studies at the Hebrew
University of Jerusalem. He is also the author, with his wife,
Nira Stone, of *Armenians in Jerusalem and the Holy Land* (Peeters,
2002) and, with various other authors, of *Report of the Survey of
a Medieval Jewish Cemetery in Eghegis, Vayots Dzor Region, Arme-
nia* (Oxford Centre for Hebrew and Jewish Studies, 2002),
Album of Armenian Paleography (with Dickran Kouymjian and
Henning Lehmann, Aarhus Universitetsforlag, 2001), and
many others.

RECOMMENDED READING

The Antiquities of Constantinople, by Pierre Gilles (Italica, 1988).
This notable work is a second edition of John Ball's 1729 English translation of the *Four Books of the Antiquities of Constantinople*, written by Pierre Gilles and published posthumously in
1561. No other edition of an English translation has been available since that time, which is odd only because this is "a fundamental text on one of the principal cities of both East and
West," according to Eileen Gardner of Italica Press, which has
a series of historical travel guides. The oft-quoted Gilles, or
Petrus Gyllius in Latin ("While other cities are mortal, this one
will remain as long as there are men on earth"), left France in
the service of François I on a fact-finding mission to Constantinople, which at the time of his visit in 1544 "was the largest
and wealthiest city of the Mediterranean, in fact of the Western
world," according to Ronald Musto in the introduction.

Constantinople: City of the World's Desire, 1453–1924, by Philip
Mansel (St. Martin's, 1996). The subject of this book, writes

Mansel in his foreword, "is the story of a city and a family. It is written in the belief that dynasties have been as decisive in shaping cities as nationality, climate and geography. . . . *Constantinople* is the story of what was, for a long time, the greatest dynastic city of all." Mansel, a historian and biographer of courts and royal dynasties, brilliantly argues his thesis. Without giving away the epilogue, I do want to share one of Mansel's conclusions: Istanbul is beginning to resume its role as meeting place. He writes, "For the first time since the 1920s the city is part of the world economy, with a fully convertible currency. In 1995 the Istanbul Stock Exchange, equipped with the latest technology, opened at Istinye on the Bosphorus. Most Istanbullus accept modern international culture as whole-heartedly as the city's nineteenth-century élite accepted French culture. Only the occasional dome and minaret distinguishes part of modern Istanbul from other European cities. Clothes, music, night-clubs, in most of the city, are the same as in Paris or New York."

1453: The Holy War for Constantinople and the Clash of Islam and the West, by Roger Crowley (Hyperion, 2005). "I shall tell the story of the tremendous perils . . . of Constantinople, which I observed at close quarters with my own eyes," notes Leonard of Chios, one of the many who claim to have accurately recorded the fall of the city. Crowley expertly sets the stage for the siege and recounts what he can from the sources available ("the band of witnesses is actually quite small," he notes, "and largely Christian"), and it seems he leaves no second of the siege unrecorded. Yet Crowley reminds us that even with all accounts we have today, we still do not know exactly how Constantine XI died: "Constantine was glimpsed for the last time surrounded by his most faithful retinue . . . his last moment reported by unreliable witnesses who were almost certainly not present, struggling, resisting defiantly, falling, crushed underfoot, until he vanished from history into the afterlife of legend." In paperback, and at 305 pages, this is a great bring-along volume of "the prototype of global ideological conflict."

Istanbul: City of a Hundred Names, with photographs by Alex Webb and an essay by Orhan Pamuk (Aperture, 2007). Webb first visited Istanbul in 1968, for one day, and didn't return for thirty years. By this time, he had become drawn to "borders and the edges of societies, where different cultures come together, sometimes clashing, sometimes fusing." The book opens with a black-and-white photo he took in '68, while all the other photos he later took are in color. The Pamuk essay is actually from a chapter in his *Istanbul: Memories and the City* book, about *hüzün*, and pairs exceptionally well with the photos.

Istanbul: Cradle of Civilizations, Collective Memory/Spatial Continuities, by Kent Belleği (Mekânsal Süreklilikler, 2007). I bought this book in the gift shop at Topkapı Palace, but I later saw it in bookstores all around Istanbul. It's divided into seven sections, for each of the seven hills of Istanbul, and it's a fascinating book packed with color photographs and maps—there is even a separate foldout poster of the Istanbul skyline (which I promptly hung above my desk) that I didn't even realize was part of the package until I took off the shrink-wrapping.

Istanbul Constantinople: An Album, by Nuri Akbayar; English translation by Sylvia Zeybekoğlu (Oğlak Yayıncılıl ve Reklamclılıl, 2000). I found this pretty little book, in the shape of a small photo album, at Robinson Crusoe, the wonderful bookstore on İstiklâl Caddesi. Besides featuring hand-colored images of the city, the accompanying text is quite interesting and many of the entries reveal little-known facts about particular monuments or moments in history.

Orhan Pamuk's two works of nonfiction are also essential reading. He might disagree (perhaps preferring that one read his fiction first) but these books, to my mind, go hand in hand with his fiction. *Other Colors: Essays and a Story* (translated from the Turkish by Maureen Freely; Knopf, 2007) is, as he describes, "a book made of ideas, images, and fragments of life that have still not found their way into one of my novels. . . . Sometimes it surprises me that I have not been able to fit into my fiction all the thoughts I've deemed worth exploring: life's odd moments, the little everyday scenes I've wanted to share with others, and the words that issue from me with power and joy when there is an occasion of enchantment." I love that description, and I feel certain many other writers would say the same thing. Some of these essays are very personal and autobiographical; others are about books, reading, and art; still more are devoted to Europe, Turkey, and Istanbul; two are about his time in New York.

The last three in the book are my favorites: "To Look Out the Window," an unforgettable story; "My Father's Suitcase," the lecture he gave for his Nobel Prize in Literature, awarded in 2006; and the *Paris Review* interview, conducted in two sustained sessions in London and by correspondence in 2004 and 2005, two months after his arrest. He had been charged under Article 301.1 of the Turkish penal code, which states that "a person who explicitly insults being a Turk, the Republic or Turkish Grand National Assembly, shall be imposed to a penalty of imprisonment for a term of six months to three years." Additionally, Article 301.3 states, "Where insulting being a Turk is committed by a Turkish citizen in a foreign country, the penalty to be imposed shall be increased by one-third." As this charge came about after an interview he had with a Swiss newspaper, when he'd said,

"Thirty thousand Kurds and a million Armenians were killed in these lands and nobody but me dares to talk about it," he would face an additional penalty for having made the comment abroad. In September 2005, Pamuk was officially indicted for having "blatantly belittled Turkishness." As Salman Rushdie noted at the time (timesonline.co.uk, October 14, 2005), "On both sides of the Bosphorus, the Pamuk case matters." The charges were dropped after intense international pressure and vigorous protests by European Parliament members and International PEN, but at the time of the *Paris Review* interview, Pamuk was still slated to stand trial on December 16, 2005.

Istanbul: Memories and the City (translated from the Turkish by Maureen Freely; Knopf, 2005) is Pamuk's tribute to the city where he's lived nearly all his life. He begins the book with a quote by Ahmet Rasim, a newspaper columnist from the early 1900s: "The beauty of a landscape resides in its melancholy." The quote is quite apt, as Pamuk's overall summary of Istanbul is indeed melancholy—this is not a bright and sunny memoir. *Hüzün* is the Turkish word for "melancholy," and the word appears often throughout the book. By the next-to-last chapter, when we find him at a crucial moment in 1972, the point at which he has come to the realization that he will not pursue a career in painting, he says:

> *If I had come to feel deeply connected to my city, it was because it offered me a deeper wisdom and understanding than any I could acquire in a classroom. . . . Here amid the old stones and the old wooden houses, history made peace with its ruins; ruins nourished life and gave new life to history. If my fast-extinguishing love of painting could no longer save me, the city's poor neighborhoods seemed prepared, in any event, to*

become my second world. How I longed to be part of this poetic confusion! Just as I had lost myself in my imagination to escape my grandmother's house and the boredom of school, now, having grown bored with studying architecture, I lost myself in Istanbul. So it was that I finally came to relax and accept the hüzün *that gives Istanbul its grave beauty, the* hüzün *that is its fate.*

Many black-and-white photographs by Ara Güler are showcased in this book, reason alone to pick it up. Pamuk says of Güler's archive that it is first and foremost a tribute to his art and "also a superb record of Istanbul life from 1950 to the present day and will leave anyone who knew the city during those years drunk with memories." I briefly considered including some of Güler's photographs in my own book, but I didn't want to be a copycat, and his work (rightly) comes at a price that is well beyond what I can afford.

John Freely's Istanbul, by John Freely with photographs by Erdal Yazıcı (Scala, 2005). Like Freely's *Stamboul Sketches*, the writings of Evliya Çelebi, the seventeenth-century Turkish chronicler, are often quoted from in this book. Çelebi's *Seyâhatnâme*, or *Narrative of Travels*, "contains a lengthy, detailed and frequently fabulous description of Istanbul during what was apparently the most colorful period of Ottoman history." I bought this illustrated paperback in Istanbul and saw it in several bookstores; I don't believe it's available in North America, but it's very much worth keeping an eye out for in Turkey. In combination with Çelebi's notes, Freely has organized this book based on the seven hills of Istanbul. This book is a wonderful continuation of *Stamboul Sketches*, with color photographs.

Bookstores in Istanbul

Istanbul has some terrific bookstores with lots of English-language titles that are unavailable in North America, so they're very much worth visiting. Most are on or near İstiklâl Caddesi. Among my favorites:

• Homer. With more than thirty thousand titles specializing in art, archaeology, architecture, and history, this is a store one can stay in for hours. (Yeniçarşi Caddesi 28A, Galatasaray / +90 212 249 5902 / homerbooks.com)

• Pandora. Aptly named, it's hard to leave this three-story box of wonders. (İstiklâl Caddesi, Büyükparmakkapı Sokak 3, Beyoğlu / +90 212 243 3503 / pandora.com.tr)

• Robinson Crusoe. In addition to being the hero of Daniel Defoe's novel, Robinson Crusoe is, according to the description on its shopping bags, "A *bookstore* with a distinctive style of its own, located in Pera, Istanbul on İstiklâl Street, no. 389. A *warehouse* established in September 1994 containing choice books. An *archive* where books are displayed & accessible to all. A *town square*, the gathering point not only of those who look & listen but of those who see & hear as well. A *library* where one goes not only for buying books but also to search for them & ask about them & browse around, sniffing the pages of & encountering, discovering & even writing books." The shop carries more than forty thousand titles. (+90 212 293 6968)

• Turkuaz. This is the store for rare and out-of-print books on Istanbul, Turkey, and the Ottoman Empire. It opened in 2001 and also stocks beautiful old photographs, engravings, etchings, lithographs, and postcards, as well as books in Armenian and Greek. (Emir Nevruz Sokak 12, Galatsaray / +90 212 245 4588 / sahaf-turkuaz.com)

Living in Istanbul, with photographs by Jérôme Darblay and texts by Kenize Mourad, Lale Apa, Teresa Battesti, Caroline Champenois, John Freely, Nedim Gursel, Tim Hindle, Arzu Karamani, and Gérard-Georges Lemaire (Flammarion, 1994). This is one of those so-called coffee-table books that is so very much more than a book for a coffee table. I've been a fan of Flammarion's *Living in* series since its inception, because the books are very well written, revealing, and interesting; the photographs are fantastic; and the visitor's guide at the back of each book is very useful and often includes things to see and do that aren't mentioned in guidebooks. John Freely's chapter, "A Day in Istanbul," is superb and filled with detail. He writes of a village on the Asian shore, Kuzguncuk, reminiscent of what Istanbul was like at the time of the Ottoman Empire. "The inhabitants of this village have always lived together in harmony, no matter what their race or religion, which is why, a few yards from Muzaffer Bey's shop, stand a Turkish mosque, a Greek church, an Armenian church and a synagogue."

Sinan Diaryz: A Walking Tour of Mimar Sinan's Monuments, by Ann Pierpont (Çitlembik, 2007). Pierpont visited Istanbul several times before she realized there was no guide written exclusively about Sinan and his works, so she decided to write one herself. This unique book is written from Sinan's perspective, and she planned the walking tours to illustrate Sinan's architectural development chronologically. I saw this in several bookstores in Istanbul, though I ordered my copy from Nettleberry, the distributor of Turkish books in the United States (See Miscellany, page 566.)

Travel Guide to Europe 1492: Ten Itineraries in the Old World, by Lorenzo Camusso (Henry Holt, 1992). This is one of my favorite books, truly a one-of-a-kind volume. Camusso presents ten real (or probable) journeys in chronological order, one

of which is "From Genoa to Istanbul." The sea voyage "took at
least thirty days, but it could easily become forty or sixty,
depending on the number of stops made at ports and the
weather conditions. One departed in May to arrive at the
Golden Horn in early July (and make the return voyage in
autumn). What kind of experience could it have been to cross
a calm Mediterranean between late spring and early summer?
The itinerary will be the route of prestigious cruises. At that
time one traveled on the sea for a living, out of necessity, in the
hope of gain. Whether or not there was also a portion of pleasure, no one can say. But the host of images—light, sea,
promontories, islands, and bays—one can imagine seeing from
the gently rocking vessel appears marvelous to us." This unique
book deserves more than short-lived appreciation.

The Wilder Shores of Love, by Lesley Blanch (Carroll & Graf, 1954,
    last reprinted edition 2002). This is actually a biographical quar-
    tet of brave nineteenth-century females who found their "wilder
    shores" in the Near and Far East. Only one ended up in Turkey
    (the others were Isabel Burton, Jane Digby, and Isabelle Eber-
    hardt), and she actually didn't arrive by choice: Aimée Dubucq
    de Rivery, a cousin to Empress Joséphine, was on her way home
    to Martinique from her convent school in Nantes when she was
    abducted by pirates and presented as a gift from the Dey of
    Algiers to the Sultan at Topkapı. She became the mother of Sul-
    tan Mahmoud II, known as the Reformer, whose sweeping
    (Western) changes laid the first foundations of the new Turkey.
    Interestingly, as Blanch notes, "there seems to have been some-
    thing in the air of Martinique which bred a race of queens.
    Joséphine, who was to become Empress of the French, her
    daughter Hortense, who became Queen of Holland, Madame
    de Maintenon, morganatic wife of Louis XIV, and Aimée, the
    Sultan Valideh, or Queen Mother, of Turkey—all these seductive
    women were Creoles from Martinique." Even if you read just

this one chapter, it's worth it—Blanch leaves out no detail of Topkapı intrigue and politics.

Guidebooks

As with books on all of Turkey, I peruse quite a number on Istanbul, too. Two I must separate from the pack are:

Imperial Istanbul: A Traveler's Guide, by Jane Taylor (Tauris Parke, 2007). This outstanding guidebook and *Strolling Through Istanbul* (just below) are the two most highly recommended books for a visit to Istanbul. You absolutely *must* read one of them, but they are different enough that reading both is best. This volume includes chapters on Iznik, Bursa, and Edirne. Taylor is a writer, photographer, and former television producer who lived in Istanbul in the early '70s and writes, "The 'Queen of Cities' continues to exercise her fascination. Despite changes (not all beautiful), this extraordinary city, with the garland of the seas that surround her and the Istanbullus who inhabit her, still makes any return to her a delightful renewal of discovery."

Strolling Through Istanbul, by Hilary Sumner-Boyd and John Freely (Redhouse, Istanbul, 1972). This is the veritable bible of the city. Robert Ousterhout, writing in *The Freely Papers*, says that "it remains the best guidebook ever written about Istanbul, setting a standard for travel writing that is rarely matched." It's not only the main text of the book that make this so valuable; with the lists of emperors and sultans, notes on Byzantine architectural forms, Ottoman architectural forms, and Sinan's works in Istanbul, this package is unsurpassed. In the final chapter, "A Last Stroll," the authors conclude that "Istanbul is much more than just an inhabited museum, for the old town has a beauty and fascination that go quite beyond its history and its architecture. One is apt to feel this when seated at a *çayevi* or *meyhane* in a sun-dappled square or while taking one's *keyif* in a vine-shaded café beside the Bosphorus. Little has been said of the Stamboullus themselves, but the visitor will surely have experienced innumerable examples of their grave friendliness and unfailing hospitality. . . . How can one not feel sad when leaving this beautiful city?"

The other guides I use fall into two categories: those I bring along and those I don't. Heavy tomes stay at home (I take notes from these) while one or two others go in my carry-on bag. All I consult are below:

Blue Guide: Istanbul because it's written by John Freely. Renowned travel writer Jan Morris once wrote that she preferred to peruse old, out-of-date guides over new ones because she liked to see how a place had changed (and when she says "old" she means decades old, not just a few years). I completely agree with her, and though the *Blue Guide* edition I have is from 1983, I still consult it. (And I am fortunate to own a Baedeker's guide to the Eastern Mediterranean that dates from the 1930s).

Eyewitness Travel: Istanbul for the time lines that run along the bottom of some of the pages in the History section, and the bird's-eye-view maps (I am nuts for these).

A Hedonist's Guide to Istanbul, otherwise known as *Hg2 Istanbul*, for its terrific and useful listings.

Insight Guides: Istanbul for the History and People section and the Travel Tips at the back.

Knopf Guides: Istanbul and Northwest Turkey for the early sections of each book—covering history, writers, painters, and relevant

topics—and the architectural cross-sections of historic buildings and private residences.

Knopf MapGuides: Istanbul for its size, portability, and good recommendations. MapGuides aren't published for every destination in the world, but when there is one in existence I never
leave without it (except when I go to Paris, for which nothing
beats the *Plan de Paris*). No more standing on a street corner
looking like a dork with a map: each volume measures about
5 × 7½ inches and the city is presented in neighborhood-by-
neighborhood maps, each of which opens up to about 9½ × 13
inches.

Louis Vuitton City Guide: European Cities for its remarkably succinct and spot-on listings. Istanbul is included in a volume with
Moscow, Saint Petersburg, Athens, and Nicosia, and it is not
sold individually—it must be purchased with the other books
in the boxed set, available at Louis Vuitton stores or online at
Louisvuitton.com. The surprising treat about the LV guides is
that a great number of listings feature plenty of good-value
choices.

Luxe City Guides: Istanbul for its size (about 3 × 6 inches) and great
recommendations. "The best of the best, stylish, brutally frank,
and sometimes, frankly brutal" is this series' motto. Each edition is nothing more than an accordion-style foldout pamphlet
geared mostly toward visitors who have only a few days in
Istanbul.

StyleCity: Istanbul for its abundance of fabulous and idiosyncratic
listings for places to sleep, eat, drink, shop, and retreat.

Time Out: Istanbul for its small size and great coverage, especially
in the Arts & Entertainment, Shops & Services, and Resources
sections.

Wallpaper City Guide: Istanbul for its unique, interesting, hip, and worthwhile suggestions for things to see, do, and experience.

Fiction

Arabesk (Headline, 2001), *Belshazzar's Daughter* (Felony & Mayhem, 2006), *Harem* (Headline, 2003), and *The Ottoman Cage* (Thomas Dunne, 2000), all novels by Barbara Nadel, all set in Istanbul.

Enlightenment, by Maureen Freely (Overlook, 2008).

Halide's Gift, by Frances Kazan (Random House, 2001).

Istanbul: Poetry of Place, edited by Ateş Orga (Eland, 2007). Among the poets featured are Lord Byron, Ivan Bunin, İrfan Orga, Orhan Veli Kanik, Robert Liddell, Roza Eskenazi, Théophile Gautier, and Nâzım Hikmet.

Kamil Pasha novels by Jenny White: *The Abyssinian Proof* (Norton, 2008) and *The Sultan's Seal* (Norton, 2007). Like Barbara Nadel's mysteries, these are all set in Istanbul—though in the 1890s—and each is incredibly atmospheric.

Leyla: The Black Tulip, by Alev Lytle Croutier (Pleasant Company, 2003). For children, but a good read for anyone of any age.

The Palace of Tears, by Alev Lytle Croutier (Delacorte, 2000).

Stamboul Train, by Graham Greene (William Heinemann, 1932; Penguin, 1992).

INTERVIEW

Gamze Artaman

When I asked Tom Brosnahan to recommend a tour guide for me, he immediately suggested Gamze Artaman. Before I met Gamze (pronounced GAHM-say), I assumed Tom had chosen her because I was a repeat visitor and because I had my own list of things I wanted to see and do. Gamze was happy to accommodate me, but she is as terrific for things to see and do that are a little off the well-trodden path as she is with first-time visitors and major sites. Her enthusiasm is the same for the monuments of the old city (Sultanahmet) as for the neighborhoods of Balat, Fener, and Eyüp. Gamze became a licensed guide in 1991.

Q: I understand that the process of becoming a tour guide in Turkey is quite intensive. What is required?

A: When I began, in 1990, the ministry of tourism organized courses every year. Exams had to be first taken on general knowledge, language skills, etc., and then, if you could pass the tests, you would qualify to attend a nearly eight-month course. After this was the traineeship, when for a whole month we were taken around Turkey to see the major sights (professors accompanied and lectured us all the way). Now, things have changed: it's even more difficult, and one must earn a four-year academic degree!

Q: As demanding as the process is, there are a *lot* of guides in Istanbul. But as with other aspects of travel, there are good guides and then there are superb guides. What are some characteristics that define a superb guide?

A: I personally separate tour guiding in two parts: guiding groups and guiding individuals (private tours). This might not make a lot of sense to some people, but the way I consider my profession they actually are two very different things. As 90 percent of my tours are private, I will speak to this type. I think that to lead a private tour, first of all, a tour guide has to be alert all the time and judge from the reactions of his or her guests what's most appealing to them. Some of my guests like to see as much as possible, some of them like to spend a whole day in Topkapı Palace, some would like to shop till they drop! So I think a good private tour guide should first of all be able to understand in the shortest time possible what kind of tourists he or she is with, especially if he or she is with them for only one day. Some very knowledgeable guides are those that just lecture and walk and follow a set itinerary planned in advance. Instead, I prefer to get to know my clients as much as possible in advance of their arrival—that is, if they are referred directly to me. If they are referred to me through Travelium, one of the leading travel agencies in Istanbul that I've been working for since 1994, we do the classical tour (Blue Mosque, Hagia Sophia, Topkapı, Grand Bazaar) on our first day. In this way, I am best able to learn how busy they want to be when they get here and also learn of some of their particular likes and dislikes. Most of the time, I'm right when it comes to guessing what people will like. I believe that private guiding, especially in a city like Istanbul, is not just informing my guests about the history of buildings but also satisfying all kinds of requests and needs, from finding the right battery charger to taking them to a place where we can find the right size Halloween costume for their grandkids. My other priority is that I like to make sure my clients enjoy their time in my country, so I help them to appreciate the Turkish approach to life and grasp details of our honorable past. And I like to do this in an enjoyable way. After all, visitors are supposed to be on vacation, not taking history or architecture classes, so ever since I started doing this job, I have been making some jokes. They must be really good jokes because, after all these years, new clients still find them funny!

Q: I've read that, on average, the maximum number of days tourists spend in Istanbul is three days. What would you consider to be an ideal three-day itinerary?

A: I can easily fill seven days, nine to five, and every day will be completely different. It's not difficult to fill the time in Istanbul! But here's what I suggest: first day would include Hippodrome, the Blue Mosque, the Cistern, Turkish and Islamic Art Museum, lunch, Hagia Sophia, the Spice Market, Rüstem Paşa Mosque. Second day: Topkapı Palace, the Archeological Museum, lunch, the Grand Bazaar. Third Day: Bosphorus boat ride, lunch, either the Mosque of Süleyman the Magnificent and the Chora Church or Taksim Square, İstiklâl Caddesi, and Galata Tower.

Q: How about day trips outside of Istanbul?

A: Normally, I would say, Stay in Istanbul, don't go anywhere else, there's so much to see and do here! But I do recommend the Princes' Islands (in the summer), and year round, Edirne is very worthwhile. If you're on your way south, the Gallipoli battlefields are exceptionally interesting. Gallipoli is approximately a five-hour drive from Istanbul, which is why it makes sense as a destination if you're headed to Ephesus or the coastal resort towns. A visit can be made from Istanbul in a (very long) day, but it's really better to spend the night in Eceabat or Çanakkale and return to Istanbul the next day. Bursa is also great, but if you're going just for the day it is essential to take the catamaran across the Sea of Marmara instead of the regular ferry boat, which is significantly longer.

Q: Where are most of your clients from?

A: Most are North American, many from New York and California especially. What I like about American travelers in particular is that they have a curiosity and an open mind. They might not know much about Turkey when they come here, but at least they don't show up with a negative view. I work with other nationalities too, and many of them, especially Europeans, already have an opinion of Turkey and it isn't a positive one. They find fault with everything. North Americans are here to really enjoy themselves and to enjoy Turkey—they are a pleasure to work with! Something I have gained in my job is an outsider view of my own country, to look at things from a foreigner's point of view, you know, to really notice and appreciate things that are peculiar to us but things which normally wouldn't mean much to another Istanbulite. I mean, how would I otherwise know to notice and appreciate a *simit* vendor in the streets of Istanbul? Or the exceptional view going over the Bridge of Bosphorus? I think my job has made me love my country even more, with all its pluses and minuses. Also, having worked with five-star hotel guests most of the time, I've met many celebrities, CEOs, some leading people in world politics and economics. Each experience has been unique, and I became a friend, temporarily, with some important people.

Q: What are your busiest times of year?

A: May, June, September, and October.

Q: What are your top five favorite things to show visitors in Istanbul?

A: Hagia Sophia, the Chora Church, the Grand Bazaar, the Mosque of Süleyman the Magnificent, a Bosphorus ride.

Q: Which hotels do most of your clients frequent in Istanbul?

A: Number one is the Four Seasons, and more than 50 percent of my guests stay there. Also popular are the Çırağan Palace Kempinski, the Hyatt, the InterContinental, and Conrad Hilton. Among these, one of the best concierge services in the world is at the Four Seasons. Whatever you need, the staff will get it for you!

Q: When clients ask you for some recommendations for places to eat, what are some of your suggestions?

A: This is almost impossible for me, a foodie with a very sensitive stomach, to answer! I've got too many places in Istanbul where I just love to eat! In the old city, my top two favorite places are Hamdi, the kebab house, and Balıkçi Sabahattin, the seafood place. There's also of course the world famous Sultanahmet Koftecisi. *Köfte* is the Turkish name for "meatball," and that's a very local thing to eat. Around Taksim/İstiklâl, my two favorite are İmroz, a seafood place with a few dozen *meze* choices (Imroz is off İstiklâl in the little street Nevizade), and Zencefil, a vegetarian restaurant, again off İstiklâl, with very yummy food. Trendy places in this area are Mikla and 360, and also Tike is a special kebab place. Another favorite place, on the Asian side, is Çiya, which is a restaurant of Turkish southeastern and east Mediterranean cuisine. It is really a reflection of a vast geography from Anatolia to Mesopotamia and the variety of culturally prosperous people that have existed on that land. Here, all the Azerbaijani, Georgian, Turkish, Arabian, Armenian, Ottoman, Syrian, Seljukian, and Jewish dishes are prepared according to the original customs and beliefs. Farther afield, I like Bebek

Balıkçısı a lot (another seafood place) and I should not forget to mention Asitane, in the old city but not in the heart of the tourist district. This is a place for visitors really looking for something different, a restaurant whose menu is inspired by a book from the sixteenth century called *A Book of Banqueting*. This is where you'll taste authentic Ottoman cuisine.

Q: When you have a day off, what are some things you look forward to doing in Istanbul?

A: Modern art museums are a new trend in Istanbul. Most of them are private museums and they are all very dynamic establishments. For me, since most of my guests prefer to see the ancient things, the modern art museums are more exciting. I also love movies, and in the summer I'm a big follower of the International Istanbul Music Festival. (iksv.org/muzik/english/)

Readers may contact Gamze directly via e-mail at artaman@superonline.com. More information about her, and other highly recommended guides, may be found online at Turkeytravelplanner .com.

Travelium, established in 1989, is a major travel agency in Istanbul specializing in private guides and limousine service. The agency is the exclusive travel company for a number of top hotels in the city, including the Çırağan Palace Kempinski, Four Seasons, Hyatt Regency, InterContinental, Sheraton, Hilton, W, and many others. (+90 212 240 8820 / travelium.com.tr)

Personalities
Natives, Expatriates, and Passionate Visitors

The country's tumultuous history has left a deep legacy. People who've never had to suffer for an idea or fight for a patch of land can be overwhelmed by the passion of ordinary Turks for their country. But for ordinary Turks that passion finds its outlet, not in martial ardour, but in simple pleasures: family, food, music, football, and friendship. Turks have an inspiring ability to keep things in perspective, to get on with everyday life and to have a bloody good time in the process. Sharing their joy in the simple things is a highlight for every visitor.

—LONELY PLANET TURKEY

Moving Freely

MAUREEN FREELY

തയ

In 1960, Maureen Freely's family moved from Princeton, New Jersey, to Istanbul. To eight-year-old Freely their destination was a complete unknown, but it was to become the place she still thinks of as home.

In addition to writing novels, Freely has also translated *The Black Book* and *Snow* by Orhan Pamuk. In her very interesting afterword to *The Black Book*, Freely talks about the "more innocent" Istanbul she knew as a child growing up there, in the 1950s and '60s: she describes a city rather down at the heels, where in every square there was a statue of Atatürk.

A quarter century after his death, Turkey was not yet the prosperous, Westward-looking republic he envisioned. The economy was all but closed, to protect its fledgling industries. We all used Omo detergent, İpana toothpaste, Job shaving cream, and Sana margarine. I remember a man on a donkey delivering milk straight from the farm. Another man with a horse-drawn cart delivered water. We bought glassware from Paşabahçe, Turkey's only glassmaker. Our shoes came from the dozen or so shoe shops lining İstiklâl Caddesi, and our silk scarves from Vakko, Turkey's only department store. There was almost no ready-made clothing, but the city's seamstresses, rumored to be the best in the world, were slavish and resourceful followers of Western fashion. The city's mechanics needed to be just as resourceful, for every taxi in the city was a 1956 Chevrolet.

She adds that in the 1960s, the radio was state-controlled, and at 8:15 p.m. there was a forty-five minute "light Western music" request program that was, for many, the only time they got to hear the Beatles.

Almost fifty years after she first set foot in Istanbul, Freely looks back on her childhood there in this piece, which originally appeared in *Cornucopia: The Magazine for Connoisseurs of Turkey*.

MAUREEN FREELY is the author of *The Life of the Party* (Warner, 1986), *The Other Rebecca* (Bloomsbury, 2000), and, most recently, *Enlightenment* (Overlook, 2008), a novel set in Istanbul.

MY FAMILY moved to Istanbul just a few weeks after I turned eight, in September 1960. I had no idea why. When I asked my father, he said, "Because it's there." By the time we left, I could locate Istanbul on the globe, but all I knew about Turkey was that it was half a world away from Princeton, New Jersey, and colored purple.

It took us eighteen hours to cover that distance in a prop plane. It was a Near East Colleges Association charter, carrying faculty and their families to Robert College, Robert Academy and the American College for Girls. Many of our fellow travelers went on to become my friends and teachers, but that first day they hardly saw us. They were too busy having a wild party at the back of the plane while my family sat in the nose, facing a blank wall.

I filled the empty hours with questions from *Treasure Island*, *Robinson Crusoe* and all the other books my father had read my sister and me to inspire an interest in the great beyond. What was the true purpose of our journey? What secrets did the future hold? I couldn't even guess, nor did I want to. We were on an adventure. That meant never knowing what would happen next.

But first we had to get there. The sun was low in the sky and I was running out of hope when my father leaned across the aisle to announce that we had entered Turkish airspace. I looked down, expecting an oriental landscape in all its purple splendor, but all I saw were brown and empty hills. Yeşilköy Airport was no better, a mustard-yellow building surrounded by more brown hills. We were soon on a bus that took us through Edirne Kapı, across the Galata Bridge and down the Bosphorus Road to Rumeli Hisar. There were so many surprises coming at me now that I had no time to notice the scenery. I was too worried about the cars careering towards us on the wrong side of the road, and the donkey carts they almost crashed into, the stench of the tanning factories, the gypsies camped along the walls, and the hordes of men wearing identical brown caps.

And what did *Yapı ve Kredi Bankası* mean, and why did every sign in the city and every bench along the shore carry those words? Before I could ask, our bus veered off the Bosphorus road to climb a steep hill that took us past a cemetery and a castle. We went through a gate and all of a sudden we were back in Princeton. Except it wasn't Princeton. It was Robert College, on the other side of the globe. That night, and the night after, and the night after that, I cried myself to sleep.

<hr>

After that I cried only on Friday nights. That was because I knew we would be getting up early the next morning to go on an all-day prowl of the old city. I'm told we took the ferry, but that's not what I remember. What I remember are the hundreds of honking cars bearing down on us as we crossed over from the Eminönü ferry station to the Yeni Cami mosque. My parents were just as shaken by this weekly ordeal, but they were in no doubt it was worth risking death for the prizes waiting on the other side. Years later, when I

had to memorize *On First Reading Chapman's Homer*, I had no trouble imagining how stout Cortés and his men must have looked as they stood silent on a peak in Darien. I knew they wore the same rapt expressions as my mother and my father when they set eyes on Ayasofya or Kariye Camii or Topkapı or Sultanahmet. "Can you believe it?" they would say. "We've made it. We're actually here."

They were surprised and disappointed when my sister and I didn't feel the same way. They were even disappointed, I think, in our baby brother. But we couldn't see things the way they did. We had not spent half our lives reading and dreaming about these places. We had not had to scheme and plot and drive our families to distraction to get here. As far as we were concerned, the less we knew, the better. If we fell in love with the marble lions of Side and the caves of Göreme and the crusader castle of Bodrum, it was because they were *there*.

Wherever we went, the question we asked was "Are they going to let us play here?" And for the most part, they did. In the years that followed, we got to play in churches, mosques, museums, fountains, and ancient temples, not just in Istanbul and Anatolia, but in Greece, Egypt, Lebanon, Syria, Cyprus, Italy, and Spain.

ɷɔɿɷɔɿɷɔɿ

So I can tell you with authority that the best place for hide-and-seek is the Valley of the Kings. The best floors for running and sliding are in the Prado. And the Acropolis is the breeziest place to play house on a hot afternoon if you are stuck in Athens waiting for money. We were always running out of money in Athens, then waiting weeks for the slow-moving First National Bank of Princeton to wire new supplies to what we called the American Depress.

But even when we were rolling in money, we always stayed in seedy hotels and traveled third class, often in buses with failing brakes and on ships that listed forty-five degrees. This sent my grandparents into a panic when they got word of it and even shocked the wild party people from that charter flight who had gone on to become my parents' dearest friends. What they didn't see was how much fun it was to travel deck class on a ship where no one spoke your language, because when you found out how to sneak into first class and they caught you, you couldn't under-stand a thing they said. They could not imagine the thrill of play-ing with newfound friends in the *platia* (main square) of a Greek village, even though your only words in Greek were "green light, red light." They could not know how much fun it was to play in a defective hotel lift while your parents thought you were in your room sleeping. We would have hated it if they'd done the done thing and left us at home with the maid. We loved having our parents' almost full attention day and night. We loved it that they found our company exciting, preferable to anyone else's. We loved eating meals at midnight. Most of all, we loved never know-ing what was going to happen next.

Even now, my idea of bliss is to arrive in a place about which I know next to nothing and to find my way around it by first get-ting lost. Or to return to a place where I got lost as a child and lose myself in it again. But I almost never can. The more adult responsibilities I accumulate, the harder it is to go anywhere with-out a huge amount of plotting and scheming. It's hard even to get back to Istanbul, despite being able to disguise this pleasure as a "family visit." So I'm more impressed than ever about the great leap my parents made in 1960. But how had they done it? *Why* had they done it? Last summer, when I was having a drink with my father in my parents' house in Rumeli Hisar, I decided to ask.

What possessed them to leave behind everything and everyone they knew to move to a city about which they knew nothing? It was, I knew, a question they had been asked many times by their own families. My father's parents were Irish. Travel for them was something you undertook to see relatives or find work. No one in the family had ever considered university. They wanted my father to become a fireman. They were appalled when, after returning to Brooklyn from the war, he decided to become a physicist.

My mother's family, who also lived in Brooklyn, never actually told her what to become. But they were hoping she would marry a nice man and settle down in a nice house within walking distance of their own. They couldn't understand why she wanted to ruin her eyes reading Proust and Herodotus, or why she was so obsessed with opera. They were apoplectic when they found out she'd been stopping off on her way home from her Manhattan secretarial job to train with Mabel Horsey to be a blues singer.

 logologolog

When my mother met my father at The Welcome Inn in Ridgeway, the first thing she did was to make him promise to take her round the world. They later drew up a contract on parchment and signed it in blood. My father had already been round the world during his two years in the navy, and he couldn't wait to get back. But first he had to finish his education. Then I was born, and then my sister and my brother. My parents ended up spending the first nine years of their marriage in New Jersey.

My father's first job as a physicist was with the signal corps at Fort Monmouth. After that he moved to a laboratory at Princeton University. Three nights a week he commuted to NYU to do his doctorate. As soon as he got his doctorate, Princeton offered him a tenured research position, and he must have been tempted.

My mother had a nice life, too. By this time she had joined hundreds of book clubs and tennis clubs and had thousands of friends. They were all set up, as people say. But that, apparently, was the problem.

They had arrived at a point when they could read the future like a map. "I was doing really exciting work on how to control thermonuclear fusion," my father told me. "I was publishing papers, so intellectually it was very stimulating. But I could see what the future would bring. We knew we had to get out before it was too late."

Why Istanbul? "Oh, we were looking into all sorts of possibilities. Australia was appealing, and so was the Fen Country. But then one day I was admiring a flowering cherry tree on the Princeton campus. I was with my dear friend Ed Meservey. He said, 'Those flowering cherry trees are nothing compared with the judas trees on the Bosphorus.' I said, 'Tell me more,' and he said, 'Let the Garwoods tell you.' " The Garwoods, who had been teaching at Robert College for years, were in Princeton on sabbatical. They invited my parents to supper.

By then my father had read an article in *National Geographic* that had pictures of Robert College. From these he could see it was a "place that was terribly different from anywhere we had been. But there was enough about it that was the same. I thought, here I can actually teach and do research and learn about history and also travel and write." There was only one worry. The faculty in the pictures seemed so very earnest. The Garwoods were quick to dispel his fears with stories of legendary parties.

My parents went on to give many legendary parties of their own during our first years in Istanbul. People still tell stories about them, but these rarely capture what they were really like. What I remember best is the rollercoaster laughter. It was as if they had just been released from tiny boxes and still couldn't quite believe they could put one foot in front of the other without bumping into a wall. Everyone was welcome at my parents' par-

not happen overnight." When I looked into obtaining the books mentioned in the article below, I learned they are all quite rare, and fairly expensive.

STEPHEN KINZER is a veteran foreign correspondent and was named the first bureau chief in Istanbul for *The New York Times* in 1996. (He is now based in Chicago.) He is also the author of *Crescent & Star: Turkey Between Two Worlds* (Farrar, Straus & Giroux, 2001).

THIS IS the Turkey of the photographer Ara Güler: A confused child peers from behind decaying tombstones inscribed with ornate Arabic script. Laborers unload hulking freighters. Couples walk down foggy streets lined with old wooden houses. Men gaze out over their drinks or contemplate rugged landscapes. Autos jam broad avenues. Horses pull carts up snowy hillsides. And Muslim worshipers bow in prayer by the hundreds.

One of the few Turks to have reached an internationally acknowledged pinnacle of creative achievement, Mr. Güler is driven by a passion for his native land and especially for Istanbul, where he has lived all his life. The rich archive he has produced has made him one of the few Turks with an international reputation. His photographs hang in many private collections and museums, including the Bibliothèque Nationale in Paris and the George Eastman House in Rochester. [In March 1997] he was in Washington to open an exhibition of forty-three of his Istanbul pictures at Cities, a restaurant in the Adams-Morgan section whose décor represents a different world metropolis every six months.

Because Ara Güler's photographs penetrate so far below the city's surface, they convey a deeper sense of the true Istanbul than most visitors can absorb. They are unsentimental, often starkly so, but still full of emotion. Sometimes their contrasts seem to reflect Mr. Güler's disgust with a country that he believes has thrown away much of its cultural richness. Always, however, they are infused with a poignancy that has made their creator the leading graphic interpreter of this city and this country.

"Ara Güler is a great creative artist," Turkey's most prominent living writer, Yashar Kemal, wrote in a recent tribute. "He delves deeply into both nature and man. The picture he captures in a single moment is the result of years of research. For years perhaps he carries within him a certain face, a certain smile, a certain expression of pain or sadness. And then, when the time is ripe, he presses the button."

Mr. Kemal compares Mr. Güler's talents to those of Cézanne, Turner, and Gauguin. They are rich in flowing patterns, and he acknowledges having learned his technique through years of studying great painters. But in an interview at his cluttered studio in downtown Istanbul, he insisted that he is merely a "press photographer." (He works regularly for major magazines, including *Time*, *Paris Match*, and *Stern*.)

"If it's art, it's art," he said with a shrug. "If it's not, it's not. Other people will decide that one hundred years from now. Photography looks like art, but art has to have some kind of depth. Painting is art. Music is art. Who is an artist, Yehudi Menuhin or Vivaldi? One is only an interpreter. Photography is interpretation. I can stand for an hour in front of a picture by Ansel Adams or Eugene Smith or Cartier-Bresson. You can see that they have a visual education. But that does not make them artists. I hate the idea of becoming an artist. My job is to travel and record what I see.

"Art is something important," he continued. "But the history of humanity is more important, and that is what press photographers record. We are the eyes of the world. We see on behalf of other people. We collect the visual history of today's earth. To me, visual history is more important than art. The function of photography is to leave documentation for coming centuries."

Mr. Güler spends much of his time seeking to document what he calls "the lost Istanbul," which he believes is not appreciated or even known to today's young people.

"What they know is the junk of Istanbul," he said. "The poetic, romantic, esthetic aspect of the city is lost. I understand the smell of Istanbul. Istanbul became my subject because I was born here, grew up here and know this place intimately. But the great culture I knew is gone."

It is a truism that everything everywhere was better in the old days, but Mr. Güler's lament for Istanbul is shared by almost everyone of his generation here.

"The real population of Istanbul is one million," he asserted. "Today, thirteen million people live here. We have been overrun by villagers from Anatolia who don't understand the poetry or the romance of Istanbul. They don't even know the great pleasures of civilization, like how to eat well. They came, and the Greeks, the Armenians and the Jews—who became rich here and made this city so wonderful—left for various reasons. This is how we lost what we had for four hundred years."

Not everyone remaining in Istanbul is an Anatolian peasant or even an ethnic Turk, however. Mr. Güler himself is of Armenian ancestry, though he says he has always considered himself "just a Turkish person like any Ahmet or Mehmet."

 logologon

Mr. Güler dreamed of becoming a film director, but his father gave him a thirty-five-millimeter camera when he was a child, and he became obsessed with it. In 1948 he got his first job, as a photographer for an Istanbul newspaper, and since then he has made his living taking pictures. For a while his work appeared regularly in the Istanbul daily newspaper *Hürriyet*, and in 1961 a

British magazine, *Photography Annual*, named him one of the world's seven greatest photographers.

Yet today his pictures are rarely published in Turkish newspapers. "A shame for the Turkish press," lamented one of his younger colleagues, Burhan Ozbilici, an Associated Press photographer based in Ankara.

In recent years Mr. Güler has published three lavish books. One is a survey of the works of the great sixteenth-century Ottoman architect Sinan, who remains perhaps the most influential designer in the Muslim world. The other two books, both of which appeared in 1995, are *All the World in Their Faces*, a vivid portrait of Anatolia, and *Vanished Colors*, an ode to Istanbul and the Constantinople that lies beneath it.

In his studio, amid portraits of figures ranging from Churchill and Bertrand Russell to Picasso and Tennessee Williams, Mr. Güler is hoarding 615 slides for what he hopes will be his next and most ambitious book. They make up a collection of brilliant color pictures he has taken during a lifetime of world travel, with large selections from India, Bangladesh, Myanmar, the Philippines, Kenya, Senegal, and other countries that he describes as "paradise for photographers." An Istanbul printer has told him, however, that it will cost at least $150,000 to produce the book.

"What publisher will pay that much for a book that will be so expensive to buy that people will only look at in bookstores for half an hour and then put it back on the shelf?" he mused. "If Kodak sponsors it, it will come out. Otherwise who knows? But the pictures will always exist. My pictures are what I leave to the world."

In the Thick of Change
Where Continents Meet

BRIAN LAVERY

℘

BY NOW, even if you've never read a single book by Nobel Prize winner Orhan Pamuk, he needs little introduction. The only other Turkish writers to have achieved similar levels of acclaim are Yashar Kemal, author of *Memed, My Hawk*, and Nâzım Hikmet, who is primarily a poet—and neither has become quite as internationally renowned as Pamuk, whose books have been translated into fifteen languages.

Pamuk is, by all accounts, a true bibliophile. It's been said of him that his source of inspiration is more literature than life, and his reading is encyclopedic. At the end of an interview that appeared in *The New York Times Magazine* (May 4, 1997), writer Fernanda Eberstadt asked Pamuk if he had considered living elsewhere. He replied that, yes, he could easily move to New York or Paris, "with guilty conscience." He adds, "All of us Turkish intellectuals have moments of exile, feeling estranged by the coups or by this new fundamentalism. My first thought is always, how will I take my library?"

BRIAN LAVERY was a staff writer for *The New York Times* from 2000 to 2006 and is now an associate at McKinsey & Company.

DUBLIN—As a Turkish writer who is also published in the West, the novelist Orhan Pamuk is often laden with an ambassador's burden, and in the two years since the September 11 attacks it has grown only heavier.

Mr. Pamuk, who grew up in a wealthy Istanbul family, has lived in Switzerland and Manhattan and keeps up with trends in American modern art. Through research for his books, he also knows better than most of his countrymen Turkish Islamic traditions and history, which were all but erased by secular twentieth-century reforms.

As Turkey weighs its political relationship with the United States and aspires to European Union membership, life in Istanbul is a constant balancing act between conflicting influences, which makes change inevitable, Mr. Pamuk said. But he rejects the ambassadorial role, he said in a recent interview here before accepting the International Impac Dublin Literary Award. Rather than accommodate and explain differences between two cultures, he chooses to probe the feelings of people caught up in that change.

"I don't believe in, say, a clash of civilizations," he said. "I am living in a culture where the clash of East and West, or the harmony of East and West, is the lifestyle. That is Turkey."

Regardless of what it is called, that mix can be violent. Mr. Pamuk's most recent book, *My Name Is Red* (published by Knopf in 2001 in an English translation), is about the impact of European Renaissance painting on the insular world of sixteenth-century Islamic illustrators, and the characters in that atmosphere of flux principally feel confusion and pain; by the end of the novel they are left either blinded, crippled, decapitated or, at least, scorned and humbled.

The plot of *Red* is propelled by a murder mystery and a love story, as a handful of miniaturist painters work in secret on what is rumored to be a heretical book for the Ottoman sultan Murat III. The novel recounts the details of an essential yet forgotten Turkish art. When the painters are chosen to narrate the book, the illustrators describe mixing pigments or preparing finely carved reed pens. There is also the lewd banter among adolescent apprentices in an artists' workshop. Fitting Mr. Pamuk's tendency to write long prose poems, *Red* has nineteen narrators, including a dog, a corpse, a counterfeit gold coin, and of course, the eponymous pigment.

More important than the texture of that forgotten world is how it adapted, Mr. Pamuk said. In 1591 ambitious young miniaturists grappled with the seductive allure of Venetian painting, and

felt intense shame when they rejected the tradition of their fathers and workshop masters. The masters resisted change so stubbornly that they preferred to blind themselves rather than be corrupted by the infidel and selfish styles of the West, even as they realized their techniques were disappearing.

One painter envisages the downfall of Muslim illustrations. "For the rest of your lives you'll do nothing but imitate the Franks for the sake of an individual style," he tells his colleagues. "But precisely because you emulate the Franks you'll never attain individual style."

In the tradition of Islamic illustration, such paintings almost always accompanied the text of a historical story or ancient legend. Mr. Pamuk includes numerous anecdotes and parables, which come up so often that even Western readers eventually come to know the stories—like how Shirin fell in love with Hüsrev when she saw his portrait hanging from a tree—as well as familiar fairy tales.

Very few Turks today show an interest in such aspects of their country's cultural history, partly because they know nothing about it, Mr. Pamuk said. He began research for this novel—he called it a "walk around in those forgotten woods"—in 1992. It was published in Turkish in 1998. This June *Red* received the Impac prize, which is worth about $100,000, making it the world's largest award for a single work of fiction.

Mr. Pamuk has rejected official titles, as he did when the Turkish government tried to honor him with a state artist position five years ago. But he has willingly, even eagerly, accepted the celebrity status that his eight novels have brought him in Istanbul. (The eighth, *Snow*, was published in English translation in 2004.) After he won the Impac prize, he said, strangers there, indignant on his behalf, stopped him on the street to ask why a quarter of the purse went to the American translator, Erdag M. Goknar.

The seeds for *Red* were sown in childhood, Mr. Pamuk said, when his parents encouraged his fumbling attempts at painting with undeserving praise. Even into his twenties he wanted to be a painter, despite an admitted lack of talent and the absence of paintings around him for inspiration.

In Turkey in the 1950s and '60s, scholars had no enthusiasm for Islamic painting, and two or three curators managed museum collections that served as mere storage vaults. Reproductions of masterpieces in art books were primitive. "Even Picassos you would see in black and white," he said.

Now Mr. Pamuk regularly travels to New York to indulge his passion for contemporary Western culture just as he engages with his own national heritage in Istanbul. He said: "You go to the past and try to invent a pure image of yourself, then you understand the vanity and romanticism of it. Then you go to the West and are shamelessly inspired by the newest postmodern form. Then you also realize the vanity of it. And your pendulum goes back between East and West.

"What is important is that you don't have to be too problematical and ethical about this. That is how life is at that corner of the world, and I accept it. My happiness is that I can make a melancholy music out of all these comings and goings."

INTERVIEW

John Freely

One of the highlights of my last visit to Istanbul, and indeed of my life, was meeting John Freely. I was accompanied by my friend of twenty-seven years, Peggy Harrison, a freelance photographer, and my wonderful Istanbul guide and friend, Gamze Artaman (see interview, page 189). We sat with John in his study on the campus of Boğaziçi University (Bosphorus University), surrounded by his library and watercolors of Istanbul that were painted by his wife, Dolores, while he regaled us with story after story, of which I could only keep up with half.

Q: How long have you lived in Istanbul?

A: Since 1960, but my wife and I left for some years, thinking we might live in Venice, but when we returned in 1993 we knew we would never leave again.

Q: What are some things that are different, and some things that are the same, in Istanbul since you first came here?

A: *Everything* is different! The city is very international now, with so many different people from all over the world. Do you know we have sixty-two different countries represented at Boğaziçi University? This city is teeming with all kinds of interesting people! We all change but we're all the same persona, and the persona of Istanbul is still the same. When I came it was a very gentle, dreamy city, and much more interesting; it was really like an Ara Güler photograph. Istanbul has lost its soft experience, its Greeks, even the restaurants are different. . . . It will never be the same. The city's a meat grinder . . . it's another city now, but it's still a great city.

Sometimes when people ask what has changed, in lieu of an answer I refer them to a chapter in *Stamboul Sketches* called "A Café on the Bosphorus." The chapter is named for a now-vanished *meyhane* called Nazmi's. A fisherman there named Riza Kaptan once explained to us the unchanging cycle of seasons and their ever-recurring winds that has implanted itself deeply in the subconscious of the city, so that those of us exiled here have attuned ourselves to it just as the departed generations did who lived here in times past. When I returned to Istanbul in 1993, I found that Nazmi's had closed and that Riza Kaptan had passed away. I sat on a park bench on the quay opposite the site of Nazmi's, now occupied by an apartment house, and from there I could see two old fishermen sitting in a shack they'd built on a bit of strand beside a seaside *yalı*. After a while one of the fishermen joined me, having no idea who I was, though I recognized him as one of Riza's younger cronies, his beard now as white as mine. He said he'd never spoken to a foreigner before except for one strange guy who was also American and who used to love hanging around disreputable dives and talking to low-life types—someone like me, he said, but with a reddish beard rather than a white one. Then I realized he was talking about me, but I let it pass, so that he could think of me as I was.

Q: What are some things you would suggest first-time visitors see and do in Istanbul?

A: Visitors should absolutely see the Blue Mosque, Aya Sofya, and Topkapı, but they should also do things like take the little rowboat across the Golden Horn from the ferry station next to Galata Bridge, near the Spice Market. I first took this boat in late September 1960, while eating a fried-fish sandwich. I'm pleased that, even now, in the early years of the twenty-

first century, both the fried-fish sandwiches and the rowboat are still aspects of life in Istanbul. Visitors should not miss walking around the old neighborhoods that have hardly changed: Fener, Balat, Samatya. They should also have dinner at a *meyhane* on Nevizade—Refik is my favorite. Also, visitors should see some villages on the Bosphorus, and go to the wonderful villages on the Asian side, like Üsküdar. Beyoğlu is terribly interesting, aside from its nightlife—look for authentic Turkish music.

Q: You have written more than forty books, including *A History of Robert College* in two volumes; you teach physics; you write articles; you lead walking tours and boat trips; you research ancient civilizations; you're a father and a husband; you allow people like me to come and interview you. How do you do it all?

A: I don't sleep! You get an extra life that way.

Monuments

In what is a hallmark of the greatest cities, Istanbul offers a vibrant present set within a captivating past and visitors are advised to neglect neither.

—HG2 ISTANBUL

"My flight from Istanbul shall resemble Ibn Shakir's flight from Baghdad under Mongol occupation."

"In that case, you must head West instead of East," said jealous Stork.

"To God belongs the East and the West," I said in Arabic like the late Enishte. "But East is east and West is west," said Black.

"An artist should never succumb to hubris of any kind," said Butterfly, "he should simply paint the way he sees fit rather than troubling over East or West."

—ORHAN PAMUK,
My Name Is Red

With bygone eras piled in archaeological layers one on top of the other, history oozes from the city's every pore. On the surface, designer shops and trendy cafés appear and vanish at the speed of light, but underneath another world of architectural splendour remains beautiful and timeless. But in the face of such contrasts, and despite recent decades of ambitious and unsympathetic city planning, Istanbul has somehow managed to hang on to its undeniable charm.

—STYLECITY ISTANBUL

The Grand Seraglio

MARY CABLE

ℒℴℛℴ

O F A L L the many pieces written on Topkapı, to my mind this is
the very best one, for everything is here: descriptions of those
who inhabited the palace, the sheer beauty of the buildings and
the grounds, the cruelty, observations by visiting Europeans, the
harem, the chief executioner, the intrigue, how dinner was
served. . . . My favorite stories of Topkapı are those about the
fancy dinners during the *Lâle Devri* (Tulip Period), during the
reign of Sultan Ahmed III (1703–1730). As the author relates
here, dinner guests were treated to a spectacle worthy of a day
dream. In his book *Middle Eastern Food*, Harry Nickles describes
these dinners in greater detail: "When the April moon was full
and floods of tulips burst into bloom in the palace garden, Sultan
Ahmed's table was set on a balcony overlooking an opulent scene.
Lamps were hung about, along with caged canaries and glass
globes filled with colored water. Sometimes whirling dervishes
entertained the sultan with their madly spinning dance, or girls
played catch with a golden ball. And lumbering among the tulip
beds were turtles by the hundreds, each with a lighted candle
mounted on its shell." I, for one, cannot remove the image of
those turtles from my head! If one has any doubts about how
sumptuous life inside the palace was, training turtles to carry lit
candles on their backs is all the proof one need produce!

It is stories like this that bring Topkapı to life, which is the key
to making your visit meaningful and memorable. As with most
other historic palaces in the world, there are few furnishings at

Topkapı, so you really have to use your imagination or you'll leave wondering what was so significant about it. I urge readers to visit the palace with a knowledgeable guide or with John Freely in hand.

I really like this piece not only for all of the fascinating details but also because it was written fifty years ago, when, as the author relates, Turkey wasn't yet used to tourism, and even Topkapı was a bit damp and shabby—not at all like the spruced-up and shining treasure it is today.

MARY CABLE has written for *The New Yorker, Harper's Bazaar*, and *Horizon*, where this piece appeared in 1959.

TRAVELERS WHO arrive in Istanbul by sea have a good view of the Grand Seraglio: a huddle of low, unprepossessing gray buildings built on a bluff at the point where the Bosporus and the Golden Horn meet the Sea of Marmara. Nearby, and outbidding it for attention, are the six spectacular minarets of the Blue Mosque and the great dome and minarets of Hagia Sophia—the ornaments of the Istanbul sky line and the great attractions for sight-seers. A tourist who asks about the low gray buildings will be told that they are the Topkapı Museum; with luck, he will also learn that until 1851 this was the Sultans' residence, a palace known to Europeans as the Grand Seraglio. But the chances are that a tourist of no more than average inquisitiveness will never learn that this palace was once more splendid than Versailles, more bloody than the Kremlin, and, though in Europe, as mysterious to Europeans as the Imperial Palace in Peking. Its extraordinary history shaped millions of lives, from the Arabian peninsula halfway across Europe and the Mediterranean, and took place among brainwashed slaves behind an iron curtain that remained drawn from shortly after the conquest of Constantinople, in 1453, to the middle of the nineteenth century.

The Marmara side of Seraglio Point, a steep, four hundred-foot ascent, was once guarded by a sea wall built of Byzantine rubble, but the wall is tumbled down now to make way for the railway to Bulgaria, and gypsies and beggars live in the ruins. The other side of the point slopes down to the Golden Horn, which is now a raffish dock area, but in the days of the Sultans was beautiful with palaces and gardens. The unadorned stone buildings of the palace, clustered and sprawled together without aesthetic consideration, suggest a military camp; the tented armies of the Seljuk Sultans must have camped like this as they swept across Anatolia from the Asiatic steppes. To modern visitors the whole palace, inside and out, seems drab and rattletrap, and it is hard to understand how the seventeenth-century French traveler Michel Baudier could have reported, "the baths, halls and galleries of this place surpass in their Magnificence the force of the imagination." Few travelers from the West in those days ever got inside the palace, and fewer still got out again—trespassers anywhere on the premises were beheaded, while trespassers in the harem were skinned alive and their skins tacked to the harem gate. But those who saw it agreed with Baudier: the place was dumbfoundingly splendid.

"Now come with me," said a French ambassador to the court of Süleiman, "and cast your eye over the immense crowd of turbaned heads, wrapped in countless folds of the whitest silk, and bright raiment of every kind and hue, and everywhere the brilliance of gold, silver, purple, silk and satin." Lady Mary Wortley Montagu, who passed that way in 1717 when her husband was a British envoy, wrote that the royal gardeners were so gaily dressed that "at a distance they appeared like a parterre of tulips." Entertained at dinner by a wife of the Sultan, Lady Mary observed among the trinkets her hostess was wearing "200 emeralds, every one as large as a halfcrown piece," and four strings of pearls "every one as large as the Duchess of Marlborough's." The knives were of gold set with diamonds and the tablecloth and napkins were embroidered with silk and gold.

The significant point about the Turkish court seems to be that its dazzle was not created by architecture, which had no particular appeal to a race so recently out of tents in Central Asia, but by the portable grandeur inside the buildings. The silks have worn out, the gold and jewels have been nearly all dispersed, and the Grand Seraglio, where three centuries of extraordinary drama were enacted, comes down to us as a bare, dark stage.

Except for the Sultan and his children, every soul in the Grand Seraglio—even the Grand Vizier, the General of the Armies, and the Queen Mother—was a slave, and not one of them was a Turk by birth. They were brought to the palace as children, between the ages of ten and fourteen. The girls were obtained through slave dealers and the boys, under a law of the land, were kidnapped from subject Christian states in lots of two to three thousand every three or four years. The most intelligent, most prepossessing boys were taken, and their kidnapping was by no means always opposed by their parents, for a place at the Sultan's court was the one available route to wealth and power.

The brightest of these bright children were enrolled in the Palace School inside the Grand Seraglio. Here they underwent a twelve-year brainwashing from which, if they survived, they emerged oblivious of their earlier life, devoted to the sultanate, and fanatical followers of Islam. A seventeenth-century Venetian, Ottaviano Bon, reported of this school that "There is great severity used in all the orders of discipline, the government of them being in the hands of the masters, who are all white eunuchs for the most part, and very rough and cruel in all their actions; insomuch that when one cometh out of that *Seraglio*, and hath run through all the orders of it, he is, without all question, the most mortified and patient man in the world; for the blows which they suffer, and the fastings which are commanded them for every small fault, are to be admired: nay, some of them are so cruelly handled, that although their time of being in the *Seraglio* be almost expired, and that they should in a few years come forth to be made great men, yet not being able to endure such cruelty any longer, they procure to be turned out, contenting themselves with the title, and small pay of a *Spahee* or a *Mutaferraka* [common soldier] rather than be so often punished and made weary of their lives."

The first thing the new students learned was to keep quiet, for in the inner palace, where the school was, only the Sultan might speak above a whisper. From the Sultan's mutes the boys learned sign languages. "Both the Grand Signor, and divers that are about him," said Bon, "can reason and discourse with the Mutes of any thing as well and as distinctly *alla Mutescha*, by nods and signs, as they can with words; a thing well befitting . . . the gravity of the better sort of Turks, who cannot endure much babbling."

The academic system was excellent, but for the ultimate welfare of the Turkish Empire it had one fatal flaw: it ignored the West. The boys learned Turkish, Arabic, Persian, and Tartar; athletics, riding, and warfare: and a special occupation or skill such as hawk-keeping or turban-folding. According to the Koran, "He who learns is the dearly beloved friend of Allah," and a state law required that every Turk, including the Sultan, should learn how to do something. Mohammed II, the conqueror of Constantinople, was an accredited gardener, and Abdül Hamid II did cabinetwork.

During their training the boys acted as pages. After graduation they became eligible for positions of trust: Private Secretary, Chief Huntsman, Chief Barber, Chief Accountant, Chief Bath Attendant, and so on. If they were gay and amusing fellows, they might become Boon Companions, who hunted with the Grand Seigneur, read to him, and tried to keep him amused. Eventually they might hope to receive the title of pasha and be sent out to govern a province or to spy on some other provincial governor, for the government was a network of spies and counterspies, with the chief officials in a constant welter of plotting against one another and obtaining one another's downfall. "He that is even greatest in office is but a statue of glass," says a Turkish proverb. A popular Turkish curse still is "Mayst thou be vizier to Sultan Selim," for during the eight-year reign of Selim the Grim seven Grand Viziers (prime ministers) lost their heads.

When Sultans decided that this or that vizier must go, their method of dispatching him was often bizarre. Murad IV used to send for the victim, entertain him with a particularly nice feast, and then hand him a black robe and call in the executioner. A number of Sultans gave the condemned man an opportunity to save himself if he could run faster than the executioner from the inner palace to a certain gate on the Marmara shore. If he won the race (he rarely did, most viziers being fat and out of training) he was allowed to keep on going through the gate into exile. Sultan Ahmed I, wishing to dispose of his Grand Vizier, one Nassuf Pasha, sent him two letters by the hand of the Chief Executioner. The first read, "Fail not presently upon the receipt hereof, to send me the Seals of my Empire," the seals being the symbol of his office. Nassuf having handed over the seals, the Chief Executioner gave him the second letter which said, "After that thou hast sent me my Seals, send me thy head by him that shall give thee this note." Michel Baudier, who reported this story in the West, observes, "This command was rough and the style of his letter troublesome, yet he must obey. Nassuf suffered himself to be strangled and the *Bostangibassi* [Head Executioner] carried away his head in the view of all his great family, whereof the least scullions might have broacht him with their spits. Yet no man moved, seeing the people of the Serrail, and knowing that it was the Prince's pleasure."

Heads, whether of viziers or of other slaves, were the usual adornment of the Seraglio's second gate, which was called the Gate of the Executioner. Anyone on legitimate business might enter the first gate, but beyond the Gate of the Executioner no one went except by invitation or duress. At this gate, which leads through a wall some twenty feet thick, modern tourists buy their museum tickets and check their umbrellas. There are a few axes on display, but the fountain where the headsman washed up after work is overgrown with weeds, and there is no sign of the "seventy-seven instruments of torture—nails, gimlets, razors, matches for scorching . . . different powders for blinding, clubs for breaking the hands and feet," which a court historian ascribed to Black Ali, Chief Executioner to Murad IV. Of Black Ali's assistants, the record says, "No light shines from their faces, for they are a dark set of people." Foreign ambassadors arriving to present their credentials were customarily kept waiting at this gate for hours and sometimes days in the society of this agreeable crew.

ﭢﭢﭢﭢﭢﭢ

The Chief Executioner, for a reason whose significance seems to have been forgotten, was also the Chief Gardener and Chief Helmsman of the Royal Caïque, thus combining in his duties the two most striking characteristics of the Ottoman Turk: extreme ferocity and a touching pleasure in the out-of-doors. The Grand Seraglio was surrounded by gardens—not formal ones like those at Versailles and Schönbrunn, but rambling woods and orchards, like English parks, kept in good order by four thousand gardeners. "Nor indeed doth a *Turke* at any time shew himself to be so truly pleased, and satisfied in his senses, as he doth . . . in a pleasant garden," reports Ottaviano Bon. "For, he is no sooner come into it but he puts off his uppermost Coat and lays it aside, and upon that his *Turbant*, then turns up his sleeves and unbuttoneth himself, turning his breast to the wind. . . . Again, sometimes standing upon a high bank to take the fresh air, holding his arms abroad, courting the weather, and sweet air, calling it his soul, his life, and his delight; with whole flowers he stuffes his bosom and decketh his *Turbant*, shaking his head at their sweet favors; and sometimes singing a song to some pretty flower, by whose name peradventure his mistress is called."

The favorite flower of the Turk was the tulip, once a wild flower of the Asiatic steppes. Holland never heard of tulips until 1562, when a shipment of bulbs arrived from Constantinople; the word "tulip" comes from *tulbend*, meaning "turban," a Turkish nickname for the flower. It was said of Ahmed III, a Sultan of the early eighteenth century, that he valued human life less than a good tulip bulb. He devoted himself to importing new varieties

from Europe and the Orient and, from Venice, glass vases to put them in. At tulip time every spring official business came to a standstill, while Sultan Ahmed put on all-night tulip fetes in the Seraglio gardens. Guests dressed up in tulip colors, caged birds sang in the tree branches, and here and there among the tulip beds tortoises with candles strapped to their backs provided ambulatory illumination. One particular night of the fete was reserved for the ladies of the harem, who organized a bazaar at which the Sultan was the only customer. They all looked for candy, hidden Easter-egg style among the flowers, and received prizes handed out by the Chief White Eunuch.

White eunuchs came from among the kidnapped slave children, and, it appears, chose of their own free will to be castrated in order to obtain certain powerful positions in the palace. Eunuchs were believed to be less corruptible than other people (says Ottaviano Bon: "though not of great courage, yet of the greatest judgment, and fidelity; their minds being set on business, rather than on pleasure") and were thus entrusted with the treasure, the mail, and the secret documents. The governing of the harem was carried on by black eunuchs, most of whom came from the Sudan where they had been captured and castrated as small boys of six or seven. The uglier their faces and persons the more highly they were valued.

Those kidnapped children who showed an aptitude for ferocity were not sent to the Palace School but put into the Janissary Corps. The janissaries were a sort of private army of the Sultan who took the field only when he did and acted as his personal bodyguard. They were first organized in 1330, when the Turks were still living on the plains of Anatolia, and were called *yeni chéri*, meaning "new soldiers." A legend says that a holy man passed his wide sleeve over their heads, blessing them, and for this reason they wore a cap that hung down behind like a sleeve. They were Spartan in their habits, celibate, and forbidden to quarrel with one another. Native Turks and children of former janissaries were not allowed to join the Corps. They were a brave and valuable lot until the great period of Turkish conquests was over and the Sultans became more interested in dallying at home in the Seraglio than in leading troops. Their number swelled from twelve thousand under Süleiman the Magnificent to forty-nine thousand a hundred years later, as more and more captured children entered their ranks and no great wars killed them off. From admirably disciplined assault troops they turned into a rowdy and dangerous mob of hoodlums, always discontented, looting, starting fires, and prone to start revolutions. By 1826, when Mahmud II succeeded in abolishing them, there were 135,000 of them, including many native Turks and sons of janissaries. Six Sultans in two and a half centuries had been dethroned or murdered, or both, by the Corps that was supposed to guard them. Lady Mary Wortley Montagu, on her visit to Constantinople in 1717, observed that the Grand Seigneur "trembles at a janissary's frown. [The Turks have] none of our harmless calling names! But when a minister here displeases . . . in three hours time he is dragged even from his master's arms. They cut off his hands, head, and feet, and throw them before the palace gate, with all the respect in the world; while that Sultan (to whome they all profess an unlimited

him he would do so through a vizier, who would refer to the ambassador's sovereign as "my brother" in order to make clear the Sultan's exalted position among rulers. The audience concluded, the visitors were attended back to their embassy by a great many janissaries and whirling dervishes, all of whom required tips.

The Throne Room Without was as far into the Seraglio as any foreigner or any Turk who did not belong in the palace was supposed to go. Beyond lay the Grand Seigneur's private apartments; the harem; the privy gardens; the quarters of pages and eunuchs; a mosque containing a mantle, a tooth, and some of the beard of the Prophet; and the Sultan's private treasury. All of these regions were so sacrosanct that in 1600 a Venetian who peered at the walls through a spyglass from the other side of the Golden Horn was put to death at once. One of the few outsiders who got this far was an Englishman named Dallam who was sent by Queen Elizabeth to set up the organ she had given the Sultan. He managed to bribe a eunuch to let him peer through a grille into a courtyard full of harem girls. "At the firste sighte of them I thoughte they had bene young men," he reports, "but when I saw the hare of their heades hange doone on their backes platted together with a tasle of smale pearle . . . and by other plaine tokens I did know them to be women, and verrie prettie ones in deede. Theie wore . . . a little capp . . . faire cheans of pearle . . . and juels in their ears; their coats weare like a souldier's mandilyon, som of red sattan and som of blew . . . britches of . . . fine clothe made of coton woll, as whyte as snow and as fine as lane . . . Som of them did weare fine cordovan buskins, and some had their leges naked, with a goulde ringe on the smale of her legg. I stood so longe looking upon them that he which had showed me all this kindnes began to be verrie angrie . . . and stamped his foote to make me give over looking; the which I was verrie lothe to dow, for that sighte did please me wondrous well."

The organ he set up was sixteen feet high and had a clock on top of it with a "holly bushe full of blacke birds and thrushis,

which . . . did singe and shake their wynges." When Dallam
demonstrated this to the Sultan, His Majesty asked an attendant
"yf it would ever doo the lyke againe." The attendant answered
that "it would doo the lyke again at the next houre." "I will see
that," said the Grand Seigneur and sat down to wait. As the birds
were adjusted to sing every fourth hour, Dallam, feeling dread-
fully ill, had just sixty minutes to make intricate changes in the
clockwork. He managed to get the birds in line and caught the
next boat back to England.

Clocks were greatly prized in Turkey. They were not allowed to be
made there or set up in public places for fear of lessening the
importance and authority of the muezzins' five daily calls to prayer.
Clockwork toys were coveted even more. Among Mohammed the
Conqueror's favorite booty at the taking of Constantinople was a
pair of golden lions that roared and a golden tree, big enough for a
man to sit under, full of singing birds. A French merchant in 1685
was able to get a look inside the harem by bribing the Chief Black
Eunuch with a mechanical man playing a drum.

The Turks acquired from the Byzantines not only mechanical
toys but a good many habits now regarded as typically Turkish: the
seclusion of women, the use of eunuchs as palace functionaries,
the seclusion and semideification of the Royal Person, strict hierarchy and ceremony at court, and the luxury and fierce intrigue
among powerful officials. The early Turkish rulers had been easily
accessible to their people; but by the time of Süleiman the Mag-

nificent, in the century after the conquest of Constantinople, the only remnant of the Sultan's ancient accessibility was in his riding out every Friday to the mosque of Aya Sofia (formerly the great church of Hagia Sophia). At this time any subject of the realm had the right to present a petition. He did so by writing down his grievance, tying the paper to the end of a long stick, and prostrating himself in the street. When the Sultan rode by on a horse whose mane was tied with diamond tassels, the petitioner, face to the ground, agitated the stick in the air and his petition was collected by an attendant.

When he got back to the palace dinner would be served, the monarch eating alone and in silence, as nobody was worthy to eat with him. Because of the ban on noise, mutes were his favorite companions. At table he was surrounded with them, and he conversed with them in sign language, threw them scraps from the table, kicked them, and tossed them gold pieces. He sat at a low revolving table resembling a Lazy Susan and covered with Bulgar leather. According to Ottaviano Bon, who was reporting second-hand but had his information from a Chief White Eunuch, he had a "very rich wrought towel cast before him upon his knees to save his clothes," as he ate with his fingers. "He useth no salt at his Table, neither hath he any *Antepaste*; but immediately falls aboard the flesh, and having well fed, closeth up his stomach with Bocklava, or some such like thing."

Serving the royal dinner required two hundred waiters. These arranged themselves in a long line, which extended through courtyards and corridors a hundred yards or so from the kitchen to the table. The dishes were passed from hand to hand, rapidly and without the smallest clatter. The royal service was always celadon, because this porcelain was supposed to have the property of rendering poisoned food harmless. Dropping a dish was punishable by death, not because of the value of the dish but because of the inexcusable racket, which may explain why the present-day museum has a vast collection of intact celadon.

After dinner the Grand Seigneur might go for a row in his seventy-eight-foot caïque. This was propelled at high speed by twenty-four specially assigned palace pages, who wore loose white garments and blue caps with red tassels. The Sultan sat in the stern under a gold-fringed crimson canopy, the only canopy allowed on the Bosporus. An eighteenth-century French ambassador who tried having one too received word from the Seraglio that diplomatic relations with France would be null and void until he got rid of it. Each foreign ambassador was allowed a ten-oar caïque and might fly his national flag, but he was not allowed to open an umbrella over his head. He might, if he wished, fan himself with a swan-feather fan.

Six caïques attended the large one bearing the Sultan. In the second was the Turban Bearer, who held up a turban and inclined it right and left to save the Sultan the effort of bowing. The oarsmen rowed standing, but the helmsman, who was also the Head Gardener and Chief Executioner and a very influential pasha, was allowed to sit in order to handle the rudder. Only he was permitted to converse with the Sultan as they skimmed along, and while they spoke, slaves rolled on the bottom of the boat and howled like dogs so that no one might hear what was being said.

The inner and residential part of the Seraglio was called the House of Happiness. It is hard to imagine who was happy there—certainly not the fifteen hundred women of the harem. For most of them life was like that in a strict boarding school from which there was never any graduation. Unless they were royal favorites they slept in dormitories accommodating ten or fifteen pallets on the floor, under the supervision of an old Moorish woman. Their education was limited to such matters as embroidery and dancing, the proper manner of bowing before the Sultan, or the playing of the *saz*, a long-necked, four-stringed affair that produced a plunking sound like a banjo. They could read the Koran and could write a little, although they had nobody to write to, having forever severed connection with their

families. Each woman had one particular duty in the housekeep-
ing arrangements: the First Mistress of the Coffee, for instance,
took care of handing the Sultan his coffee when he visited the
harem, and wore on her headdress a diamond pin in the shape of
a coffeepot. They never went out of the palace except for occasional rides in a closed carriage or caïque. Any manservants
who entered the harem—wood carriers, for example—walked
between closed ranks of black eunuchs, and wore long woolen
curls hanging down on each side of their faces to act as blinders.
A doctor was sometimes allowed in the harem in case of serious
illness, but he might examine only his patient's hand and pulse,
the rest of her being smothered in quilts. If she was one of the
Sultan's concubines, a silken veil covered her hand.

Many of these women lived and died without so much as a
smile from His Majesty; others were smiled at, and for this reason
promoted to the rank of *gözde*, meaning "in the eye" (of the Sultan) but never got any further than that; others were invited to
the royal couch one or more times, which made them *ikbal*, or
royal favorites, and entitled them to an increase in jewels and
silk dresses and a private bedroom; and at the top of the ladder

were the *kadins*, the first four concubines who produced children. The
Sultan by tradition did not marry, but
a *kadin* had the rank of wife except
that no dower was settled on her, as is
required in the Moslem marriage
contract. The chief reason for this
arrangement was to save money for the state, since a suitable
dower for a Sultan's wife would have seriously embarrassed the
treasury. Süleiman the Magnificent defied tradition and married
his favorite, Roxelana; and it was she who moved the women's
quarters—formerly in another part of the city—into the Seraglio.
When Süleiman died, Roxelana became the power behind the
throne of her son Selim the Sot, and for a hundred and fifty years
thereafter a succession of ruthless, conniving queen mothers were
the real rulers of Turkey. They were abetted by a verse in the
Koran which reads, "Paradise is under the feet of thy Mother."
Ottoman "momism" was particularly unattractive because these
old ladies were not only dominating but as evil as could be. They
had to be evil or they would have been trampled in the general
rush of some fifteen hundred women for the most powerful position in the world.

In selecting a concubine, a Sultan held a regular weekly levee at
which the virgins of the harem were brought in for his inspection;
he dropped a handkerchief at the feet of the one who pleased him
most, indicating that she was *gözde* and might hope for a summons to the royal bedchamber. When this came she was dressed
in silk and jewels and perfumed with ambergris, with kohl on her
eyes and henna on her fingernails, and conducted to the Sultan by
the Chief Black Eunuch, all in strict secrecy so that the other
women wouldn't be waiting to scratch her eyes out the moment
she got back. The Sultan's bed had wrought-silver bedposts
topped with crystal lions holding in their teeth a gold cloth
canopy. He liked the idea of owning a bed, like European rulers,

but he slept, as his ancestors did in their tents, on a mattress spread on the floor. Two old Moorish women stood at his head with burning torches so that he might have light to say his beads at the last and the first hours of prayer, as the Koran frowns on praying in the dark. "Thus he rests," soliloquized Baudier, "which troubles all *Europe*, disquiets Asia and afflicts Africa."

A concubine arriving to spend the night was required to enter the bed from the foot, inching her way up under the covers until she lay level with the Sultan. This performance was also expected of husbands of the Sultan's daughters. These princesses, who wore a silver dagger at their belts to remind their consorts of who outranked whom, were in no demand at all as brides, for their husbands not only took orders from them, but could claim no special familiarity with their father-in-law. Children of such unions were not allowed at court at all, and the princesses' dowries could not be inherited by husband or children but reverted to the sultanate, as, indeed, did all the wealth of even the greatest pashas in this slave state.

 басбасбас

The strange life of the Grand Seraglio began to languish after the destruction of the janissaries and the partial Europeanization of the Sultans. A new, elaborate palace was built on the Bosporus, and after 1851 the old Seraglio was used only to house the harems of Sultans who had died. One of the last official events there took place in 1909, after Abdül-Hamid II had been deposed and forcibly retired to Adrianople together with fifteen concubines, a guard of eunuchs, and his favorite cat. A public notice appeared in the newspapers, stating that anyone having a relative who was a member of the Imperial Harem might, by calling at the Seraglio, reclaim her. Telegrams bearing this news were sent to the headmen of villages in the Caucasus, since many of the women had come from there.

On an appointed day the entire harem, numbering nearly

twelve hundred, was assembled without veils in a large hall, while hundreds of Caucasian mountaineers and other Christian people from outposts of the Turkish Empire filed through, seeking to recognize in these elegant ladies their daughters and sisters. Not all of the women were claimed or wanted to be. Some had been spoken for by rich pashas who were anxious for beautiful and delicately bred wives; some nobody came for; some quailed at the prospect of a peasant's life and chose to spend the rest of their days in reduced but genteel circumstances there in the old Seraglio, which thus ended as an old ladies' home.

Sultan's Supper at Topkapı

It isn't very often that the Topkapı powers that be allow ordinary subjects into the palace after hours. But the clients of Sea Song Tours are not interested in doing ordinary things in Istanbul, and Sea Song is no ordinary agency. In fact, it is in every way extraordinary. A ten–course Ottoman dinner for two at Topkapı (as well as a cocktail party for a special celebration) can be arranged by Karen Fedorko and her dedicated staff at Sea Song, for a price: about $6,000 for dinner for two, with a portion of the money donated to the palace. "Our goal is to create a totally unique experience for our clients," says Karen, owner of Sea Song. "We want to provide a level of service that meets all expectations, so we follow through and pay attention to every single detail. That's how we've built our reputation." That reputation has come mostly by word of mouth and through membership in the prestigious Virtuoso network, an invitation-only organization of more than six thousand travel specialists with more than three hundred agencies in twenty-two countries.

Sea Song works mostly with travel agents and private

groups, and lately the agency is working more with high-profile celebrity guests. Almost no request is considered unusual—private *yalı* and museum visits, trips outside of Istanbul, etc.—and all the staff wear many hats (including that of resident historian: one American client enlisted Sea Song's help in tracing a family member's past from an old photograph, which they did by examining the Ottoman medals the subject is wearing in the photo). Sea Song maintains two offices in Turkey, one in the Fındıklı neighborhood of Istanbul and the other in the pretty coastal town of Kuşadası.

As for many other visitors, the Rüstem Paşa Mosque is my favorite in Istanbul. I love that it's a little hard to find, tucked away as it is on a street just off the Egyptian Spice Market, and I absolutely love the Iznik-tiled interior—I really can't get enough of those tiles! The tiles cover virtually every inch of the mosque's surface, from floor to cupola, and they are dazzling. The mosque is just one of Mimar Sinan's grand constructions, built for Rüstem Pasha, the grand vizier of Süleyman the Magnificent. Rüstem Pasha was known to be difficult, mean-spirited, and tightfisted, but he was found to be a suitable choice as husband of Süleyman's daughter Mihrimah. They married in 1538, the same year in which Sinan was named royal chief architect. In *Sinan Diaryz*, Ann Pierpont notes, "We are aware that Rüstem collected thousands of tiles, some said as another investment; but without this greed the visitor would not have such an exciting experience, for the Master was usually modest in his use of faience and desired it as a decorative highlight more often

than as a focal point, reserving it for the kıbla wall surrounding the mihrab. Entering the mosque one is overwhelmed
with splendor; there is no doubt that this is a fitting memorial for the miser." In the bookstore at the Istanbul Archaeology Museum, I found a lovely hardcover book, *Tiles of
Rüstem Paşa Mosque*, which has barely any text but page after
page of the beautiful tiles.

When I asked Robert Ousterhout—author, frequent visitor to Turkey, professor of Byzantine Art and Architecture, and director of the Center for Ancient Studies at the University of Pennsylvania—what some of his favorite memories of Istanbul were, he asked if he could ponder the query for a while, and later he shared this special recollection: "During the intermission at the Istanbul Music Festival in Aya İrini, I enjoy waylaying my guests, leading them through the darkened aisles to the west doors, where through the crack we have a narrow view into the atrium of the church. Lustrous in the half-light of the evening is the huge porphyry [purple granite] sarcophagus of Constantine the Great, all but forgotten in its present location. As a historian of Byzantine art and architecture, the experience at Aya İrini is emblematic of how the Byzantine city is seen today—dimly, unexpectedly, out of context—often no more than a provocative glimpse through the cracks of the Ottoman and contemporary city." (Note: Aya İrini [Hagia Eirene] is open to the public only during the annual International Istanbul Music Festival in June.)

Mimar: Architecture in Development was an excellent bulletin published from 1981 to 1992, and it was the only international architecture magazine to focus on architecture in the developing world. One edition featured an absolutely fantastic guide to the history and architecture of Istanbul. It's available online, complimentary, along with all forty-three issues of the magazine. Go to Archnet.org/library/documents/collection.jsp?collection_id=87, or simply type "Mimar: Architecture in Development" in Google to access all *Mimar* editions online.

The Istanbul essay was a collaboration by four authors who'd participated in the Turkish workshop of the Oriental Cities Program. I very much wanted to reprint it here, but it's quite lengthy—however, don't let that prevent you from downloading the report! It's outstanding. It takes readers through the many historical periods with articles such as "Byzantium from Antiquity to the Middle Ages," "The Classic Ottoman City," "Cosmopolitan Istanbul," and "Istanbul—Capital in Spite of Everything (after 1922)." You may find lots of other articles of interest as well, notably "The Arsenals of Venice and Istanbul" and "Individual Houses: Turkey."

T.C.
Kültür ve Turizm Bakanlığı

Ministry of
Culture and Tourism

TOPKAPI SARAYI HAREM DAiRESi
TOPKAPI PALACE HAREM

- BU BiLET YALNIZCA TOPKAPI SARAYI HAREM DAiRESi İÇİN GEÇERLİDİR.
  THIS TICKET IS VALID IN ONLY TOPKAPI PALACE HAREM.
- KAPALI MEKANLARDA FOTOĞRAF ÇEKİMİ VE VİDEO KAYDI YASAKTIR.
  PHOTOGRAPHY AND VIDEO RECORDING IS FORBIDDEN IN ALL SECTIONS.
- SATILAN BiLETLER GERİ ALINMAZ.
  TICKETS ARE NON-REFUNDABLE.
- BiLETİNİZİ GEZİ SÜRESİNCE SAKLAYINIZ.
  PLEASE KEEP YOUR TICKET DURING THE VISIT.
- BU BiLET YALNIZCA BiR KİŞİ VE BiR SEFER İÇİN GEÇERLİDİR.
  THIS TICKET IS VALID ONLY FOR ONE PERSON AND ONLY FOR ONE TIME.
- BU BiLET TOPKAPI SARAYI GiRiŞİ İÇİN KULLANILAMAZ.
  THIS TICKET CAN NOT BE USED FOR THE TOPKAPI PALACE ENTERANCE.

Istanbul's Caravan Stops

JOHN K. McDONALD

ಬಂ

THIS HAS long been one of my favorite articles in my files, and after reading it I became completely obsessed with Turkish *hans*. My idea of a great day out in Istanbul would be to make a tour of all the *hans* that are accessible to visitors. A *han* and a caravansary are the same thing, but a *han* may be thought of as an urban way station while a caravansary is more of a "truck-stop-for-camels" in the words of Tom Brosnahan.

This piece originally appeared in the travel section of *The New York Times* over twenty years ago. Though I haven't made a tour of the *hans* mentioned in this piece recently (and I'm not positive they are all still open to visitors), I included the piece more for the history of and information about the *hans*. If you really want to see these particular *hans,* you should ask the concierge at your hotel or a guide to find out for you in advance if they are all open; but there are some *hans* within the Grand Bazaar that I can confirm are open and are definitely welcoming to visitors.

JOHN K. MCDONALD studied Egyptology at Cambridge University and the Oriental Institute of the University of Chicago. He worked for many years as assistant curator of Egyptian art at the Metropolitan Museum of Art in New York.

UNTIL THE dissolution of the Ottoman Empire after World War I, and the subsequent move of the Turkish capital to Ankara, Istanbul was the seat of Ottoman power. Built on the remnants of Constantinople and Byzantium, it was as grand a city as it was powerful, for the sultans fully intended it to be a majestic capital and commissioned the finest architects to make it so.

Between the conquest in 1453 and the completion of the Nuruosmaniyeh Mosque in 1758 no fewer than ten imperial mosques were constructed, each of such proportion and grace that the city ranks with Isfahan and Cairo as one of the great repositories of Moslem architecture.

Yet cheek by jowl with the grand mosques are dozens of little-known *hans* that served a large and flourishing community of foreign traders by offering both lodging and warehousing—and were amply provided with stout doors and massive stone walls for the purpose. Some *hans* provided for the spiritual well-being of the merchants as well, by including a small mosque. Istanbul benefited from being both at the doorstep of Europe and at the western terminus of the silk routes: it was at the *hans* that the caravans from Asia, laden with spices, silks and porcelains, were put up.

At one time there were scores of *hans*. Evliya Chelebi, the most peripatetic of seventeenth-century Turkish chroniclers and a man who wrote extensively about Istanbul, describes two dozen of the largest *hans*. Most were known primarily by the goods traded within: woolens, cloth, slaves, honey, furs. Still others were known chiefly by the peoples living there: Bulgarians, Egyptians and Persians.

The neat distinctions of commodity and nationality no longer apply, and those *hans* that survive are given over to many small and frequently unrelated industries. They are often in sad disrepair and somewhat ill used by the tinkers and merchants who tenant them.

But the *hans* are loud with echoes of the past and, to any tourist determined enough to seek them out, convey a deep and indelible impression of the daily life of Istanbul as it was four centuries ago.

The old *hans* are situated for the most part on the slopes of the Golden Horn and all are within easy walking distance of the Spice and Covered Bazaars. They are quite safe but they are not often visited by tourists; hence the souvenirs and luxury goods so readily available in the bazaars are nowhere to be found in the *hans*. Trying to chat with the local people in English is apt to be futile, but French and German are useful.

One of the larger, the Vezir Han, is midway between the column of Constantine and the enclosure wall of the Nuruosmaniyeh Mosque. It is reached through a small passage on the right leading through a pair of enormous arched, iron-battened doors. For security, the outer wall has only small windows set with iron grills.

The courtyard is spacious and is surrounded by a two-story arcade. Many of the ground floor rooms, formerly stables and storehouses, have been converted to small living spaces each with its own door and windows. The arcade roof doesn't exist in some places and in others is dotted with hardy tufts of grass. The Vezir Han, probably built in the 15th century, has an aura of venerable decrepitude.

The road in front of the Vezir Han descends and stops just outside the grounds of Mahmud Pasha Mosque. This is one of the oldest private mosques in the city, built in 1463 by Mahmud Pasha, a grand vizier who was calumniated by jealous officials, eventually lost the trust of the sultan, was denounced and executed in 1474. His mausoleum behind the mosque offers a consolation since it is entirely revetted in blue and turquoise Iznik tiles, named after the Turkish town in which they were produced from about 1454 onward. These are some of the oldest examples in Istanbul.

Just before the grounds of the mosque and leading off to the left is Kilichilar Sokayi, the street of the sword makers. It is teeming with small shops sandwiched in between the precincts of Nuruosmaniyeh and the Chuhagilar Han of the cloth merchants. This *han* is entered via a low, vaulted passageway midway down the street and on the right-hand side. The passage is apt to be choked with people, but with polite persistence one eventually emerges into a small, bustling courtyard.

Like the Vezir Han, this also has a two-tiered arcade. If one mounts the staircase on the left and walks to the back of the arcade there is a fine view to be had of the busy han in the foreground, which is dominated by the gray granite dome of Nuruosmaniyeh. The contrast of the secular and the sacred is very effective and particularly so around noontime when the men leave their work for God's and attend to their prayers across the street.

Other *hans* worth a visit are lower on the slopes of Istanbul and are most accessible from Mahmud Pasha Yokshu, the principal thoroughfare joining the Spice Bazaar with the lower gate of the Covered Bazaar. About three hundred yards down the street is the Kurkchu Han: the *han* of the furriers. It is by far the most ancient standing *han* in Istanbul and is easily recognized in Evliya's seventeenth-century accounts.

Built in 1460 as still another benefaction of Mahmud Pasha, it originally consisted of 120 rooms arrayed around a double courtyard and at one time had a small mosque in the first court. That

has long since disappeared. The interior is not much to look at, but the facade and gateway are well preserved and are unencumbered by surrounding buildings.

Descending down Mahmud Pasha Yokshu, the first turning on the left is Chakmakchilar Yokshu, a fairly steep, narrow way, off which are three eighteenth-century *hans*. The two on the left, Buyuk Yeni Han (Big New Han) and Kuchuk Yeni Han (Small New Han), are foundations of Sultan Mustafa III and were constructed about 1760.

The Buyuk Yeni Han is distinguished by an extremely long, slim courtyard more than one hundred yards in length and it possesses a three-tiered arcade, the only such surviving. The effect of the court is spoiled by the later addition of a crosswall. But the triple arcade with its alternating brick and stonework is very handsome. The Kuchuk Yeni Han, on the other hand, is totally eclipsed by its far grander contemporary, save for one feature: a tiny red mosque perched high on its roof.

Continuing up the Chakmakchilar Yokshu, there is a large portal on the right leading to what is unquestionably the largest and most celebrated of the Istanbul *hans*: the Valide. It is described in considerable detail by Evliya. The Valide was built in 1646 by Kosem, the Greek mother of the Sultans Murad IV and Ibrahim I, with the endowment of five royal domains. She was principal wife of Sultan Ahmet I, who built the Blue Mosque, and was a savvy politician but ran afoul of the Janissaries, the palace guard, in 1651 and was strangled with a curtain cord.

In Evliya's day this *han* had over 350 storerooms and boasted stables that could accommodate more than one thousand mounts. The very irregular shape of the *han* testifies to the ancient street plan to which the builders had to adapt their design. A mosque in the center of the courtyard has been recently rebuilt, and the back rooms, three stories high on account of the steep incline on which the *han* sits, now house a textile mill.

The back of the Valide Han abuts Uzun Charshi Caddesi. This

street descends sharply almost to the Golden Horn but ends
abruptly before the courtyard of Rustem Pasha Mosque. This
mosque is one of the few private works of Sinan, Suleiman the
Magnificent's chief architect. It was commissioned in 1550 by the
grand vizier Rustem Pasha and is considered one of Sinan's masterpieces.

It has a jewellike perfection to its design and the matchless
exterior revetment of Iznik tiles is almost unknown in Moslem
architecture outside of Iran. The tiles are precisely set to form a
sinuous floral pattern, and one, just right of the door, bears a fanciful representation of the holy city of Mecca, replete with
minarets, pulpit, fountains, and even the Kaaba sheltering the
sacred black stone that the devout believe was given to Abraham
by Gabriel.

To the right of the mosque, at a distance of approximately fifty
yards, is the Balkapan Han, traditionally the honey market. The
han is not especially distinguished; but in Evliya's day it housed a
contingent of Egyptian traders and it was constructed over some
genuinely ancient Byzantine vaults that may be reached from the
center of the court.

This brief list of the *hans* is by no means exhaustive but is a fair
sample. There are others in Istanbul itself, and still more across the
Golden Horn in Galata. Each is an integral part of the modern
city, but just as firmly rooted in the past: modest structures hidden
in the shadow of the mosques, but fascinating in their own right.

nothing seriously, he said, "People like the legends and the stories. Don't blame me."

Barlak explained that the oil-burning chandeliers in Hagia
Sophia were hung low in order to enhance the little light they do
provide. "Thomas Edison wasn't with us then." He described a
tilted marble column as the "Turkish Tower of Pisa." Not in his
repertoire were the most enduring and evocative legends of Hagia
Sophia. It is said that two priests were celebrating Mass when the
Ottomans broke through the doors, whereupon the priests
melted into the walls, carrying with them precious artifacts; they
will not return until Constantinople is again a Christian city.
Another story has it that the original altar is at the bottom of the
sea and will rise when Constantinople becomes Christian once
more. Christians in Turkey are nothing if not hopeful.

My guide's tutelage was yet another reason for me to pity
Hagia Sophia. Even where tours are concerned, it suffers like no
other building on earth. Barlak had few things to say about the
magnificent mosaics for which Hagia Sophia is renowned—
although he did point out that the eyes of Jesus in the Deesis
Mosaic follow you as you walk away. He said little about the
mosaics because he believed that I, like most Americans, would
be bored. He might have been right. Byzantine mosaics are grim
pieces of work, and we Americans prefer lighthearted art.

Mustafa Akkaya, the director of the museum, has a different
theory as to why mosaics haven't caught our collective attention.
(I didn't want to torture him by pointing out that Americans do
like mosaic tiles—if they're part of bathroom or kitchen decor.)
"The art you love is easily transportable," he said. "Mosaics cannot be lifted and taken away." I amended his theory to suggest
that Americans tend to value only what they have a reasonable
expectation of buying, and the finest mosaic art tends to be firmly
affixed to walls.

Hagia Sophia's mosaics are primarily fragments. The few that
survive have been restored, to the credit of Turkish administrators.

Most are in the galleries, reached by walking up a crude curving ramp. (The Christian emperors rode up in chariots pulled by ponies.) I like to imagine what Hagia Sophia must have looked like a thousand years ago, when the interior was surely a wonder unequaled anywhere on earth. Apparently, the marble floors were once highly polished and the walls ablaze from the golden tiles. Now the museum is gloomy. I've always been astonished at how little light is allowed to enter houses of worship, when one would expect the opposite.

ιοοιοοιοοι

I knocked on Christian doors, curious to learn if the loss of Hagia Sophia still rankled, or perhaps even burned. The Ecumenical Patriarchate was not the only organization reluctant to speak on the record. The mere fact that after millennia the Church of Divine Wisdom can inspire so much discomfiture was a revelation.

I went to the Roman Catholic Church of St. Anthony three times before a member of the clergy would see me. On my second visit, a priest thrust a promotional pamphlet into my hands and firmly shut the door in my face. I imagined him standing with his back to the door, breathing deeply, praying that the inquisitor would not return to torment him yet again. On my third visit, I cornered a kindly priest who took me to a small room, folded his hands, and told me that he would speak to me if I did not use his name or his words. He said that the controversy over Hagia Sophia was a Greek Orthodox matter, not a Roman Catholic one. His nervousness disappeared only when I told him that the Patriarchate didn't seem any more interested in speaking openly about Hagia Sophia than he did. At this, he actually grinned.

Several other church leaders did not return my calls after I left messages explaining the nature of my inquiries. The only one who welcomed me was the Reverend Benjamin van Rensburg of the Union Church of Istanbul, who pointed out that political realities made the designation of Hagia Sophia as a museum a sensible decision. He said that however controversial the matter might be today, it is not as serious as it was just after World War I, when the defeat and dissolution of the Ottoman Empire made Muslims intensely concerned that Hagia Sophia would be reconsecrated as a church. Akkaya, the museum director, said that Ataturk's decision to create a museum was one of the most important and critical moments in the Westernization of modern Turkey, because it allowed Hagia Sophia to represent two cultures and two religions. The accomplishment seems all the more noteworthy today, considering the deteriorating state of Muslim-Christian relations throughout the world.

I find myself standing pretty much alone among devout believers in Hagia Sophia because I can accept whatever religion it happens to represent. I'm certain that both Muslims and Christians would be comfortable with my form of devotion. I do not pray for Hagia Sophia simply because I don't think that way. But I do worry about it all the time.

Saint Mary of the Mongols

A visit to the Fener district of Istanbul is considered a bit off the beaten path, but it deserves to be better known, not least because of one particular church, Saint Mary of the Mongols. Of the two dozen Byzantine churches in Istanbul, Saint Mary's is the only one that is still in use as a house of worship (it was never converted to a mosque), and the story behind it is one of the city's more colorful. While most of the world was shaking in their shoes over the arrival of the Mongols, the Byzantines were less fearful (all the peoples the Mongols terrorized were their enemies) and they shrewdly smelled an opportunity for some kind of friendship. Emperor Michael

VIII Palaiologos decided to send his illegitimate daughter, Maria Despina, as a bride-princess to Hulagu Khan, the chief Mongol khan in Baghdad.

Maria began her journey eastward in 1265, reportedly in a church-shaped tent bedecked with images of saints, but when she finally arrived, the khan had died. So, Maria married his son, Abaqa Khan, instead. Abaqa was not Muslim, and Maria was successful at protecting Christians when the khan began to persecute his Muslim subjects. Abaqa was assassinated by his brother (who was Muslim) in 1282, and after fifteen years, Maria decided it was time to return to Constantinople (though not until after her half-brother, now Emperor Andronicus, offered her hand to another Mongol, Charbanda; he marched west to fetch Maria in Nicaea, where she was waiting, but the city fell to the Ottoman Dynasty before he arrived, and he turned around and went home). Upon her return, she rebuilt the nunnery that had been started in 1261 and enlarged in 1266, and she retired there until her death. The exterior is a dark red color, said to date from May 29, 1453, when the neighborhood streets were filled with Greeks desperately fighting the invading Ottomans—the Turkish name for it is Kanlı Kilise, or Church of the Blood. The name of the street that leads to the church is still called Ascent of the Standard-Bearer, in honor of a Muslim standard-bearer who was killed in the fighting.

The church is not freely open to the public—though my visit was spontaneous—so it is advised to ask your concierge or guide to arrange a visit. Once inside, you'll see that it is most unusually shaped, due to the rebuilding. Of significance are the framed *fermans* (official decrees), of Mehmet II and Beyazit II that granted the ownership of the church to the Greek community in perpetuity: Mehmet reportedly endowed the church to the mother of Christodoulos, the Greek architect of the mosque of Fatih, in acknowledgment of his work. Beyazit extended the *ferman* in recognition of the services of the nephew of Christodoulos, who built the Beyazit Mosque.

In an article in *Time Out Istanbul*, Scott Newman observes that "the Church of Saint Mary continues as a functioning church, but with few Greeks left in the city, especially in Fener, it sits alone and little visited." My visit to Saint Mary of the Mongols was one of my most memorable, and I encourage visitors to wend their way up the steep hill to see this historic site and interesting neighborhood, which is a UNESCO urban renewal project.

The Museum of Turkish and Islamic Arts (located in the İbrahim Paşa Sarayı) is little-visited but is very much worthwhile. It sits north of the Hippodrome and is one of the few surviving examples of Ottoman domestic architecture of the sixteenth century. I admit I might not have visited the museum if it weren't on the suggestion of Ömer Eymen (see Arasta Bazaar in Miscellany for a description of Ömer, page 494). At the time, I was serious about learning more about Turkish *kilims* and rugs and Ömer, who owned a shop specializing in nomadic weavings (and had already spent the better part of a day teaching us about vegetable dyes, chemical dyes, and types of weaving) recommended the museum for its ethnographic displays of the Yörük tribes, one of the few semi-nomadic tribes left in Anatolia. Ömer was right—the displays showed how wool was dyed and how a *kilim* was woven, and a complete *topak* (a roundhouse) was constructed with all the objects of daily life on view. It was very well done, and I now had a visual understanding of how functional the weavings were: the fact that they were also decorative was secondary to their usefulness in the nomadic tradition. Remarkably, I was practically the only visitor there.

Jane Taylor, in *Imperial Istanbul,* says it is "one of the most superbly planned and displayed museums in Turkey," and the palace's great hall she describes as a "magnificent room, far grander than any at Topkapı Sarayı." Taylor also relates that İbrahim Pasha (first grand vizier to Süleyman the Magnificent) once told an Austrian ambassador, "Although I am the Sultan's slave, whatsoever I want done is done. . . . I can give kingdoms and provinces to anyone I like, and my master will say nothing to stop me. Even if he has ordered something, if I do not want it to happen, it is not done; and if I command that something should be done, and he happens to have commanded the contrary, my wishes and not his are obeyed." (Except, apparently, the Sultan's wish that he should be strangled.) The museum also features an interior of a well-off Bursa household of the nineteenth century as well as a twentieth-century Istanbul mansion.

T.C.
Kültür ve Turizm Bakanlığı

Ministry of
Culture and Tourism

• BU BİLET YALNIZCA AYASOFYA MÜZESİ İÇİN GEÇERLİDİR.
  THIS TICKET IS VALID ONLY IN HAGIA SOFIA MUSEUM.

• AYAKLI KAMERA VE FOTOĞRAF MAKİNASI İLE
  PROFESYONEL ÇEKİM YAPMAK ÜCRETE TABİDİR.
  PROFESSIONAL CAMERA RECORDING IS
  SUBJECT TO A FEE.

• SATILAN BİLETLER GERİ ALINMAZ.
  TICKETS ARE NON-REFUNDABLE.

• BU BİLET YALNIZCA BİR KİŞİ VE
  BİR SEFER İÇİN GEÇERLİDİR.
  THE TICKET IS VALID ONLY FOR ONE PERSON
  AND ONLY FOR ONE TIME.

• BİLETİNİZİ GEZİ SÜRESİNCE SAKLAYINIZ.
  PLEASE KEEP YOUR TICKET DURING THE VISIT.

AYASOFYA MÜZESİ / HAGIA SOFIA MUSEUM

Türkiye

Little Aya Sofya, or Church of the Saints Sergius and Bacchus, is a little gem, south of the Hippodrome and separated from the Sea of Marmara by a railway line and the coastal road. It was begun by Justinian in 527 and, according to John Freely, the story goes that during the reign of his uncle Justin I, an old soldier, Justinian had been accused of plotting against the throne and had been sentenced to death. But Saints Sergius and Bacchus appeared to the emperor in a dream and told him that his nephew was innocent. The next morning Justin ordered that Justinian be freed, and Justinian thereupon vowed that he would show his gratitude to the saints by building a church dedicated to them. When he succeeded to the throne he did just that. Sergius and Bacchus were two Roman soldiers who'd been martyred for their faith and who later became the patron saints of Christians in the Roman army.

The church very much resembles Aya Sofya, and in fact Freely writes that "it thus belongs to that extraordinary period of prolific and fruitful experiment in architectural forms that produced, in Constantinople, buildings so ambitious and so different as the present church, Haghia Sophia itself, and Haghia Eirene—to name only the surviving monuments—and in Ravenna, St. Vitale, the Baptistery, and St. Apollinare in Classe. It is as if the architects were searching for new modes of expression suitable to a new age." The church became a mosque during the reign of Beyazit II from 1506 to 1513. In 2006, after an extensive restoration resulting from a UNESCO designation as an endangered monument, the mosque reopened to the public and to prayer.

The Pera Museum, in Beyoğlu (Meşrutiyet Caddesi 141 / 212 334 9900 / peramuzesi.org.tr), opened in 2005 and is a don't miss on your itinerary! The museum is beautifully installed in a historic building that dates from 1893 and was until recently the Bristol Hotel. The permanent collection includes Portraits from the Empire: The Ottoman World and the Ottomans from the 18th to 20th Century, which belong to the Suna and İnan Kiraç Foundation, patrons of the museum. The Anatolian Weights and Measures collection is on a different floor and is truly fascinating, as is the collection of Kütahya Tiles and Ceramics. The Kiraç Foundation's Orientalist Painting collection consists of more than thirty paintings, including the famous work (and my favorite) by Osman Hamdi *The Tortoise Trainer*. (Remember all those turtles walking around the Topkapı grounds with lit candles on their backs?) The Pera is not a large museum, perfect for an hour or two of delightful browsing.

Byzantium Preserved

PATRICK BROGAN

ഇ

JOHN ASH, in *A Byzantine Journey*, opines that the former Church of the Savior in Chora—the Chora Church, or Kariye Camii—and its mosaics and frescoes "constitute one of the supreme masterpieces of European art, and deserve to be placed on a level with the nearly contemporary work of Giotto or the greatest achievements of the High Renaissance." He concludes that "without the art of the Chora the world would be an impoverished place." Like Aya Sofya, this beautiful monument is deserving of several hours of your time. (A tip: you may want to bring binoculars if you have them for closer observation of the mosaics and frescoes, most of which are on the ceiling.)

By the way, a morning visit would be supremely topped off by lunch at Asitane, the restaurant of the Kariye Oteli hotel, right next door. Since 1991, Asitane has been collecting authentic recipes from sources such as the kitchen registers of Topkapı, Dolmabahçe, and Edirne palaces; books and memoirs by visiting overseas officials; and a book dating from 1539 detailing the circumcision ceremony of the two sons of Süleyman the Magnificent. The restaurant now has an archive of more than two hundred original recipes and serves the dishes, in season, with their original Ottoman names. Whether you eat inside or in the outdoor courtyard, you will not only experience one of the most unusual meals of your life, you will enjoy it literally in the shadow of one of the world's most beautiful museums. (The Kariye Oteli, once under the auspices of the Touring and Automobile

Club of Turkey, is a lovely place to stay as well, with a tasteful, early-1900s décor and all contemporary conveniences at a reasonable price. (Kariye Camii Sokak 6, Edirnekapi / 190 212 534 8414 / kariyeotel.com; more about Asitane may be found on its Web site, asitanerestaurant.com)

PATRICK BROGAN has penned many pieces for *Connoisseur* (no longer published), where this piece originally appeared in 1983.

THE TWENTIETH century has been hard on Istanbul. A queen among cities, on seven high hills surrounded by water, facing Asia and the Bosporus, Istanbul still boasts beautiful public monuments: Justinian's Church of the Holy Wisdom (Hagia Sophia) and splendid mosques of the Ottomans. But like Paris since 1945, Istanbul has felt the crushing weight of peasantry moving off the land and into the city. And though Turkish real-estate speculators are less wealthy and destructive than their Parisian counterparts, Turkey lacks the resources available to France for saving its architectural heritage.

As a result, the lesser monuments, particularly the Byzantine ones, are collapsing into ruin all over the city, and the distinctive wooden houses of the Ottoman period have been swept away as though Istanbul, like Dresden or Tokyo, had been consumed by fire. They have been replaced by blocks of concrete apartments, characterless and international, the sort of building to be seen in every other city on the Mediterranean coast from Barcelona to Tel Aviv.

In this wasteland, therefore, it is a delight and a relief to find one corner of the city where something is being preserved. The Touring and Automobile Club of Turkey, guided by its director,

How to Explore Istanbul's
Great Mosques

JOHN K. McDONALD

ℒℴℊ

HERE'S ANOTHER of my favorite pieces, again by John K. McDonald (whose article on Istanbul's caravan stops appeared earlier in this section). I feel this is an excellent introduction to Istanbul's imperial mosques, and it's also filled with enough detail to satisfy repeat visitors.

EVERY GREAT city possesses a distinctive architecture, as recognizable as a person's handwriting. New York has its glass and steel skyscrapers, Paris its slate mansard roofs and chimney pots. Istanbul, with its ten imperial mosques, is no exception. The great brooding monuments, flanked by pencil-thin minarets, punctuate the skyline and emphatically proclaim to any Western visitor that he has taken an enormous stride beyond the familiar and comfortable. The imperial mosques were constructed by the Sultans for themselves and their immediate families between the Ottoman conquest in 1453 and the mid-eighteenth century. They are not necessarily the most beautiful or pleasing. Frequently, the smaller mosques achieve greatness because of the constraints of money and space that the architects had to observe. But the imperial mosques are without question the largest and grandest; situated as they are on the hills of the city, they are visible for miles around.

All share certain formal characteristics: a porticoed courtyard on the west, with a *shadirvan*, or ablution fountain, in the center and the congregational portion of the mosque to the east; in the mosque proper a *mihrab*, or prayer niche, cut into the eastern wall (approximately the direction of Mecca from Istanbul), with a pulpit to its right and a loge for the Sultan and his family to its left; lastly, minarets at the corners of the building from which muezzins call the faithful to prayer.

The mosque is often the centerpiece of a complex of related structures, including religious and primary schools, hospitals and kitchens. But unlike those of their coreligionists in Damascus or Cairo, the Istanbul mosques have soaring, breathtaking interiors overarched by domes which hang weightless and in defiance of natural law.

The imperial mosque of Sultan Ahmet I, known as the Blue Mosque for its painted plaster decoration, is one of Istanbul's most famous. It is dramatically sited at the southern end of the At Meidan and stands scarcely two hundred yards from Hagia Sophia, across a pleasant park planted with flowers and trees.

Any visitor newly come from Hagia Sophia to the Blue Mosque will notice many resemblances between the two, for although Hagia Sophia opened its doors in AD 537, the Ottoman architects a millennium later drew inspiration from it and incorporated much of the overall plan in their finest designs.

The Blue Mosque was erected in 1616 on a site formerly occupied by the palace and hippodrome of the city of Septimus Severus. All traces of the palace has vanished; but the hippodrome's axis, or spina, is still marked by three monuments, the most interesting being an obelisk of the Pharaoh Tuthmosis III, which once stood near the eighth pylon of the temple of Karnak in ancient Thebes.

The edifice across the spina is the palace of Ibrahim Pasha, one of Suleiman's grand viziers. He was murdered in 1536 in Topkapi Palace at the insistence of the Queen, who was convinced Ibrahim had designs on her husband's throne. His property,

including this residence, reverted to the state and today the building is undergoing restoration. The facade is one of the finest to
survive from any private Ottoman dwelling. Seen from the west,
the mosque is tucked behind a high screen wall. When I saw it in
late autumn set against bare tree limbs and in a thicket of minarets
(Sultan Ahmet has, exceptionally, six of them), I felt I had
chanced upon the enchanted tomb of a prince long dead.

Entry to the mosque is not by the courtyard but from the north
exterior wall. There and at other holy sites visitors are required to
remove their shoes or strap on cloth slippers, and it is customary
to tip the men who tend the shoes or tie the slippers. The money
helps support the foundation, too. A donation of one hundred
liras (about fifty cents) should do.

I went into the Blue Mosque prepared to take careful note of
the celebrated painted decoration. But any such consideration of
detail was banished from my mind when I saw the vast, serene
interior. Peace and quiet reign, for any footfall is immediately
muffled in a sea of carpeting.

The mosque is cruciform, with a hemispherical dome set on
four massive, ribbed piers, each about fifteen feet thick, and semidomes at each of the cardinal points. The dome rises over 130 feet
and, unlike the vaults of most Christian churches, its hemispherical curve confers an impression of lightness and space. It is only
the chandeliers, brought down to within twenty or thirty feet of
the floor, that reestablish any sense of human scale.

In its pristine condition, the building was glazed with over 250
stained glass windows. Much is missing or has been replaced with
modern imitations that admit too much light. But the illumination does permit close scrutiny of detail, and of that there is an
abundance.

Against the eastern wall are a pulpit of marble, a tiled prayer
niche, and a windowed arcade. The shutters of the window sashes
are made of ebony inlaid with ivory. It must have delighted
Ahmet to look through the shutters down to the Sea of Marmara

and across to the Princes' Islands, a place where his more temperate successors exiled their political foes. This civility unfortunately came too late for Ahmet's son Osman II, who was executed by his brother Sultan Murat IV. Now reconciled, the brothers lie buried in garden tombs behind the mosque.

On the low wall sections is an unobtrusive but peerless revetment of tiles from the village of Iznik, where they were produced from about 1454 onward. The ones in the Blue Mosque are from the very best period, just after 1600, and are designed for the most part in the so-called *quatre fleurs* style: intertwined tulips, roses, carnations, and lilies.

About two-thirds of a mile from the Blue Mosque is that of Sultan Beyazit in the square which bears his name. It is just off the Yenicheriler Caddesi, the principal thoroughfare issuing from the At Meidan, and can be reached by a short ride on any municipal bus bound for Beyazit Square or the Edirne Kapu gate. But it is a shame to miss the chance for a walk through some of Istanbul's busiest streets and past some of her least pretentious but most charming monuments.

Just outside the At Meidan, in full view of the Blue Mosque and near the ruins of the palace of Antiochous, is the mosque of Firaz Aga. It was built in 1491 by the chief treasurer of the realm. The design of the mosque couldn't be simpler and contrasts sharply with all but the earliest imperial mosques: a dome upon a square, with a solitary minaret at the northeast corner. But the rudimentary form is probably not the result of limited means but simply that the mosque predates the borrowing of ideas from Byzantine basilicas.

Halfway to Beyazit Square on the right side is the mosque of Atik Ali. It sits askew to the surrounding buildings because it was laid out in 1496, long before the modern street and quarter were planned. Atik Ali was Sultan Beyazit's chief eunuch and for his mosque he chose the old form of two domed rooms separated by a north-south crosswall. The design has been varied by replacing

 the eastern dome by a semidome with stalactite decoration. The building is set in a flagged court with shade trees and gardens and has been little touched by time or the restorer's hand.

Several hundred yards beyond Atik Ali is Beyazit Square, near the center of the city. The Covered Bazaar and the university are within easy walking distance. The mosque of Sultan Beyazit II was an imperial foundation erected in 1506 on what was very near the grounds of the old palace (Eski Saray) of Mahmet the Conqueror. It includes the customary courtyard with domed portico and the interiors of the domes have been freshly painted in burgundy, black, and gold to bring out their floral designs. The building was reputed to be so carefully oriented toward Mecca that sailors could set their compasses and astronomers their clocks by it.

This was the first of the imperial mosques to owe a heavy debt to Hagia Sophia. Its central dome is flanked on the east and west by semidomes and on the north and south by tympanic arches. But the arches are supported on only one rather than three columns, hence the division of nave from aisle is less pronounced and the interior space is correspondingly more open. The curious wings to the south and north, both of which terminate with minarets, are also a borrowing from church architecture and give the effect of a narthex, or vestibule.

The area around the mosque is usually awash with students coming from the university or with shoppers on their way to the bazaars and is thus a favorite place to loiter and observe. If sitting on the staircase in total indolence seems too sinful, one can always visit the second-hand book market alongside the mosque. The Sahaflar Charshi, as it is known, was the book and paper market of Byzantium and, but for a brief period as the center for turban making and engraving, has continued to serve as such. It was

there that I sampled one of the delicious *semits*, or sesame seed
bread rings, on sale in the nearest things Istanbul has to automatic
vending machines: a Plexiglas box divided in two. You simply take
a bread ring from one half and deposit a ten-lira note in the other.

A short amble up the great staircase and through the university
grounds with their pines and cypresses leads to the greatest
Ottoman building Istanbul has to offer: the Suleimaniye of Sultan
Suleiman the Magnificent. Suleiman assumed the Sultanate from
his father, Selim I, in 1520. During his reign of forty-six years the
Ottoman Empire reached its zenith. What his emissaries and
statesmen in the courts of Europe could not achieve, his armies in
the field did. The Turkish court was one of the most brilliant in
the world and its manners and intrigues passed into the arts and
literature of sixteenth-century Europe.

The mosque and its associated buildings form a truly immense
ensemble and are a supreme tribute both to the Sultan and to
his principal architect, Sinan. Standing isolated on a vast, paved
terrace, the mosque and its attendant mausoleums shrouded behind
somber cypresses underscore the perishability of worldly glory, an
effect made all the more poignant
for me by the antics of a scruffy
brown bear that was dancing on
the porch of the mosque.

Still, as a monument to one
man, the mosque succeeds admirably. It is bracketed by four impressive minarets which symbolize that Suleiman was the fourth
Ottoman Sultan to rule in Istanbul. Their combined balconies
symbolize that Suleiman was the
tenth Ottoman dynast.

The mosque is entered via the
courtyard, which, with its mon-

umental western facade, is appreciably broader than it is deep. And the customary octagonal ablution fountain is here replaced by a delicate rectangular marble one. The first thing to strike the visitor upon entering the mosque itself is the wonderful lighting of the interior. The majority of the original stained glass windows survive. The glass was reputedly made by Sarhosh Ibrahim, whose sobriquet, Sarhosh, means the drunk. His personal excesses seem not to have dulled his creative energies.

The light serves to accent the astonishing range of marble veneers and stones used in the making of the mosque. And the calligraphic text adorning the *mihrab* and drum of the dome are justly praised.

All these details are set against a soaring interior over 140 feet high. The columns supporting the north and south tympanums are only two in number. They are exceedingly slender and somewhat withdrawn and as a result the interior can be seen from nearly any point. All but the western buttresses have been relegated to the outside, unencumbering the interior still more. In fact, the external buttresses have been elaborated into two-tiered arcades which mask their true function.

The garden behind the mosque contains the tombs of Suleiman and his Queen, Haseki Hurrem, and their children Mustafa and Mihramah. The Iznik tiling in the tombs of Suleiman and his Queen is lavish and should not be missed. Apply to the caretaker, whose hut stands in the corner of the garden, if you want to see it. All the buildings within the immediate view of the mosque are part of the foundation. Consisting of schools, kitchens, and hospitals, many of them still operate, although not in their intended capacities. What was originally a kitchen (*imaret*) on the extreme west of the terrace is now a museum of pottery, glass, carpets, metalwork, and jewelry. What was once a school across the broad western avenue now functions as a maternity hospital and the schools farther to the east now house a manuscript collection in excess of 32,000 pieces.

The man who wrought this magnificence was not a Turk, but a Christian youth taken from his native Greece in 1511 at the age of twenty-one. At forty-six Sinin became the chief royal architect and throughout his ninety-seven years erected mosques, baths, schools, kitchens, markets, and tombs. His works in Istanbul alone total forty-one. For his contribution to the perpetuation of Suleiman's memory he was accorded the unparalleled honor of a burial within the mosque grounds.

From Sinan's tomb the road descends very sharply, skirting the terrace on which the Suleimaniye is built. The first major turn to the left leads to Uzun Charshi Caddesi, which reaches almost to the Golden Horn but ends suddenly in front of Rustem Pasha Mosque. To the right, at a distance of perhaps two hundred yards, is a two-storied brick and mortar building. This is the Spice Bazaar. Also known as the Egyptian Bazaar, it is one of the busiest markets in the city.

It is part of the Yeni Valide Mosque, the penultimate of the imperial mosques. The Yeni Valide belongs to the final and by no means finest flowering of Ottoman architecture. But seen from the stern of one of the Bosporus ferries or from the Galata side of the Golden Horn, it is stunning. The mosque was commissioned in 1597 for the Queen Mother, but work was abandoned in 1603 and not resumed until after the structure was damaged by fire in 1660.

Like the Blue Mosque, the Valide has a centralized plan of a single dome resting on four semidomes. But in the Valide all the structural pieces can be appreciated from the exterior. In particular, the columns are brought above the level of the roof and are capped with small bonnets to form a cascade or staircase effect. The external buttressing of the walls has been articulated into porches with sharply pitched, overshot roofs. The southern porch especially is a place of congregation.

The park is a fine place to relax and there are plenty of benches for the purpose. The stalls along the verges of the park do a brisk business in the sale of exotic birds and the immediate area is something of a pet emporium. Quarantine restrictions being what they are, I decided not to buy a bird. I did, however, invest in a tin of bird seed for five cents, on sale from an old woman who traffics in such things, and I spent a pleasant quarter hour feeding the flocks of pigeons.

These four imperial mosques span the early sixteenth to mid-eighteenth centuries and represent the best in Ottoman building. Furthermore, they have the advantage of lying relatively close to one another and can be reasonably worked into a single day's tour. But if you want to spread your visit to the imperial mosques out over several days, the Beyazit and Suleiman Mosques can be seen in one tour and any visit to Topkapi Palace and Hagia Sophia can be easily extended to take in the Blue Mosque. The Yeni Valide Mosque is nearly impossible to avoid since it stands only a stone's throw from the central bus station and from the ferry slips where boats depart for the Princes' Islands, the Asian suburbs, and the villages along the Bosporus.

Bathed in Tradition

NANCY MILFORD

ౡౢ

THERE'S NO reason that the word "monument" has to designate a museum or a mosque or a statue. A Turkish *hamam* is indeed one of the true monuments of Istanbul, and in this piece we learn about the author's attempt to visit a few that the Turks themselves frequent.

NANCY MILFORD is the author of *Savage Beauty: The Life of Edna St. Vincent Millay* (Random House, 2001) and *Zelda: A Biography* (Harper & Row, 1970), which was a finalist for the Pulitzer Prize and the National Book Award and has been published in twelve languages.

IT WAS the end of the summer in 1983, and I was sitting with friends in a taverna on the harbor at Hydra, a Greek island that remains a haven for writers and painters. The waterfront, bright with gaily colored lights, looked like the setting for an operetta. So it was hardly surprising when the Egyptian cotton broker at our table turned his sly eyes on me and sang, "You must go to Istanbul and take the honey baths!" True, we were talking about travel, and we had been drinking that cold gasoline the Greeks call retsina. But I knew immediately that I wanted to go.

with exquisite gifts. I find there a small, oval, lidded soap dish
from the nineteenth century, of copper lined in tin. It's called a
hamam sabunluk, and women used to carry them into the baths
with their soaps and powders and pumice kept dry inside. And I
think my mother will fancy it. At home in Michigan I tell her my
story of the baths of Istanbul. She asks, "Is it safe? Is it clean? Do
the women really have all their clothes off?" I suddenly remember another phrase I learned from a young Turkish woman: "*Eski
hamam, eski tas*," which means, "Same old *hamam*, same old cup,"
or, things are always the same.

COMING CLEAN

Cağaloğlu Hamami (Kazim Ismail Gürkan Caddesi 34 / +90
212 522 2424 / cagagloaluhamami.com.tr) is almost adjacent to
the Hagia Sophia. Both the men's and the women's baths are
open daily.

Çemberlitaş Hamami (Vezirhan Caddesi 8 / +90 212 522
7974 / cemberlitashamami.com.tr) is off Divan Yolu near the
Grand Bazaar.

Galatasaray Hamami (Turnacıbaşı Sokak 24 / women +90
212 249 4342; men +90 212 252 4242 / galatasarayhamami
.com) is near Galatasaray Square in the Beyoğlu district. The
men's and women's baths are open daily.

Mihrimah Sultan Cami (Fevzi Paşa Caddesi 333 / +90 212
523 0487) is in the Edirnekapı district. The bath is open daily
and there is no women's bath.

Cinili Hamam (İtfaiye Caddesi 49 / +90 212 631 8883) is in
Zeyrek, near the Church of the Pantocrator and the Aqueduct
of Valens. The men's and women's baths are open daily.

Türkü (Cevdetpaşa Caddesi 226 / +90 212 265 2991), in Bebek, sells traditional Anatolian women's dresses, silver accessories, ceramic objets d'art, calligraphy, and books.

In addition to descriptions and advice about the *hamam* in guidebooks and other accounts, I will share a few tips of my own:

- All, or almost all, *hamams* have lockers for your clothes and belongings, including your valuables. If you're uncomfortable about leaving your valuables behind (though I have not heard of anything being stolen at a *hamam*), bring along only what you really need and put it in a very small plastic or waterproof bag. It's *water, water everywhere* inside the *hamam*, as well as steam, so anything that can get wet will.

- Don't show up at a *hamam* without small bills and coins. Even if you're staying at a luxury hotel and are charging the fee to your bill, you will need cash for a tip. Do not expect the *hamam* attendants to have change for large bills.

- It's useful to decide what tip you want to give before the end of your session so you can hand it to the attendant unhesitatingly, with a smile, and with a confidence that says, "Here is your tip. It is not negotiable." If you waver, you are opening the door to frowns and cries of protest, perhaps worse. It can make you feel lousy, embarrassed, or cheap, and then, if you have it, you fork over more money, contributing to this minor form of extortion. At the conclusion of a Turkish bath, everyone should feel good, so tip appropriately but not extravagantly (unless you have had the sultan's treatment and you are over the moon and beyond). If you prefer to seek guidance about tips, ask

your hotel concierge, a guide, or the person who checks
you in at the *hamam*, but ask *before* you are whisked away to
the changing room (again, you want to avoid that hesita-
tion at the end).

• The first time I had a bath, at Cağaloğlu Hamam, I was
scrubbed with a *kese* (a loofah) so hard I couldn't decide, at
first, if it was enjoyable. And it took me a while to realize
that the gray stuff on the *kese* was actually my skin. But I
did feel great at the end, though my tan was gone, and I
concluded it was indeed all worth it. Other visits to
hamams outside of Istanbul didn't have such scrub-happy
attendants, but they made me feel great, too.

When I returned to Cağaloğlu years later, the attendants
were almost all Russian and looked like they were going to
pummel me. But they preferred much softer cloths, and they
weren't aggressive at all. I still felt enormous well-being
when it was all over, but in retrospect I think I preferred the
more startling experience of my very first *hamam*.
(Cağaloğlu, by the way, is one of my favorite Turkish words
and is pronounced JAH-low-loo.) This *hamam* has become
so famous that its sign now states it is featured in the best-
selling book *1,000 Places to See Before You Die*, by Patricia
Schultz (Workman, 2003). I still think Cağaloğlu is worth
going to—the architecture of the *hamam* is beautiful—but
experiencing more than one *hamam* is ideal. Before setting
out for a bath, check on the hours and days of the week—
they aren't always identical for men and women (occasionally only one or two days of the week or certain hours are set
aside for women).

Yael Alkalay, founder of the wonderful Red Flower line of bath and body products (redflower.com), is one of the most inspiring and interesting people I've ever met—and I'm not simply saying that because I am a huge fan of her products, which are 100 percent botanical based and are found at hotels like the Mayflower Inn and Spa and the Carneros Inn. She traces her family's history back to the late fifteenth century in Turkey, where nearly all the men in the family were grand rabbis (read a fascinating story about the Turkish coins she counts as her most prized possessions in *The New York Times*, February 20, 2005). Alkalay didn't visit Istanbul until she was a teenager, but many of the smells and scents there were familiar due to her grandmother's cooking. She says that Red Flower is really an expression of the smells of her childhood, and she holds the sights, sounds, and scents of places in her mind to keep them alive. "The first two things I do when I'm in Istanbul," she told me, "are to take one of the ferries across the Bosphorus, drinking tea of course, and go to a *hamam*. Cağloğlu is my favorite." Alkalay has been to more than five hundred bathhouses around the world, and notes that "every product in the Red Flower *hamam* treatment is inspired by this ritual." In fact it was the *hamam* line that first made me a fan, and Red Flower's travel *hamam* set—mint tea silt purifier, clay, lemon coffee blossom olive stone scrub, steam room mist, cardamom amber oil, and tangerine fig lotion all tucked into a 4½-inch leather pouch—is a must-have. Alkalay adds that she believes travel is "seeing a few things very well. You can sit in front of the Blue Mosque, sipping tea, and just look at it from sunup to sundown. You'll never forget it."

RECOMMENDED READING

The Art of the Kariye Camii, by Robert Ousterhout (Scala, 2002). This is a wonderful book to look at before you visit the Chora Church. The photographs are beautiful—they will prepare you for the real thing, though they are not nearly as beautiful—and the author makes a strong case for renewed preservation of this Byzantine masterpiece. Dr. Ousterhout is one of the world's leading archaeologists and historians of Byzantine art and architecture, and is on the faculty in the Department of the History of Art at the University of Pennsylvania. Ousterhout wrote in *Cornucopia* that when he first set foot in the Kariye Camii many years ago, he fell in love. "It was the academic equivalent of a blind date—I'd committed myself, sight unseen, to write a PhD dissertation about a building I'd never seen in a city I'd never visited. Happily, the Kariye caught and held my interest." The building he refers to as the key monument of late Byzantine art and architecture—"there is absolutely nothing that can compare with it in Istanbul, or anywhere else for that matter"—has continued to hold his attention for more than thirty years. And now he is worried for its future, and recommends a fresh evaluation of the building. It would indeed be a tragedy if the Kariye were allowed to further deteriorate.

Byzantine Monuments of Istanbul, by John Freely and Ahmet S. Çakmak (Cambridge, 2004). This magnificent book is hard to find, but well worth the effort. The monuments are presented here in chronological order and are described in the context of their times. The text, accompanied by maps and photographs (most in black and white but plenty in color), really tells the *story* about each monument, which is why this book is so valuable. If you can locate this only in your local library (I had to request an inter-library loan), it's better than not reading it at all; but this is one you'll want to keep.

A History of Ottoman Architecture, by Godfrey Goodwin (Thames & Hudson, 1971). You will find references to this book in nearly every guidebook and with good reason: it is hands down the single best work on the subject—absolutely essential. It is not for light reading, however—this is a large, heavy tome of 511 pages—but even for dipping into only a few chapters I highly recommend it. Goodwin relates in his autobiographical *Life's Episodes: Discovering Ottoman Architecture* (below) that when he finished the manuscript, he turned it into Thames & Hudson "without warning since I knew nobody there. Later I learnt that they said at least it was something new and the next day they sent it to Professor Géza Fehérvári, then at the School of Oriental and African Studies. Geza brought it back to Thames & Hudson on the Thursday saying, not that it was

worth publishing, but that it had to be published forthwith." Goodwin made a pledge to himself years before when he was visiting Bursa that he would "explore every nook and cranny of Ottoman architecture and also the people who lived here over many centuries, to include the farmer sitting next to me on a bus. I did not then know that I had made such a promise but the monuments themselves did. The task is not yet finished."

İpek: The Crescent and the Rose: Imperial Ottoman Silks and Velvets, compiled and edited by Julian Raby and Alison Effeny (Azimuth Editions, 2001). This positively stunning book— about 14 × 11 inches, with hundreds of lavish color and black-and-white pattern designs and other illustrations—is a must for anyone who has a yen for textiles in particular and Ottoman history in general. Though this is a thick volume (360 pages), the author team has focused on silk (*ipek*) textiles of the sixteenth and seventeenth centuries, and the book combines immense visual appeal with the most comprehensive scholarly research to date. The authors visited all of the major collections of Ottoman textiles in the world, traveling to seventeen countries, and finding masterpieces not only in Topkapı and the Mevlana Museum in Konya but also in monasteries and museums in the Balkans, Sweden, Poland, and Russia. The book brings together an "unparalleled range of information on Ottoman silks," and examines many of the different factors that determined the history of these textiles.

Turkish silks were held in high regard by Europeans in the nineteenth and twentieth centuries, while, initially, wearing silk was considered an infidel custom (the Prophet Muhammad is said to have remarked that "he who wears silk in this world will forgo it in the next"). Eventually, silk was the preferred fabric of royal dress, and the authors relate how "the entire elaborate edifice of Ottoman court ritual and its economic

structure of salaries and rewards was built around the symbol-
ism, costliness and almost religious mystique of silk."

Part two of the book, on the Ottoman silk industry, features
a detailed description of the Istanbul *hans* devoted to the textile
industry, complete with a map of the *bedesten* (cloth hall) in the
market district.

Life's Episodes: Discovering Ottoman Architecture, by Godfrey Goodwin (Boğaziçi University, 2002). Despite what the title may
suggest, this is actually an autobiography of Goodwin, who
joined the faculty of Robert College (which later became
Boğaziçi University) and was the author of *A History of
Ottoman Architecture* (see above), still considered the standard
work of reference on the subject. He passed away in 2005, and
in his obituary in *The Guardian*, Goodwin was referred to as "a
scholar in love with the wonders of Ottoman architecture and
all things Turkish." Goodwin's passion for Ottoman architecture is evident, but I like this book more for his personal observations of people, places, and events. About his first day in
Istanbul, upon moving there on New Year's Day, 1957, he
relates:

It was raining. It went on raining every day through January and
February, when there were brief interludes of snow, and then
every day until the middle of April. It rained so much that it
was no longer a storm but a wall of water and one needed gills
like a fish. Taksim was ankle deep, achieving a flood at the top
of a hill. It shrank your socks in your shoes and I did not get to
the İstiklâl Caddesi for fear that I would never return. Both my
pairs of heavy shoes fell apart but happily there are fine cobblers
in Istanbul. I might add that all this did not stop the Turkish citizens from going about their business. It was a golden period
when the city was still as it had been and there was proof of this
when the long handle of a baker's pan laden with baked loaves

came straight out of the window and hit me in the stomach. At least I had the wit to laugh at myself. It was the period when manhole covers were stolen each night and sold back to the Belediye (municipality), so I was anxiously watching my step.

Mosque, by David Macaulay (Houghton Mifflin, 2003). *All* of Macaulay's wonderful books are appropriate for children and adults, but *Mosque* is perhaps the one with which adults feel most completely comfortable as it is quite a sophisticated book. Macaulay admits in his preface that, as he was researching construction details, he realized he knew very little about Ottoman architecture, or more specifically about Sinan, and he was convinced "that the time had come to find out where these extraordinary buildings came from, who built them, why, and of course how." He explains that the building complex in the book is fictional, as are its patron and architect; but the individual structures are modeled directly on existing examples built between 1540 and 1580 in and around Istanbul. Macaulay says that he believes the best examples of religious architecture are among humankind's proudest accomplishments: "Motivated by faith, but guided ultimately by common sense, these builders created constructions that reveal a level of ingenuity, ambition, and craftsmanship rarely found in secular architecture. The greatest achievement of the buildings, however, as well as the ultimate indication of their success, lies in their ability to impress and move even those whose personal beliefs they do not necessarily serve."

Sinan: Ottoman Architecture and Its Values Today, by Godfrey Goodwin (Saqi, 1993). For readers interested in comparing and contrasting the many works of Sinan, this is perhaps the best volume, though it is out of print. The buildings and bridges Goodwin studies here are not limited to Istanbul, and the photographs are black and white. He provides a handy abbreviated list of Sinan's buildings, which he culled from a definitive register of works attributed to Sinan by Dr. Aptullah Kuran, author of *Sinan: The Grand Old Master of Ottoman Architecture* (Institute of Turkish Studies, 1987). Interestingly, of the 477 buildings recorded, 173 no longer exist, 52 have been virtually rebuilt, 32 cannot be traced, and 25 are in ruins.

The World of Ottoman Art, by Michael Levey (Charles Scribner's Sons, 1975). There are very few books devoted to Ottoman art—oddly, I think—but even if there were many more, this one would still be the very good reference it is (it was published over thirty years ago). Levey has much enthusiasm for the subject, and he seeks to "encourage greater exploration and awareness of a rich fascinating culture"; he wrote the book "with the general reader and ordinary tourist in mind." He notes that serious appreciation of Ottoman art was long delayed, and that it still does not have the prestige of Persian art. Yet the character of Ottoman art remains its own, and it really does create a complete world, similar, says Levey, to these words of the Koran: "But those that have faith and do good works shall not lose their reward. They shall dwell in the gardens of Eden, with rivers rolling at their feet. Reclining there upon soft couches, they shall be decked with bracelets of gold and arrayed in garments of fine green silk and rich brocade." The focus in this book is on Istanbul, Bursa, and Edirne, and it's a very thorough survey of interior and exterior architecture, painting ("one of its underestimated arts"), Iznik tiles, calligraphy, and weavings.

The Turkish Table

It might almost be said that life in Turkey revolves around food. Hours of long and patient effort are spent in the kitchens and in summer all meals are served in the open. Even in the shabbiest districts of old Istanbul each small house has its own veranda and its fig tree and perhaps an ancient vine or two and honeysuckle (most delicately named by the Turks "*hanım elli*"—lady's hand) smothering the wire fences between the houses. Roughly hewn wooden tables are covered with fine linen cloths, relics of a great grandmother perhaps or made for the trousseau when the present middle aged housewife was a newly betrothed girl of ten. Cloths, napkins, cushion covers are all heavily embroidered in exquisite patterns; rich Sparta carpets cover the floors even though there may scarcely be a stick of furniture to stand on them. It is a land of carpets and prayer rugs and no Turkish family would ever be put to the shame of being without one or the other.

—Irfan Orga,
Turkish Cooking

Turks eat with relish because their religion allows them few other indulgences. But there is another reason: their food is delicious. And not because of human ingenuity. Turkish cooking is not the result of lengthy elaboration. There are no stocks taking days to make, no overnight marinades, no sauces of infinite complexity. Turkey has no use for stocks and sauces because here everything tastes the way it should: the tomatoes like tomatoes, the cucumbers like cucumbers, the eggplants like eggplants. And the bread? Why, it might have been baked in heaven.

—Eric Lawlor,
Looking for Osman

This city was a jumble of aromas, some of them strong and rancid, others sweet and stimulating. Almost every smell made Armanoush recall some sort of food, so much so that she had started to perceive Istanbul as something edible. She had been here for eight days now and the longer she stayed, the more twisted and multifaceted Istanbul grew to be.

—ELIF SHAFAK,
The Bastard of Istanbul

Turkish Food
in the Cycle of Time

AYLA ALGAR

ॐ

I HAVE long loved Margaret Visser's book *Much Depends on Dinner* (Grove, 1999). Visser borrowed her title from lines from Lord Byron's "The Island," which read, "All human history attests That happiness for man,—the hungry sinner!—since Eve ate apples, much depends on dinner." Much *does*, in fact, depend on dinner. Arthur Schwartz, in his *Jewish Home Cooking*, opens his introduction with these words: "Food can connect us to our past. In fact, food is often our very last and only connection to our pasts, enduring long after the old language has been forgotten and other traditions have died." And Ayla Algar, in her wonderful cookbook *Classical Turkish Cooking*, opens with a quote by Abdül-hak Şinasi, a Turkish writer: "One should not pass over these things, simply saying they are food. They are in reality a complete civilization."

To paraphrase Algar, when the railroad between Istanbul and Vienna was completed in 1888, a European resident of Constantinople interpreted the event as marking "the conquest of the city by foreign thought and enterprise" and its "annexation to the Western world." His estimate may have been exaggerated, but as Algar notes, the Westernization of Turkish culture had already begun by the late nineteenth century. A symptom of this was the decline of Istanbul's traditional neighborhoods and the rise of Pera, now Beyoğlu. Historically Pera was home to the city's Christian minorities and the European diplomatic community, and by this time the area had also become attractive to foreign travelers and the Ottoman elite, who frequented the European-style cafés and restaurants. Algar explains, "The emergence of the Turkish restaurant must, in fact, be dated to this period. In traditional Turkish society, the idea of eating a complete meal outside the home as a matter of pure recreation, unconnected with the exigencies of travel or the exchange of hospitality, was unknown." (As an aside, I found this to be true in Morocco as well, where historically foreigners eating in restaurants were pitied since everyone knew the best cooking was to be found in the home; this is changing, however, as more restaurants have opened in Morocco and many are quite excellent.)

It is changing in Turkey as well, Algar notes, and it's increasingly common now in urban areas for families to eat in restaurants. But she notes that the food served in restaurants is also changing, with most offering a mixture of Turkish and Western dishes. She bemoans the "disturbing development" of the proliferation of fast-food places offering pizza and hamburgers, "a sure sign that Turkey is entering the orbit of the multinational corporations." In their own homes, however, Turks follow more conservative culinary habits, and Algar says that preferred dishes, both for everyday meals and special occasions, tend to be traditional. The importance of family is still regularly expressed at the dinner table: "It is unthinkable that as a matter of course teenage children should eat at a separate time of their own choosing, and equally unlikely that a mother should make her often tiring work outside the home a reason for failing to prepare a meal. (It should be noted, however, that grocery shopping is often a male duty, in accordance with tradition.) Furthermore, it is not a disaster, to be masked with uneasy pleasantries, if an unexpected guest chances by at dinnertime. Room is made at the table, and the opportunity to feed a guest is indeed greeted as a chance to earn merit." In the twenty-first century, this familial cohesiveness seems almost urgently needed, everywhere in the world. Algar shares the thoughts of writer Ahmet Hamdi Tanpınar, in observing the changes that affected Turkish life by the late twentieth century: "Side by side with those many things which are lost when one passes from one civilization to another, there are others which themselves ruling over time are the true and lasting monarchies of this world." She concludes that it's "not an exaggeration to regard the rich traditions of Turkish cuisine, with their profound historical and cultural roots, as one of those precious and imperishable monarchies."

"Turkish Food in the Cycle of Time," an essay from Algar's book, is a wonderful celebration of Turkish food through the seasons.

AYLA ALGAR is also the author of *The Complete Book of Turkish Cooking* (Kegan Paul, London, 1995) and has written for *Fine Cooking* and the *San Francisco Chronicle*.

UPON REFLECTION, the calendar turns out to be far more than a mathematical means of marking the passage of time. With its festivals and special occasions, it is, on the contrary, a way of planting islands of meaning in the inexorable flow of days and months, times that are to be both remembered and anticipated in their punctual and welcome recurrence. On such occasions, the link between food and sociability, always strong in Turkish culture, comes fully to the fore as special dishes and foods are prepared for both family and friends.

It is only an apparent paradox that Ramadan, the month of dawn-to-dusk fasting obligatory for all Muslims, should also be a month of extraordinary culinary activity. It is not only that the appetite and the sense of taste are sharpened by the experience of fasting; Ramadan is also a month of hospitality and charity, in which the obligation to feed the hungry is taken more seriously than usual. It should also be noted that fasting is experienced not as a deprivation but as a gift, a source of abundance; the whole month, not merely the festival itself that marks its end, is joyous, and the sense of renewal that comes to those who observe it finds a natural expression in the meals taken together at the end of each day.

Each day's fast is also preceded by a meal known as *sahur*, taken before the dawn prayer, intended to fortify one against the rigors of the fast (which might last as long as fifteen hours, if Ramadan falls in the summer). Traditionally, pilaf dishes, *börek*, and poached meat served cold and sliced (*söğüş*) would be favored for *sahur*, but now people generally content themselves with leftovers from the previous day's dinner, or the regular fare eaten for breakfast.

Even the traditional *sahur* was a frugal affair compared with the quantity and variety of foods prepared in Ottoman times for breaking the fast (*iftar*) as soon as the sun had set beneath the horizon. The treasures that had been accumulated in the pantry in the weeks leading up to Ramadan would be brought forth in rich and hierarchic splendor to delight the palate of the faster. Samiha Ayverdi, the well-known contemporary writer, recalls how during her childhood in an aristocratic family foods would be gathered in advance of Ramadan from all the corners of the Ottoman realm—still a vast area, despite the progressive amputation of its outlying territories: dates from Baghdad, rice from Egypt, clarified butter from Aleppo and Trabzon, baklava from Gaziantep, dried apricots from Malatya, kasseri cheese from the Balkans, honey from Ankara, caviar from the Black Sea, figs from Izmir, cheese aged in skins from eastern Anatolia.

The time for breaking the fast was traditionally announced by the firing of a cannon in big cities or the beating of a drum in smaller localities. This was the signal to bring out an array of small dishes containing a variety of cheeses, pickles and jams, dates, and slices of sausage (*sucuk*) and dried pressed meat (*pastırma*), accompanied by sesame rings (*simit*), and a special type of *pide* baked for the season. After this prelude to the day's feast, the sunset prayer would be offered, before proceeding to the next stage of the evening meal, consisting of either rice or vermicelli soup and eggs cooked with onion or *pastırma*, a dish which for all its simplicity had originated in the kitchens of the palace. Even this did not mark the end of the proceedings, for then came a variety of meat and vegetable dishes, *börek*, and desserts. The most favored dessert during Ramadan was *güllaç*, a creamy and delicate concoction flavored with rose water, that set off to perfection the heavy meal just completed. Then pipes and coffee were prepared, serving to dissipate postprandial languor.

Outside the home, eating places would remain open throughout the night, and the special prayers performed during Ramadan, known as *teravih*, would often be followed by an outing to a locality of Istanbul renowned for a certain kind of food.

Constraints of time and finance have combined to reduce the lavishness with which *iftar* is prepared, but the three-tiered arrangements—an array of small dishes followed first by soup and then by a dinner with several dishes—is still preserved, as are, of more importance, the festive and communal aspects of the meal.

Ramadan is brought to an end with a festival known popularly as Şeker Bayramı, the Festival of Things Sweet. On that day candy and confectionery as well as traditional desserts such as *kadayıf* and baklava are offered to guests and relatives who come to pay their compliments. A special meal may also be cooked for the occasion, consisting of heavy foods not customarily eaten, such as stuffed chicken or turkey and a dish of meat and wheat known as *keşkek*.

The other chief festival of the Islamic calendar is known as Kurban Bayramı, the Festival of Sacrifice. On this day Muslims everywhere—especially those performing the hajj, or pilgrimage to Mecca—slaughter an animal both in commemoration of the readiness of Abraham to sacrifice his son Ishmael and as an act of charity. The meat of the animal slaughtered is to be distributed, in fixed proportions, to relatives, neighbors, and the poor. In Turkey it is almost always a sheep that is sacrificed, and the approach of the festival is marked by the appearance of sheep in the most unlikely metropolitan settings, tied to a tree and awaiting their fate. The meat is roasted in a dish known as *kavurma*. *Dolmas*, *börek*, and various desserts—baklava and *kadayıf* in particular—are also eaten on this occasion. It is customary in addition to prepare *helva* using the fat of the slaughtered animal.

Şeker Bayramı and Kurban Bayramı belong to the official calendar of Muslims all over the world. Distinctively Turkish, by contrast, is the celebration of six nights distributed through the calendar known as Kandil Geceleri (Lamp Nights). Each of these nights is of religious significance for all Muslims, but only in Turkey (and in some countries once ruled by the Ottomans) are they given this collective designation, which refers to the illumination of the mosques and the stringing of rows of lights between their minarets. These nights are marked gastronomically by the preparation of various special desserts, primarily *lokma* but sometimes helva, and distinctive *çöreks* adorned with sesame seeds.

The tenth day of Muharram, the first month in the Islamic lunar calendar, has also held an important place in the popular religion of the Turks. It has given rise to a sweet soup, known like the day itself as *aşure*.

Since the Islamic calendar is lunar, it regresses ten days in each year in respect to the solar calendar, and the religious festivals that are set in accordance with it move gradually from one season to another. Other festive occasions, and their gastronomic accompaniments, are fully seasonal in nature: the cherry harvest, the weaning of lambs, the beginning of the ramming season. Not surprisingly, these festivals are confined almost exclusively to the countryside, and even there they are gradually dying out. Still celebrated is the Festival of Hıdırellez, a celebration of the arrival of spring held on May 5 and 6. The name of this festival comes from a compounding of Hidir and Ilyas, two figures that symbolize fer-

tility and immortality in popular Islamic tradition. People go pic-
nicking on foods as varied as hard-boiled eggs, grape-leaf *dolmas*,
lettuce salads, and different kinds of *börek* and *çörek*. Sometimes a
lamb may be slaughtered, and its meat roasted and eaten with bulgur pilaf.

A seasonal celebration of a quite different type, one that I
remember from my own childhood, belonged to an urban milieu.
During the forty coldest days of winter (reckoned to begin on
December 22 and end on January 30), friends would invite each
other to their homes to while away the long winter evenings eating *helva*—hence the name of the occasion, *helva sohbetleri* "*helva*
conversations"—and listening to poetry. Other substantial foods
would also be prepared for the occasion, such as stuffed turkey
and *börek*. At the end of the winter, all those who had survived
the cold season without falling sick would sacrifice an animal and
organize additional "*helva* conversations"—an excuse for more
eating and conviviality!

Both these categories of festival, the religious and the seasonal,
serve to fix the pattern of social and communal life. A third set of
occasions serve as landmarks in the life of the individual and the
family; their particular quality, too, is marked by appropriate gifts
of food and drink.

This pertains particularly to marriage and all the carefully cali-
brated stages that have traditionally led up to it. In the past, when
verbal agreement was made between the families of bride and
groom, sherbet was served, followed by sweet coffee, *lokum*, and
candy, the hope being that all this sweetness would somehow be
reflected in the marriage-to-be. The formal announcement of
engagement was similarly accompanied by much sweetness! On
the night that the bride was taken to the bathhouse and the following night when she was adorned with henna, a substantial
meal was served, consisting of pilaf and meat dishes, rich desserts,
fruits, and roasted nuts. A similar ample repast would be prepared
on the day of the wedding itself; essential elements of this feast

were a meat pilaf, a warm vegetable dish, and *tepsi böreği*. If all went well on the wedding night, the family of the bridegroom would send a tray of desserts to the family of the bride the next day.

The procedures leading up to marriage in modern Turkey have been telescoped into a few simple stages, and not many people can afford the money and time required to provide such repeated hospitality on so lavish a scale. Nonetheless, the wedding and its preliminaries are still the occasion for much cooking, eating, and drinking.

A birth is, of course, a festive occasion, but it is not celebrated with the same ceremony as the circumcision of a male child, which traditionally takes place when the boy is at least four or five years old. Then he is dressed in a white suit and crown of velvet and gold thread, to help him forget his discomfort, and the guests are served a meal that should traditionally contain a meat pilaf, *helva,* and a saffron-flavored rice dessert (*zerde*) that is now almost entirely forgotten in Turkey.

Even death, the somber counterpart of the processes of generation and birth, has its culinary consequences. As the Turkish writer Nezihe Araz puts it with characteristic grace, human beings have never been able to accustom themselves to death, despite the grim regularity of its occurrence, and "those who seek to modify the nature of death by means of various ceremonies, to soften its impact, naturally have recourse to food in their efforts." Even now, it is customary in Turkey for neighbors and friends to send food to a bereaved household for three days after the occurrence of death. The trays they send will always include warm soups, but never the sweets and desserts associated with joyous occasions. However, on the evening after the funeral, *helva* is prepared by female friends and relatives of the family, to the accompaniment of prayers, and it is then distributed in the neighborhood, with the request that everyone pray for the departed in whose name it has been prepared. Seven days after the funeral, *lokma* is made and similarly eaten in memory of the departed.

Many of the rich traditions described here have diminished or been forgotten in recent times. Changes in material culture, in living arrangements, and in the overall atmosphere of society have combined to make impossible the retention of the former leisurely way of life with its ornate and sumptuous celebration of special occasions. But it may be thought that the essential has been preserved: the celebration of continuity in patterns of religious devotion, in the cycle of the seasons, and in the life and death of the individual, by means of food that nurtures the heart and the spirit even more than the body.

Istanbul's Newest Tastemaker

GISELA WILLIAMS

ℭℭℭ

STYLISH DEFNE Koryürek (profiled in "Miniskirts Meet Minarets in the New Istanbul") is one of Istanbul's ultimate food insiders. Here she shares with writer Gisela Williams her favorite restaurants.

Koryürek's husband, Vasif Kortun, is founder and director of the Platform Garanti Contemporary Art Center (İstiklâl Caddesi 115A, Beyoğlu / +90 212 293 2361 / platformgaranti.blogspot.com) and for this original article he shared information about two other favorites: Istanbul's Bilgi University opened Santralistanbul in 2007 by transforming a 1911 power plant into a sprawling modern art museum and cultural center (Eski Silahtarağa Bektrik Santrali, Kazim Karabekir Caddesi 1 / +90 212 444 0428 / santral istanbul.org). Rodeo is one of the newest additions to Istanbul's gallery scene—it's in a former tobacco warehouse and shows modern Turkish and Greek art (Tütün Deposu, Lüleci Hendek Caddesi 12, Tophane / +90 212 293 5800 / rodeo-gallery.com).

GISELA WILLIAMS is European correspondent for *Food & Wine*, where this piece originally appeared. She also writes frequently for *The New York Times*, *Travel + Leisure*, and the online travel magazine *Indagare* (indagare.com).

DEFNE KORYÜREK might just be the world's most glamorous butcher-shop owner. It's a sunny Saturday in Istanbul, and the forty-year-old Defne—in a chic minidress by Machka, one of her favorite Turkish designers—is giving me a tour of Dükkan, the butcher shop she runs with her business partner, Emre Mermer. Since it opened four years ago, Dükkan has become the local go-to source for dry-aged steaks. It also supplies veal and sausage to many of the city's most prestigious restaurants, including the one at the Four Seasons Hotel Istanbul at Sultanahmet and the trendy Ulus 29 and Kantin. Dükkan's meat is also the focus at Dükkan steak house, which Defne and Emre opened last fall two storefronts away from the butcher shop.

Defne has lots of other projects at the moment—in addition to the butcher shop and steak house, she also writes a food blog and heads up Istanbul's Slow Food chapter—but she has been pushing Turkish cuisine forward for more than a decade. She spent three years in the 1990s as a caterer in New York City, where she delivered Mediterranean comfort food like beef-and-lamb *köfte* to homesick expats and created recipes like one she named Eggs alla Kortun, poached eggs on toasted bread with sizzling feta and olives (recipe below). When Defne returned to Istanbul, she opened a restaurant called Refika in the gritty (but now gentrified) neighborhood of Tünel. There, she used fresh ingredients for Turkish dishes like a warm lentil salad with roasted red peppers and garlicky sausages.

"I still remember the first meal I had at Refika: a chicken stew with pears," says Semsa Denizsel, the chef at Kantin. "It was very clear that Defne was doing something new and different. At the time in Istanbul, there was the food you ate at home and the food you had in restaurants, which was often European, rarely Turkish. Defne's food was delicate and refined, but at heart, it was good Turkish home cooking." Refika (which is now closed) sparked a sort of Alice Waters-esque movement toward using the very best ingredients to elevate simple Turkish dishes. As a result, many local chefs consider Defne a mentor and mother figure.

Now, with Dükkan, Defne is helping locals understand how to properly grill steak. "People in Turkey tend to overcook meat, so we would have clients come back to the shop and say the steaks were too dry," she explains. "We had to show them how to do it." Opening the steak house was a natural next step.

As she walks from the butcher shop to the steak house, Defne points out the extreme contrasts in the scruffy neighborhood, Küçükarmutlu: Nearby are tiny crooked houses, with Istanbul's stock exchange building looming behind them (stockbrokers often come to Dükkan for lunch). "When we first opened, the headlines were, 'Society Butchers in a Shantytown,' " she says. "But we like the low rent."

An enormous glass case of dry-aged steaks stands just inside the door of the steak house. The waiters ask diners to select their meal from the display—like choosing a lobster from a tank. "The conversation usually becomes a little lesson about meat cuts and dry aging," Defne says, walking past several packed communal tables to reach her husband, Vasif Kortun, who's sitting in the back of the room under a large mirror decorated with a butcher's diagram of a cow. Vasif, one of Europe's most respected contemporary-art curators, is the founder and director of Istanbul's avant-garde Platform Garanti Contemporary Art Center. He is also co-curating this year's Taipei Biennial and collaborating with the Nobel Prize–winning Turkish author Orhan Pamuk on an installation based on Pamuk's much anticipated new novel, *Museum of Innocence*.

In between bites of fennel-and-apple sausages, smashed potatoes, and a T-bone steak dripping in its own juices, Defne and Vasif talk about food, art, and Istanbul. Vasif describes the growth of the city's contemporary-art scene: Two new modern-art museums—Santralistanbul and Istanbul Modern—have opened in the past four years. Defne mentions some of her favorite Istanbul restaurants, including Kantin, which has a chalkboard menu of Turkish dishes that changes daily and might include cinnamon-spiced rice pilaf with mussels and calamari. And she raves about Changa, a fashionable restaurant that she recommends for its modern reinterpretations of Turkish dishes, like pan-fried beef tongue with mustard sauce.

"It's definitely an exciting time for food here—the city is in an experimental adolescent stage," Defne says. "But we still need more markets, a good culinary school and more risk takers." With Defne helping to nurture other risk takers, Istanbul is ready to grow up.

DEFNE'S RESTAURANT FAVORITES

Boğaziçi Borsa A local institution, famed for classics like braised lamb with eggplant. (Lütfi Kırdar Kongre ve Sergi Sarayı / +90 212 232 4201 / borsarestaurant.com)

Kantin Turkish-inspired comfort food, like rice pilaf with mussels and calamari. (Akkavak Sokak 16/2 / +90 212 219 3114 / kantin.biz)

Mangerie A rooftop café in the stylish Bebek area, serving perfectly grilled sea trout and elegant snacks. (Cevdetpaşsa Caddesi 69, Bebek / +90 212 263 5199)

Dükkan Defne's lively steak house specializes in dry-aged steaks and house-made sausages, which are also sold at her butcher shop two doors away. (Fatih Sultan Mehmet Mah. Atatürk Caddesi 4, Armutlu / +90 212 277 8860 / dukkanistanbul.com)

Changa Its outpost in the Sakıp Sabancı Museum offers Scandinavian style and updated Turkish dishes like pan-fried beef tongue with mustard sauce. (Sakıp Sabancı Caddesi 22, Emirgan / +90 212 323 0901 / changa-istanbul.com)

Develi The Samatya outpost, near the airport, is Defne's favorite: "I'm not a fan of modern, lighter kebabs. A good kebab should be at least 40 percent fat, as they prepare them there." (Gümüsyüzük Sokak 7, Samatya / +90 212 529 0833)

Cibalikapı Balıkçısı Defne loves this cozy restaurant's fish *meze*: "I get the wild-herb salads, stuffed calamari, and lots of bits and pieces of cured fish." (Kadir Has Caddesi 5, Cibali / +90 212 533 2846 / cibalikapibalikcisi.com)

Poached Eggs with Baked Feta and Olives

౭౦ఁ

TOTAL: 30 MIN

6 SERVINGS

Defne Koryürek created this recipe, aka Eggs alla Kortun, when she and her husband, Vasif Kortun, were living in New York City in the '90s. He loved the combination of toasted bread, poached eggs, sizzling feta, and olives, so she decided to name the dish after him. When they returned to Istanbul, Koryürek opened a café, Refika; this was one of the first things she put on the menu. She says, "To our delight, it sold like crazy!"

6 3-inch squares of rosemary focaccia, halved horizontally
2 tablespoons extra-virgin olive oil, plus more for brushing
10 ounces feta cheese, cut into 6 slabs
Aleppo pepper or ancho chile powder, for sprinkling
6 large eggs
salt
18 pitted kalamata olives
1 tablespoon chopped sage

1. Preheat the broiler and position a rack 6 inches from the heat. Bring a large deep skillet of water to a simmer. Brush the focaccia with olive oil and broil until lightly toasted. Put a slab of feta into each of 6 individual gratin dishes. Drizzle each slab with 1 teaspoon of the oil. Sprinkle lightly with Aleppo pepper and broil for 2 to 3 minutes, until lightly browned and sizzling.

2. Meanwhile, crack the eggs one at a time into a small bowl, then slide them into the simmering water. Poach until the whites are set but the yolks are still runny, about 4 minutes. Using a slotted spoon, transfer the eggs to the gratin dishes and season with salt. Sprinkle with Aleppo pepper, the olives, and sage. Serve with the focaccia.

WINE Eggs can be difficult to pair with wine, but feta, olives, and bread make this dish much more wine-friendly. Pair it with a fruity Mediterranean rosé (a good wine for eggs in general), such as the 2006 Librandi Cirò Rosato from Italy or the perky 2006 Gaia Estate 14-18h Rosé from Greece.

I had the great pleasure of meeting Gisela Williams when she was in New York recently, and she mentioned that Defne also had a recipe for a drink called a Rakitini. With a name like that, I had to find out more, so Gisela put me in touch with Defne, who kindly agreed to share the recipe with readers of this book. She wrote to me the following:

Rakitini was created by a friend of mine, for me. It has this beautiful green color for it is made of cucumber juice, a few drops of a lemon, and rakı, the proud member of the ouzo/arak liquor family. Today it's prepared by two establish-

ments only, for the Turks are awfully conservative when it comes to rakı and fish. They don't drink "green concoctions"! But I can proudly tell you that one of the two places that prepare Rakitini is a very traditional little fish restaurant. (Perhaps new tastes need only time.) I used to ask for a jar with a lid to shake the drink myself. Nowadays they have the full set: a vegetable juicer and a stainless steel shaker! And they even insist to prepare it for me.

Rakitini

Rakitini can be prepared with ouzo as well, but *rakı* (especially the Kulüp brand) works better if you ask me. (Nothing nationalistic here, just taste.)

In a shaker combine 1½ ounces fresh cucumber juice (juice of cucumbers with their skins on) and 1½ ounces *rakı*. Add 2 ice cubes and shake.

Pour into a chilled martini glass and add a drop of fresh lemon juice. It's very green and serves one.

Interview: Şemsa Denizsel

I was so happy that Koryürek included the restaurant Kantin among her favorites as it's one of mine as well. I was introduced to it—and its warm, knowledgeable chef, Şemsa Denizsel—by John Scott, editor of *Cornucopia*. Kantin is a neighborhood place, in Nişantaşı, that's open primarily for lunch but also for an early dinner or afternoon tea (hours are 11:30 a.m. to 7:00 p.m., Monday through Saturday). The traditional Turkish treat of *simit* (sesame rings) and *kasar* (a hard, white cheese) are served in addition to tea, coffee, and cakes. Denizsel told me the name Kantin is a playful take on the English word "canteen"—she wanted to convey the idea of a small, cozy, casual place to eat but quite the opposite of a school canteen, where the food is typically dreadful. Kantin's menu is unique in that it's written in chalk on a blackboard and is divided into sections, such as Today, Everyday, Sides, Desserts, and *Citir*, which refers to a very thin crust with a selection of toppings—something between pizza and a Turkish *lahmacun*—and is a specialty of Kantin. The Today section changes every single day and includes soup, three different dishes of Turkish home cooking, and a daily fish option. Everyday items include staples, which is a sort of comfort zone—if you don't like the daily options, you always have the staples. Some of Kantin's special desserts are warm semolina *helva* with Turkish ice cream, mastic pudding with sour-cherry compote, cheesecake, and oven-roasted seasonal fruits.

Denizsel is not shy about her culinary opinions, and I asked her a few questions about the current food scene in Istanbul:

Q: Is Istanbul fare different from Anatolian fare? And is there such a thing as New Istanbul Cuisine?

A: The way Istanbul people used to cook was different from Anatolian fare. The food you usually get in restaurants these days is not the Istanbul cuisine; it is Anatolian based. Istanbul cuisine used to be and still is much more refined. Unfortunately, not many Istanbul natives live in this city, let alone professionally cook. The "New Istanbul Cuisine" is a term I use (or maybe have invented), and not many people think about it. But here is what I think: Istanbul is a great metropolis, with more than a thousand years of history attached to it. During all of its existence, Greeks, Armenians, Jews, and Turks have lived here. All the people have contributed to the cultural and social life. That includes food, cuisine, eating habits, and all. Today, with the globalization of everything, foods of different countries and cultures also affect each other. The New Istanbul Cuisine treasures its roots but at the same time reaches out to the world to update and refresh itself, uses local seasonal ingredients, combines classic techniques and recipes with contemporary needs of today, uses traditional to create untraditional, and is based on Turkish cooking but allows itself to be influenced by other world flavors.

Q: Kantin's menu seems to be very seasonal and very local. What are some examples that would only appear under your Today section?

A: Aubergine dishes, tomatoes, and sardines are in abundance in the summer, but in winter you will never see this on the menu. I have artichokes on offer almost every day from mid-March to the end of June, but then that's it until the following spring.

Q: What would you recommend first-time visitors order at Kantin?

A: It would be best if they choose from Kantin's Today section, as these dishes, which change daily, represent our approach to food best. They can always ask for a tasting menu. We would be more than happy to serve them (unless, of course, the lunch service is in a rut). We don't serve *mezes*, by the way, though we do have beer and wine by the glass. Actually, anyone who cares for good food would leave Kantin happy and content.

Q: Do you recommend any Turkish cookbooks (in English) for visitors who are serious about learning to cook Turkish dishes?

A: I can't really recommend any, but if they are willing to take any private lessons or have a class as a group, they can get in touch with me.

Q: Are you working on a cookbook of your own?

A: Yes, I am. It will be Kantin's cookbook, and I'm trying to get it ready for Kantin's tenth anniversary at the end of 2009!

Recommended Restaurants

The key to fantastic eating in Istanbul is to eat at a variety of different types of eateries. Just as in France you might alternately eat at a café, a brasserie, a wine bar, a bistro, a tea salon, and a Michelin-starred restaurant, in Istanbul you should try street food, a steam table place, a *köfte* or *kebab* place, one of the trendy new-wave restaurants, and a palace restaurant. In this way, you'll experience a wide range of flavors and ingredients and discover all the culinary specialties of Turkey, past and present. Here are some places I highly recommend, in addition to others mentioned elsewhere in this book:

Changa (Sıraselviler Caddesi 47, Taksim / +90 212 249 1348) and **Müzedechanga** (Sakıp Sabancı Müzesi, Sakıp Sabancı Caddesi 22, Emirgan / +90 212 323 0901 / changa-istanbul.com). Changa is a favorite for many locals and visitors alike, and it's hard not to feel that something exciting is happening in the kitchen here. Chef Peter Gordon, originally from New Zealand and now in London, laid the groundwork for what might be called the New Istanbul Cuisine in 1999. *Changa* means "mix" in Swahili, and it's an appropriate word for these southeast Asian/Mediterranean dishes that really work. The Taksim location is in an Art Nouveau building with an interior that's completely the opposite: slick, stark, and with a most unusual "ceiling" of sorts set in the floor, so that diners may view their food being prepared in the kitchen below. Changa was honored as the only Turkish restaurant featured among the top fifty restaurants in the world by the UK's *The Restaurant* magazine. Müzedechanga, which opened in 2005 on the beautiful grounds of the Sakıp Sabancı Museum, is equally as enticing as its downtown cousin. It opened with a splash: a dinner party in honor of Picasso's grandson Bernard-Ruiz Picasso and his mother, Christine. Wow. The hip, award-winning Istanbul design firm Autoban designed the interior and the furniture.

Most items on the menu have long names—in-house hickory smoked red mullet and pomegranate salsa in chilled red turnip soup; slow-cooked beef cheeks and *erişte* (Turkish noodles) with goat milk yogurt sauce and gremolata; green tea champagne jelly with passion fruit cream, hazelnut croquant, and pineapple curd—but are wildly delicious. The cocktail list is nothing if not mod, with the signature, The Istanbul, a cool concoction of *rakı*, vodka, and Bodrum tangerine. I've read that the bar at the Taksim outpost serves drinks in shot glasses made entirely of ice. Somehow I missed that, but you can bet I'll be there on the first night of my next visit.

Çiya (Güneşlibahçe Sokak 43–44, Kadıköy / +90 216 418 5115 / ciya.com.tr). As the *Hedonist's Guide to Istanbul* puts it, Çiya is "a restaurant worth crossing the continents for. This won't immediately be apparent as Çiya, only a few streets away from the ferry port in Kadıköy, is unassuming in appearance and most of the clientele look as if they've only crossed the road to get there. Which they have." Though tourists are onto the delicious and immensely satisfying food served up by chef Musa Dağdeviren, Çiya is beloved by locals. Çiya is actually a compound of three places, two kebab spots and one *sofrasi* (home-style restaurant). Musa himself is from southeastern Turkey, and is half Kurdish, half Turkish. His view of food is all-inclusive, with dishes ranging from "the Balkans to the Caucasus and from Asia to the Arabian Peninsula." Paula Wolfert, writing in *Food & Wine* in 2004, called him "part chef, part culinary anthropologist," and *Saveur* included him in its annual list, the *Saveur* 100, in 2006.

Musa travels all around Anatolia to track down regional recipes, often at customers' requests, and he just keeps adding them to the menu, which is enormous (he offers fifty to sixty-five or more different types of kebabs alone), and you can be assured that your meal will be different each time you come. (Note that alcohol isn't served at any of the three establishments.) According to *Saveur*, one of Çiya's early customers was journalist Zeynep Çalişkan, who was so smitten with the kebabs from her hometown, Antakya, that she soon became a regular and ended up marrying Musa. (Zeynep now manages the business.) She says, "He relates everything to food. You could say, 'It's nice weather,' and he'll say, 'Yes, good for the sunflowers, for sunflower oil.' " Making the journey to the culinary shrine that is Çiya will be one of your lasting memories of Istanbul.

Feriye Lokanta (Çırağan Caddesi 40, Ortaköy / +90 212 227 2216 / feriye.com). Feriye is not in a former palace—though it's a grand building right on the Bosphorus shore that used to belong to the Çırağan Palace—but rather in a late-nineteenth-century former police station. Chef and manager Vedat Başaran is the son of Bosnian Muslims who immigrated to Istanbul in 1956 and opened a deli-like store. It wasn't until he was studying in London, in the 1980s, when he saw a BBC documentary about how food was prepared in a traditional Aegean Sea village that he began to take an interest in Turkey's culinary history. When Başaran returned to Turkey, with a master's degree in professional cooking, he applied for a research grant from the cultural ministry but was rejected, so he decided he would have to pursue learning about Ottoman cuisine by a different route. He then was put in charge of Tuğra, the restaurant in the soon-to-open Çırağan Palace Hotel, and he persuaded the hotel's management to allow him to create a menu of pure Ottoman dishes, a departure from the Continental cuisine considered standard hotel restaurant fare at that time.

Başaran began buying every Ottoman cookbook he could find in the bazaar, but after a while word went around that "someone" was buying up these volumes and suddenly the prices were out of his reach. Still, by then he'd purchased enough (some dating from the late 1800s and early 1900s) to seriously begin his research. In an interview with writer Joanna Preuss for *Food Arts*, in 2003, Başaran noted that these cookbooks had never been translated, so the recipes and measurements were indecipherable. He had to teach himself the script and studied with one of the few remaining Ottoman scholars in Istanbul. He related that at Tuğra, "the Turks couldn't understand what I was doing, especially since no one knew what palace foods really tasted like." Neither restaurateurs nor diners were very sophisticated then, but after a few foreign food writers ate at Tuğra and praised the food, interest in Ottoman cooking suddenly took off, and other hotels noticed. By this time, Başaran had translated a large number of recipes, and he recognized there were clear distinctions between different Ottoman periods. He classi-fied the collection by century, noting, "After years and years of study, I feel that I live in the present but sleep in the past."

There is indoor and outdoor seating at Feriye, but to me the whole point is to eat outside. Even when I visited in Jan-uary, clear panels had been erected over and around the out-door terrace, and though this barrier existed between me and the water, it was still magnificent (there were small heaters installed in the tent as well). The menu is just extra-ordinary, like nothing else in Istanbul. Don't forgo the rounds of bread with black sesame seeds that are brought to the table—they are divine. The cold fisherman's platter I had was out of this world. The waitstaff is predictably attentive, but they didn't hover annoyingly, and they relished the moment when they brought our main dishes (all hot) and lifted the silver domed lids from the plates simultaneously.

My three companions agreed that every dish we had left us rather stunned, and my friend Arlene proclaimed she was sure she would likely never have duck that delicious again in her life. There is one dessert, a chicken-breast pudding (*tavuk göğsü*), about which Arlene said, "I'm sure it's delicious but it's just too weird." She was right about it being delicious, and it's only a tiny bit odd. Başaran says, "My cooking is a reinterpretation, not a replica, and that itself is part of the Ottoman culinary tradition."

5.Kat (Soğanci Sokak 7, Taksim/Cihangir / +90 212 293 3774 / 5kat.com). *Kat* means "floor," and to reach that floor in this slightly dilapidated building you get in an elevator (also slightly dilapidated) and an attendant will take you up and into a dark, plush room with a bar and about ten tables. 5.Kat has been described as "velvety," a word I think is perfect, though I'm told that in the summer the velvet is abandoned for the rooftop terrace, which I haven't yet experienced, though I'm sure I will love it. I only had drinks here, so I can't vouch for the food, but the people eating—and it was packed, and it was midnight—seemed to be thoroughly enjoying their meals. I did take a peek at the menu; it offers Turkish staples but also Asian and Italian dishes. My friend Maha tried to take a photo because the interior is hard to describe, but she was quickly and firmly asked to banish her camera from sight. Too bad, because 5.Kat is like nothing else—very bohemian, kitschy, yet definitely stylish.

The House Café (Asmalı Mescit Sümbül Sokak, Tünel Geçidi İsban 9/1, Beyoğlu / +90 212 245 9515; Atiye Sokak İskeçe Apt. 10/1, Nişantaşı / +90 212 259 2377; Yıldız Mahallesi, Salhane Sokak 1, Ortaköy / +90 212 227 2699). I wish the owners of this chain would set their sights on the

States, because everything about this concept is so unchain-like, and perhaps it could become an inspiring model for entrepreneurs interested in good food that's served up fast. The menu features mostly healthy, simple dishes, with plenty of vegetarian options, and many are good for sharing. Each dish is nicely presented—lots of towering things—and the salads are *great*. My glass of sparkling water arrived with a clutch of fresh vegetables and slices of fruit in the bottom of the glass, which I loved. Each location (though I've only been to the Nişantaşı branch) has a bright, airy interior with a communal table and other smaller tables scattered around. The House Café is great for both a quick rest and a pick-me-up or a full meal. If you like the jam, coffee, and olives here, you can buy the House brand.

Rumeli Café (Divanyolu Caddesi, Ticarethane Sokak 8, Sultanahmet / +90 212 512 0008). Rumeli is one of the few Sultanahmet favorites, with traditional Turkish, Mediter-ranean, and Greek dishes, all well prepared. The interior is warm and cozy, with exposed-brick walls and dark wood floors, and a fireplace in the upstairs room. In warm weather there is seating on an outdoor patio. Rumeli is casual and reliably consistent, with something for just about every-one—grilled fish, pasta, salads, hot and cold *meze*, vegetarian selections, chicken shish kebab, lamb, etc.—and the service is quite friendly.

Tarihi Selim Usta Sultanahmet Köftecisi (Divanyolu 12 / +90 212 513 1438). The long name simply translates to "Historical Sultan Ahmet Köfte Restaurant," and simple but very tasty meatballs are what you'll find here. In fact, the only other items on the menu are a delicious white-bean salad and *ayran*, the popular yogurt drink. The *köfte* are very fresh because there is such high turnover—as has been the case for more than eighty years. Though this is listed in many guidebooks, it's also very popular with locals (mostly men, by the way) and is inexpensive.

360 Istanbul (İstiklâl Caddesi 311, Beyoğlu / +90 212 251 1042 / 360istanbul.com). Located in the historic Mısır apartment building on the seventh and eighth floors (you take the elevator to the seventh floor and then walk up one flight to the rooftop), 360 is a trendy bar, restaurant, and club, and I am a huge fan. Everyone told me 360 is a better place for drinks than dinner, but I thoroughly enjoyed my dinner there, though I would never call it amazing. "Amazing" *is* the word I would use, however, to describe it as a venue for drinks. 360 is essentially a glass cube on top of a building, with a true 360-degree view. "Your World Is 360" is the motto of this unique space, with really cool circular sofas and a bar with unusual drinks. You can buy the menu (I did). You can buy a CD (I did). And if you are so inclined, you can sit outside on the terrace for hours and hours. (I didn't, but only because my friend Sinan was anxious to show me and my friend Maha more of Istanbul at night.)

INTERVIEW

ᘛᘚ
───────────────────────────────────

Engin Akin

Writer and cookbook author Anya von Bremzen—who has referred to Istanbul as "a hallucinatory experience"—is a frequent contributor to Food & Wine, *where her piece on Turkish cook and hostess Engin Akin (known as Turkey's Julia Child and Martha Stewart rolled into one) appeared in the April 2001 issue. As this good piece ("Engin's Empire") is easily accessible online (foodandwine.com), I decided not to include it here, though I urge you to read it as it's loaded with excellent culinary tips.*

I had hoped to meet Engin Akin when I was last in Istanbul, but she was in New York at the time, so we have been communicating ever since by e-mail. I asked her if she would still recommend the shops and restaurants she visited with Anya, since this piece appeared eight years ago, and she assured me she still frequents each one. As Akin also writes a weekly food column for the daily newspaper Vatan *and welcomes interested foodies to her cooking school in Ula, near Bodrum (details follow), I asked her about new places and culinary delights she's enthusiastic about now:*

Q: Have you been shopping at any new food markets, and can you recommend some places to eat that are your current favorites?

A: Istanbul has changed since the *Food & Wine* piece. People are more seriously interested in food than before and in fresh produce markets. So markets are once again a serious business that is a requirement of quality living. Bodrum has a great market on Fridays—fresh produce, wild greens and mushrooms, dried fruits, vegetables, and also the ladies from the villages bring their homemade specialties like *erişte* (ancient Turkish homemade pasta), *bazlama* (homemade bread), and *gözleme* (*yufka* filled with greens baked over a *saj*). All around Bodrum one can find a market to go to each day of the week. One of my favorites is the Muğla market on Thursdays. This is where I do my vegetable shopping for my classes in Ula. I find a huge variety of the freshest cured cheeses here, like the cured cheese of Bergama and curd, *çökelek*, which I prefer to use in my pasta on *börek* dishes. I never miss a cone of salep ice cream made with the ever-unchanged recipe of Yalabık, the famous deceased ice-cream maker of Muğla. [Salep is orchid-root powder that, when frozen, becomes ice cream and, when hot and mixed with milk, becomes a popular winter drink.] In Istanbul I take my salep ice cream on the delicate *su muhallebisi* of Sütiş in Emirgan, which leaves the taste of milk in my mouth. Sütiş is also my latest Turkish breakfast address—I love their tea, *kaymak* with their delicious honey, and their cheese, *pide*, and all the rest—everything is yummy. Also the İstinya Park Shopping Center has one of my favorite shops, Malatya Pazarı, where I go for dried fruits and spices. My most delicious and recent find, Cafer Erol Turkish Delight shop, also has a branch here. Cafer Erol, with its history and years of expertise, is a wonderful family business where each product is mouthwatering. I go there for the pistachio *çifte kavrulmuş lokum* and the *kaymak*-filled ones, which have a shop life of only two days. I would not miss their orange peel, eggplant, and green walnut version, and not to be missed for all the things in the world are the rose-petal jams. Close to the Black Sea is Sarıyer, a neighborhood where I go for my meat *böreks*. Even though I make the same at home, these are somehow more special, with expertise of over one hundred years. The Sarıyer *muhallebicisi* is also a special shop, established in early 1900, where I stop for lemonade and *tavuk göğsü* (chicken-breast pudding). Hacıbey is my steady address in Teşvikiye for Bursa kebab, which is mentioned in the travel book of the famous seventeenth-century Turkish traveler Evliya Çelebi—the owner moved to Istanbul over thirty years ago. Also the Balık Pazarı at İstiklâl Caddesi still has its charm. My spice shop, Bünsa, is there and I always find the freshest spices. Kadıköy, on the Asian side, also offers the best quality produce. I enjoy going there. I would not miss the *su börek* with *ayran* (a traditional yogurt drink) or Turkish tea at Güllüoğlu's new shop in Karaköy. Visiting Güllüoğlu also gives me an opportunity to bring home baklava and other syrupy desserts to be savored by the family. They have the best Turkish pastry desserts in Istanbul. When I am around the Grand Bazaar, I either indulge myself at Şehmuz for the purest of kebabs (his meat *pide* is unsurpassed so far) or if I want a more delicate and classic taste, I choose the small shop near the Nuruosmaniye gate of the Grand Bazaar, Çarşı Muhallebicisi (Çarşıkapı Nuruosmaniye Caddesi 5–7), where I have chicken soup and chicken over rice with a special yogurt on the side. Hünkar is great for grand Turkish tastes like the *hamsi pilav* or *manti*, lamb knuckle soup, and *puf börek*. For a more elegant address in the area I like Şamdan, where I get the purest Turkish dishes like *köfte* and bread *kadayıf*, though they also serve continental food. For evenings, Club 29 is still my favorite with its Turkish *mezes* of small *lahmacun*, *köftes*, etc. Really I could just go on and on. . . .

Q: You are not a professional chef in that you don't cook in a restaurant, but you seem to value pure and sophisticated cuisine and perfect results, and you believe in aesthetics as well. Who were your mentors or people that you found inspiring?

A: My mother, grandmother, and aunts are my mentors. I am quite like my grandmother, who would not let anyone else go in the kitchen, even though she had help. None of my mentors would start cooking unless all the ingredients were the best. I learned from them that good food *looks* good, too— you have to play around with some dishes to make them look appetizing. Presentation is important, but one must remember that it's like earrings on a beautiful girl—they don't change the girl. Also, I learned that good food *smells* good, so today the aromas connect me with the wonderful food the women in my family cooked. I know by smell what the food is going to be like. The new style of serving may be fine but I stick to the essence of taste and do not play around and add a lot of unnecessary extras. To me it feels like covering up something. I like honest food in every respect. Turkish food is more about taste than presentation.

Q: If you were preparing a Turkish dinner for guests in your home, what would be on the menu?

A: I love to start with *mezes* and then move on to main dishes. I think of a meal like a *sofra*, a special Turkish word for a table with all its food in the proper place, similar to a play with all its acts. I like to highlight seasonal specialties, so here are two seasonal menus. *Summer:* Assortment of *mezes*, including white cheese and honeydew melon (these are a must with *rakı*, the preference of Turkish people for summer nights and dinners); fried eggplants and peppers with tomato sauce; purslane salad with walnuts and crumbled *tulum* cheese, preferably of Erzincan [*tulum* refers to the goatskin bag this ewe's milk cheese is cured in]; and Turkish tomato salad. The main dish may be okra with chicken and tomato rice with cold yogurt and cucumber soup on the side. For dessert, fresh fruits like watermelon or *kazandibi* with Turkish ice cream (it is made with salep). *Winter: Mezes* would include celeriac with green lentil braised in olive oil and spinach *börek* cut into squares, followed by lamb shoulder braised with sour dried plums or sour-plum paste and Turkish spices, dressed with *pekmez.* Butter *erişte* on the side, and pumpkin dessert over semolina *helva.*

Q: What are some of your favorite sources in Istanbul for table-top items and decorative accessories?

A: I have a number of favorites at the Grand Bazaar: Eğin Teksi-til for towels and textiles for home like bedcovers [Yağlıkçılar Caddesi 1]; Timuçin is my jewelry place for modern items [Kalpakçılar Caddesi 24–26]; Adiyaman Pazari for textiles and special *hamam* covers that may be used for tables and throws [Yağlıkçılar Caddesi 74–76]; Em-er for Turkish tiles and ceramics [Takkeciler Sokak 100]; Derviş for handwoven modern shawls in lovely pastel colors and items for the home [Keseciler Caddesi 33–35]; Dhoku for modern *kilims* [Takke-ciler Sokak 58–60]. Also at the Grand Bazaar, if you need to stop and take a break, I like Gül-ebru, a small *büfe* (a place where you get your food and eat it wrapped in bread; there are small stools here) for *döner* of beef cooked over charcoal. For the boxwood spoons (*şimşir* spoons) mentioned in Anya's article, I go to Bizim Ahşap [Kutucular Caddesi 27–29, Eminönü], which is very close to the Mısır Çarşisi (Spice Market).

Q: You wrote a cookbook with Mirsini Lambraki entitled *Two Nations at the Same Table,* which was published simultaneously in Turkish and Greek and was honored with a 2006 Gour-mand World Cookbook Award. Do you and Lambraki plan on writing another book?

A: So far Mirsini and I have no plans for another book. I have been working on a book of Turkish cuisine from its roots to the empire and present, and I may be doing a book on yogurt and *yufka* dishes, both savory and sweet, because I feel these are the richest points of Turkish cuisine that can also con-tribute to world gastronomy.

Q: What are some features about your cooking school that make it different from others in Turkey or Greece?

A: First of all, we learn to cook in traditional and practical ways with certain contemporary additions. We learn to cook from the freshest vegetables that we pick from my garden. Our nomadic roots have taught us to make do with the least to make the most. We cook seven dishes during the day, and the atmosphere is as it always has been in Turkish homes. We cook together and have our Turkish coffee in between. It is also a cultural experience, nothing like the soulless schools. Food has always been about sharing, in every culture. It's about enjoying life through making food as well as eating it. I want to keep it that way.

Akin was included in the *Saveur* 100 in 2007, and six of her recipes for a Turkish dinner menu were featured in the May 2007 issue of *Bon Appétit* (her recipes may be found online at epicurious .com). Details of her cooking school in Ula, on the Aegean Sea, may be found on her Web site, enginakin.com. Though I've not yet been to Ula, a visit there would be a perfect post-Istanbul respite, not only because of Engin, the food, and the beautiful accommodations in Engin's family home, Nabiye Konak, but also because the program is just four days, allowing visitors to plan an extended Mediterranean Turkey trip and not be locked into a weeklong commitment.

Circassian chicken is a renowned Turkish dish, and recipes for it are plentiful. In *Life's Episodes: Discovering Ottoman Architecture*, Godfrey Goodwin relates that he had once been invited to a dinner where this dish was the pièce de résistance. He asked his host how the dish had been made, and the host replied that Circassian chicken was "an Ottoman

dish which could not be made much longer because first of
all one needed eight grandmothers. These set to work one
day earlier shredding the breasts of young chickens, thread
by thread. Others were crushing the juice out of fresh black
walnuts. Then a rectangular terra-cotta flower pot had a line
of chicken threads laid across it and these were painted with
walnut juice. Another layer of chicken followed and was
painted in turn. By evening the dish was full and a brick was
placed on top. It was set by an open window and would be
ready for lunch next day."

You will see Hamdi Restaurant (Tahmis Caddesi Kalçin
Sokak 17, Eminönü / +90 212 528 0390 / hamdirestorant
.com.tr) recommended often in guidebooks and articles, and
with good reason: this renowned place serves delicious specialties from the southeastern part of Turkey *and* has a view
of Istanbul to die for. Founder and owner of the restaurant
Uncle Hamo left Birecik (near Urfa) over forty years ago and
came to his uncle's house in Istanbul. He attended Haydarpaşa high school for a total of twenty-six days, and that
was the end of academe for him—he dabbled in carpentry
after school and then completed his military service before
starting work at a kebab restaurant. Hamdi has been at its
present location, in a five-story historic building that once
was a porter's office, for over 140 years. In case you wonder
why you have to step into an elevator when you enter the
building, it's because the breathtaking views of the Golden
Horn and Galata are obviously to be had from the top floor!
In warm weather, request a seat on the outdoor terrace. It
may seem hard to imagine until you've tasted them, but the
kebabs and *köfte* here are absolutely among the best in all of

Turkey. There are five choices of kebab: hashish (I'm not entirely sure that's what you might think it is), aubergine, pistachio, garlic, loquat, and *testi*. *Testi* is prepared for at least ten people; the filling—meat, tomatoes, shallots, garlic, and green pepper—is put inside a pot which is closed with pastry, and then it is served by breaking the pot. Hamdi's tomato, walnut, and mint salad with pomegranate molasses is out of this world. But the real surprise is the baked goods: never, ever have I tasted baklava as good as Hamdi's. Since Hamdi doesn't ship overseas, one would be wise to consider packing a box of this in your carry-on.

"The first time I went to Istanbul was in 1957. I was the only woman visible on the street and in restaurants. Istanbul was only three million people at that time. I returned thirty-five years later to a city with twelve million people, a three-hour

'rush hour,' and women driving tractors in the countryside, wearing the head scarf and veil. Quite a change!

"There is great food in Istanbul—I loved eating fried mussels with *tarator* sauce served from street carts, and I loved the *meze* joints on the Çiçek Pasajı. My most memorable meal was in Kadıköy at Şiribom. I went with Chef Len Allison and we ate for three and half hours. The food was so magnificent I cried. What *meze*, *esme* sauce, *köfta*, pastries! I will never forget those flavors. I love the Spice Market, walking through the bazaar (I am wearing a necklace today that I haggled for and still love). Seeing those amazing kitchens at Topkapı was also memorable. What feasts they must have served. And those magnificent mosques!

"The skyline at night in 1957 was magic. The lights shimmered at night when you looked at the Princes' Islands. The skyline is still quite wonderful with minarets and bridges and modern buildings. I'm looking forward to going back with my grandson."

—Joyce Goldstein, a food writer, chef, and owner of the former Square One restaurant in San Francisco, and author of over a dozen cookbooks, including *The Mediterranean Kitchen* (Morrow, 1998), *Italian Slow and Savory* (Chronicle, 2004), and, most recently, *Mediterranean Fresh* (Norton, 2008)

Simply Sensational

BERRIN TOROLSAN

ʓʊʒ

BERRIN TOROLSAN, publishing director of the outstanding and gorgeous magazine *Cornucopia: The Magazine for Connoisseurs of Turkey*, also writes wonderfully interesting articles about Turkish cuisine for the magazine, and following are two of them.

This first focuses on a ubiquitous Turkish classic, the *börek* (*börekçi* is the word for a *börek* shop or seller), a heavenly marriage of featherlight pastry and cheese, meat, vegetables, or just about any filling you can conceive.

BERRIN TOROLSAN lives in Istanbul and is publishing director of *Cornucopia*, where this piece originally appeared.

MY GRANDMOTHER was a fine lady with a taste for the good things in life and boundless energy for creating those little pleasures that make life more enjoyable. Besides big lunches on festive days, one of those pleasures was her impromptu midweek *börek* lunch parties. They would often be announced at short notice, but I don't remember a single invitation being turned down. Appointments were shifted around, and my father and uncles would be sure to come home from work specially.

There was usually one savory pastry dish on the menu, along with plenty of salad and fresh fruit. Sometimes it would be *Tabak*

Börek, sometimes *Tatar Börek*. But it was *Puf Börek* that reigned supreme (see recipes). We would gather round a mountain of these puffed-up *böreks* displayed in the center of her large dining table. Sometimes the pile was so high that I couldn't see the person sitting opposite me. Amid the jolly chatter, there were occasional sighs of "I've lost count" as someone reached for yet another golden puff. And as soon as one mountain vanished, another pile appeared from the kitchen, freshly fried, to take its place. "Mother, who is going to eat all this?" my mother and aunt would exclaim. But my grandmother would take not the slightest notice and, more often than not, at the end of the meal not a single *börek* remained. On the rare occasions when any were left over, they would be wrapped and given to a guest to take away as a welcome snack for later.

What exactly is a *börek*? Put simply, it is a savory pie: a filling, usually of cheese or meat, is sandwiched between sheets of thinly rolled-out dough. It is baked, or pan-fried, or deep-fried, which allows the ingredients to combine in a delectable marriage as the filling melts, blending to a creamy consistency inside a crisp casing of pastry.

Although *böreks* come in an almost infinite variety of shapes and sizes, the common denominator and chief inspiration is the fine sheet of pastry known as *yufka*. A *yufka* (or *yupka*, as it is spelled in Mahmut al Kashgari's eleventh-century lexicon of Turkic languages, *Divanü Lûgat-it-Türk*) is a thin sheet of dry-cooked unleavened dough. *Yufka* was an ingeniously practical invention. These dry, featherlight leaves of bread could not have been more appropriate for people with a nomadic way of life.

The French nobleman Bertrandon de la Brocquière, "first esquire carver to Philippe le Bon," who traveled across "Turcomania" on his way from Palestine to France in 1433, came across Turkmen nomads near Adana, in southern Anatolia. With their customary hospitality, they offered the passers-by cheese and grapes and "a dozen of thin cakes of bread, thinner than wafers:

they fold them up as grocers do their papers for spices, and eat them filled with the curdled milk, called by them Yogort." A few days later he "lodged" at another Turkmen encampment of round felt "pavilions." "It was here I saw women make those thin cakes I spoke of. They have a small round table, very smooth, on which they throw some flour, and mix it with water to a paste, softer than that for bread. This paste they divide into round pieces, which they flatten as much as possible with a wooden roller [oklava] of a smaller diameter than an egg, until they make them as thin as I have mentioned. During this operation, they have a convex plate of iron [saç] placed on a tripod [sacayak], and heat it by a gentle fire underneath, on which they spread the cake, and instantly turn it, so that they make two of their cakes sooner than a waferman can make one wafer."

Yufka is still a rural staple today, and a coarse homemade yufka is as widely consumed as bread in most Anatolian villages. Yufka rolled around a spread of grape molasses is a popular shepherd's snack. The village woman's quick meal of katlama (literally "folded")—crumbled cheese and butter wrapped in yufka and toasted on a hot griddle—is still hugely enjoyed in the countryside.

Finer leaves of yufka are sold to make börek in markets, bakers, and yufkacı shops all over the country. Rolled out into large circular, gauzelike sheets, 60 centimeters (2 feet) in diameter, they will have been lightly dry-cooked on both sides on a hot iron griddle, exactly as Bertrandon described six centuries ago. The ingredients, even the utensils, are the same. Only the fuel has changed, as campfires have given way to electricity.

Simple snacks evolved over time into more complicated tray-baked böreks, employing ever more varied ingredients and cooking facilities, and, above all, calling for a large, well-organized community to gather round the börek tray and enjoy a shared meal.

Plain yufka dough made with wheat flour and water came to be enriched with eggs to create a softer pasta dough. Flaky pastry came from working in butter, fat, or oil, leading in turn to strudel and puff pastry. All could be used to envelop a delectable filling and be baked or fried as neat parcels of every shape and size.

The *börek* has an extensive place in Turkey's culinary repertoire, and the choice of fillings is infinite. Something that is protein-rich to complement the carbohydrate of the pastry makes for a perfect nutritional balance. From cheese to spicy ground meat or sautéed meat cubes with nuts and raisins; from chicken or turkey to fish and lentils; from offal such as brain or tripe to vegetables—the list is almost endless. Spinach, leek, potato, aubergine, courgette, pumpkin, cabbage and spring greens, sorrel, and nettle can all be included. And fillings are often further enhanced with butter, yogurt, milk, eggs, and fresh herbs.

As to the cooking, theoretically one needs an oven, whether modern or rustic, in which to bake *böreks*. But delicious tray *böreks* are still cooked, as they would have been in earlier times, on an open fire and covered with an iron lid, with the embers piled on top to create an ovenlike effect. Or else they can be simply cooked very fast on an open flame, then flipped over like a pancake and cooked on the other side.

ꙮꙮꙮꙮꙮ

Perhaps the forerunner of all pastries, *yufka* must have opened up a whole new culinary horizon, leading the way to a constellation of *böreks*, and a further galaxy of baklavas—for that is what you have when the pastry is given a nut-based filling, sweetened with honey or sugar syrup. Baklava calls for *yufka* rolled out into paper-thin leaves so fine that you can almost see through them: it may have anything from forty to eighty leaves, with a nut filling in between, yet be no thicker than two fingers. Another sweet idea is to take little morsels of fried *börek* and saturate them in syrup or honey; the result is crisp sweetmeats oozing with sweetness. But these call for a well-equipped kitchen, more time, and helping hands to tend to the frying while others are being served.

As the *börek* evolved, increasingly intricate dishes were devised in palaces and wealthier households, and above all by Ottoman sufi dervishes, for whom cuisine played a symbolic role on the path to perfection. By the fifteenth century the *börek* was already a classic dish. We know that Mehmet II, one Saturday in 1474, was served a *börek* that had been baked in the imperial bread ovens and was therefore called *furun böreği*, or "oven *börek*," which suggests that other techniques were also practiced.

By the seventeenth century, according to the chronicler Evliya Çelebi, there were a staggering four thousand specialist *börek* shops in Istanbul. These were strictly not to be confused with bread and biscuit shops. Even the mills producing the quality white wheat flour for the *börek* shops were different from those supplying the bakers.

Börek shops nowadays are less specialized. Tray *böreks* are sold in baklava shops by the portion or the kilo; others made from flaky pastry are sold individually in patisseries, along with croissants and mille-feuilles. A 1780 decree governing Istanbul's *börek* sellers stipulates that *böreks* should contain no less than 250 *dirhem* (802 grams) of mutton which must be "unadulterated with other meats." (Offenders would be severely fined.) Some things have changed little. Judging by the quantity of filling, *böreks* must have been baked in large trays and sold cut into rectangles, as they are to this day, for a *börek* with a savory filling, then as now, makes the perfect quick meal.

I still miss my grandmother's *böreks*, the delicious smells wafting from the kitchen, and the gasps of delight as a mound of hot, golden pastry puffs appeared at the table. And above all I miss the conviviality of those carefree *börek* parties.

A Note on Yufka

A variety of buttered paper-thin pastry—known by its Hellenic name, filo or phyllo—is well established in Western cuisines. Filo is manufactured around the globe, and *böreks* made from it are very popular outside Turkey, especially on London restaurant menus.

The first two *böreks* described here are made with ready-made *yufka* dough, which is less brittle than filo and lighter when fried or baked. If you cannot find ready-made *yufka*, use filo pastry, or better still make your own with flour, water, and a pinch of salt.

Sigara Böreği
(Cigarette *Börek*)

ı' o̧

1 leaf of yufka *dough*
Filling:
1 egg
100 grams white or feta cheese (crumbled)
1 cup fresh parsley (finely chopped)
oil for frying

This, the easiest and most rewarding *börek*, keeps in the fridge or freezer but can also be prepared in no time and served as a snack, starter, or main course. Classic fillings are the cheese one described here, or minced meat (as in *Muska Böreği*). But depending on how imaginative you wish to be, countless variations can be tried, using different ingredients.

1. Spread the circular *yufka* on a flat surface. Halve and quarter it with a knife, and place the quarters on top of each other. Halve and quarter these, to obtain 16 identical wedges from one leaf (depending on your needs, you can increase the quantity). Pile the wedges on top of each other.

2. To make the filling: break the egg into a bowl. Reserve a

little egg white for later to seal the *böreks*. Beat the rest
and mix in the cheese and parsley.

3. Spoon a little filling onto the broad end of each wedge,
   fold the sides over the filling, and roll up the *börek* on a
   board like a cigar, using a touch of egg white on the
   pointed end to seal it.

4. Heat plenty of oil in a deep pan and deep-fry the *böreks*.
   They are best served hot, when they are at the peak of
   their crunchiness, with a creamy heart.

Muşka Böreği
(Amulet Triangle *Börek*)

2 leaves of yufka *dough*
Filling:
stick of butter
1 onion (grated)
150 grams minced meat (veal or mutton)
freshly ground black pepper
parsley and dill (finely chopped)
oil for frying

Quick to prepare, this *börek* is another winner. Choose from
a broad range of fillings, from spicy cheeses to vegetables,
from shrimps to mushrooms (for the classic white cheese filling, see *Sigara Böreği* recipe). This recipe uses the traditional
minced-meat filling.

1. Spread the *yufkas* on a work surface. Cut into even-sized
   strips, about three fingers (5 centimeters) wide and 20
   centimeters long.

2. Prepare the filling by heating the butter in a skillet and

sautéing the onion until translucent. Stir in the meat, season with pepper and sparingly with salt (because *yufka* is already salted), and stir-fry until all the juices are absorbed. Remove from the heat, add the chopped herbs, stir, and set aside to cool slightly.

3. Spoon a little meat filling near one end and fold the nearest corner over the filling to make a triangle. Continue folding, securing the open sides in a neat triangular parcel. Finish by dampening the loose end with a little water to seal.

4. Heat the oil and deep-fry the *böreks* until deliciously puffed up. Serve at once as an appetizer, or with a robust green salad and a glass of red wine as a complete meal.

Puf Böreği
Puff *Börek*

about 4 cups wheat flour
1 cup water
salt
1 egg
½ cup olive oil

Filling:
1 egg
parsley and dill (finely chopped)
250 grams white or feta cheese
oil for frying

This puffed-up *börek* is the superstar in the constellation of *böreks*. Its delicate, flaky, melting-in-the-mouth texture makes it addictive. The use of a traditional *oklava* makes it easy to roll out the pastry into a large, fine sheet.

1. Knead the flour, water, salt, one of the eggs, and the olive oil into a pliable dough. Cover and leave to rest for about an hour.

2. Divide the dough into six identical pieces. Roll each piece into a circle about 20 centimeters in diameter. Brush with olive oil and place them one on top of each other.

3. When finished, fold up this stack of circles, knead briefly once more, and roll into a ball. Divide into two equal pieces and cover with a damp cloth.

4. Prepare the filling by breaking the second egg into a bowl. Beat it with a fork and add the parsley, dill, and cheese. Blend well to a creamy consistency.

5. On a spacious surface lightly dusted with extra flour or, better still, rice flour, roll out one of the balls as finely as possible with a rolling pin or *oklava* into a sheet about 60 centimeters (almost 2 feet) in diameter. Down one side of this sheet of dough, about four finger-widths in from the edge, place small mounds of filling in a row, spacing them evenly about four finger-widths apart. Leave enough space at the edge to fold the dough over the filling. Flip the outer edge over the filling, and press the rim of a glass or small metal lid into the dough to cut small semicircles around the mounds of filling. This seals the filling inside. Transferring cut *börek* pieces to a clean kitchen towel, repeat, row by row, with the rest of the dough and again with the second ball of dough. Knead the trimmings into another ball and repeat with the remaining filling.

6. Heat plenty of oil in a deep pan and deep-fry the *böreks* on both sides. Serve hot and puffed up, perhaps accompanied by a refreshing compote freshly made with seasonal fruit.

The Milky Way

BERRIN TOROLSAN

ಬಂ

TURKISH *MUHALLEBI* (milk pudding) satisfies children and adults alike, and some *muhallebi* are far too sophisticated for a child. In this piece, Torolsan revives the stars of Istanbul's vanishing pudding shops.

TWENTY YEARS ago in Istanbul they were everywhere, and there are still a few around—special little shops with a couple of marble-topped tables and Thonet chairs, not there in the name of fashion, but simply because that was when the place was last refurbished. A white-aproned waiter hastily wipes a table to make room for another customer. In a way these shops are as much a part of Istanbul life as cafés are in Vienna, though the food and the concept are entirely different, and there is not the same panache, of course. These simple shops offer only one specialty: milk puddings. Called *muhallebici*, they are pudding shops—milk parlors, if you like—and they operate quite separately from restaurants and patisseries.

Muhallebi is a sweet, milk-based cream, thickened only with starch (unlike custards and *crème pâtissière*, it contains no eggs), and it is a familiar dish from the Crimea to North Africa, from the Balkans to India. Even the name varies little from place to place. Only in Europe is it unknown, or perhaps forgotten.

In Turkey *muhallebi* forms part of everyone's diet, from babies to grandmothers, for it is wonderfully nourishing. It has two essential ingredients: pure starch—whether from the flour of rice, wheat, corn, or potatoes—which is entirely digestible; and milk, which is rich in protein, calcium, and vitamins.

In the distant past, before ready-made rice flour existed, and corn and potatoes were waiting to be discovered in America, rice flour was made at home. Whitened, short-grain rice grains, which contain more starch than long-grain rice, were ground or pounded and sifted to the desired fineness. To obtain the pure starch—*nişasta* in Turkish—the powdered rice was washed in hot water and filtered through layers of muslin.

The consistency of the *muhallebi* varies according to taste. Personally, I prefer a fairly creamy, rather than a dense, texture. You can obtain a thicker cream by increasing the ratio of rice or other flour to liquid. One kind of *muhallebi*, known as *taş* (or stone) *muhallebisi*, not surprisingly, is pretty solid.

Inexpensive, healthy, delectable, *muhallebi* itself is the cream, as it were, of a whole variety of milk puddings, all of which share much the same method of preparation. Because they all take their flavor from the milk, which is the main ingredient, a creamy full-fat cow's milk is preferable. Modern dieticians may frown at this, and at the addition of sugar and starch. Yet not one of the puddings featured here has anything like as much in the way of calories or fat as, say, a crème brûlée.

An entire food culture grew up around *muhallebi*. The special heart-shaped silver spoons with the maker's stamp that you find in antique shops are just one reminder. When the puddings had cooled, it used to be the custom to cover them with a paper stencil and shake powdered cinnamon over them. When the stencil was removed, the puddings might bear—in stylized calligraphy—the words *Afiyet olsun* ("*Bon appétit*") or "Long live the Sultan" or some such greeting. Later, under the Republic, they were replaced by a cinnamon crescent and star. Today, only the sprinkling of cinnamon remains.

I vaguely remember in my childhood seeing these stenciled crescent and stars in *muhallebi* shop windows. Less blurred is my memory of dozens of china dessert bowls, some delicate, others plain, all filled with *muhallebi* left to cool on the table in my grandmother's kitchen. Later I would be served with my own bowl with my initial, B, in cinnamon. My grandmother had cut a stencil for every one of my cousins, too.

The first mention of the dish as a dessert dates from 1473, when the imperial kitchen accounts of the Ottoman sultan Mehmet the Conqueror record that he and his retinue were served *muhallebi*. This is the very same dish that we know today. But *muhallebi* was not always such a simple affair. Medieval Arab cookery books give recipes for a dish of the same name that was a complicated confection of milk, rice, almonds, saffron, and chicken breast or other meat. This bears a striking resemblance to the medieval English *blancmanger*.

In the *Oxford Companion to Food*, Charles Perry writes, in the entry on blancmange: "The fourteenth- and fifteenth-century

English *blancmangers* were made of shredded chicken breast, sugar, rice, and either ground almonds or almond milk." Where did the dish originate—with the Romans, with the Arabs, or elsewhere? The question remains open. Colman Andrews tells us in *Catalan Cuisine* that Catalan monks claim to have invented *menjar blanc* near Tarragona in the eighth or ninth century. But did the influence of their new rulers, the Moors, have anything to do with it? This was not a dessert, but a thick gruel made of finely ground chicken or seafood steeped in spices and almond milk. In time, as it passed from court to court, and progressed from Barcelona to England, this savory was transformed into a fine dessert.

Turkey has three delicious but distinct "white" puddings, all related to *muhallebi*: *tavuk göğsü* (literally chicken breast), which is made, as its name suggests, with milk and shredded chicken breast and is eaten as a dessert; *sütlaç*, a rice and milk pudding of a creamy consistency; and *keşkül*, which is prepared with milk and almonds.

In the past *keşkül* required endless work and considerable expense. Large quantities of sweet-almond kernels were blanched and pounded in huge stone mortars. The milk had to cook with the almond extract for hours so that it would become glutinous and set. The top of the resulting cream was then decorated with edible gold and silver leaves.

This most luxurious of milk puddings is also sometimes called *keşkül-ü fukara*, the fakir's bowl. *Fakir* in modern Turkish means "poor," and is derived from the Arabic *faqir*. So how did this extravagant dish acquire such a contradictory name? *Fakirs* were also Indian ascetic mendicants, who would have been familiar in the Ottoman Empire. Abstaining from all worldly things, they had nothing but a loincloth and an elliptical bowl in which to receive donations of food. This bowl was usually made from the shell of coco-de-mer, the giant nuts that are often washed up on Indian shores. Just as the coconut was known as *hindistan cevizi*, or Indian nut, in the Ottoman Empire, so the coco-de-mer came to be called *keşkül-ü fukara*, the fakir's bowl. Could this association with the begging bowl, and the fact that the flesh of the ripe coco-de-mer is a sweet, creamy delicacy—not unlike this heavenly pudding—explain the name?

One of the many variations on *muhallebi* is *su* (water) *muhallebisi*, an opaque unsweetened jelly made with water and rice flour. It is sometimes eaten with grape molasses (*pekmez*), which suggests a rural rather than royal origin. A more refined version is a jellied cream prepared with milk and a little sugar, and served with lashings of rose water and icing sugar.

Alas, *muhallebi* shops are dwindling in number with every year that passes, replaced by posh cafés and pizzerias. This is a great shame, because their wares are simply delicious. Many years ago a friend who was working on a London fashion magazine was on a visit to Istanbul. One day we stopped in a *muhallebi* shop, where for the first time she tasted a water *muhallebi* with a large spoonful of salep ice cream on top, all liberally sprinkled with icing sugar and rose water. Ever since, whenever she sees me, she recalls the experience with enthusiastic sounds and gestures of immense pleasure.

These are a few of the specialities the milk pudding shops have to offer.

A Note on Rice Flour

Known as rice starch in America and *crème de riz* in France, rice flour is a staple in Turkey but may be harder to find elsewhere. Asian or Middle Eastern shops are good sources. Otherwise, corn starch, potato flour, or a mixture of the two makes a perfectly good substitute. The starch should be fresh and kept airtight, otherwise you will find greater quantities are required to thicken the pudding. You can also make the rice flour yourself the old-fashioned way. Rinse white short-grain rice and leave it to dry on a kitchen towel. Grind while still moist in a clean coffee grinder.

Quantities

The quantities given below (3 tea cups = 500 milliliters) make four small portions, but there are no hard-and-fast rules. The consistency and sweetness can be adjusted to taste.

Muhallebi
Milk Pudding

ιϽϽ

3 cups milk
4 tablespoons sugar
3 tablespoons rice flour
ground cinnamon

Much easier to make than any custard or mousse, *muhallebi* can be made with any starch available if rice flour is not at hand. Vanilla, mastic, lemon rind, cocoa powder, or ginger can be added to flavor the *muhallebi*, which also makes a practical cream for filling cakes and lining tarts.

1. Combine the milk and sugar in a heavy saucepan, and heat over a medium–high heat, stirring a little to dissolve the sugar.
2. Meanwhile, mix the rice flour in a small bowl with a little cold water, using a teaspoon, until it is well blended and forms a thin batter the consistency of single cream.
3. When the milk is hot and steaming, add the rice flour mixture to the pan, stirring constantly with a wooden spoon to prevent lumps from forming. Continue stirring until the mixture comes to a boil and is the consistency of a thick sauce. Cook for a further 3–4 minutes until it no

longer smells of raw flour, continuing to stir so as to prevent it sticking to the pan.

4. Remove from the heat and ladle the *muhallebi* while still hot into individual bowls. Hold the ladle high while pouring to create the bubbles on the surface appreciated by connoisseurs.

5. Serve cold, sprinkled with powdered cinnamon. This dessert tastes best the day it is made, but can be stored for up to three days in the fridge.

6. If you wish to stencil the top, cut the desired motif out of wax paper, place it on the surface of the *muhallebi* after it has cooled and set, and lightly sift powdered cinnamon over it. Remove and repeat with the remaining bowls. Alternatively, you can lightly stamp the tops with a biscuit cutter dipped in powdered cinnamon.

Sütlaç
Rice Pudding

3 tablespoons white short-grain rice
4 cups cold water
salt
3 cups milk
6 rounded tablespoons sugar

There are two secrets to an ambrosial *sütlaç*: rich, creamy milk and a long simmer over a very gentle heat (in the old days the pan was left on the dying embers overnight, as with porridge). It is also wise to leave it at least one night before serving. In some households and restaurants today, with time and patience in short supply, *sütlaç* is thickened with extra rice flour. But a long, gentle simmering allows the rice grains to break down and release their starch into the milk to form a gooey, homogeneous texture Mahmut bin Tosun, writing in 1893, recommended adding a piece of beeswax the size of a chickpea for an even creamier color.

1. Place the rinsed rice in a heavy pan with the cold water and a pinch of salt. Bring to a boil, then turn the heat to minimum and leave it, uncovered, for an hour or so, checking from time to time and giving it a stir, so that the rice doesn't stick to the bottom. Cook until the rice grains have almost dissolved and all the water has been absorbed.
2. Pour in the cold milk, bring to a boil, and turn down the heat as before. Allow to simmer very gently for 20 minutes, stirring occasionally.
3. Add the sugar and cook for a further 5 minutes, this time stirring constantly with a wooden spoon until all the sugar has dissolved and the pudding has reached a creamy consistency.
4. Pour into individual dishes and serve chilled. Alternatively pour into earthenware or ovenproof bowls. When it is cold and has formed a skin, scorch the surface under a hot grill. Serve cold.

Çukulatali Muhallebi
Chocolate Pudding

3 cups milk
4 tablespoons sugar
2 tablespoons cocoa powder
2 teaspoons instant coffee (optional)
2½ tablespoons corn starch
bitter chocolate shavings to garnish

This chocolate pudding is a winning version of the traditional favorite *muhallebi*. It is delicious and light and, unlike chocolate mousse, does not involve raw eggs. The coffee is optional, but it makes the taste of the chocolate more pronounced.

1. Heat the milk in a heavy saucepan.
2. In a bowl, combine the sugar, cocoa powder, and coffee, if used. Blend thoroughly with a teaspoon so that the fine cocoa powder coats all the sugar granules. Only then will the cocoa dissolve evenly in the milk.
3. Stir the mixture into the hot milk.
4. Dissolve the corn starch in a little extra cold milk or water to form a smooth batter. Add to the hot milk, increase the heat, and cook, stirring, until the mixture comes to a boil and thickens so that it coats the back of the spoon. Cook, stirring, for a further minute or two, and remove from the heat.
5. Ladle the hot mixture into individual bowls. While still hot, garnish the tops with the bitter chocolate shavings: rub a piece of chocolate against the chip blade of a hand-grater. The chocolate will half melt.
6. Serve chilled.

"When I first went to Istanbul thirty years ago, Istanbullus saw the cooking of the Anatolian provinces as crude and basic and full of garlic, spices, and hot red pepper. They saw their own cuisine as more European and refined. No one was interested in regional foods. But now their best restaurants serve foods from areas such as Gaziantep, Konya, and the Black Sea. My friend Nevin Halici (who was the first to travel around the country collecting regional recipes) and her brother Feyzi Halici (a poet and longtime senator who promoted regional cuisines by organizing cooking competitions and gastronomic congresses) took me to their favorite restaurant—Borsa.

"There are four Borsas. The famous old Borsa is in Beyoğlu, İstiklâl Caddesi. We went to the one in the İstinye Park luxury mall. It is like a grand old-style French restaurant with wood paneling and Murano chandeliers. The owner, Rasim Özkanca Bey, serves traditional dishes from different regions, especially from the Black Sea, where he is from, and presents them in an elegant way that can compete with any international nouvelle cuisine. Here is a list of what we had: aubergine salad; *su boregi beyaz peynirli*—baked pastry with creamy cheese; *manti*—tiny pasta stuffed with minced lamb with yogurt sauce and a sprinkling of melted butter and red pepper; maize flour fried in butter with a special Black Sea cheese; black cabbage stuffed with minced meat and rice with sumac; Jerusalem artichokes and leeks in olive oil, grilled turbot, anchovies, and baby red mullet; roasted baby lamb shanks served with *hünkar begendi*, an aubergine purée, and *iç pilav*, rice with raisins and tiny bits of liver; and veal meatballs with yoghurt. We finished with a heavenly assortment of fruits and pastries. It was paradise."

—Claudia Roden, author of *Arabesque: A Taste of Morocco, Turkey, and Lebanon* (Knopf, 2006) and *The New Book of Middle Eastern Food* (Knopf, 2000), among others

Albondigas

MATTHEW GOODMAN

ෆෞ

HERE IS a piece that originally appeared in one of my favorite food magazines, *The Art of Eating*, referred to as "the must-have foodie quarterly" by National Public Radio and by me as one of the best publications of any kind, ever (1 800 495 3944 / artofeating .com). The piece eventually became a chapter in the writer's very good cookbook *Jewish Food: The World at Table*, one of the most refreshing and enlightened Jewish cookbooks in print. In the cookbook, the author reminds readers to really, *really* squeeze out all the excess water from the potato and leeks or the meatballs won't have the proper consistency. Additionally, he notes that "correctly prepared, *albondigas* come out of the frying pan crisp outside and remarkably light inside, almost fluffy. The surprising softness of the interior results from the ground meat having been mixed not just with starch, as in most other meatballs, but also with some form of cooked vegetable. These meatballs are, in fact, mostly vegetable." I made these with ground turkey, instead of beef or lamb, and the results were delicious.

MATTHEW GOODMAN wrote the "Food Maven" column for *The Forward* for ten years and is the author of *Jewish Food: The World at Table* (Morrow, 2005), with recipes from thirty different Jewish communities around the world. His food writing has also appeared in *Bon Appétit* and *Brill's Content*, among others. He recently wrote *The Sun and the Moon: The*

Remarkable True Account of Hoaxes, Showmen, Dueling Journalists, and Lunar Man-Bats in Nineteenth-Century New York (Basic Books, 2008), a nonfiction narrative about a newspaper hoax in 1835 claiming that life had been discovered on the moon and involving P. T. Barnum and Edgar Allan Poe.

IT MAY not be possible to read the future in tea leaves or coffee grounds, but it is possible to read the past in meatballs. Certain ones, anyway—like the delicious Turkish Jewish meatballs called *albondigas*.

Correctly prepared, *albondigas* come out of the frying pan crisp outside and remarkably light inside, almost fluffy. The surprising softness of the interior results from the ground meat having been mixed not just with starch, as in most other meatballs, but also with some form of cooked vegetable. These meatballs are, in fact, mostly vegetable. It is not unusual for *albondigas* to contain potato, spinach, celery, or eggplant, but the most famous and popular kind is certainly *albondigas de prasa*: leek meatballs. A single mashed potato may also find its way into the mix along with a handful of ground walnuts, which not only add flavor but provide a contrasting texture to the softness of the rest. Usually the *albondigas* are first dredged in flour and then dipped in beaten egg—the reverse of most Western cookery—which turns them a somewhat mottled golden brown. Less often, they are dredged in flour alone, which gives the chestnut brown color we usually associate with meatballs. After frying, the *albondigas* are further enlivened by a dash of fresh lemon juice.

As someone who writes about Jewish food, I had long heard about *albondigas*, but I had never tasted one until a year ago, when a Turkish friend sent me a photocopy of *Sefarad Yemekleri*, "Sephardic Food." That cookbook, sadly now out of print, was published in 1990 by members of Istanbul's Jewish community, which today numbers about fifteen thousand, to raise money for a senior citizens' home. The book is a fascinating compilation of traditional Turkish Jewish recipes, among them such favorites as eggplant gratin, sweet-and-sour celery, and the sweetened rice-flour pudding called *sütlaç*.

Of the book's 141 recipes, seven are for *albondigas*, which suggests their importance to the community. *Albondigas* are perhaps the most beloved of all Turkish Jewish foods, served on the Sabbath, on holidays, at weddings, or, for that matter, on almost any other festive occasion. So it has been for a very long time. Some months ago I called up an acquaintance, Klara Perahya, a writer for the Istanbul Jewish weekly newspaper *Shalom* and a venerable *albondiga* maker. "When I make *albondigas*," she told me, "they are the same as my grandmother's *albondigas* from seventy years ago. A lot of things have changed, but *albondigas* never did." Perahya admits to having grown children, but she never reveals her age. When asked, she says only, "Old, old, old."

Adding chopped vegetables to meatballs appears to be one of the distinctive features of Jewish cuisine, commonplace in Jewish communities throughout Turkey and the Balkans but unknown outside them. Claudia Roden notes this in her exemplary *Book of Jewish Food*, and the cookbook author Nicholas Stavroulakis, the leading authority on Greek Jewish food, told me recently, "I can't say that we are the only people to do this—but we certainly do, and mixing vegetables and meat together to form meatballs is certainly neither Turkish nor Greek nor Bulgarian."

Why Jewish meatballs contain vegetables has never been answered definitively, but it likely has to do with the very popularity of the meatball among Jewish cooks. For them, the generally tenderer cuts of meat in the back of the animal are outlawed by the dictates of kashruth. (Jewish law forbids the consumption of the sciatic nerve, located in the hindquarters. The nerve can be removed, but the time and expense is, practically speaking, prohibitive.) As a result, Jews adopted various methods of tenderizing the mostly tougher meat from the forequarters. This resulted in the celebrated Jewish affinity for long-stewed pot roasts. But many times whole cuts were unavailable, and cooks could obtain only scraps, flavorful but very tough. They required chopping or grinding. Even this humble meat was relatively expensive for those in the lower reaches of society, and so a thrifty cook naturally sought to stretch the meat by combining it with cheaper, more plentiful ingredients. Meatballs were a perfect medium for incorporating bread crumbs, cooked rice, or mashed potato. In this way, meatballs are like that other classic forcemeat, gefilte fish. And like gefilte fish, meatballs could, if necessary, be made ahead of time and served cold on the Sabbath, when cooking was prohibited. So the meatball proved a special boon to Jewish cooks, who over time found that adding finely chopped vegetables to the meatballs not only further stretched the meat but also gave variety to a dish that might otherwise have become too familiar. In Turkey, the result was *albondigas*.

And that brings us to the name itself—it isn't Turkish. Turkish meatballs (which can include chopped onions, but not the wide variety of cooked vegetables in *albondigas*) are called *köfte*, from the Persian verb meaning "to pound," which is also the root of the Greek *keftedes*. The word *albondigas* probably comes from the Arabic *al bundaq*, meaning "round," though it might be a corrupted form of *albidaca*, meaning "chopped meat." As the British food historian John Cooper notes in his excellent *Eat and Be Satisfied: A Social History of Jewish Food*, the Arabs of the early medieval period, like the Jews shortly afterward, often used the toughest meat by chopping it and turning it into meatballs. Both the name and the practice, then, indicate that these meatballs originated in the Middle East and migrated west with the Moorish conquests, until they arrived in Spain, where they became known as *albondigas*.

Albondigas were extremely popular with the Jewish community in Spain, so much so that during the trials of the Inquisition in the fifteenth and sixteenth centuries, the preparation of *albondigas*, like the Sabbath stew *adafina*, was presented by prosecutors as evidence of secret Jewish practice. Of course, only Jews who stayed in Spain and converted to Catholicism were ever put on trial. The vast majority had long since fled, bringing their recipes for *albondigas* with them wherever they went, including Turkey, where they were welcomed by the Sultan Beyazit II—and where, half a millennium after the Spanish exile, Jews still call their meatballs *albondigas*.

These recipes, so little changed by time, exist today as enduring reminders of the capacity of the poor to become, if momentarily, rich: to overcome the strictures of poverty and turn the rudest fare into something delicious. The meat, tenderized by chopping and grinding, reveals the struggle to craft pleasing sustenance from seemingly forbidding ingredients, while the vegetables are the response to an otherwise wearying routine. The very name *albondigas* expresses broad swaths of European history, from the Arab conquests of the West to the exile of the Spanish Jews in the wake of the Inquisition. The present-day use of the name, too, shows the efforts of the Jews of Turkey to maintain their historical connection, over long centuries, to the homeland they so fervently loved and from which they fled in terror. Seemingly among the lowliest of foods, these meatballs are among the most glorious.

Albondigas de Prasa kon Muez
(Leek Meatballs with Walnuts)

ᗧᗤᗤ

This recipe is adapted from the cookbook *Sefarad Yemekleri*. Today, the meat is either pulverized in a food processor or chopped by hand with a knife, which gives a rougher texture, and, rather than olive oil, for a long time the meatballs have been fried in sunflower oil. Some Turkish recipes for the same leek meatballs call for adding soaked white bread to the meat instead of potato. For Passover, the meatballs are dredged in matzo meal instead of flour.

2 pounds (900 grams) medium leeks
1 large potato (about 1 pound, or 450 grams)
¾ pound (340 grams) ground beef or lamb
3 tablespoons coarsely chopped walnuts
3 eggs
salt and freshly ground pepper to taste
oil for frying
flour for dredging
a lemon

Discard the dark green portion of the leeks, and carefully wash the white and pale green part to rid it of all grit. Cut into ½-inch pieces. Peel and quarter the potato.

Bring a large pot of salted water to a boil. Add the leeks and the potato, and cook until soft, about 20 minutes. Drain well and cool. Squeeze as much water as possible from the leeks, and mash the potatoes.

In a large bowl, combine the leeks, potato, ground meat, walnuts, 1 egg, and a generous seasoning of salt and pepper. Place the mixture in the bowl of a food processor and pulse just until it comes together in a soft paste. Roll into balls about 1 inch in diameter.

Place a large serving platter in a 200° F (90° C) oven. Beat the remaining 2 eggs in a bowl and spread some flour on a plate. Heat ½ inch oil in a large skillet over medium-high until it is almost but not quite smoking. Roll the meatballs in flour, shaking off any excess, and then dip them in the egg. Place them gently in the hot oil, working in small batches so as not to cool the oil too much. Fry the meatballs, turning as necessary, until they are golden brown and cooked through—about 10 minutes. Drain them on paper towels, and keep them warm on the platter in the oven. When all the meatballs are done, squeeze lemon juice over them and serve hot. Serves 6.

"We in the States have only the barest idea of how rich and varied Turkish food is," notes Margo True, food editor at *Sunset* and formerly of *Saveur*. True was in Turkey for several weeks when she was working for *Saveur* and says she was "knocked out" by the depth and breadth of Turkish cuisine. There is no better place to experience this culinary depth and breadth than at Istanbul's Egyptian Spice Market, Mısır Çarşısı. The market, shaped like a giant letter L, is so named because when it was built, in 1648, all the goods sold there came from Cairo. The market was constructed as part of the Yeni Cami complex, with the rent from the shops used for the upkeep of the mosque (I always smile when I think that the Yeni Cami, or New Mosque, is so named because it was the last large mosque—in other words, the most recent—built during the classical period of Ottoman architecture, in 1663!

To clarify the dates: the full name of the mosque was Yeni Valide Camii, the Valide Sultan being the mother of the reigning sultan. It was begun in 1597, but in 1599 the architect died, so a new one carried on until 1603, when the death of Mehmet III halted construction as his mother then lost her power in the palace. The new sultan, Ahmet I, and his immediate successors weren't interested in completing construction, so the mosque sat, unfinished, for more than half a century, when it was destroyed by fire in 1660. The mother of Sultan Mehmet IV decided to rebuild the mosque as an act of piety.

According to John Freely, the Spice Market as we see it today was part of a much larger market, with birds and animals, that stretched to the shores of the Golden Horn. So if walking around a food market doesn't sound appealing to you, view the journey as a walk through a historic area where a market has existed for two thousand years, again according to Freely. It's also incredibly colorful (great for picture taking), with all the pyramids of ground spices, the hustle and bustle, and signs for "Turkish Viagra."

Ayla Algar, in *Classical Turkish Cooking*, tells us that the Spice Market had a central function in provisioning the whole city, but that, simultaneously, many districts were famous "for one or more particular commodity, so that the truly discriminating shopper had to tour much of the city to find all his needs: Çukurçeşme was celebrated for its pickles, Eyüb for its clotted cream, Kanlıca for its yogurt, Karaköy for its *poğaça* (enriched flaky rolls), and so on." Algar refers to the Spice Market as "an outpost of Anatolia situated in the heart of Istanbul. Most of the wares sold there originate in Anatolia, and the dominant atmosphere is the same one of businesslike sobriety that prevails in so many small Anatolian towns." Plenty of locals still shop at the Spice Market, and high-profile chefs, too.

A few specialty items to consider buying are: hazelnuts, pistachios, red-pepper flakes, ground sumac, pomegranate molasses or syrup, walnut oil, honey, dried figs, dates, apricots, rose petals, a brass or copper *cezve* for making coffee, brass pepper grinders, and handwoven baskets, traditionally lowered to the street from apartment windows above as a means of delivery for fresh bread and small grocery items. And if you run out of one of these foodstuffs once you're back home, Kalustyan's, in New York, is a longtime purveyor of Near and Far Eastern specialties (123 Lexington Avenue / 212 685 3451 / 800 352 3451 / kalustyans.com).

The prices are lower the further you delve into the market from the main entrance, especially on the side streets, appropriately named Street of the Coffee Roasters, Street of the Scale Makers, Street of the Wicker Weavers, etc.—one is never in doubt about what is for sale in which street. Time your visit to end with lunch at Pandeli (open only for lunch; Mısır Çarşısı 1 / +90 212 527 3909), located down the stairs to the left of the main entrance of the market. It's one of the oldest restaurants in Istanbul, dating from 1901, and though both the staff and the food receive mixed reviews, you'll have a fine meal there. If your timing is off, at least step inside to see its turquoise-aqua tiled interior, which elicits lots of wows.

Eating in Istanbul

ANYA VON BREMZEN

৪৫

FROM STREET food to chic new restaurants, Anya von Bremzen shares a true cornucopia of choices for visitors in this piece. *Afiyet olsun!* ("Bon appétit!") (And the phrase to thank the people who have prepared your food is *Elinize sağlık!*, "May God give health to your hands.")

ANYA VON BREMZEN, introduced previously, is the author, most recently, of *The New Spanish Table* (Workman, 2005). She wrote this piece for *Departures*, the magazine exclusively for American Express Platinum Card holders.

STANDING ON the Galata Bridge eating a peach, I'm only half looking at the lineup of imperial mosques along the Golden Horn. Instead I'm contemplating my new purchase, which isn't a gold bracelet from the Grand Bazaar or a *kilim*—though I certainly need one. What I've bought is an apartment, a little place with a beautiful Bosporus view in the neighborhood of Cihangir, Istanbul's leafy hub of café life. The thought of my acquisition has me in a state of simultaneous gloom and euphoria. Gloom because Turkey's currency is fluctuating like crazy, because the prospect of the country's joining the

EU seems real one day and phantasmagoric the next, because the local Ikea has sold out of the extralong curtain rods I need. Euphoria because to me Istanbul is the most fascinating, most ravishing city on earth, a feeling that hasn't wavered since I first ate a peach on the Galata Bridge twenty years ago.

Everything one hears about Istanbul is pretty much true. Yes, the Hagia Sophia is big and byzantine, the Grand Bazaar both a treasure trove and a tourist trap. Yes, this metropolis of twelve million people physically and metaphorically straddles Europe and Asia. It is by turns provincial and cosmopolitan, Muslim yet resolutely secular, exhilarating and exasperating. Even the rumors of Istanbul's transcendent new coolness aren't vastly exaggerated. Beyond the clichés, though, what keeps luring me back is the texture of everyday life. The ferry ride at dusk as the skies flare cinematically over the minarets. The tulip-shaped glasses at my corner tea garden. The courtly smile of my local pistachio vendor. And the food.

With the endless grills, the subtle spicing, the celebration of yogurt, legumes, and sun-ripened vegetables, Turkish cuisine is the last frontier of healthy Mediterranean cooking. The kebabs and savory pastries called *börek* alone are reason enough to move here. While Istanbul isn't the next capital of Spanish-style avantgarde cooking—so fashionable in Europe these days—its hedonistic high society ensures that there are plenty of spots that outglamour anything in Miami Beach or Hong Kong.

It's a sprawling city, divided into three parts by the Bosporus strait and its offshoot, the Golden Horn. Though many tourists tend to stick close to the Old City—especially the historic Sultanahmet district around Topkapı Palace, the Hagia Sophia, and the Blue Mosque—to truly experience Istanbul's food, you have to go a bit farther afield. Best of all, meals often come framed by views so breathtakingly beautiful, it's hard to shake the feeling that this city is a mirage.

SEARCHING FOR STREET FOOD

On my first day back in Istanbul, I enlist my friend Engin Akin to accompany me on a street food tour. A columnist for the Turkish newspaper *Vatan*, Engin has been my guide to the city's foodscape for more than a decade. In the mood to do something unabashedly touristy before eating, we visit Topkapı Palace, built by Sultan Mehmet the Conqueror after he seized Constantinople in 1453. Separate buildings house the palace kitchens under domes that bring to mind giant meringues. Ottoman sultans clearly had a serious food fetish: A staff of more than a thousand cooks was organized into guilds, each specializing in a particular item, say, halvah or kebabs. Over six centuries of refinements and codification, the Ottomans developed a culinary culture every bit as sophisticated as that of the Chinese or the French.

But today the Sultanahmet district is not exactly the seat of sophisticated Ottoman dining. What one eats here is *köfte*, the addictive grilled meatballs that are a staple of millions of working-class lunches. The Hagia Sophia of *köfte* joints, as it were, is **Tarihi Sultanahmet Köftecisi**, founded more than eighty years ago and still run by the same family. Packed in behind the old marble tables, everyone orders the meatballs—crusty, springy, and suffused with smoke—served with *piyaz*, a lemony white-bean salad. To drink, there's a tart, thin yogurt beverage called *ayran*. It's good to be back.

"Turkish cuisine marries palace finesse with rugged nomadic traditions. Think of all the grills, yogurt, and butter," Engin says as her driver whisks us across the Galata Bridge and over the Golden Horn to the port area of Karaköy. Our grail is the shop **Karaköy Güllüoğlu**, renowned for its baklava and *börek*. These incomparably flaky pastries are fashioned from *yufka*—phyllo, to the Greeks—a multilayered dough of Turkish nomadic origins rendered perfect and paper-thin by Topkapı chefs. Güllüoğlu's pistachio-infused, not-too-sweet baklava puts the leaden Greek version to shame. A few bites of the buttery spinach *börek* and we're off again, heading into the heart of the Beyoğlu district.

We stop for a quick *lahmacun*, the wafer-thin pizza with a smear of spicy ground lamb that's baked in a wood-burning oven. Next we buy *simit* from a mustachioed street vendor. These dense, chewy bread rings, Istanbul's most traditional and ubiquitous street snack, are brushed with molasses, encrusted with sesame seeds, and baked to a deep amber tan.

Winding down, we stop at **Mado**, opposite the Lycée Galatasaray, once Turkey's Eton. This smart café with locations all over town specializes in ice cream thickened with salep, a powder milled from wild orchid bulbs grown in the Anatolian mountains. It gives the ice cream, made without cream or eggs, its exotically elastic texture. Mado's flavors are almost surreally vivid. Licking on our cones, we stroll on, arguing about which is best: pistachio, sour cherry, or mulberry. The word *salep*, Engin informs me, comes from the Arabic term for "fox testicles."

Istanbul's Foodscape

The easiest way to get around this sprawling city is by taxi, though if you're heading across to the Asian side or up the Bosporus, ferry rides can be magical—especially at sunset. Fares are cheap, but be sure to have your concierge write down directions. Of course, Istanbul is a magnificent place to wander on foot, making occasional stops for *çay* (tea) at the ubiquitous tea houses. At better restaurants, at least some English is typically spoken and English menus are often available. Perhaps the two most invaluable Turkish words to learn are *teşekkür ederim*, or thank you.

---

360 Istanbul Dinner, $200. İstiklâl Caddesi 311, Misir Apartments, eighth floor, Beyoğlu / +90 212 251 1042 / 360istanbul.com

Boğaziçi Borsa/Loft Dinner, $200. Darülbedayi Caddesi, Istanbul Convention Center, Harbiye / +90 212 232 4201 / borsarestaurants.com; +90 212 219 6384 / loftrestbar.com

Çiya Dinner, $40. Güneşlibahçe Sokak 48B / +90 216 336 3013 / ciya.com.tr

Hünkar Dinner, $100. Mim Kemal Öke Caddesi 21, Nişantaşi / +90 212 225 4665

Kale Çay Bahçesi Breakfast, $25. Yahya Kemal Caddesi 36, Rumeli Hisarı / +90 212 257 5578

Karaköy Güllüoğlu *Börek*, from $5 per pound. Rhıtım Caddesi 29, Karaköy / +90 212 293 0910 / gulluoglu.biz

Köşebaşi at Reina Dinner, $110. Muallim Naci Caddesi 44, Ortaköy / +90 212 258 0683 / kosebasi.com.tr

Mado Ice cream, $6 per pound. İstiklâl Caddesi 186/2, Beyoğlu / +90 212 244 1781 / mado.com.tr

Mikla Dinner, $125. The Marmara Pera, Meşrutiyet Caddesi 167–185, Tepebaşı / +90 212 293 5656 / istanbulyi.com

Tarihi Sultanahmet Köftecisi Lunch, $35. Divanyolu Caddesi 12, Sultanahmet / +90 212 520 0566

BEYOĞLU: TWENTY-FIRST-CENTURY ISTANBUL

Much has been said about the rampant gentrification of Beyoğlu, formerly Pera, the European quarter first settled by Genovese traders. Back in the nineteenth century, İstiklâl Caddesi, the district's thronged pedestrian thoroughfare, was a glamorous cosmopolitan boulevard known as the Grande Rue de Pera. Once flanked with cafés, embassies, and Parisian-style arcades, the street has recently been repaved with ungainly slabs of granite, while its weathered pâtisseries and old *döner* dives are yielding to latte pushers and international chains.

A few hours on İstiklâl can be an exercise in *hüzün*, the melancholy yearning for a crumbling past that pervades Nobel Prize–winning novelist Orhan Pamuk's *Istanbul: Memories and the City*. Still, the district is home to some of the city's most stylish and sophisticated restaurants.

Typifying Beyoğlu's thrust into the globalized future is **360 Istanbul**, a restaurant-cum-club that resembles a postindustrial glass house set atop a nineteenth-century building overlooking the Bosporus. At the stoves is the indecently handsome South African chef-owner Mike Norman, whose menu—tandoori chicken pizza, beef carpaccio, zucchini blossom *dolmas*—is as giddily international as the crowd.

Some of the fickle Turkish beau monders who couldn't get enough of 360 when it opened three years ago have since migrated to **Mikla**, owned by Mehmet Gürs, the lanky charismatic grand vizier of Istanbul's restaurant scene. Following the success of his previous ventures, Lokanta and NuTeras, which jump-started the revitalization of the downtrodden Tepebaşı Boulevard near İstiklâl, Gürs opened Mikla on the seventeenth floor of the Marmara Pera hotel in 2005. The thirty-eight-year-old Gürs, who has a Finnish mother and a Turkish architect father, grew up shuffling between Stockholm and Istanbul. ("We celebrated *bayram* with a Turkish feast and Christmas with pig's feet and moose roast," he recalls.) In 1994, after graduating from Johnson & Wales, he settled in Turkey, bringing with him a flair for Scandinavian design and a sharp minimalist cooking style that defines his nine restaurants.

Mikla is his masterpiece, commanding Istanbul's most breathtaking panorama from its glassy perch. Striped marble, dark wood, and Alvar Aalto chairs set the scene for food that fuses

Turkish ingredients with Gürs's Nordic penchant for raw fish and smoky-salty flavors. There's a luminously fresh sea bass carpaccio sprinkled with salmon eggs, lemon, and dill. *Hamsi*, anchovies from the Black Sea, are ingeniously laminated onto gossamer slices of toast and highlighted with a lemony foam. Gürs's shank of grass-fed Turkish lamb is slowly cooked to a melting tenderness and accented with lingonberries. Still, it's hard to concentrate on the plates when the domes and minarets of the Old City are glowing below and you can play Name That Landmark. Far left? The stubby tower of Topkapı Palace. To its right? The eternal Hagia Sophia. Looming over it all is the swelling vision of the Süleymaniye Mosque, Istanbul's masterpiece by Mimar Sinan, the Michelangelo of Ottoman architects.

ASIAN SPICE: CROSSING TO KADIKÖY

Too few Americans bother to make the trip across the Bosporus to Istanbul's Asian side. Bourgeois Turks, meanwhile, find little reason to go to the Old City unless they wish to have curtains made on the clamorous alleys of Mahmud Paşa or visit a certain goldsmith inside the Grand Bazaar. My own treks to Asia usually revolve around meals at **Çiya**, the most intriguing restaurant in the folksy Kadıköy quarter.

Getting there by the hulking public ferry is part of the thrill. Unceremoniously, I elbow my way to the open upper deck and accept a glass of *çay* (tea) from a vendor. For the next twenty minutes I'm sailing to Byzantium. As the boat casts off, Süleymaniye's cascading domes rise behind and the conical-capped Galata Tower swings into view on the Beyoğlu side. Soon the Topkapı Palace assembles itself and the profile of the Blue Mosque joins in as the twilight sky turns a dazzling orange behind it. We sail to the sounds of seagulls squawking and the muezzins' echoing calls to prayer. It's the most magical public-transport experience you can have for less than a buck, plus thirty cents for the tea.

After landing, I cross the street and veer into a buoyant mercantile hub, where the aroma of roasting coffee mingles with that of briny grape leaves. Çiya, which sits on a market street, is actually a mini empire: two kebab places and the cafeteria-style Çiya Sofrasi, where diners help themselves to cold snacks, then order hot specials dished out from bubbling pots. The mischievous fortyish owner, Musa Dagdeviren, is a chef as well as publisher of a Turkish food and culture magazine. He serves up regional specialties such as tiny meatballs in sour-cherry sauce; a lemony salad of mastic leaves; and dried eggplant *dolmas* with a rice filling sweet and sour from pomegranate molasses. At the larger of Çiya's two kebab places—be sure to book on the rooftop terrace—the braziers turn out beautifully marbled cylinders of minced lamb grilled with loquat, quince, or spring onions. I like to end with the *tahinli ekmek*, a paper-thin disk of dough flash-baked with tahini and sugar. I'm amazed this brilliant dessert pizza idea has never occurred to Wolfgang Puck.

ON THE BANKS OF THE BOSPORUS

Come warm weather, locals flock to the Bosporus with the determination of migrating birds. This narrow, nineteen-mile-long strait, stretching from the Sea of Marmara to the Black Sea and separating Europe from Asia, just might be the world's most adored and fully utilized body of water. Locals wax rhapsodic about its hilly green shores and vigorous breezes. They love the genteel villages lined with wooden waterfront mansions called *yalılar*, some of them freshly painted, others in a state of romantic decay. And they'll invariably recommend that you spend a languorous weekend morning at one of the outdoor cafés near the Rumeli Hisarı Fortress, erected in 1452 by Mehmet the Conqueror as he plotted the siege of Constantinople. If you're coming from Sultanahmet, it's a beautiful half-hour taxi ride along the Bosporus.

I usually gravitate to **Kale Çay Bahçesi**, which serves an exemplary Turkish breakfast of feta, olives, crunchy cucumbers, slender green peppers, *simit*, and jam. Over endless glasses of tea, I take in the Bosporus promenade, where suntanned men fish, couples nuzzle, chic twenty-somethings in dashing sunglasses and designer headscarves loll about alongside tattooed beauties with bare midriffs. Ignoring warnings about treacherous currents and boat traffic, small boys leap into the steely waters. Giant freighters glide up and down. It's easy to sit and stare forever.

Another ritual here is eating fish at the waterside restaurants. For outsiders, it's hard to understand why locals maintain such fierce loyalty to a particular fish house, say, Kiyi or Iskele. The menus are fairly identical. Small dishes, or *meze*, such as smoky eggplant spread, feta with melon, and buttery *lakerda* (cured bonito), give way to fried calamari and warm eggplant with yogurt. It's all washed down with *rakı*, the anise-scented Turkish spirit. Then pick your catch—mackerel, sea bass, bluefish—fried or grilled.

Busy by day, the road along the strait is bumper-to-bumper on warm summer nights as Istanbul's jeunesse dorée inch their Mercedes convertibles toward waterside nightspots. The traffic comes to a lurching standstill at **Reina**, whose valets are blamed for notorious bottlenecks. Reina is actually a bazaar of six restaurants that morph into one giant after-hours club. Inside, the open-air space is breezy and sultry, filled with decorative-looking people ogling each other in the glint of a vast chandelier.

Those who come here to eat book at **Köşebaşi**. Some ten years ago the owner of the original Köşebaşi in the Levent district had the smart idea of serving ur-traditional eastern Turkish kebabs on white tablecloths in modern surroundings. It was a huge success, spawning an army of imitators and a chain of Köşebaşi restaurants. Ordering is a no-brainer. First, let the waiters mosaic your table with plates of spicy dips, mini *lahmacun*, and herbaceous chopped salads with tangy pomegranate. Then move on to the signature dish, *çöp şiş*, small tender lamb cubes marinated in a recipe that is more zealously guarded than the formula for Coca-Cola. Sprinkle with spices, wrap in lavash bread, plop it in your mouth, and savor the scene. As soon as the blaring Anatolian pop starts up, flee.

TRULY TURKISH IN NIŞANTAŞİ

When Istanbul residents are not eating kebabs or grilled fish or sushi at glamorous spots, they pine for their mother's stews and stuffed vegetables, lamenting how difficult it is to find good home cooking at restaurants that aren't outright dives. **Hünkar**, tucked away on a side street in the chic shopping neighborhood of Nişantaşı, is an exception. Foreigners love the place because owner Feridun Ugümü—imagine a Turkish Zero Mostel—personally guides them through the cold *meze* case and the display of tender braises and stews. The moneyed Nişantaşı locals go for Hünkar's cosmopolitan ambience. With dark wainscoting, red lanterns, and piles of fruit by the entrance, this could be a bistro in Buenos Aires or Zurich. That is, until you taste the handmade *manti* (thimble-size meat dumplings) under a tart cloak of yogurt; the Hünkar *begendi*, a velvety warm eggplant purée enriched with milk and cheese; or a stunning fresh anchovy pilaf studded with currants and pine nuts. And it would be reckless to pass on dessert, perhaps *sütlü kadayıf*, a crunchy shredded wheat nest with a walnut heart framed by a delicate milk sauce. Very Ottoman.

My own favorite Turkish dish is one of the simplest, never mind its tongue-twisting name, *zeytinyağlı* (*zey*-tihn-*yah*-lih). It's a wondrous silken veggie confit in which broad beans, artichokes, and celery root are braised for an eternity in olive oil and a secret pinch of sugar that teases out their natural sweetness. It'll forever ruin your appetite for al dente green beans.

Every place in town serves decent olive oil braises, but those by **Boğaziçi Borsa** (in Harbiye, adjacent to Nişantaşı) are in a league of their own. So is its red bean *pilaki*—a tomatoey Armenian stew cooked for twelve hours—and the deeply satisfying *keşkek*, a kind of creamy wheat berry risotto with shreds of lamb. This big, handsomely modern place was conceived by restaurateur Rasim Ozkanca because he, too, pined for great Turkish home cooking. His authentic regional menu is laced with a strong preservationist streak and a good deal of ingredient fetishism. That crumbly, stinky *tulum* cheese is from a special maker in the city of Erzincan; the pomegranate syrup is produced in Mardin; the fish is caught in the cold Black Sea, where they're fattest. Esoteric sweet wines made from sour cherries or Turkish Çalkarası grapes complete the meal. Ozkanca's son Umut, who trained in the States, presides over the creative Mediterranean fusion menu at **Loft**, downstairs from Borsa. His clubby, on-the-scene sister, Bahar, runs the smart restaurant at the Istanbul Modern museum near my home.

Here, overlooking the Bosporus and the Hagia Sophia, I can have trendy salads and sandwiches alongside *manti* and stuffed purple cabbage that taste just like Mom's. It's perfect, especially after a day of haranguing contractors and comparing faucets at hellish hardware emporiums for my new apartment. As I eat, gloom gives way to euphoria.

Engin Akin has said that "palace cuisine is the trunk of the tree, while all the other influences constitute the tree's roots." The chefs of the sultans duly earned the title "Frenchmen of the East," yet no one really knows *exactly* what was prepared in the Topkapı Palace kitchens; the archives house no recipes, and cooks during that time may not have been literate. But one can glean something of the scope of what was prepared by reviewing a list of kitchen ingredients purchased in a single year, 1640. Harry Nickles, in *Middle Eastern Cooking*, notes that meat was preeminent, at 1,131 tons. He continues:

> *The spinach ordered came to 92 tons; carrots, evidently not in favor, to less than a ton; and a category of unspecified "vegetables" to 94 tons. In a feat of caterer's accounting, separate entries were made for 320,350 heads of lettuce and 11,720 cabbages. Rice far outstripped wheat, 265 tons to three. Among dairy products, 14 tons of yogurt were listed, and four of cheese, along with 2,720 plates of kaymak [a very rich clotted cream extracted from six times its volume of milk; the word also refers to a flattering description of a pretty girl]. Egg purchases exceed 18,000 dozen. And tartness apparently won out over sweetness, with 59 tons of vinegar and 19 of lemons against ten tons of sugar (a golden abundance of honey probably corrected the imbalance, but does not appear in the record).*

Nickles goes on to say that written menus of the time reveal that the soup chef alone had nearly forty soups in his repertoire, but the names, surviving in the Arabic writing of that day, have no equivalents in modern Turkish and defy translation. Some of the dishes were reportedly magnificent: gold and precious stones were sometimes pulverized and added to the sultans' more ambitious dishes!

Sharon Croxford and Ozge Samancı are the team behind the Istanbul Food Workshop, which offers hands-on cooking classes and gourmet food walking tours. Croxford trained as a dietitian in Australia and then as a chef at Leith's School of Food and Wine in London, where she has been teaching cooking, food science, nutrition, and dietetics at King's College for part of the year. She's now at the Yeditepe University gastronomy department to teach cooking practice. Samancı is a renowned food historian specializing in Turkish-Ottoman cuisine and she is also on the faculty of Yeditepe University. Together they wrote *Flavours of Istanbul* (see Recommended Reading, page 394, for more details) and they are passionate about sharing knowledge and experiences of Turkish food with those who want to learn. They emphasize that scholars and gastronomes consider Turkish to be one of the world's finest cuisines, and that Turkish cuisine is, in essence, Istanbul's cuisine, which in turn represents the culinary tradition of Ottoman palace cuisine.

The complexity of Turkish food is the result of the varied culinary traditions in lands that were once part of the Ottoman Empire. Though many of these old recipes are still made in contemporary Turkish kitchens, others have been lost, and Sharon and Ozge aim to recover and reintroduce some of these. Programs are seasonal, with options for sessions of a half day to several days. Classes are of three to six people and are held in a semiprofessional kitchen in a charming home where the neighborhoods of Fener and Balat meet. (The Tahtaminare Mosque is directly across the street; Balat's Tuesday food market is a short walk away; traditional bakeries of bread and biscuits are steps away; and sites nearby include the Greek Patriarchate, Ahrida Synagogue, and Saint Stephen of the Bulgars Church.) Gourmet walking tours—which are proving to be as popular as the classes—include visits to local markets and specialist shops and are typically followed by preparation of an Ottoman feast. Customized programs are happily arranged, and special classes for Ramadan and Kurban Bayramz are also offered. (+90 212 534 4788 / istanbulfoodworkshop.com).

I asked Sharon if there were many kitchen utensils used in

preparing Turkish dishes that are typically Turkish, perhaps found only in Turkey. She replied that in fact she had written an article, "10 Essential Items for Your Turkish Kitchen," for *Today's Zaman*, an online newspaper, and they appear below with slightly condensed descriptions (to read the full article, visit Todayszaman.com):

- *Saç*: A *saç* is a rounded griddle, available in many sizes, that's used to make a simple snack called *gözleme*, thinly rolled pieces of dough (*yufka*) sprinkled with a filling of cheese and parsley, minced meat, or spiced potato. You can buy a complete kit that comes with a gas inlet attached or a roughly prepared single griddle that doubles as a convex wok-style pan (and referred to as both *tava* and *saç*). Griddles and larger pieces of cooking equipment are found beyond the end of Hasırcılar Caddesi on Sobacılar (Stove Makers) Caddesi, near the main road along the Golden Horn across from the Istanbul Commerce University in Eminönü and at local markets.

- *Oklava*: This is the word for the long, thin rolling pin used to make *yufka*, which in turn is used not only for *gözleme* but also for baklava and *börek*. Varying lengths of *oklava* are available, and they're found in the same streets where a *saç* is sold. The larger the *oklava*, the easier to work the dough, so opt for one that's at least sixty centimeters long.

- *Sahan*: A *sahan* is a small, shallow pan in which *menemen*, the classic breakfast dish, is cooked. More traditional *sahans* are made of tin-lined copper with ornamental handles, but there is a range of conventional pans available with or without lids.

- *Copper pots and pans*: Chefs attest to the superior flavor and texture of pilafs cooked in a copper pan, along with the multitude of stewed and braised dishes found in Turkish cuisine. These come in sizes large and small, the smaller ones used for melting butter that tops İskender kebab as well as for a multitude of other uses. The trick when buying these pans is to check that the weight of the handle is in proportion to the base. There is nothing worse than setting a carefully prepared dish that you intend to present in the pan on the hot plate only to find it tip all over the stove.

- *Copper bowls*: A unique addition to your Turkish kitchen is the small, silver looking bowls, some with ornamental handles, used for sipping *ayran*, the savory drink made from yogurt and water in southwestern Turkey. They can stand in as a sherbet bowl for your Ottoman-themed dinners or serve as attractive soup-bowl holders in winter. Usually accompanied by small silver ladles, these are difficult to find in stores outside the region but can be found in markets, especially those set up for special occasions.

- *Şiş skewers*: The *şiş* and the *döner* kebab are two international Turkish food icons. For a real taste of Turkey and the Ottoman Empire before it, look for skewers with figures of the famous shadow puppets, Karagöz and Hacivat, or other Ottoman and Turkish symbols.

Here's Sharon's recipe for a great chicken and bay leaf *şiş* for two:

2 chicken breasts, chopped into large cubes
2 garlic cloves, crushed
2 tablespoons olive oil

2 tablespoons onion juice, extracted from one small onion,
   grated
12–15 bay leaves.

Place all ingredients in a large bowl or plastic bag, massage together, and allow to marinate for 1 to 2 hours. Remove and thread chicken pieces and bay leaves on *şiş* skewers. Cook on reheated oiled griddle or charcoal grill for several minutes on each side and serve.

- *Turkish coffee set*: Coffeepots (*cezve*) of varying sizes are available at many market stalls, especially in the streets around the Spice Market. Buy according to the number of cups you usually make or a little larger for the unexpected guest. Coffee cups come in a bowl style without handles, as well as those that resemble espresso cups. Look around for those that suit your style and budget.

- *Turkish tea glasses and double teapot*: A double teapot (*çaydanlık*) is a must for serious tea drinkers. Choose one that will be large enough to boil water for your usual number of cups. Keep in mind that the bottom pot is where the water is boiled; then it's transferred into the top pot that contains the tea. After the tea steeps, it's poured into individual glasses.

- *Wooden spoons*: Wooden spoons in an impressive range of sizes can also be found in most markets across Turkey as well as small shops around the Spice Market. Many of the large ladles are characteristically hand-carved.

- *Porcelain*: If stepping back into the past with Ottoman-flavored menus appeals, try out some of the glassware and porcelain based on that used in the Topkapı and Dolmabahçe palaces. To find these items, you will need to step away from the hustle and bustle of Eminönü and visit one of the many shops and outlets that specialize in re-creating these touches of the past.

Kitchen Supply Stores

Bozaydin (Nalburlar/Sobacılar Sokak 11, Eminönü / +90 212 522 3134). For a range of griddles and pastry trays.

Kütahya Porselen (kutahyaporselen.com.tr). For a range of traditional-style coffee cups, pitchers, and service plates.

Paşabahçe (pasabahce.com.tr). Paşabahçe has many stores; the Butik section houses a range of traditional Ottoman-inspired pieces.

TBMM Milli Saraylar Depo-Müze (Located in the old Dolmabahçe kitchens in Beşiktaş / +90 212 227 6671 / millisaraylar.gov.tr). This museum of items, many from the Dolmabahçe Palace kitchen, also sells reproduction pieces.

Ünal Cam (Tahmis Sokak 68, Eminönü, just outside the Spice Market / +90 212 511 2551 / unalcam.com). The Web site lists a range of traditional-style glass containers, but the shop sells just about any kitchen item available.

"In 2000, I was invited to Istanbul to study the cuisine. I immediately fell in love. It's a city that I return to over and over for inspiration. My favorite restaurant in the world is Çiya. When I dine there, I'm so excited about what I'm eating, I can't stay seated. I dream about *börek* and *kaymak* in the Beşiktaş Market, one of my favorite markets to stroll around in. I could die eating *manti* and *puf börek* at Hünkar restaurant. The generous and hospitable people had me charmed more than any other place I've traveled. I miss the view and sounds from the roof deck of the Empress Zoe Hotel, and sipping tea in my favorite carpet shop, Noah's Ark. I could go on and on. . . ."

—Ana Sortun, the chef and owner of Oleana Restaurant, in Cambridge, Massachusetts; named Best Chef: Northeast, 2005, James Beard Foundation Awards

---

David Rosengarten, in his book *Taste: One Palate's Journey Through the World's Greatest Dishes*, shares some words of advice about eating while traveling that could easily have been written by me, and as I feel they are worth repeating, I will share some of them with you. Rosengarten acknowledges that travelers may have to try hard to create what he refers to as a "meaningful and authentic brush with the local food." He mentions he knows some dedicated foodies who have resorted to McDonald's in other countries on occasion. Sometimes even adventurous eaters, when traveling, start craving hamburgers and bacon and eggs because nostalgia and desire for familiar creature comforts get the better of them. Rosengarten admonishes us to put these temptations out of our minds, and says (and I completely agree), "If you want to eat as you do at home . . . stay at home! Travel is your single greatest chance to understand the food of another country—but you will squander your chance if you don't completely dedicate yourself to the food of that country while you're there!"

He recommends throwing yourself into the gastronomic reality of a country: "Eat the breakfast they eat. Eat the lunch they eat. Eat the dinner they eat. Eat these meals at the times they eat them. Eat between meals only as they do. Drink what they drink, when they drink it. . . . After a week of following their schedule and habits, you will begin to have insights into that country's food that you would never have had otherwise."

Among his list of ten tips (which, again, you may consider my own as well) are: read everything you can about the food of the country in advance—include cookbooks, travel and restaurant guides, and food dictionaries; talk to people who are gastronomically knowledgeable before you leave; be an investigative reporter when you arrive, asking questions, taking notes, listening; take cooking classes; even if you're not staying in accommodations with a kitchen; don't fail to walk around the local food markets—you can always buy some things for a picnic and you'll see what's local; and don't eat exclusively at the famous-name restaurants if you want to experience a country's most authentic food.

RECOMMENDED READING

Cookbooks

Arabesque: A Taste of Morocco, Turkey, and Lebanon, by Claudia
Roden (Knopf, 2005). Roden notes in her excellent book that
a sophisticated, aristocratic cuisine developed in Constantinople when it was, for more than four hundred years, the glittering capital city of the Ottoman Empire. "That cuisine came
to be considered on a par with those of France and China.
While many of the more elaborate dishes have disappeared,
what you find in homes in Istanbul today and on the standard
menus of Turkish restaurants are simplified adapted versions of
that high style." Regional cuisines of Turkey were barely
known outside of their localities, Roden says, until the arrival
of millions of migrants from rural and eastern Turkey over the
last decades.

Roden also notes that the specialization in the food industry
is a legacy of the organization in the Ottoman palace kitchens
where cooks were entrusted with one type of food only, such
as soups, kebabs, or jams. So *pideci* specialize in *lahmacun*, a
Turkish type of meat pizza; *börekçi* specialize in all kinds of pies;
işkembeci are tripe soup eateries; *muhallebicis* offer milk puddings;
and *baklavaci* sell baklavas and other pastries. Note: in addition
to these there are also *pastahaneler* (European-style bakeries or
patisseries) and *lokantalar* (singular is *lokanta*, referring to a place
serving the Turkish version of comfort food; in recent years
newfangled versions of these have opened, notably Lokanta,
one of the restaurants under the helm of celebrity chef
Mehmet Gürs, now sadly closed).

The Art of Turkish Cooking: Or, Delectable Delights of Topkapı, by Neşet Eren (Doubleday, 1969) This may be among the first Turkish cookbooks to be published in the States. The author grew up in a home that was the headquarters of the Bektaşi Order of Dervishes, of which her family were the heads. The house was kept open day and night to all the members of the sect who came by, and therefore it was a real challenge to the cook since no one ever knew how many people might be sitting around the table. This is more interesting to read for the anecdotes—"In Turkey you never order peaches. You must specify whether you want Bursa peaches or Izmir peaches"— and explanations than for being a must-have recipe book.

A Book of Middle Eastern Food (Vintage, 1974) and *The New Book of Middle Eastern Food* (Knopf, 2000), by Claudia Roden. It may seem unnecessary to recommend *both* of these books as the second is a reedition of the first, and perhaps I wouldn't if I weren't so attached to Roden's original edition; but if you can look at both of them, I think you'll agree that they're a little different from each other. There is something so, well, *exotic* about the first book that I can't imagine not having it in my kitchen. That said, Roden's updated edition is very welcome. As she says, "Cooking does not stand still: it evolves. Life is different, and different choices are made to adapt to new circumstances." The recipes in the first edition employed no home ovens, blenders, food processors, or freezers, for example, so Roden updated and revised some of them, but with no loss of flavor.

The good recipes aside, what is most valuable about these books is the introduction, which is divided into essays such as "Origins and Influences," "Social Aspects," "The Traditional Table," "Muslim Dietary Laws," "The Ottoman Empire," and "General Features of Middle Eastern Cuisines." Roden grew up in a Jewish family in Cairo and her grandparents were originally from Syria and Turkey. She relates that when she ate at friends' homes they enjoyed a range of dishes from various countries. "I am sometimes asked how a Jewish woman can be fascinated with Arab food and Islamic civilization, and I reply that it was also ours (with some differences) and we were part of it."

Classical Turkish Cooking: Traditional Turkish Food for the American Kitchen, by Ayla Algar (HarperCollins, 1991). To the best of my knowledge, this was really the first Turkish cookbook published in the States to receive attention. As I have introduced Algar previously in this section, I won't go on and on about this book except to say the recipes are indeed "classical"—you won't find any newfangled dishes here—but that is not a drawback: this is the book with which to begin learning about Turkish cuisine.

Contemporary Turkish Cooking, by Filiz Zorlu (Çitlembik, 2007). Zorlu tell us in her introduction that she never intended to write down all the recipes she's been cooking for nearly forty years, but at her sons' insistence, she finally did. Her recipes incorporate traditional Turkish home cooking with more modern takes and also include some innovative dishes with Western ingredients. As this is published in Turkey, it's not that easy to find (my copy was found through an inter-library loan) but it's also not a book I would call essential. However, I did make three recipes and they were winners: Cucumber and Zucchini Salad, Green Lentil and Cabbage Salad, and Zucchini Pancakes.

Flavours of Istanbul: A Selection from Original 19th Century Ottoman Recipes, by Özge Samancı and Sharon Croxford (Medya+ik, PMP Publishing, 2007). This fully illustrated paperback, from the team behind the terrific Istanbul Food Workshop, features recipes for dishes chosen from Ottoman cookbooks published between 1844 and 1900. The recipes are not complicated, nor particularly time-consuming, and any home cook could prepare a complete Turkish meal from this selection of recipes. The introductory chapter, "Cuisine of Istanbul in the 19th Century," is fascinating and worth the price of the book alone. Note that this book isn't readily available—I ordered my copy from Nettleberry (see Miscellany, page 566).

Middle Eastern Cooking, by Harry G. Nickles (Time-Life, 1969; revised 1979). As readers of my previous books already know, I'm a *huge* fan of the *Foods of the World* series published by Time-Life. There are few out-of-print books that grant me such pleasure as a volume in this outstanding series. Unfortunately, the editors of this series did not see the need to devote an entire book to the cuisine of Turkey, so "A Treasury of Turkish Delights" is one chapter in this Middle Eastern book. "My picture of Turkey's lavish food," Nickles writes, "often comes to a focus in the memory of one or another great meal."

He and his wife, Muriel, experience dining at the homes of friends and in restaurants fancy and simple. At one banquet lunch served in a private waterfront *yalı*, with dish after splendid dish, a vodka bar, Turkish wine, and animated conversation until four in the afternoon, he learned a Turkish saying: " 'When a moment of silence falls during a meal, somewhere a girl is born.' Surely, only boys were born that afternoon."

Spice: Flavors of the Eastern Mediterranean, by Ana Sortun with photography by Susie Cushner (ReganBooks, 2006). The title of this wonderful cookbook is a bit misleading, which is why it's here instead of with the other Mediterranean titles. Ana Sortun went to Turkey in 1997 and it's no exaggeration to say it changed her life—she fell in love with the food and learned the cooking traditions from local women and was "inspired beyond measure." What impressed Sortun most about Turkish cuisine were delicious, multicourse meals after which everyone left feeling energized instead of feeling heavy and tired as after a southern French, Italian, or Spanish meal. After earning a degree at École de Cuisine La Varenne in Paris and stints at three restaurants in the Boston area, Seattle-born Sortun opened Oleana in 2001 in Cambridge, Massachusetts, where she is chef and co-owner. Catherine Reynolds, a longtime writer for *Gourmet*, writes in *The New York Times* of Oleana that it "is at once rustic-traditional and deeply inventive." *Spice* received a nomination for Best International Cookbook by the James Beard Foundation, and in 2005 Sortun was honored with a Best Chef: Northeast award from the James Beard Foundation.

On her first Turkey trip, she went to Gaziantep, generally considered to be the country's gastronomic capital, and studied Turkish cuisine with Ayfer Unsal. "Travel is far and away the biggest influence on me," Sortun says. "When I went to Turkey for the first time I had genies and magic carpets in mind. When I got there it changed everything I ever thought about the country and food." *Spice* is wisely arranged by spice and herb groupings or families. This is so much more sensible to me because we often have an abundance of one herb or another, or want to buy a new spice and try it out, but then have to wade through dozens of recipes before finding one that might be suitable. One small quibble: Sortun often refers to "the Arabic Mediterranean" and "Arabic foods," but the Turks are not Arabs, a fact about which you will be swiftly reminded.

Among my favorite recipes in this book are Arabic Coffee Pot de Crème; Cranberry Beans Stewed with Tomato and Cinnamon; and Greek Salad with Winter Vegetables, Apple, and Barrel-Aged Feta Cheese. Also Oleana offers its own assortment of spice towers online, one of which is *baharat* (Arabic for "herbs and spices" as well as for "spice shop"). Though Sortun offers a recipe for *baharat* mix in her book, it is far easier—and just as fresh-tasting—to use the one from Oleana. Because I don't like lamb, I didn't use the Oleana *baharat* for Lamb Steak with Turkish Spices, but following some of Sortun's recommendations, I did use it on grilled mushrooms with olive oil, in a chickpea soup with farro, in a tomato sauce, and in a carrot soup . . . and it was great each time. Each spice blend (the others are Ras El Hannout, Persian Spice Mix, Za'atar, and Dukkah) is $15 plus shipping and handling (617 661 0505 / oleanarestaurant.com).

Turkish Cooking, by Irfan Orga (Andre Deutsch, 1958). In the afterword to *Portrait of a Turkish Family*, Ateş Orga notes that *Turkish Cooking* was quite successful when it was originally published, and was still in print twenty years later. This piqued my curiosity, and I felt I had to track it down. I'm glad I did: it's an interesting little book, though I have only made very few recipes from it. It's for the herbs and spices list and the preface for which this book is really worthy. Orga notes that the craze for "vitaminising" food—balancing meals so the greatest dietetic value may be extracted—is lost on the Turks as they have for centuries served well-balanced meals quite by accident. They have been experts on vegetable dishes for generations, and "unknowingly vitaminised themselves by simply serving their vegetables in the liquor in which they were cooked."

Turkish Cooking: Authentic Culinary Traditions from Turkey, by Bade Jackson (Chartwell, 1998). Jackson notes in her introduction that historical documents reveal that the basic structure of Turkish cuisine had been established during the nomadic period of the sixth to the eleventh century AD. "Culinary attitudes toward meat, dairy products, vegetables, and grains that characterized this period still make up the core of Turkish cuisine." Jackson provides a variety of meat and vegetable recipes with (mostly) readily available ingredients, and many are those that would be prepared in an average Turkish home.

Turquoise: A Chef's Travels in Turkey, by Greg and Lucy Malouf (Chronicle, 2008). I discovered Australian gourmands Greg and Lucy Malouf a few years ago through their books *Artichoke to Za'atar: Modern Middle Eastern Food* and *Saha: A Chef's Journey Through Lebanon and Syria*, not because I've been to Australia (yet). *Turquoise* is a special book—first of all, it's gorgeous, with photographs that will make you want to buy a plane ticket to Turkey immediately, and secondly, as the Maloufs point out, it's definitely not a traditional Turkish cookery book. "After all, there are plenty of these around, many of them written by people far better than we are. In *Turquoise* we wish to share the story of our journey with you, to inspire you to learn more about this country and about the aromas, flavours and textures of its wonderful cuisine." The recipes are indeed not what you'll find in any other Turkish cookbook, though they fully respect traditional Turkish ingredients.

The Maloufs note that "food is, of course, both the product and expression of a culture, and in Turkey we found this to be profoundly different from and more exciting than anything we had been expecting."

World Food: Turkey, by Dani Valent (Lonely Planet, 2000). Not only does this essential book include an English-Turkish glossary and a forty-three-page Turkish culinary dictionary, but it also features background information on the specialties of each region of the country, essays on various customs and traditions, and recipes. (I love that the one for *aşure* is referred to as "40-Ingredient Pudding, or Stuff in a Bowl.") Plus, it's pocket-size, taking up almost no room in your luggage.

A number of recipes for Turkish dishes are found in general Mediterranean cookbooks. This happens to be my favorite kind of cookbook, simply because I am a big believer in the Mediterranean diet, and as a result these are the most-used cookbooks in my kitchen. I use the following books *all the time* and highly recommend them:

• *A Book of Mediterranean Food*, by Elizabeth David (Penguin, 1988). I actually read from this classic volume more often than I cook from it.

• *The Cooking of the Eastern Mediterranean*, by Paula Wolfert (HarperCollins, 1994). Recipes from Istanbul, Izmir, Konya, and Gaziantep are plentiful in this terrific book, and as Wolfert says, "Turkish home cooking is simple to prepare, easy to like, healthy to eat."

• *The Essential Mediterranean: How Regional Cooks Transform Key Ingredients into the World's Favorite Cuisines*, by Nancy Harmon Jenkins (William Morrow, 2003). Jenkins expands upon a handful of core ingredients—salt; olives and olive oil; wheat, pasta, and couscous; wine; chickpeas, lentils, and fava beans; peppers and tomatoes; and cheese and yogurt—that are fundamental to all of the Med's diverse cuisines.

• *Mediterranean Cookery*, by Claudia Roden (Knopf, 1987). I remain particularly fond of this book because Roden includes many recipes for popular street foods and common dishes that regular people eat and travelers will encounter often, as opposed to fancier restaurant dishes. Also, I learned a great tip: when the weather doesn't permit you to light your outdoor grill and you don't want to permeate your house or apartment with the smell of roasting red peppers on the stovetop, put them in a baking dish, uncovered, and roast in a 400-degree oven. Trust me, they come out *almost* as good as those cooked over a flame.

- *A Mediterranean Feast: The Story of the Birth of the Celebrated Cuisines of the Mediterranean, from the Merchants of Venice to the Barbary Corsairs*, by Clifford A. Wright (William Morrow, 1999). Books don't get more definitive than this one, and his *Mediterranean Vegetables* (Harvard Common, 2001) and *Little Foods of the Mediterranean: 500 Fabulous Recipes for Antipasti, Tapas, Hors d'Oeuvre, Meze, and More* (Harvard Common, 2003) are equally essential for Mediterranean food enthusiasts.

- *Mediterranean Fresh: A Compendium of One-Plate Salad Meals and Mix-and-Match Dressings*, by Joyce Goldstein (Norton, 2008). I have so many of Goldstein's cookbooks it was hard for me to think how she could write another one that I would consider a must-have in my kitchen; but she did, and this is it. Here's what I didn't pick up from Goldstein's other books: she loves Turkey, and especially Istanbul! There are seven named Turkish recipes here and about two dozen more that are easily recognizable on any Turkish table (plus three recipes for pomegranate dressings).

- *Mediterranean Grains and Greens*, by Paul Wolfert (HarperCollins, 1998). There aren't *quite* as many Turkish recipes in this volume as in Wolfert's Eastern Mediterranean book, but there are enough to warrant an appearance on this list.

- *The Mediterranean Kitchen*, by Joyce Goldstein (William Morrow, 1989). I think I may have made just about every recipe in this very excellent book. One of its unique features is that Goldstein indicates how, by changing only an ingredient or two, a recipe can go from being Italian to, say, Turkish, Portuguese, or Moroccan, allowing for more mileage out of nearly every recipe.

- *The Mediterranean Prescription*, by Angelo Acquista, M.D. (Ballantine, 2006). This book received a quiet reception, but it deserves more notice. Its subtitle is *Meal Plans and Recipes to Help You Stay Slim and Healthy for the Rest of Your Life*.

- *Mediterranean Street Food: Stories, Soups, Snacks, Sandwiches, Barbecues, Sweets, and More from Europe, North Africa, and the Middle East*, by Anissa Helou (HarperCollins, 2002). Streets foods deserve pride of place as they are so much a part of the Mediterranean lifestyle. Helou's recipes are great for cocktail parties or light lunches and dinners.

- *Mediterranean Women Stay Slim, Too: Eating to Be Sexy, Fit, and Fabulous!*, by Melissa Kelly (Collins, 2006). Though the title is a nod to another favorite book of mine, *French Women Don't Get Fat*, by Mireille Guiliano (Knopf, 2005; Vintage, 2007), this book is quite different, filled with many recipes as the author is also the co-owner and executive chef of Primo, a restaurant in Rockland, Maine, where I had one of the best meals of my life.

- *Meze: Small Plates to Savor and Share from the Mediterranean Table*, by Diane Kochilas (William Morrow, 2003). In this great volume, Kochilas has divided the chapters by specific types of *mezes*, such as dips, spreads, and relishes; small egg dishes; meatballs and kebabs; and finger foods and fried treats.

- *The New Mediterranean Diet Cookbook: A Delicious Alternative for Lifelong Health*, by Nancy Harmon Jenkins (Bantam, 2009). A revised and updated edition of the groundbreaking volume, first published in 1994.

- *Olives: The Life and Love of a Noble Fruit*, by Mort Rosenblum (North Point, 1996). Though Turkish olives don't figure in the book, this is a fascinating read. "Next time the sun is bright," Rosenblum observes, "and the tomatoes are ripe, take a hunk of bread, sprinkle it with fresh thyme, and think about where to dunk it. I rest my case."

- *Secrets of Saffron: The Vagabond Life of the World's Most Seductive Spice*, by Pat Willard (Beacon, 2001). Though Turkey is no longer a source for it, saffron, mostly from Iran, is sold in many markets in Istanbul, so this is a worthwhile read to learn more about this tiny flower, from which "so little is needed to turn life into a sumptuous feast."

- *The Slow Mediterranean Kitchen: Recipes for the Passionate Cook*, by Paula Wolfert (Wiley, 2003). There are a number of Turkish recipes in this book, and two I particularly love are Turkish Red Lentil Soup with Paprika and Mint Sizzle, and Melt-in-Your-Mouth Green Beans with Turkish Pepper.

Eveline Zoutendijk

Eveline Zoutendijk, originally from the Netherlands, went to Istanbul for the first time in May 1997 and has been living there since October 2001. She holds a Grand Diplôme with honors from Le Cordon Bleu in Paris and cooked for a year in a Michelin-starred restaurant in the Netherlands as the only female in a kitchen with sixteen men. She then attended hotel management school in Glion, Switzerland, and began working for the St. Regis Hotel in New York. Five years later she decided to take a year off and travel the world, which was when she discovered Turkey. Toward the end of her second visit of what would turn out to be eleven visits in twenty months, she had already decided she wanted to move to Istanbul, but finding a decent job turned out to be more difficult than expected. She received an offer to open the Four Seasons George V in Paris, and accepted it. But during those two years she couldn't get Istanbul out of her mind, and eventually she decided to move there and try to start her own little hotel. The timing was bad—right after September 11, 2001—but this didn't stop her from signing a rental contract with the Sarnıç Hotel in Sultanahmet, which she operated for six years. Here, she created Cooking Alaturka, featured in The New York Times *("Have Spatula, Will Travel," April 15, 2007). A collection of Eveline's recipes has been featured in* Food & Wine *accompanying an article by Chandler Burr ("Sailing Through Byzantium," May 2005), and she is one of the contributors in the wonderful* Tales of the Expat Harem *anthology.*

Q: During your year "off," you traveled all over the world, and could have chosen to live anywhere you wanted. What made you decide on Istanbul?

A: It was sort of love at first sight. After living in New York and Paris, Istanbul seemed to have just the perfect combination of energy, culture, history, and physical beauty. It was all so new, so different and exciting, I became quite obsessed by wanting to live there. Istanbul easily becomes an obsession, an addiction that gets into your blood and keeps you on a continuous high.

Q: You've said it was difficult to find a job initially. Was there a point when you wanted to give up?

A: Yes, in fact I did give up, initially, and that's when I accepted the job in Paris. But I couldn't stop thinking or talking about Istanbul. No one around me could understand why I wanted to move there so badly, and I used to reply that I could think of a hundred reasons. . . . One night I sat down and wrote out those one hundred reasons—I still have them somewhere. I needed a little cue to go, and this came in the summer of 2001, when a friend of mine sent an e-mail announcing he was moving out of his apartment. He had this fabulous place with a 270-degree view of the Bosphorus, starting with the Bosphorus Bridge and Ortaköy, moving over the Dolmabahçe Palace, the Maiden's Tower, the Sea of Marmara, Sultanahmet, and the entire neighborhood of Cihangir. That's where I'm still living today.

Q: How did September 11 affect your plans?

A: It rendered all my hotel ideas ridiculous, of course. Tourism was at an all-time low, so investing in it didn't seem a very logical idea. But I decided that if I didn't move then, I never would and I would regret not doing it for the rest of my life.

Q: Once you finished redecorating the Sarnıç Hotel, how did you get the idea for cooking classes?

A: Food is *really* important to me, so I hired a very capable chef, and he didn't have enough to do. This—combined with the fact that we had a large kitchen in the hotel, there were no Turkish cooking classes available yet for travelers passing through, plus of course my own cooking background and my love for Turkish food—made me come up with the idea. The marketing of it was a lot harder than I thought it would be, though. Progress was slow but steady, and over the years, the classes have become very popular.

Q: How are your classes structured, and how much does every-one participate?

A: The ideal class size is between six and ten people. I divide up the basic tasks, such as chopping tomatoes and onions, which provides a chance for participants to get to know one another, but each person gets to do the important stuff: preparing egg-plant for *imam bayıldı* and stuffing it, or filling a chicken breast Topkapı style. We start at ten-thirty a.m. and make a five-course menu, and then have lunch around one p.m. Upon request, we arrange evening classes as well, but my experience

is that the concentration level is lower at night after a full day of sightseeing. Prior to cooking, I explain the recipes, which usually consist of three appetizers, a main course, and dessert. I also offer a *meze* class, which consists of five *mezes* and a dessert. Any dietary restriction can be accommodated and I do my best to include special requests, provided they are of interest to the whole group. We've also done Turkish cooking demonstrations for private groups of fifteen to thirty people on a wooden boat on the Bosphorus. These are not hands-on, though, due to lack of space. Each participant receives the recipes to take with them.

Q: What are some of the dishes you make?

A: I stick to dishes that are typically Turkish, so specialties with lamb, eggplant, and other vegetables are popular. *Imam bayıldı* is a regular, and flat green beans cooked in olive oil, too. Warm stuffed vine leaves with rice and minced meat, lamb stew in tomato sauce on smoky eggplant purée, and red lentil soup with bulgur and lemon yogurt soup with mint are also regular menu items. An old Topkapı Palace recipe, adapted to modern times, is our chicken breast stuffed with rice, pistachios, tomatoes, and dill. Okra is a popular seasonal vegetable here, but I don't include it so often since people may have trouble finding it in their home country. The aim is really to work with ingredients they can easily find outside of Turkey, so that they can invite their friends for a real Turkish meal.

Q: What are some typical Turkish ingredients that are a must for visitors to take home with them?

A: Definitely the Turkish red-pepper flakes, since they have such a different flavor than regular chili pepper. Red bell pepper purée is used a lot in Turkish cooking; it keeps in the fridge for about a year, but could be substituted by adding more tomato paste. The peeled pistachios from Gaziantep are wonderful, and of course hazelnuts—Turkey is famous for these, and they taste so much better here! Any type of nut or dried fruit is good here, and relatively inexpensive, though one must be warned that Istanbul's cheap days are over. The dark, unsulfured apricots are amazing, and Turkish delight always makes a nice present. People ask me often about saffron, but it's hard to find the real high-quality saffron here. In any case, it's not so commonly used in Turkish cuisine, just in a few dishes and desserts.

Q: What are some of your favorite restaurants you would recommend to visitors?

A: Everyone should try some different types of Turkish restaurants, of course; then, if there is time left, some more contemporary options can be included as well. A good kebab house is a must: Hamdi or Develi are great, and not far from Sultanahmet; farther away there are Tike and Venge, among others. There's a *meyhane* on Nevizade Sokak in Beyoğlu called Boncuk, which has great food and live music, with reasonable prices, and Sofyalı, with its myriad *mezes*, in Tünel. Fish lovers can go to Doğa in Cihangir, Balıkçı Sabahattin in Sultanahmet, or one of the posh fish places on the Bosphorus. As for fusion food in a hipper atmosphere, my favorite is Changa, close to Taksim, which specializes in inventive cuisine in a minimalist décor, contrasting perfectly with the historical building. 360 on İstiklâl is a must for soaking in an amazing view over cocktails. A great new place is Moreish, in the historic district of Pera. The chef is very talented (and is a friend of mine) and he isn't afraid to introduce new combinations of flavors that aren't typically Turkish. Moreish is a fine example of what's going on in the more avant-garde world of Istanbul restaurants.

Q: You've described some of your experiences as a business-woman in Istanbul as difficult. Do you still feel the same way about the place that captured your heart?

A: It's undeniably true that it's hard to set up and run a business successfully in Turkey. Whereas in New York you can go against the current and get a million things done every day, in Istanbul you have to go with the flow and hope for the best. If I accomplish one task in a day, I consider myself lucky. I'm a perfectionist, but "perfectionism" isn't a word that translates easily into Turkish. And after all these years, I've stopped looking through my pink glasses—I get irritated by so many things! Nevertheless, I still love this city.

Eveline may be contacted directly at info@cookingalaturka.com or through her Web site, Cookingalaturka.com. Cooking Alaturka is now located at Akbiyik Caddesi 72A in Sultanahmet; phone +90 212 458 5919. She is currently working on a book about her adventures at the Sarniç Hotel and hopes to write a Turkish cookbook one day as well.

The Bosphorus

[Turkey's] moves towards Europe . . . started a long time ago. When Abdul Mecit inaugurated his Euro-palace at Dolmabahçe in 1856 it was as if he was saying: "Look! We're part of Europe." A decade later Beylerbey Palace on the Asian shore yelled back: "And so are we, but we still have a touch of the Orient."

—CHRIS HELLIER,
Splendors of Istanbul:
Houses and Palaces
Along the Bosphorus

This is the only city that straddles two continents, and the Bosphorus is what divides and unites it. Without this strait Byzantium/Constantinople/Istanbul would be unimaginable. It would not have been so enormously important over so many centuries, so eagerly sought after by so many of history's greatest conquerors. Nor would it be nearly so rich, beautiful or romantic.

—STEPHEN KINZER,
Crescent & Star

Mansions on the Water
The *Yalıs* of Istanbul

CHRIS HELLIER

ΩΩ

Yalıs (the name is derived from the Greek word *yialos*, "seashore,") were built as waterside summer residences by the Ottoman aristocracy between the seventeenth and eighteenth centuries. They were "sandwiched conveniently between the cool shade of their gardens and the cool ocean breeze," according to Arzu Karamani in *Living in Istanbul*, and "their large airy rooms enabled their residents to escape from the stifling heat of the city." Karamani also notes that to live in a *yalı* is, for all intents and purposes, "to live with water, to invite the sea into your front room. . . . But above all it is to live on shoreline, and here on the Bosporus it is the shoreline of one continent facing the shoreline of another. It is, in short, to live on intimate terms, and on a daily basis, with the unique feature of Istanbul, the one that gives the city all its magic: the fact that it lies between East and West, at the meeting point of two worlds."

Pierre Loti wrote what was nothing less than a death knell of this famous waterway in the early 1900s:

> The European shore of the Bosphorus is already for the most part abandoned to our modern barbarity, with the worsening effect of Levantine bad taste. On the other hand, the Asian shore, which lags at least a hundred years behind the European shore, will retain for some years at least some of its peace, charm and mystery. Passing along it on a *caïque* (traditional Turkish

borrowed from the French—that produced several of the largest *yalıs*. Toward the close of the nineteenth century, this was over-shadowed by an eclectic "cosmopolitan" style wherein several *yalıs* became ensembles of European towers and Ottoman onion domes, each ornamented with Islamic motifs. Finally, during the decade prior to World War I, a Turkish expression of Art Nouveau influenced some of the last of the Ottoman *yalıs* to be built.

Yalıs were rarely built for longevity. In Ottoman Turkey there was no hereditary aristocracy that bequeathed property from one generation to another, as was the custom in Europe. A pasha's position depended on his relations with the sultan: Should the pasha fall from grace or the sultan fall from power, the family's fortunes fell as well, and the *yalı* often became impossible to maintain.

Indeed, temporality is intrinsic to timber buildings. Winter rains and the moist sea air both encouraged rot. On an unseasonably chilly July day in 1910, the romantic French novelist Pierre Loti, staying at the *yalı* of his friend Count Ostrorog, noted that "a balmy dampness fills my bedroom overlooking the sea, like an old ship whose hull is no longer watertight."

Simple forms of heating, such as the common open brazier, or *mangal*, caused several devastating fires. Later, in the 1940s and 1950s, rising land prices took a further toll. Thus only a handful of eighteenth-century *yalıs* have survived, and a number more from the nineteenth century. During the 1980s, some of these received new leases on life as a new class of monied Turkish entrepreneurs revived the prestige of a historic Bosporus summer home.

Today, the remaining *yalıs* are protected buildings, divided into several categories according to their architectural importance. One, the eighteenth-century Bostancibaşi Abdullah Ağa Yalı at Çengelköy, has been acquired by the Ministry of Tourism, and it is being remodeled to accommodate a restaurant and a souvenir shop.

The future of the best eighteenth-century *yalıs* now seems brighter than at any time this century. Several have actually remained in the same family for generations, and the current owners are committed to their upkeep. The Çürüksulu Yalı at Salacak, for instance, is maintained largely as it was originally conceived by one of Turkey's leading industrialists.

Istanbul socialite Ayşegül Nadir is restoring the Sa'dullah Pasha Yalı. Farther up the Asian coast, plans are again afoot to restore the dilapidated 1698 Köprülü Pasha Yalı. Restoration of this oldest of the *yalıs* was first planned in 1915, but was derailed when, following World War I, the Ottoman era ended with the establishment of the modern Republic of Turkey.

Editor's note: Hellier ended this piece with a final sentence noting that if the Köprülü Yalı's facelift was completed in 1998, it would also be its three hundredth anniversary. Sadly, however, things didn't turn out that way. According to Jane Taylor in *Imperial Istanbul*, "A few years ago the Turkish Touring and Automobile Club was given permission to renew the wooden props that held the front of the room above the water, and to replace the broken windows. Since then nothing has been done. Yet it is a unique monument of great historic and artistic interest, and it would well repay careful restoration."

Sadberk Hanım Museum

Among my favorite Istanbul museums is the Sadberk Hanım Museum, up the Bosphorus in Büyükdere. I originally wanted to visit the museum because it's in a beautiful *yalı*, and as I didn't know anyone who owned a *yalı* I thought it might be my only opportunity to see the inside of one (so far, I was right about that). The original building is a three-story wooden mansion that is generally believed to date from the late nineteenth century, and it was purchased by the wealthy and influential Koç family in 1950 and used as a summer house. It opened as a museum in 1980, and what a gem of a museum it is! The collection consists of artifacts of Anatolian civilizations dating to 5400–4750 BC; Greek artifacts (mostly terra-cotta items and figurines); Roman artifacts; Byzantine art; coins; early Islamic art; Seljuk art; Ayyubid and Mamluk art; Timurid and Safavid art; Ottoman art; enamelware; Chinese celadons and porcelains; Iznik and Kütahya ceramics; European and Turkish porcelains; glassware; calligraphy (this collection isn't large, but it is gorgeous); embroideries, needlework, and silk fabrics; women's costumes and fans; and excellent ethnographic displays on Turkish customs, including the coffee service, the bridal bath, the henna party, the shaving of the bridegroom, childbed customs, and a circumcision bed. Definitely worth a detour.

The Sadberk Hanım is not far from the also excellent Sakıp Sabancı Museum. This villa was built in 1927 by Italian architect Edouard de Nari, commissioned by Prince Mehmed Ali Hasan of Egypt. Later it served as the Montenegran embassy, and in 1950 it was bought by industrialist Hacı Ömer Sabancı. It came to be known as the Horse Mansion because a statue of a horse was installed in the garden. Another horse on the grounds is the cast of one of the four horses taken from Sultanahmet when it was looted by the crusaders of the Fourth Crusade and sent to the Basilica of San Marco in Venice. The Sabancı houses a permanent collection and mounts temporary exhibitions as well. Its calligraphy collection is outstanding (examples from over five hundred years); the painting collection focuses primarily on works created between 1850 and 1950; furniture and decorative arts are on the entry level of the museum in rooms that were in use when the Sabancı family lived in the mansion; archaeological and stone pieces are showcased in the garden; and of course there is also the Müzedechanga restaurant!

If you prefer to tour the Bosphorus shoreline in more privacy—and have the advantage of getting much closer to the shore than when on the large ferry boats—a reliable private guide is Erol Aydin, proprietor of Enjoy Cruises. His boat, *Enjoy*, is fifty feet long with a seating capacity of eight people. *Enjoy* cruises along at about five to seven miles per hour (ten maximum), and trips can be arranged for daytime cruises, sunset journeys, half days, or full days. Princes' Islands cruises are also popular. Aydin is very much in demand—he is often recommended to hotel guests of the Four Seasons—so contact him as far in advance as possible (mobile +90 532 595 1252 / aydinerol@hotmail.com).

RECOMMENDED READING

From the Bosphorus, by Richard Hinkle and Rhonda Vander Sluis (Çitlembik, 2003). This is a little book you *positively must have* if you're going on a Bosphorus cruise. It's lightweight, fully illustrated in color, and packed with descriptions about nearly every site and building along both banks from the Sea of Marmara to the Black Sea. Both Hinkle and Vander Sluis were U.S. State Department staffers in Istanbul when they hatched the idea for this book. Hinkle also worked as a volunteer coordinator for the consulate motor launch, *The Hiawatha*, and he gave countless tours on the Bophorus for visiting friends and government officials. The authors are careful to state that this volume is necessarily brief and is not a definitive work. However, they also note that due to multiple ownership, patchy record-keeping, and the lack of surnames until after the establishment of the Turkish Republic in 1923, there are conflicting accounts about some of the structures along the Bosphorus. They made every effort to vet the accuracy of the information, but sometimes it was educated guesswork: "Legend, rumor, and intrigue have been part and parcel of Bosphorus history and Ottoman tradition for centuries; it defies our Western attempts at organization." Happily, Hinkle confirms that "a tour along the Bosphorus will find more of the old shore houses being restored than ever before." This book is only available in Turkey or through *Cornucopia* magazine, which is how I came by my copy (U.S. and Canada: 971 244 8802 / cornucopia.net).

Splendors of Istanbul: Houses and Palaces Along the Bosphorus, by Chris Hellier with photographs by Chris Hellier and Francesco Venturi (Abbeville, 1993). "The shores of the Bosphorus," writes Hellier in this excellent book's first chapter, "its waters alive with ferries and fishing boats, motor launches and luxury yachts, are still one of the most enchanting aspects of this seductive three-in-one city: Byzantium-Constantinople-Istanbul." Five chapters (including one fully devoted to the Grand Seraglio) paired with exterior and interior photographs tell the fascinating history of residential building on the Bosphorus. My favorite chapter is "Wooden Mansions," about *yalıs*. Though these grand wooden houses passed through several distinct architectural phases as the city adapted to new ideas largely imported from abroad, in their original form they were perched on the water's edge and had cantilevered bay windows jutting out over the water.

Interestingly, Hellier notes that the eighteenth-century Fethi

Ahmet Pasha Yalı, which is raised up on slender timber columns, impressed Le Corbusier when he visited Constantinople in 1911 and ultimately influenced the design of some of his buildings, notably the Unité d'Habitation in Marseille, which is supported on gigantic concrete pillars. Hellier also tells us that, as early as the 1720s, the Turkish chronicler Küçük Çelebizâde Asim Efendi noted the traditional color of the *yalıs*—rust red, or "Ottoman rose"—was beginning to change in the direction of pastel shades, which were introduced through increasing contact with Europe. He also notes that different ethnic communities in the city could often be identified by the color of their homes. "Along the Bosphorus, Turks, Armenians, and Greeks lived in separate villages, rarely meeting each other except for business. The Turks' houses were painted in fanciful, gay colours prohibited to other groups. Armenians confined themselves to red; the Greeks, to a lead colour; while the Jews, descendants of the Sephardic community expelled from Spain in 1492, were compelled to colour their houses black. Some of the Porte's wealthiest ministers and businessmen painted their spacious homes in two distinct colours, giving the effect of separate but attached dwellings."

After the formation of the Turkish republic in 1923, many of the Bosphorus palaces were abandoned or neglected, viewed as unwanted symbols of the Ottoman past. Happily, some are now museums, some have been restored by the Turkish Touring and Automobile Association, and others have caught the eyes of both Turks and foreigners who recognize and appreciate their value and uniqueness.

The Beauties of the Bosphorus: Illustrated in a Series of Views of Constantinople and its Environs, by Julia Pardoe with illustrations by W. H. Bartlett (George Virtue, London, 1838). I have never seen a copy of this book, so I suppose this can't truly be a recommendation. But when you read about a book that is mentioned by everybody as the absolute best, you begin to think so, too, and that's the case with this one. When I last checked, copies of this very rare volume were priced between $862 and $2,263. Some reprinted editions were published in 1840 and 1855. Some volumes feature seventy-eight steel engravings by Bartlett; one has the addition of an appendix on the Crimean War; others feature marbled endpapers and gilt-edged pages. Though Pardoe has been referred to as "dull," this chronicle of her travels to Turkey with her father in 1835 has been described as "one of the most popular and attractive of all books on the Bosphorus." Author Chris Hellier says that Pardoe "sought to record the traditional customs and the settings of the city before they changed beyond recognition." It seems a paperback edition was published not long ago, also by George Virtue, but I can't bring myself to buy it as it can in no way live up to the hardcover editions. So I mention this undoubtedly valuable book for those who may be able to purchase a copy without making too great a dent in their savings. (If you are lucky enough to secure a copy, I hope you'll write to me, describing it in full. I thank you in advance!)

My parents stopped in Istanbul for a few days in 1991 with eleven friends before boarding their chartered *gület* for a once-in-a-lifetime sail along Turkey's Mediterranean coast. My mother, Phyllis, told me, "We were much younger then and wanted to experience 'real' Istanbul so we booked rooms at a modest hotel in Sultanahmet, a perfect decision . . . charming, quaint in so many ways. And one of my best memories was the dinner prepared for us in the hotel's garden: the food was wonderful, the wine never stopped flowing, service was outstanding, and it was altogether a magical night. Another great memory—and I have so many—is sighting a very large

Russian ship on our ride up the Bosphorus. The first Gulf War had just ended, and the Cold War was over, so seeing that Russian flag and knowing how close we actually were to the Black Sea . . . well, the geography of Istanbul really hits you." After their trip, the group continued to get together periodically for fun evenings of reminiscing. They even wrote their own lyrics to songs, like this one, sung to the tune of "The Battle Hymn of the Republic":

> *Mine eyes have seen the seven hundred jewelry stores*
> *of gold,*
> *Leather shops where jackets, pocketbooks, and shoes and*
> *belts are sold,*
> *Among the brass you're apt to find Aladdin's Lamp, I'm*
> *told,*
> *It's Istanbul's Bazaar!*
> *Glory, Glory, Hallelujah!*
> *Merchants grab you like they knew ya . . .*

And so on. (Perhaps you had to be there.)

Edirne

Edirne is rarely considered by tourists as anything other than a stopover on the road to Istanbul. Luckily, the town seems entirely unperturbed by this "neglect," and remains a bustling centre of modern Turkish life in all its forms, with the added colour of constant through traffic from Greece and Bulgaria. Visitors who do pause to take an interest will find a surprising amount of impressive architecture—Edirne was briefly the capital of the Ottoman Empire, and many of the key buildings are still in excellent shape.

—*Lonely Planet Turkey*

Edirne's Architectural Feast

GODFREY GOODWIN

ເວລ

EDIRNE MAY BE long past its zenith, but its hoard of great Islamic buildings is still unparalleled, as the author details in this piece that originally appeared in *The New York Times*.

GODFREY GOODWIN was the author of *A History of Ottoman Architecture* (Thames & Hudson, 1971), *The Janissaries* (Saqi, 2006), *The Private World of Ottoman Women* (Saqi, 2007), and *Sinan: Ottoman Architecture and Its Values Today* (Saqi, 2001), among others. He passed away in 2005.

IN THE golden age of Süleyman the Magnificent, the verdant city of Edirne, founded by the Roman Emperor Hadrian, was the second capital of the Ottoman Empire and three times its present size—its monumental architecture and gardens a brilliant setting for grandees and ambassadors on horseback, its stone pavements thronged with dervishes and merchants.

Today, the once-major city peters out amid a vision of trees and greenery—an appealing country town within sight of both the Greek and Bulgarian frontiers. But within its shrunken borders are exquisite mosques and public baths, and market halls still line its spacious avenues.

Approaching Edirne on the highway from Istanbul, a four-hour trip, I like to stop and look down on the center of the city, just beyond the immense sixteenth-century caravansary built by Rüstem Pasha. The grand vizier of Süleyman the Magnificent, he married Süleyman's daughter Mihrimah, a woman of extraordinary ability and riches. The caravansary is one of the largest ever built, with endless domed chambers set around two courtyards. Above these on the skyline ride the great cupolas of five major mosques with their minarets ranging from delicately slim to fatter brick versions.

Well beyond the city center is the island palace of Sultan Süleyman, pillaged in the nineteenth century by Russian invaders who destroyed its romantic pavilions and gardens; all that is left are the ruins of the kitchens. The island itself, called Saray, has been deserted by the modern Edirne, which has receded behind the banks of the Tunca River.

Although the streets of the city are no longer thronged, as they were until the eighteenth century, they are still lively, the bazaars crowded with local inhabitants in search of necessities like pots and pans, cutlery and sensible clothes. The charm of Edirne today is in the pleasure of gentle walking—from the city's center, with its cafés and shops, down Talat Pasha Avenue, to the Gazi Mihal bridge and the meadows beside the banks of the Tunca, where children swim and play.

I have visited Edirne at least forty times because of its rich architectural heritage, most recently last July, but I like to begin each visit with the same walk. Leaving the main road just before the modern bridge over the Tunca, I park the car in a small village, from which a broad dirt track reaches the fifteenth century double bridge on the left. From the bridge I can imagine the miles of orchards lining the river where, until a century ago, the townsfolk came on warm evenings to picnic, dance and sing.

The bridge leads to the high dike that protects the great hospital built by Beyazit II in the 1480s. The dike offers a superb view of the hospital—a grand complex that is a tribute to Ottoman charity. The halls where the patients were lodged are on one side of a paddock filled with wildflowers, the handsome storerooms and kitchens are on the other, and the mosque with its courtyard is set between. The mosque is no more and no less than one astonishing dome over a monumental square hall. On each side of it are the quarters for the dervishes, one of the mystic sects that were responsible for nursing the patients, who were fed fresh fruit and vegetables and soothed and cheered by musicians three times a week.

Getting back into the car, I cross back over the river and proceed down the long Talat Pasha Avenue to the great mosque of Selim II, one of the noblest of all Ottoman buildings, splendidly set on the site of the first Ottoman palace built in the 1360s. It was from here that Mehmet II set out to conquer Constantinople at the age of twenty-one. Designed by the greatest of Islamic architects, Sinan, the mosque is striking because of its four minarets—which at more than 230 feet are the tallest in Islam—and its great dome, about 103 feet in diameter, visible long before reaching town.

The proportions within are just as breathtaking. Semidomes have given place to eight piers that open up the interior. One appreciates that this building (1569–74) is brother to the masterpieces of the High Renaissance. The key to this relationship is shared mathematics, but here, also, inventiveness finds its apogee. I usually can persuade an officer of the mosque to allow me to mount the central singing gallery, where his few notes from the call to prayer prove the acoustics are without reproach. Under the gallery is a marble fountain in a pool, the navel of the building, symbolic of the source of life.

The tiles in this mosque hug the windows of the mihrab apse where the imam leads the faithful in prayer. They are panels of the richest color and brilliant execution. In the 1570s the potteries at Iznik (Nicaea) reached a perfection that achieved a dazzling range of colors and unblemished white grounds. The reds, in particular, were the envy of European ceramicists. There are unique designs set into the shoulders of the many arches, but the glory is in the royal box (*hünkar mahfili*). Having asked the officer of the mosque for permission to see them, I make a modest donation of about two dollars and follow the guide up the stairs in the wall. Apart from the looted panel now in the Hermitage, all the tiles are still there and of pristine beauty, with imaginative floral designs. The center panel of the mihrab is formed of inlaid wooden shutters that open magically so that sultans, on their knees, could look out on nothing but the heavens.

There is a small museum in the former teaching complex of this mosque, but the energetic should press on for a little less than a mile up the hill to the mosque of Murad II, father of Mehmet the Conqueror, which was once the center of a Mevlevi dervish convent. The highly intellectual and esthetic order is still famous for the mystical dance in which seven participants slowly gyrate like spheres, each with one hand pointing to heaven and the other to earth. Sadly, all but the mosque is gone, and the building is often shut at the whim of the imam. But the view across the plain to the foothills of Bulgaria is still fine, and a mood of medieval fantasy survives.

Returning down the hill to the center of town, I visit the bazaar below the Selim II mosque, where stout country boots, an Edirne specialty, are sold. The city is also known for quality soaps, some modeled into animals to amuse children. Beyond that visitors will find little that is not available in Istanbul. But the opening price, before bargaining begins, is likely to be much lower.

ɔɔɪɔɔɪɔɔɪ

Outside the bazaars are numerous open-air cafés, one of which has tables on the slope beneath the Selim II mosque. Although this café is cooled by a pool sparkling with jets of water, the umbrellas over the tables are sometimes not enough and it is best to have a hot or iced tea in one of the tree-shaded cafés along the main street; one of my favorites is the café in the piazza formed by the caravansary and the Old Mosque (Eski Cami). The Eski Cami has an interesting independent minaret of monumental proportions built of brick. Although the mosque is under repair, you can still see the astonishingly large inscriptions on the walls, added in the nineteenth century. The mosque itself dates from around 1400, but there is a cocky little later brother built of stone, added at the far corner of the portico.

The Turks have always been a practical people who erect what they need where they can without attempting to imitate an older style. Nowhere does this work better than at the nearby Üç Şerefeli Cami (the Mosque of the Three Balconies, used by the muezzins who make the call to prayer). In the sixteenth century—the time of Süleyman the Magnificent—there was not just one singer for each balcony but four, at each of the cardinal points. For this mosque, which was the royal mosque of Murad II, the first two minarets were built at the corners where mosque and

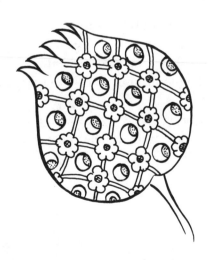

courtyard meet. This is the usual position in a sultan's mosque and traditionally these minarets should form an identical pair.

But here the minaret with the three balconies is over 223 feet tall and its companion shorter. Both are built of brick like the minaret of the Old Mosque, which this one supplanted as the Friday Mosque of Edirne; they were joined by two more unmatching minarets at the other corners of the rectangular courtyard. The first added is flamboyant, its trunk twisted like barley sugar, but the last is built in finest cut stone, which is why it is the slimmest, with the traditional dignity that became universal after 1500.

Built about 1440, Üç Şerefeli Cami represents the initial step in the evolution of classical Ottoman domes; its dome is almost seventy-nine feet in diameter, but is low and built cautiously with massive supports. Though the mosque is closed for repairs, one may still peer into the charming courtyard, which was spared the prominent canopy added to most other royal fountains by Murad IV in the mid-seventeenth century.

From the mosque of Murad II it is about a mile to Edirne's two better hotels. I've had comfortable if far from luxurious stays in both of them, but I decided to drive the 150 miles back to Istanbul that evening by way of Büyükçekmece. This is the greatest of Sinan's bridges—a broad, undulating span carried by seven arches built across the marshes in the mid-sixteenth century after Süleyman had to climb onto the roof of a peasant farmhouse to escape a flood.

Halfway to the bridge, I saw endless sunflower fields and several strange hillocks. These were, I knew, unexplored archaeological sites, promising further glories.

Another, more recent article about Edirne I regret I couldn't include is "Edirne: The Forgotten City," by Caroline and Andrew Finkel (*Cornucopia: The Magazine for Connoisseurs of Turkey*, Spring 2007). The authors recommend browsing the Web site of Ayhan Tunca (edirneden.biz), a writer and photographer who publishes a magazine on Edirne, *Yöre*. The Web site is in Turkish only, but the photographs featured—including some old ones from the days when the city was known as Adrianople—are fantastic. The Finkels also recommend *The Age of Sinan: Architectural Culture in the Ottoman Empire* (Princeton, 2005) and Godfrey Goodwin's *A History of Ottoman Architecture* (Thames & Hudson, 1987).

SEFER SAATİN̄**511103837533323833196**SİI ZORUNLUDUR

080110/PZYY/266 1/1

İDO
İstanbul Deniz Otobüsleri
San. Ve Tic. A.Ş.
Ulaştırma V.D. 4700019571

MALİYE
T.C.
BAKANLIĞI

YOLCU BİLETİ

A 105981

İL MÜDÜ 34

YENIKAPI/YALOVA

SEFER TARİHİ :

SEFER SAATİ : 11.01.2008 CUMA
YKAPI 09:30

DÜZENLEME TARİHİ :

ADI / SOYADI :   10.01.20

ADRESİ..........: MAHA GAM

V.D/V.NO.......:

KATEGORİ ....: YOLCU(TA

SALON ....: ARKA SALC

YOLCU ....: 1

KOLTUK ....: P28

ÜCRET......: 12,00 YTL.(I

7F079743

Satım yeri İstanbul Deniz Otobüsleri Yenikapı/İstanbul U

BURSA BÜYÜKŞEHİR BELEDİYESİ

BuKART

TÜM
HATLARDA
GEÇERLİDİR

Katlamayınız, buruşturmayınız, manyetik
ortamlardan uzak tutunuz. Yolculuk süresince saklayınız.

BURULAŞ   e-kent

Bursa

Bursa used to be one of the loveliest cities of western Asia. It is now a large, and sometimes heavily polluted, industrial city, but, if it is no longer as beautiful as it once was, it nevertheless still contains many beautiful things, which it would be foolish to miss.

—JOHN ASH,
Turkey: The Other Guide: Western and Southern Anatolia

Broussa lay mapped out in all its extent, the sober-coloured buildings overshadowed by lofty trees; and the three hundred and eighty mosques of the city scattered in the most picturesque irregularity along the side of the mountains, and on the skirts of the valley.

—JULIA PARDOE,
The City of the Sultan, 1837

The Birthplace of Empire

HEATH W. LOWRY

ΩΩ

It's true what John Ash says about Bursa, and the beautiful architecture of this once-famous Silk Road city is often forgotten. You have to try harder in Bursa—its beauty is not readily apparent; its treasures are hidden away. Among its noted monuments are those of Sultan Yıldırım Beyazit (or Thunderbolt), his son Mehmet I, and his grandson Murad II. Beyazit was the son of Murad I, who on the morning of 15 June 1389 was preparing to do battle with a Serbian army under the leadership of Prince Lazar in the Battle of Kosovo. The story has come down to us that before the battle began, a Serbian nobleman claiming to be a deserter with information that would be useful to the Turks was admitted to Murad's tent, and he plunged a knife into the sultan's heart. Beyazit then took command and killed Lazar and routed the army, and according to legend, there were seventy-seven thousand Serbians dead. As Hugh and Nicole Pope note in *Turkey Unveiled*, the Serbs "never forgot or forgave their great defeat at Kosovo." (Positively the best book to read about this battle—and about the former Yugoslavia and the origins of the Bosnian conflict—is *Black Lamb and Gray Falcon,* by Rebecca West, Viking, 1941.)

In 1396, Beyazit was faced by an army of a reputed one hundred thousand crusaders. They had invaded his Balkan territories, and he promised his God that he would build twenty mosques if he were granted victory, but having disposed of the crusaders with ease at the Battle of Nicopolis (in Bulgaria), he began to

439

have second thoughts; twenty mosques seemed a tall order. His architect came up with a solution: the Great Mosque of Bursa was one of the largest structures the Turks had ever built. It had more domes than any other mosque in the sultan's territories and their number was at least an allusion to the terms of the pledge. (John Ash notes that "architectural historians have generally been unkind about the results, finding the mosque clumsy. . . . This may be true, but it will not concern an unprejudiced person who has spent some time in Beyazit's mosque.") Later, Beyazit went head to head with Timur (Tamerlane) and became Timur's captive. Rumor has it that he became Timur's slave, and after Timur pillaged and burned Bursa, Beyazit killed himself. The Yeşil Cami and Yeşil Türbe in Bursa are the mosque and tomb of Mehmet I, and Murad II is buried in the pretty Muradiye Cemetery complex, probably the most peaceful spot in the entire city.

Cornucopia published a special thirty-six-page feature on the city that gave the Ottoman Empire its first capital, "Bursa: Home of the Sultans" (2007). I urge readers to order a copy as the accompanying photos reveal just how gorgeous Bursa's architectural gems truly are, and the other essays in the special issue are essential reading (cornucopia.net). This piece is the opening essay of the special section.

HEATH W. LOWRY is Mustafa Kemal Atatürk Professor of Ottoman and Modern Turkish Studies at Princeton University. He contributed this piece to *Cornucopia: The Magazine for Connoisseurs of Turkey* and is also the author of numerous books, including *Ottoman Bursa in Travel Accounts* (Indiana University/Ottoman and Modern Turkish Studies, 2003), *The Nature of the Early Ottoman State* (SUNY, 2003), and *Fifteenth Century Ottoman Realities: Christian Peasant Life on the Aegean Island of Limnos* (Eren, Istanbul, 2002).

ALONG THE skirts of the Bithynian Mount Olympus (known for half a millennium by the Ottomans as Keşiş Dağı, or Monk's Mountain), lies what remains of the first capital of the early Ottoman state. Once home to the most flourishing silk industry of the Middle East and fabled for its three hundred minarets, it was a city dedicated in equal parts to commerce and religion. From the fourteenth until the early twentieth century, its inhabitants never numbered more than fifty thousand. Today it is a sprawling metropolis of over 1.5 million which is home to Turkey's automotive industry and still a major center of textile production, although the famed Bursa towels have long since out-paced its renowned silks. As for its minarets, which really only numbered three hundred in the writings of travelers, they are still there, though one sometimes has trouble spotting them amid the apartment blocks and stores that mar what was once a vista of dozens of graceful spires rising above the maze of two-story lath-and-plaster dwellings.

Equally famed were its natural hot springs, known in Turkish as *kaplıca*, which abound in the western suburb of Çekirge, and which by the end of the eighteenth century had been discovered by a handful of adventurous Europeans, who built a number of small spa hotels, immediately attracting parties of hardy visitors. This meant that Bursa soon became a popular weekend retreat for Europeans living in Istanbul, who sailed for eight to twelve hours to the port town of Mudanya on the Marmara Sea and were then transported by horse-drawn wagons over the forested hills and through fifteen kilometers of mulberry and fruit orchards to Bursa and its baths.

By the end of the nineteenth century the journey was made somewhat easier by the construction of a narrow-gauge railway connecting the two towns. Even that trip, however, was not with-out adventure: travelers reported how at steep grades along the way the male passengers were asked to disembark and walk on foot to the brow of the next hill, as the little engine didn't have quite enough steam to get itself and a full load of riders over the hills that surrounded the fertile Bursa plain.

Today, a pleasant (and quick) way to get from Istanbul to Bursa is the new fast ferry service from Yenikapı (along the sea walls of Istanbul) to Mudanya in a surprisingly quick seventy-five minutes. From there one takes a bus or taxi to Bursa and the whole trip takes less than two hours. If you travel with one of the several dozen books written by nineteenth-century visitors in hand, you will end up fully disoriented. For in place of the forested hills that once gave way to the vast Bursa plain, covered as far as the eye could see by plantations of mulberry trees (the leaves of which fed the silkworms on which the city's economy depended), the hills are now covered with the villas of Bursa residents who have escaped the city. In place of the mulberries are factories, outlet stores, car dealerships, and row upon row of not always attractive apartment blocks. Such is the price of progress.

However, as one approaches the city, it is still possible to imagine how it came to be known as Yeşil (Green) Bursa, for the rivers and rivulets of icy water running down the slopes of Ulu Dağ (Great Mountain)—the not-so-romantic name by which the Mountain of the Monks has been known since 1925—still feed the remaining foliage and convey a sense of what once was. Against the backdrop of the forested mountain itself, green is still the prevailing color. Although at the rate human settlement is moving up the mountain, that too may soon be a thing of the past.

One of the less pleasant aspects of modern life is the plethora of automobiles, which make getting around (let alone parking) an exciting and often frustrating task. The twenty-first-century visitor is advised to leave the driving to the hundreds of bright yellow taxis which always find a way through the traffic jams threatening to surpass even the congestion of Istanbul.

Bursa as described by visitors in earlier centuries was a warren of small, often dead-end streets with no apparent rhyme or reason to their makeup. What larger streets (dare I say boulevards) there are today are indirectly the result of the horrendous earthquake of 1855, which destroyed most of the city, and in whose wake an energetic governor, Ahmed Vefik Pasha, redesigned the grid and added what passes for main thoroughfares today. He also reconstructed most of the damaged historic monuments and introduced the residents to other aspects of Western civilization, including the theater. Indeed, Ahmed Vefik truly deserves credit as the father of the modern city. Without his tireless effort it is difficult to imagine what Bursa would look like today.

After countless visits in forty-plus years, Bursa still remains a personal favorite. I never come here without finding something new—not such a difficult task given that there are still well over a hundred minarets.

Should one tire of mosques, the massive courtyard caravansaries that once housed the city's artisans and manufacturers, including the impressive Koza (Silk) Han, with its dozens of venues offering goods made from the city's famous silks, are there to be visited. Anyone who thinks that silk is not still an important aspect of the city's life will be quickly disabused of the idea with a visit to this site. Where by the late fourteenth century the city was home to several dozen silk and wool merchants from Venice, Genoa, and Florence, today buyers are more likely to fly into the city in the morning, place their orders, and return to their Western European offices by late afternoon.

Today's answer to the vigor and vision of Ahmed Vefik Pasha is an equally energetic businessman and collector named Ahmet Erdönmez. Almost single-handedly in the past decade he has goaded and shamed the city fathers into taking a long-overdue interest in protecting what remains of Bursa's Ottoman heritage. He began by creating the Kent Müzesi (City Museum). This is a labor of love containing a street in which the shops of craftsmen of an earlier era have been beautifully re-created. He was also involved in the restoration of the city walls and, most recently, with the restoration of the sixteenth-century Balibey Han, a unique four-story edifice which clings to the slopes of the walled city. Indeed, my first stop on every visit to the city is the Kent Museum, where I learn from Ahmet Bey what has been done since my last visit.

Among the things that are a must for every first-time visitor to Bursa is a visit to one of the city's *kaplıcas* (hot springs). My personal favorite is the Eski Kaplıca (Old Hot Springs), just below the Hüdavendigâr Mosque in Çekirge. Originally a Roman bath, today's structure was built in the fourteenth century by the third Ottoman ruler, Sultan Murad Han, known as Hüdavendigâr (the Ruler). We know of its past from nineteenth-century travelers, who described the Roman mosaics that lined the large bathing pool in the men's section until the 1855 earthquake. In the rebuilding, the mosaics were covered by the marble one sees today. Meticulously maintained, this bath has separate sections for men and women; the women's section (even without the mosaic floor) is reportedly just as pleasant as the men's.

This bath was renowned in Byzantine times as a cure for leprosy and by the Ottomans for syphilis. One Greek legend has it that the city was founded by the leprous daughter of a Byzantine emperor who was miraculously cured after a visit to the hot springs. Fortunately, I am unable to vouch for the accuracy of these claims. What I can attest to, however, is that after a busy day of exploring Bursa, there is nothing better for my spirits than a pleasant couple of hours in the Eski Kaplıca. The Kervansaray Termal Hotel forms a U shape around these baths, and one can actually walk directly from the hotel into the baths.

Bursa was conquered following a ten-year siege in 1326 by Orhan Gazi, two years after the death of his father, Osman, to become the first capital of the fledgling Ottoman polity. When the Byzantine official who surrendered the city was asked by the new ruler why they had finally capitulated after holding out so long, he replied: "Your father had taken all our villages, and our former peasants who live in them are happy. We, too, wanted to share that happiness." Therein lay one of the secrets of Ottoman success: good treatment and a fair tax burden (often less than under a strapped and weakened Byzantium) made it possible to rule a population most of whom shared neither the religion, the language, nor the culture of their new rulers.

Writing some fifteen years after the fall of Bursa, the Byzantine chronicler Nicepheros Gregoras described the melding of the region's Muslim and Christian populations: "Therein all the Bithynians came together, all the barbarians who were of his [Orhan's] race, and all the *mixobarbaroi* [offspring of mixed Greek and Turkish unions] and in addition all those of our race whom fate forced to serve the barbarians." This must have accounted for the quick conversion of Byzantine "Prusa" into Ottoman "Brusa," and then to the name which has come down today as "Bursa."

Even after the Ottoman center moved west, first to Dimetoka and Edirne in the Balkans in the early 1360s, then to Istanbul in 1453, Bursa remained a center of learning and in many ways the spiritual core of the state. This is reflected in the large number of surviving *medreses* (theological seminaries), ever-present mosques, and the ornamental *türbes* (domed tombs) of the first six rulers, all of whom were buried in Bursa, and in the signs of royal patronage still evident throughout the city.

Sultanic mosques abound, including the unique twenty-domed Ulu Cami (Great Mosque) built by Yıldırım Bayezit, at the heart of the present-day city. To its east is the Yeşil Cami complex erected by his son Çelebi Mehmet (Mehmed I). To the west, in Çekirge, is the beautiful complex of buildings endowed by his father, Murad Hüdavendigâr. It includes what is today known as the Hüdavendigâr Camii (Ruler's Mosque), which was designed as a multipurpose building (as were most early Ottoman mosques), containing under one roof a *zaviye* (hostel for dervishes), a *medrese*, and the actual sanctuary itself. Next to it still stands the *imaret*, where twice a day those who worked in the complex, students of the *medrese*, dervishes staying at the *zaviye*, travelers (rich and poor), and the local indigent were fed free of charge. No longer in existence is the hospital. In its garden is the tomb of Murad himself and, lower down the hill, the Eski Kaplıca. In the center of the town once stood an imposing *han*, also endowed by this ruler, as were numerous others built by his descendants (which do survive). In short, here is an encapsulated version of early Ottoman history.

The story it tells is not the one recorded by the sixteenth-century chroniclers, who lived at a time when the dynasty had already achieved its aspiration to be recognized as the successor of the earlier great Sunni (Orthodox) Ummayid, Abbasid, and Seljuk empires. As part of that goal the sixteenth-century rulers had fully embraced orthodoxy (this also set them apart from their eastern enemy, the Shii Safavids in Iran), and the early history of their enterprise was conveniently rewritten accordingly.

Far from what they had become by the time these mythologized eulogies were penned, initially the fourteenth-century sultans ruled over a state the overwhelming majority of whose inhabitants were Christians, reflected in the fact that the services

of the hospitals and soup kitchens endowed by Murad Hüdavendigâr and other rulers were available to subjects regardless of
religion. This largesse impressed several European visitors.
The facilities provided for the Muslim mystics, the dervishes,
which included free lodging in the *zaviyes* and free food in the
imarets, likewise reflected their key role in conquests of the
period. Their spiritual leaders, known as *Babas* (Fathers) or *Sultans* (Rulers), led the Ottoman troops into battle, and it was the
moral authority they conferred on early Ottoman rulers that
enabled them to maintain the loyalty of the seminomadic Turcoman tribesmen whose support was key to early Ottoman success.

It is no coincidence that the oldest Ottoman document to survive is the foundation charter, or *vakfiyye*, drawn up by Orhan
Gazi in 1324, endowing a *zaviye* for these wandering mystics, and
placing its management in the hands of a converted freed eunuch
named Sharaf al-din Muqbil. The document's careful wording
(reflecting the fact that the eunuch had no offspring) states that he
will be succeeded as administrator of the foundation by the ablest
of the children of the Christian slaves who serve the facility. This
was the milieu within which Christians and Muslims, slave and
free alike, mingled. It was this milieu which served to create the
new race of Ottoman Turks, whose heritage is still so visible.

Viewed against this background, the surviving early Ottoman
monuments of Bursa take on a special meaning. Their scope and
numbers are truly impressive, even more so when we factor in the
series of man-made and natural disasters of the past half millennium. Three times Muslim armies occupied, looted, and burned
up half the city (Tamerlane's army in 1403, the forces of Karamani Mehmet in 1413, and the rebels known as the Celalis in
1609–12). Earthquakes, always a bane in Bithynia (which lies
across a major fault line), frequently took their toll as well. Fires, a
perennial problem in a city whose residences were built primarily
of lath and plaster, frequently ravaged whole quarters. Finally, in
the twentieth century, the rejection of everything Ottoman in the

new Republic of Turkey meant the destruction or neglect of monuments that stood as silent reminders of the past one was not supposed to remember. What is amazing is less how much is gone than how much has survived. No visitor to Turkey can ever really gain a feel for the wonders of the Ottoman past without a visit to Bursa.

EXPLORING BURSA

It is easy to find your way around Bursa, because wherever you are the mountain of Uludağ is visible behind the city. The key districts are some distance apart, built as they were on different ridges by successive sultans in the fourteenth and fifteenth centuries. But getting around is easy by cab or *dolmuş*, or by car using the small lanes above the city to avoid the traffic.

Around the Yeşil Mosque and Emir Sultan

The place for aesthetics: if time is short, spend it at the **Yeşil Cami** and **Yeşil Türbe**, the mosque and tomb of Mehmet I. From here you see why Bursa was known as Green Bursa: you get the most perfect view of the hilltop mosque of **Emir Sultan**, surrounded by cypresses, just a ten-minute stroll away. A sleepy museum in a box-hedged garden occupies the Yeşil *medrese*, alongside a row of prettily painted houses, now antique shops. Emir Sultan's courtyard, with its wooden arches, has a nineteenth-century Caucasian feel. Birdhouses are built into all the walls; fine stones and cypresses fill the cemetery below. Itinerant sellers outside the mosques sell leather slippers and earthenware pots. Encourage them.

- Not the place for a meal. Try tea with a pastry from **Arzum**, opposite the museum: buttery bread enriched with sesame oil (*tahinli çörek*), or poppy-seed pastries (*haşhaşlı burma çöreği*). **Yeşil Timsahlar**, at Namazgâh Caddesi 34, has walnut bread

(*cevizli lokum*) and shortbread sculpted like pears, with cloves
for stalks.

Around the Ulu Cami

The bustling heart of town, with the **Ulu Cami** (Great Mosque)
and its herculean calligraphies, the bazaars brushing up against it,
the **Kent Müzesi** (City Museum) for local arts and crafts, and
loads of places to eat. Fire and quakes have taken their toll of the
Covered Bazaar, but it is still choc-a-bloc with Bursa towels,
loofahs, *kese* (massage gloves), clogs, bowls, and soaps. You can
still buy silk at the most famous caravansary, Koza Han, and sip tea
or lemonade (*gazoz*) under the plane trees. Stock up on local
cheese and honey at Tahtakale, behind the Ulu Cami. Chewy
Mihaliç (pronounced "mah-lich") cheese is good at **Polatgil
Gıda** (Veziri Caddesi 11).

- For eighty years the **Iskender Kebabcısı** by the State Theater—all whitewash and gleaming sky-blue paint—has been
  home to the eponymous Iskender kebab, *döner* on *pide*, with
  tomato sauce, yogurt, and melted butter poured over.

- **Çiçek Izgara** (by the town hall) is famous for another Bursa
  treat, *Inegöl köfte*—succulent veal-and-lamb patties, which
  you sprinkle with paprika and eat with *piyaz*, a bean and
  onion salad.

- **Ömür Köftecisi**, up at the Ulu Cami's west door, is a more
  lively *Inegöl köfteci*. Also does chops, good French fries, and
  sweet, milky *kadayıf*.

- **Namlı Ciğerci** (behind Ömür in Ertaş Çarşısı), hidden
  among the towel shops, does meltingly delicious fried liver.

- For slow cooking, visit **Abidin Usta** in Tuzpazarı, near
  Çiçek: stews (*yahni*), cabbage leaf wrapped around rice,

raisins, and chestnuts (*kestaneli lahana dolması*), and, on Fridays, liver and rice wrapped in caul (*ciğer sarması*).

- **Lâlezar** (Unlü Caddesi 14, near the Kent Müzesi) also offers local home-cooked delicacies: pit-roasted lamb (*kuzu tandır*), lamb in puff pastry (*talaş kebabı*), and aubergine purée (*hünkar beğendi*).

- **Bağdat Hurmacısı** pastries ooze syrup. **Kafkas** is king of *marron glacé* (*kestane şekeri*).

The Muradiye

Escape the concrete in a beautiful, shady garden with loads of history. Take a book on a fine spring day. The **Muradiye Camii**, with its fine brickwork portico, is the last of the great early Bursa mosques. The gardens' imperial mausoleums open during museum hours. Across the square, in the Şair Ahmetpaşa Medrese, is the **Esat Uluumay Museum**, with its costume and jewelry collection.

Tophane

This is the old citadel area. The walled city itself is built up and the walls are being (over-) restored, but get a map and take a stroll. Serious anoraks hunt here for interesting early mosques amid the concrete. **Yaniçoğlu** has a fountain-minaret like a bell tower, **Kavaklı** a five hundred-year-old plane tree. Mystics gravitate to the sufi **Üftade**. Here Orhan Gazi built his palace. He and his father, Osman Gazi, founder of the Ottoman Empire, lie here in stately tombs.

- **Bursa Kebabçısı** is perfectly placed in the square by the tombs, in an old wooden house rescued by Ibrahim Ünal Avşar, a math teacher, who does good Iskender kebab, grilled *köfte* on *pide,* and delicious puddings: milky *kadayıf,* dried figs stuffed with walnuts (*incir tatlısı*), pumpkin pudding (*kabak* *tatlısı*). Order a mix and add a dollop of cream (*kaymak*). The grape juice (*şıra*) and coffee cannot be bettered. If the garden is full, step upstairs for an even better view.

Çekirge

This is bathhouse territory. Çekirge, once a distant suburb on the road to Uludağ, grew up around **Hüdavendigar Camii** and the famous hot springs. There used to be *hamams* of every shape and size, and a few survive. Most have a hotel attached.

- Survive the noisy wedding parties at the **Kervansaray Hotel**, and in the morning head in your dressing gown to the Eski Kaplıca. At the **Gönlüferah Hotel**, a revamped grande dame with the best private *hamams* (domed pools and lion's heads), step into the lift. The **Çelik Palas** has a Goldfinger pool, but the water is heated.

- Çardak and its fab potato *köfte* are no more; smart hotels spurn Turkish food. On a fine day take the Uludağ road and try an open-air *kendin pişir kendin ye* ("cook-yourself, eat-yourself") place. Lamb by the kilo comes to the table with a charcoal *mangal*. Sprinkle with oregano and order a drink.

Yildirim Bayezit and the Lower Town

Motorways and malls march across the plain with little for culture vultures except **Yıldırım Bayezid Camii**, 1399, model for the Yeşil Cami—with the portico it lacks—and good places to eat.

- Kurtuluş Cad (Yıldırım Belediyesi) has Bursa's best offal soup (*paça*) shops: the immaculate **Paçacı Hüsnü** (no. 219) and earthy **Çorbacı Salih** (no. 187). Like many Bursa citizens, Hüsnü is from the Balkans. Veal, vinegar, and garlic are the ingredients of his soups, always rich but delicate: there's tripe, finely chopped (*işkembe*) or chunky (*tuzlama*), head (*kelle*), tongue (*dil*), trotter (*ayak*), or brain soup, or a mix. The late

Çorbacı Salih served tripe soup for thirty years. Korkut, his grandson, has added pilav, beans (*kuru fasulya*), and *malak ciğeri*, tender female water-buffalo liver.

- The lower town has two fine *lokantas*: affable **Selim Usta** (Demirtaş Paşa Hamamı, Inönü Caddesi 70) offers steaming broths, stews, pilav, beans, silky *helva*. Olive-oil dishes include artichokes and vineleaf dolma. **Hayat** (by the Almira Hotel) attracts factory owners and a conveyor belt of SUVs.

- Iskender's heirs now own the trademark and are busy opening emporia, including the tourist group–friendly **Botanik Bahçesi**—Hollywood Bursa. **Hacıbey** is a plush place at a BP station on the Istanbul road. For the real thing, join the queue in the old Garaj spare-parts district—**Uludağ Kebabçısı** is owned by brothers Cemal and Cemil, old Iskender hands.

Short Trips

Bithynia, as the province was called when Pliny was governor, is prosperous, fertile land, far from the tourist trail. To the north, between Yalova and Bursa, the hills are draped with olive groves and Umbria comes to mind. East, the road to Ankara leads to the sterner Anatolian plateau, softened in spring by drifts of cherry blossom. This is border country, littered with the tombs of *babas* and *sultans*, the spiritual leaders of the nomadic Turcomans, who settled here in the twelfth century. They are still places of pilgrimage. Along the Marmara west of Bursa is flatter, even more fertile land—good dairy country; hence Bursa's excellent cheeses, worth stocking up on for picnics. The sites are rarely ends in themselves, but are good excuses to roam. Behind every giant plane there's a story (and often a café).

- Uludağ: Coffee under Inkaya's giant plane tree is the first stop, then on you drive, up through forests, first of chestnut then of fir, with places to eat, until you reach the national park. The road ends above the tree line at the huge ski hotels. Only then do you get a view.

- East: the Ankara road. First stop **Cumalıkızık**, an untouched seven hundred-year-old Turcoman village minutes from Bursa: a lovely wander (avoid weekends). Spring water rushes down the streets, cooling the air and watering orchards. A few villagers rent rooms and offer delicious snacks. Next, **Babasultan**: no longer pretty, but the drive is. Baba Sultan, mounted on a deer, helped Orhan Gazi conquer Bursa and planted the tree in the citadel at Kavaklı Cami before going home to this lovely spot. No politics for him. His tomb is beside another giant plane. Over the door hang antlers. On to poor, ugly, bespoiled **Inegöl**. **Beşer** is the home of the *Inegöl köfte*, next to Ishak Pasha's once-perfect mosque.

- West: **Gölyazı** is a sleepy island village on **Lake Uluabat**. Further along is **Issızhan** caravansary. Another twenty minutes and you are in **Karacabey**, famous for its horses. Visit the fair (*panayır*) in May, full of lively gypsies. The lamb's the thing, borne in on a spit, eaten with your fingers—no other meat compares. One last stop in spring: Lake Manyas—where ancient Persians built a paradise garden to watch the birds.

- North: the coast road to **Trilye** (Zeytinbağı) winds through pretty olive groves—very slippery in the harvest season. Buy kilos of olives and eat fish by the harbor at Savarona. The road to **Iznik** via Yenişehir is also beautiful: soothing lake, lovely city walls, glorious sunsets.

When to go: any time but high summer. In bleak midwinter, heaven is tramping through the snow to a marrow-warming *hamam*. Getting there: by *vapur* to Yalova, or high-speed *hızlı feribot* to Mudanya (ido.com.tr). If driving from Istanbul, take the calming Eskihisar ferry to Yalova.

THE BATHS OF BURSA

The seventeenth-century Turkish traveler Evliya Çelebi wrote that Bursa consisted purely of water. Springs, hot and cold, gushed out of the hillside, and they still do.

Before World War I, Bursa was the height of fashion. Each water had its peculiarity, and visitors spent weeks taking them in sequence. One governor found himself looking after the Duke of Schleswig-Holstein, Prince Victor Napoleon, and Duke Carl Edward Saxe-Coburg in quick succession.

The two most famous baths are the Yeni Kaplıca (New Hot Springs) and the Eski Kaplıca (Old Hot Springs). The heavily renovated Eski Kaplıca is now virtually part of the luxury Kervansaray Hotel, and you are likely to have the place to yourself. On the other hand, the Yeni Kaplıca, barely changed since 1894, is bustling from dawn to dusk.

Some hotels in the Çekirge area still have their own springs and baths, from the plush, such as the Gönlüferah, to the delightfully old-fashioned, such as the Selvinaz, sadly threatened by developers.

Many other handsome *hamams* are dotted around the city, including the Timurtaş Paşa and the Mahkeme, which both heat their water—the latter using sawdust.

RECAPTURING OLD BURSA

With a population of over two million, Bursa has already been swamped by concrete. Fortunately, "Green" Bursa's swan song coincided with the rise of photography. The Kent Müzesi (City Museum) always has interesting displays on the social history of the city, and several good albums of photographs have been published.

Bursa in the Ottoman Period, by Neslihan Türkün Dostoğlu (Akmed; in two volumes, in Turkish, French, and English), has images from the Suna and Inan Kıraç Collection and the Albert Khan Museum, Paris. Engin Özendeş's *Bursa: Osmanlı'nın İlk Başkenti* (Bursa: First Ottoman Capital) is a good collection of photos in paperback.

On the historical front, the birth of the Ottoman Empire is best explained in Heath Lowry's *Nature of the Early Ottoman Empire*. His *Ottoman Bursa in Travel Accounts* uses untapped sources that historians have largely ignored. *Osman's Dream*, by Caroline Finkel, is a good general history.

Devlet Ana (Mother State), Kemal Tahir's classic saga set in the early Ottoman years, awaits translation. The only detailed guide-book to the area in English, *Mini Tours*, by Betsy Harrell (Red-house), is out of print but well worth finding.

Gallipoli

The band played softly and mournfully and my father kissed us children, then said his good-bye with lips that were wooden and stiff. An old man came forward and handed him the Turkish flag and the people all shouted "Padişahim çok yaşa" and my father stepped into his place, amongst the other recruits. . . . Then they turned the corner, out of our sight, only the sound of the cheering and the singing voices and the noise of the band, coming ever fainter back to us.

> —IRFAN ORGA,
> *Portrait of a Turkish Family*

The drama of the Dardanelles campaign by reason of the beauty of its setting, the grandeur of its theme and the unhappiness of its ending, will always rank amongst the world's classic tragedies. The story is a record of lost opportunities and eventual failure.

> —BRIGADIER GENERAL C. F. ASPINALL-OGLANDER,
> *History of the Great War Based on Official
> Documents* (a twenty-eight-volume series
> covering the military operations of the British
> Army during World War I, usually referred to
> simply as the *British Official History*)

The *History of the Great War Based on Official Documents* referred to on the previous page was written as a technical history for military staff rather than for the general public. The first volume was published in 1923, the last in 1949. British historian John Keegan has been critical of the work's dry prose, and has remarked that "the compilers . . . have achieved the remarkable feat of writing an exhaustive account of one of the world's greatest tragedies without the display of any emotion at all." Regarding Gallipoli, anyone who's seen the movie knows the conflict was gushing with human emotion.

For a very basic and succinct summary of the campaign, one would have to search hard for a better one than that provided by "Gallipoli 1915: The Drama of the Dardanelles," an excellent Web page compiled by the Imperial War Museum in London: "Early in January 1915 matters came to a head when Russia asked for help in its fight against the Turks in the Caucasus. Britain and France began a naval campaign to break open the Dardanelles, the narrow strip of water that led from the Mediterranean into the Sea of Marmara and divided European from Asiatic Turkey. The ultimate aim was to knock the Turks out of the war by threatening their capital, Constantinople. When the most concerted attempt to smash the central defences of the Dardanelles failed on 18 March, a military force was assembled and plans were made to capture the shoreline of the Gallipoli Peninsula and so allow the naval campaign to be resumed." As Napoléon remarked in a letter to his aide-de-camp Marquis de Caulaincourt in 1808, "Essentially the great question remains: who will hold Constantinople?"

One would have to search equally as hard for a more heartbreaking scene than this one, from *Portrait of a Turkish Family*. The author has learned about the fate of his father from a captain, who disclosed that, on the march to the Dardanelles, his father had suffered from foot trouble. When his feet began to swell they had to cut his torn boots off him, and they found that his two feet were so badly infected up to the ankles that he was left by the roadside, as was the custom, and a message went back down the lines that a wounded man was lying under a tree. "And eventually this message would reach the end of the marching lines where a horse-drawn cart lumbered for the express purpose of picking up the sick and wounded. But if the cart was already full to overflowing with all the other sick soldiers who had dropped out on the way? Ah well—in that case a man just lay by the side of the road under the blazing sun and waited for the next lot of marching soldiers to take up the same old cry, that a man lay wounded under the trees by the side of an alien road. Down, down the weary lines the cry would go, but perhaps by the time the sick-cart reached the spot a man would be dead and there was not much point in carrying a dead man—when there were so many living who still might be saved."

Though it is best recommended as an overnight journey, a visit to Gallipoli is most definitely worth a detour.

Gallipoli
Landscape of Sacrifice

CATHARINE REYNOLDS

♋

THE COMMONWEALTH War Graves Commission information sheet referred to in the following article is excellent, and is available as a complimentary download from the Commission's Web site. Go to cwgc.org; then click on Publications, Free Publications, and Information Sheets, and scroll down alphabetically to Gallipoli.

CATHARINE REYNOLDS wrote the wonderful "Paris Journal" column for *Gourmet* for more than twenty years, and the column was honored with a James Beard Foundation Award in 1998. She also was a longtime contributing editor of the magazine, and she now divides her time between Paris and Boston while working on a biography of Nicolas Fouquet, Louis XIV's first minister of finance.

GALLIPOLI. FOR many of us the name summons scenes of Mel Gibson and his fellow Australians in Peter Weir's film of that name, struggling onto Turkey's shores under fire in one of World War I's bloodiest campaigns.

History buffs may think of Winston Churchill's support for the operation conceived to bring Constantinople and all Turkey into

Allied hands: to enable the Allies to gain access to Russian grain, and to supply the Eastern front, thus easing pressure on the Western trenches.

Neither approach conveys the totality of this complex and horrific battle. The 259-day campaign in 1915 and early 1916, described by one who fought in it as "hell heaped-up," resulted in more than half a million casualties. Still controversial, the campaign is generally considered an imaginative strategic ploy botched by such catastrophic incompetence that not even the dazzling heroism of Allied troops could redeem it.

Last autumn I set out from Istanbul with three friends to visit the battlefield at Gallipoli and to understand better the struggle for the sixty-mile-long peninsula that juts off Turkey's European coast, separating the Aegean Sea from the Dardanelles.

Approaching from Çanakkale on the boat across the Dardanelles to Kilitbahir, a ten-minute trip, I was immediately struck by the difficulty of the peninsula's little-populated scrub-covered terrain—which seems to have bemused the Allied commander, the British general Sir Ian Hamilton, who reported to his Secretary of State for War, Lord Kitchener: "Gallipoli looks a much harder nut to crack than it did over a map in your office."

Hamilton's objective was to clear the peninsula of the Turkish troops allied with Germany, so silencing the artillery and clearing the mines that had foiled naval attempts to win the Dardanelles in February and March. His plan called for a double blow by British, French, Australian, and New Zealand forces at the southern tip of the peninsula, at Cape Helles, and a landing south of Arı Burnu on the west coast, with two diversions: a landing at Kumkale on the Asian shore and a demonstration at Bolayır near the neck of the peninsula.

Planning our visit, we had noted the relative compactness of the battleground, an area roughly twenty miles from north to south. Fighting was confined to three sectors, the Cape Helles landing beaches, Anzac Cove on the Aegean coast, and the Suvla Bay beaches north of Anzac.

Signs to orient visitors are so few that we were glad to have an excellent map on the information sheet issued by the Commonwealth War Graves Commission. And we were relieved that our car was a rental as we edged off the ferry onto washboard roads.

The beautiful and desolate Gallipoli countryside has largely been returned to the grazing land that has sustained its few inhabitants, many of them nomads, since ancient times. A national park encompasses the area around Anzac Cove, although Commonwealth, French, and Turkish authorities maintain the cemeteries and national monuments scattered over the hills.

That first afternoon, we made for the Cape Helles landing beaches first so that we could orient ourselves and appreciate the strategic situation. On April 25, 1915, Helles defenses were incredibly undermanned, with only two Turkish infantry battalions and an engineer company. But that was not apparent to the men of the Royal Dublin Fusiliers rowing at daybreak toward V Beach to the west of the old fort of Seddülbahir. One described the day as "a beauteous morning, calm and free," an illusion dispelled as a "tornado of fire swept over the incoming boats, lashing the calm waters of the bay as with a thousand whips." Hamilton had overestimated the ability of Allied naval guns to knock out the entrenched gun emplacements.

The next wave included the refitted collier River Clyde, conceived as an amphibious Trojan horse to be run aground along the shore, spilling 2,000 British infantrymen onto the 400-yard-long beach. Few made it, wiped out by machine-gun fire from the Turkish troops dug into the surrounding slopes. Allied commanders had failed to appreciate that the six weeks taken to muster troops and transport had permitted German field marshal Otto Liman von Sanders's Turkish conscripts to entrench themselves and to train.

Today, the beach at Cape Helles is curiously domesticated, with whitewashed buildings dotting the inlet. I asked myself whether the youngsters playing soccer along the beach knew anything of the men little older than they who had lost their lives grappling ashore nearly a century ago.

To the west of the beach the austere 100-foot Helles Memorial obelisk marks some of the first ground taken by British soldiers on April 25—and the last from which they withdrew on January 9, 1916. The names of 20,763 British, Australian, New Zealand, Newfoundland, and Indian dead are engraved in honey-colored stone alongside the names of formations and ships that participated in the campaign. The late-afternoon sun refracted across the approach to the Dardanelles, as if to emphasize the unattained goal.

Less than two and a half miles east stands the French War Cemetery, commemorating the 10,000 Frenchmen who died establishing and holding the right end of the Helles line, and the more recently erected Turkish Çanakkale Martyrs Memorial. In keeping with local custom, the 25,000 Turkish dead had long gone uncommemorated, buried in communal graves in the seasonal watercourses that scar the landscape.

Today the Turkish government is trying to make Gallipoli a focus of nationalism. It has erected the Martyrs Memorial and a variety of other monuments, as well as a highly informative modern museum at Kabatepe, a twenty-minute drive from the French cemetery. Although the one-story building is architecturally uninspired, the museum's collection is absorbing. Exhibits, labeled in Turkish and English, illustrate the squalid conditions under which Allied and Turkish troops operated.

Despite the torrid summer, the former were often outfitted in woolly uniforms. Rations of bully beef, butter, and tea were no more suitable, and, for the Allies, who never reached the inland wells, water was scarce. The Turkish infantryman, nicknamed Mehmetçik, was better nourished—on legumes and vegetables—

than his British counterpart. Flies plagued everyone, and dysentery was rife; Allied casualties from disease were double the battle casualties.

Anzac Cove, a few miles northwest of the museum, is the most visited site of the battlefield, a place of pilgrimage for Australian backpackers and other young people. It takes its name from the 16,000 men of the Australian and New Zealand Army Corps—or Anzacs—who were put ashore on April 25 at this second landing zone. The dash and tenacity of these soldiers became the stuff of epic.

Approaching the area, we paused at Beach Cemetery, a poignant spot where 391 graves cling precariously to the shore. The Commonwealth dead were mostly buried where they fell, so there are thirty carefully tended cemeteries in addition to this one scattered across the peninsula.

In the second prong of the April landing, an uncharted current swept the craft carrying the Australian and New Zealand battalions a mile north of their intended landing place to an inhospitable crescent beach backed by steep bluffs cut with deep, bewildering ravines that became Anzac Cove. Within hours the sliver of beach became a welter of pack animals, stores, ammunition, and the wounded waiting to be evacuated, with shells arcing across the sky.

Turkish machine-gun emplacements pinned the troops down within yards of the beachhead. General Hamilton directed: "There is nothing for it but for you to dig yourselves in and stick it out." Dig they did, chipping miles of trenches out of the crumbly earth. In them they found what shelter they could for the next eight and a half months, knowing that the defender's trenches were only yards away.

Glad we had worn boots, we walked up the tangled gullies near Anzac, where we found it hard to see the outlines of the old trenches. But in the surpassing stillness we could imagine the young soldiers, their bare shoulders blackened by sun and grime, carrying ammunition to the firing line. Repeated attempts to break out ended in failure. Throughout the campaign the Allies never managed to penetrate much beyond the foothold they gained in those April days, an area no more than two miles long and three-quarters of a mile deep.

One reason the Anzacs failed to achieve their objectives that first day was the intervention of Lieutenant Colonel Mustafa Kemal, who rushed reinforcements to Chunuk Bair, securing the northern end of the Turkish line and gaining control of the heights. The reputation earned at Gallipoli enabled him to go on to win his more familiar title, Atatürk, Father of the Turkish People.

Kemal was also instrumental in thwarting the Allies' last serious bid to turn the tide, the landing on August 6 and 7 at Suvla Bay, five miles up the coast, when three fresh divisions were put ashore in an attempt to outflank the Turks, which proved a fiasco due to the staggering ineptitude of the corps commander, Lieutenant General Sir Frederick Stopford.

Circling inland from Suvla and driving back into the hills, we joined a handful of Turkish and English-speaking tourists visiting the monument to Atatürk and his troops on the heights of Chunuk Bair, one of the best points from which to survey Gallipoli. Close by, the New Zealand Memorial reminded us that valiant New Zealanders held the top of this vital 850-foot hill for a few hours on August 7.

Under a glaring September sky we took in the whole battleground: the Dardanelles to the east, Anzac to the west, and the Helles memorial to the south, as well as the corrugated landscape made more sere by a fire in 1994. It sleeps peacefully under a mantle of scrub and pine, broken by few roads. I scrambled through the elaborately reconstructed trenches nearby to inspect the view of Suvla but found the shelter unconvincingly tidy and curiously unevocative.

To the southwest, marking the left flank of the Anzac salient, the Nek was the scene of the assault dramatized in the movie *Gallipoli*. Although the film erroneously implies that British nonchalance at Suvla fruitlessly cost Australian lives, it nonetheless offers a powerful picture of battlefield conditions.

For the Australian and New Zealand troops Gallipoli was a national rite of passage. Today Australians make up the majority of visitors, though only 15 percent of the soldiers at Gallipoli were Australian nationals, making the legend forged from their bravery all the more phenomenal.

The road past the cemeteries at Quinn's Post and Johnston's Jolly more or less follows the course of the opposing trenches. As little as five yards separated Anzac and Turkish lines—a tenth of the no-man's-land typical on the Western front.

We completed our two-day visit at the far end of the heights over Anzac Cove. Lone Pine Cemetery and Memorial stand above the trenches taken at appalling sacrifice in early August. The panoramic view confirms the vulnerability of the entire Anzac salient. In hindsight, withdrawal of all Allied troops seems to have been inescapable, as General Hamilton's replacement,

General Sir Charles Monro, persuaded by storms and cold, finally concluded.

In one of the most brilliant logistical exercises in military history, the 120,000-man garrison of Anzac-Suvla and Helles was withdrawn in late December and early January without a single casualty.

Only in visiting Gallipoli did I come to appreciate the futility of the enterprise and the tragedy of its failure. With painful prescience Sublieutenant Rupert Brooke—the young English poet who died only two days before the first landings—penned this encomium for his fellows:

> *These laid the world away; poured out the red*
> *Sweet wine of youth; gave up the years to be*
> *Of work and joy, and that unhoped serene,*
> *That men call age; and those who would have been,*
> *Their sons, they gave, their immortality.*

Though it's possible, as Catharine Reynolds did, to tour Gallipoli on one's own, hiring a guide is a more multilayered experience and usually results in a more efficient visit as visitors can tour the battlefield in a single day. On Kenan Çelik's Web site he refers to himself as "Probably the best guide for Gallipoli battlefields," but he is *without doubt* the very best guide to Gallipoli. Çelik has been a guide to the battlefields of the Gallipoli Peninsula for more than twenty-five years, and he's been featured in several documentaries about the Gallipoli campaign. He speaks English very well, having earned a Fulbright scholarship at Oregon State University, where he received an MA in literature for his study of the works of Edwardian poet Rupert Brooke. In 2000, Çelik was awarded the OAM, Medal of the Order of Australia—established in 1975 by Queen Elizabeth II of Australia—and was the first Turkish citizen to receive this honor. Kenan Çelik may be reached directly at kcelik@ttmail.com and through his Web site, Kcelik.com. Though he specializes in Gallipoli, Kenan also offers guided tours of nearby Troy. Kenan also arranges for visitors to be picked up in Istanbul.

If he's fully booked during the time you'll be in Turkey (he is in great demand) or if you're looking for an experience that isn't *quite* so scholarly, a great company to contact is TJs Tours & Hostel, in Eceabat (anzacgallipolitours.com / enquiries@anzacgallipolitours.com). TJs is operated by a Turkish-Australian couple, and their goal is to "bring the ANZAC legend to life; to open travelers' eyes to the wonders that Turkey has to offer; and to widen the friendships that started in WWI." TJs offers tours daily, every day of the year, and, conveniently, the company owns both the Eceabat Hotel and TJs Hostel. TJs has over fourteen years of experience on the battlefields and the guides know the area inside and out. The guides also don't rush visitors through the battlefields, and all speak English and Turkish. Details of all the tours are found on the Web site, along with some very useful tips, such as: there are very few toilets in the battlefield area, nor shops, so buy water and snacks beforehand; take sunscreen and a hat as there is little shade; the ANZAC area is an alcohol-free zone. TJs also organizes special ANZAC Day tours (essential to book ahead) and can assist in locating a grave—it's the only agency with a set of registers for the Gallipoli Peninsula. The books were given to them in recognition of their work for the Commonwealth War Graves, and they can thus locate the burial site of any Commonwealth soldier who fell in the campaign.

Gallipoli
The Dardanelles, April–December 1915

Upon the margin of a rugged shore
There is a spot now barren, desolate,
A place of graves, sodden with human gore
That Time will hallow, Memory consecrate.

There lie the ashes of the mighty dead,
The youth who lit with flame Obscurity,
Fought true for Freedom, won thro' rain of lead
Undying fame, their immortality.

The stranger wand'ring when the war is over,
The ploughman there driving his coulter deep,
The husbandman who golden harvests reap—
From hill and ravine, from each plain and cover
Will hear a shout, see phantoms on the marge,
See men again making a deathless charge.

JOHN WILLIAM STREETS
The Undying Splendour, 1917

ATEŞ ORGA, in *Istanbul: Portrait of a City*, tells us that Sergeant Streets was of the 12th Battalion, York and Lancaster Regiment, and he was one of the unsung poets of the 1914–18 conflict. Streets was reported "wounded and missing" on the first day of the Battle of the Somme, July 1, 1916, and then reported "killed" on May 1, 1917. *The Undying Splendour* was published posthumously. Orga notes that, in Gallipoli, "no sides are taken, there is neither victory nor defeat, accusation nor judgement: Johnny Turk and Bulldog Brit, 'the mighty dead,' are one and the same, separated only by uniform—cannon fodder and conscripts on a short road to the afterlife."

RECOMMENDED READING

~~~~~~~~~~~~~~~~~~~~~~~~~~~~~~ ෪ ~~~~~~~~~~~~~~~~~~~~~~~~~~~~~~

A very thorough Gallipoli bibliography, featuring forty titles from the Imperial War Museum's Department of Printed Books, may be found by a link on the Gallipoli 1915: The Drama of the Dardanelles Web page, Iwm.org.uk/upload/package/2/gallipoli/index.htm.

Catharine Reynolds and guide Kenan Çelik (see text box on page 468) highly recommend the following: *Gallipoli*, by Robert Rhodes James (Macmillan, 1965), which Catharine says "remains the benchmark," and *Gallipoli*, by Alan Moorehead (Harper Perennial, 2002). Additionally, Catharine also recommends *Gallipoli*, by Michael Hickey (John Murray, 1995), and Kenan adds *Birds Without Wings*, by Louis de Bernières (Knopf, 2004), as well as *Gallipoli*, by Les Carlyon (Macmillan 2001), whom Kenan actually assisted in the writing of this book.

I weigh in heavily on Alan Moorehead's volume. I have been a huge fan of Moorehead's books on the Nile, and this work on Gallipoli is just as lively and informative. Moorehead (1910–1983) was a foreign correspondent for the *London Daily Express* and became internationally known for his coverage of World War II campaigns. He writes in the introduction to *Gallipoli* that, by August 1914, "the setting could hardly have been better for the complicated intrigues that now began: the foreign ambassadors, installed like robber barons in their enormous embassies along the Bosphorus, the Young Turks in the Yıldız Palace and the Sublime Porte, and everywhere through the sprawling decaying beautiful capital itself that hushed and conspiratorial air which seems to overtake all neutral cities on the edge of war. It was the atmosphere of the high table in the gambling casino very late at night when every move takes on a kind of fated self-importance."

In the epilogue, Moorehead quotes from a moving preface given by General Sir Ian Hamilton to the Gallipoli soldiers:

> "You will hardly fade away until the sun fades out of the sky and the earth sinks into the universal blackness. For already you form part of that great tradition of the Dardanelles which began with Hector and Achilles. In another few thousand years the two stories will have blended into one, and whether when 'the iron roaring went up to the vault of heaven through the unharvested sky,' as Homer tells us, it was the spear of Achilles or whether it was a 100-lb shell from Asiatic Annie won't make much odds to the Almighty."

Hamilton was given command of the Gallipoli Peninsula in April 1915, a post he held until the following October. During his tenure, he visited every front line of the trenches, and his dispatches from the Dardanelles remain models of their kind.

Troy

I regret that I haven't been to Troy. For a long time I just thought that huge replica of the wooden horse was somehow too corny, but on my next trip to Turkey I will definitely be making the journey there. After all, it's one of Turkey's World Heritage sites, added in 1998, and, as the Lonely Planet guide states, for anyone who's read the *Iliad* or who's heard the tales of the Trojan War, Troy has "a romance few places on earth can hope to match." All the guidebooks have fairly thorough visitor information, but to get the most out of a visit, I recommend reading any of the following: *The*

Complete and Unabridged Bulfinch's Mythology, by Thomas Bulfinch (Modern Library, 1998); *Mythology*, by Edith Hamilton (New American Library, 1940); *Gods, Graves, and Scholars*, by C. W. Ceram (Knopf, 1951), in which Troy is included in the first chapter; *The Landmark Herodotus: The Histories*, edited by Robert Strassler and with a new translation by Andrea Purvis (Pantheon, 2007)—though this greatest classical work of history encompasses a much larger geographic area than the Levant, it's still a great reference for Troy, and it's such a pleasure to dip into this book; *The Odyssey*, by Adrian Mitchell (DK Classics, 2000), and *D'Aulaire's Greek Myths* (Delacorte, 1962) are great for children but perfectly suited for adults, too.

Finally, the stellar translations of *The Iliad* and *The Odyssey* by Robert Fagles (both published by Viking). Fagles, who passed away in 2008, was a renowned translator of Latin and Greek. His versions of *The Iliad* and *The Odyssey* became "unlikely best-sellers" according to his obituary in *The New York Times*, and together with his translation of *The Aeneid*, sold millions of copies. Their success, according to the obituary, "was due largely to Mr. Fagles's gifts as a writer. He was not an exactingly literal translator but rather one who sought to reinterpret the classics in a contemporary idiom."

A TURKISH MISCELLANY

I think of this section as an informative and interesting source-book, one that could almost be published as a separate volume. I say "almost" because the original version I wrote was over two hundred pages, which *is* just about the size of a separate book, and which my editor said was too long. So I had to delete many entries, kicking and screaming all the while. Happily, however, you'll find those entries—along with updates, more recommendations, and all kinds of worthy tips and noteworthy trivia—on my corner of the Vintage Web site, randomhouse.com/vintage.

A

Accommodations

Unlike France, for example, with its *chambres d'hôtes, auberges, hôtels de charme, gîtes,* and *châteaux-hôtels* (among others), Turkey does not have as many different *types* of lodgings—most everything is a hotel, a *pansiyon* (pensione), or a simple room in someone's house. Istanbul, however, has an astounding variety of hotels, in all price ranges, and so many of them are so appealing that it may prove difficult to choose among them—I love the hotels of Istanbul! I also believe that choosing where to stay is as important as any other trip-related decision. I do not buy into the idea that accommodations are only places to sleep—where you stay can be one of the most memorable parts of your trip, and the staff at a hotel can be enormously helpful in making your trip special. Deciding where to stay should not be taken lightly and deserves your best research efforts.

Because the city is so spread out, and because it is next to impossible to select just *one* place to stay, I recommend making reservations at two or possibly three places. In this way visitors may experience different neighborhoods as well as lodgings, perhaps choosing a moderate inn initially and then splurging on one of Istanbul's splendid palace hotels. Additionally, keep in mind that Sultanahmet, a great neighborhood to stay in due to its proximity to all the major sites of the Old City, is not known for great restaurants, so if you stay here you may find yourself taking a lot of cabs to Beyoğlu and the neighborhoods north of the Golden Horn.

When I first visited Istanbul, in 1990, the Hilton was the nicest hotel in town; it still is a fine hotel, and in fact it was the very first deluxe hotel in the city, built in 1957. But nineteen years later the list of world-class hotels in the city is long, a sign that for both business travelers and vacationers Istanbul's lodgings are now equal to those in any of the world's major cities. I myself do not generally prefer chain hotels, especially American ones, but those who do will find not only Hilton represented but also Marriott, Hyatt, Sheraton, Ramada, and Best Western, among others.

It is not my intent to visit dozens of hotels in Istanbul and report on them—that is within the purview of guidebooks, Web sites, and accommodations guides (one I particularly like is Alistair Sawday's *Special Places to Stay: Turkey*). But as someone who pays close attention to the tiniest details, has stayed in accommodations ranging from campgrounds to five-star hotels, is practically allergic to must and dust, has an exacting idea of the words "customer service," and who has been known to rearrange the furniture in a few hotel rooms, I do think I have something valuable to share with readers. Therefore, I move around when I travel, changing hotels and arranging visits to those that are either fully booked or that I otherwise might not see. I make sure to see lodgings both moderately priced and expensive, so that readers have personal recommendations for both. Most often, I am drawn to the moderate places that also represent a good value as I've found that these sometimes receive the least attention. It's never hard to find out about the budget or luxury places to stay, but the places in between—which I believe suit the pocketbooks of the majority of travelers—are often overlooked or given cursory consideration.

I also prefer to consult specialty hotel groups, assuming there is one for the destination I'm visiting. One of my favorites is the Association of Historical and Boutique Hoteliers of Turkey (historicalhotelsofturkey.org; there is also a nice booklet, but it's available only in Turkey). This association represents unique hotels with distinct features, and all are independently owned and managed. There are sixty-one members, with forty-eight in Istanbul, many of which do not appear in any guidebooks. I also very much like Small Hotels of Turkey, founded by Sevan and Mujde Nisanyan and on the Web at nisanyan.net. More than three hundred small, charming hotels and guesthouses are featured, and they are all vetted by Sevan and Mujde, who are very committed to a good quality-price ratio. They also publish a popular annual guide, *The Little Hotel Book*, which may be ordered online directly from their site or from *Cornucopia* (cornucopia .net). Other hotel groups I like are Small Luxury Hotels of the World (currently with only one property in Istanbul, Les Ottomans; see below) and Leading Hotels of the World (also with only one property in Istanbul, Çırağan Palace Kempinski; see below).

Here is a selection of lodgings that I particularly like and that I believe will make your stay in Istanbul special:

- Turing Ayasofya Konaklari, Sultanahmet (Soğukçeşme Sokak / +90 212 513 3660 / ayasofyapensions.com). This unique inn is actually made up of a row of nine individual wooden houses on a picturesque cobblestone street that is closed to traffic. The name of the street translates to Street of the Cold Fountain, one of several streets in Istanbul named for a fountain. Each "house" has between four and ten bedrooms and each has a lobby that is meant to be used for entertaining. Mine had a large sitting room, dining room, small kitchen, and bathroom, and could easily have accommodated twenty-five guests (my traveling companions and I kept joking that we were going to host a cocktail party here and invite all our new Istanbul friends—we never did, and I greatly regret it every time I think about it!). The interiors are nicely furnished in nineteenth-century Turkish style, and because each "house" has room for approximately ten people, staying here is *perfect* for families or friends traveling together. A few of the suites have their own private white marble *hamam*. An ample breakfast is served in a glass-roofed conservatory.

This wonderful inn was a pioneering project of the Touring and Automobile Club of Turkey, which took on this renovation in the 1980s. Part of this venture, but in a separate annex, is the Konuk Evi, just above the conservatory. Rooms are elegant and larger than in the row houses, and the building is a replica of an eighteenth-century wooden Ottoman house. (Another Touring Club inn that I also highly recommend is the Yeşil Ev, Green House, also in Sultanahmet. The Club also maintains the Sarniç Restaurant and Istanbul Handicraft Center, in Sultanahmet, as well as the Bebek Café, and the İskele Café and Kültür Evi Inn, both on the Princes' Island of Büyükada.) The location of the Ayasofya Konaklari and Konuk Evi—right next door to Aya Sofya and a five-minute walk to Topkapı—in combination with a can-do staff and a reasonable price, make this one of my favorite hotels. I'm already planning a family and friends reunion. (Note that the Touring Club published a book, in 2002, called *Soğukçeşme*

Street, featuring pictures and engravings before and after the renovation.)

• Çırağan Palace Kempinski, Beşiktaş (Çırağan Caddesi 32 / +90 212 326 4646 / ciraganpalace.com). Hotel of choice for many heads of state, sports stars, singers, movie stars, royalty, and at least one former astronaut (Neil Armstrong), the Çırağan is the only imperial palace hotel in all of Turkey and is a sponsor of Istanbul 2010. It was once the home of Sultan Abdülaziz and was designed by the noted Armenian palace architect Nigoğayos Baylan. During this time (1863–1867) it was customary for sultans to build their own palaces rather than using those of their ancestors. The Çırağan Palace is the last such example of this period. In May 1876, Abdülaziz was found dead (possibly by suicide) in the palace shortly after he was dethroned. He was succeeded by his nephew, Sultan Murad V, but Murad only reigned for ninety-three days before he was deposed by *his* brother, Abdülhamid II, though he lived out his days here under house arrest until his death in 1904. After several nonimperial uses, the Çırağan was finally restored in 1991, and a large, modern hotel was built next to it in the garden.

The hotel was then and is now palatial in every sense. It's luxury defined, and romantic—the hotel hosts a great number of extravagant weddings every year—and surely has the most to-die-for swimming pool in the city (it may have been Istanbul's first infinity pool). The Çırağan underwent a second renovation in 2007—the previous renovation had apparently been criticized for not being faithful to the period—and now the adjacent sultan's palace is a lavish abode consisting of all suites (twelve of them).

Before the Four Seasons Bosphorus opened in the spring of 2008, there was talk about it possibly surpassing the Çırağan Palace. As wonderful as the new Four Seasons is, I consider it to be very different. The Çırağan Palace is magical. You feel like royalty yourself when you walk around inside this wedding cake of a building. I doubt this feeling can ever be erased, no matter what a future interior designer may envision. In addition to the Çırağan's Laledan Restaurant and the Gazebo Lounge, its award-winning Tuğra Restaurant—serving classical Turkish and Ottoman cuisine—is a favorite with locals, too, so make sure to reserve.

The hotel's breakfast buffet is rather renowned among hotel guests, and one of its signature dishes is *menemen* (Turkish scrambled eggs with tomatoes and feta). A few years ago, this recipe was featured in *Gourmet*, and I've been making it ever since. I love it. It's great for a few people or a crowd. And it's yet another way to immerse yourself in Turkey before you leave and when you come back. The public relations staff of the hotel has graciously allowed me to share the recipe with you:

Menemen

2 ripe tomatoes
1 green bell pepper
1 small onion, chopped
7 tablespoons unsalted butter (I prefer to use olive oil, or a
   combination of butter and oil)
6 ounces feta cheese
8 large eggs, beaten lightly with a fork
chopped parsley, to taste

1. Peel and cube tomatoes.
2. Cube finely the rest of the ingredients.
3. In a copper sauté pan that will hold all the ingredients (well, okay, I don't have a copper pan, but you'll have to

just trust me that in a regular skillet this turns out delicious), melt the butter and sauté the onion over moderate heat, stirring until softened. Then add the bell pepper and feta.

4. Add the eggs and stir and cook until they're fairly firm, but the entire dish should be slightly moist due to the vegetable juices.
5. Sprinkle with salt and pepper.
6. Serve immediately with chopped parsley on top. (I also can't resist sprinkling a teaspoon of Turkish red-pepper flakes on top before the dish is served.)

The awards the Çırağan has garnered are an embarrassment of riches, and throughout the year, the Çırağan offers special rates and packages—be sure to inquire when arranging your stay, or check the hotel's Web site periodically. Outside guests are welcomed at the Çırağan's restaurants and its Bosphorus Pier Lounge—I promise you will *not want to leave* this spot—so even if you can't splurge for a reservation, you should stop by. A brief visit or a stay at the Çırağan is one you'll never forget.

• Four Seasons Hotel, Sultanahmet (Tevkifhane Sokak 1 / +90 212 638 8200 / fourseasons.com/istanbul). It's easy to joke about wanting to be kept a prisoner here in this lovely Sultanahmet paradise once you learn that this building *really was* a prison, built in what was known as the Turkish New Classical style between 1918 and 1919. But the architect who envisioned the leap from a prison to a deluxe hotel created nothing less than an extraordinary architectural exploit. The Four Seasons is almost as worthy of touring as its next-door neighbors, Aya Sofya and the Blue Mosque—even if you don't stay here, you should add the hotel to your sightseeing itinerary. The building served as a prison until 1970, detaining dissident Turkish politicians and writers, such as Nâzım Hikmet. On the facade of the southwest wing, facing Tevkifhane Street, original tiles and eaves decorations as well as original stone and woodworks have been preserved. The phrases "going to Sultanahmet" or "being taken to Sultanahmet" once meant being imprisoned here. The hotel's beautiful saffronlike yellow color acts like a beacon, making it easy to find in this part of the neighborhood. Guest rooms, some with balconies or terraces, nicely combine contemporary Western amenities with an Eastern character, and are refreshingly not overdone.

In an interview with *Architectural Digest*, architect Sinan Kafadar noted, "I think people need to be soothed rather than stimulated after a day's sightseeing, so I set out to create an atmosphere where the design and the decoration don't force themselves on you." Kafadar also tried to evoke Turkey's history and traditions throughout the hotel, believing that it's "very important to give people a sense of the place they're in." It is this that, for me, fixes the Four Seasons on my short list. The name Four Seasons alone isn't enough to woo me. That a Turkish ambience hasn't been abandoned in this historic building is impressive and is what makes this Four Seasons property stand apart. Touches I particularly admire include: the original iron locks and keys hung on the wall of the breakfast room; the paintings in the bar area by Timur Kerim İncedayı, who founded the Metropolismo movement in Italy in the 1990s but now focuses on Seljuk, Byzantine, and Ottoman themes (if you love his work as much as I do, his number in Istanbul for French and English callers is +90 533 525 0792; otherwise his studio in Rome is reachable at +39 06 855 1907 / +39 335 65 79 774); and that no two guest rooms are alike, each filled with one-of-a-kind antiques and objets d'art.

Of the hotel's sixty-five guest rooms, eleven are suites and all rooms have windows that open! Children are warmly welcomed here—with bedtime treats, special gifts, and complimentary items for infants, this is definitely a family-friendly hotel. Its meeting and banquet facilities, for business events or special celebrations, are also renowned. The hotel's inviting courtyard is among the nicest you'll ever see, but its rooftop terrace may make you decide to take up permanent residence. Since 2000, the Four Seasons has been honored with a ridiculous number of awards, including Best Restaurant in Istanbul by Zagat in 2002 and 2003. (My own dinner at Seasons Restaurant was memorably delicious; outside guests are welcome.)

- Four Seasons Hotel Istanbul at the Bosphorus (Çırağan Caddesi 80, Beşiktaş / +90 212 381 4000 / fourseasons .com/bosphorus). When I heard the Four Seasons was opening a second Istanbul hotel, I thought it couldn't possibly be as nice as the one in Sultanahmet, figuring it was going to be a new construction with no real personality. I was happy to learn that this beautiful new hotel, opened in the spring of 2008, was created by joining the nineteenth-century Atik Pasha Palace with two contemporary buildings. It might not be *quite* as unique as the former prison in Sultanahmet, but here's what it has that the other location doesn't: great waterfront views—almost one-quarter of the 166 guest rooms, including twenty-five suites, open onto the Bosphorus; others face garden or city scenes. The hotel also features a heated outdoor pool, an indoor pool, and the Urban Spa and Turkish Bath; and meeting and banquet facilities with a seating capacity of up to eight hundred. The guest rooms facing the Bosphorus have fantastic floor-to-ceiling windows, and four of the Palace Suites offer rooftop terraces and expansive views. A very great and handy perk now is the private ferry service between the two hotel locations—this alone might be worth the stay as the opportunity to see Istanbul from the water is unparalleled (except perhaps on par with Venice), and taking the ferry ensures you won't get tangled up in the sometimes horrific traffic.

• İbrahim Pasha Hotel (Terzihane Sokak 5, Sultanahmet / +90 212 518 0394 / ibrahimpasha.com). Taking its name from the former palace home of İbrahim Pasha directly across the street (now the Turkish and Islamic Arts Museum), this hotel is my current favorite in Istanbul. The building itself is a four-story nineteenth-century Ottoman town house set on a quiet street in Sultanahmet, steps away from the Hippodrome. There are only sixteen guest rooms, and everything about the inn exudes style, from the inviting lobby with its fireplace, library, and glass reception desk atop a beautiful (and genuine) Corinthian capital to the unique bedrooms that so wonderfully blend modern conveniences with antique décor. Though I loved my room— one of four deluxe rooms on the top floor, with a view out one window of the obelisk in the Hippodrome—my favorite feature of the hotel is the square-shaped shaft in the center of the building that allows one to peek all the way up or down, from the first floor to the fourth. With the pretty tiles surrounding the square openings (enclosed by a metal rail), the effect is kaleidoscopic and beautiful. Framed sepia-toned photographs of old Ottoman families adorn many walls, and the small rooftop terrace affords a nice view of the Blue Mosque, the Bosphorus, and the Hippodrome. Breakfast typically includes yogurt, fruit preserves, bread, dried fruit, cucumbers, tomatoes, olives, cheese, tea, coffee, and fresh squeezed orange juice (for an extra fee). Staff members are friendly and incredibly helpful, and enjoy sharing the names of their favorite restaurants and sites. The İbrahim Pasha is charming and a great value, and I am counting the days until my return. I hope the owner's lovable dog, Godot, will be waiting for me (no pun intended).

• Hôtel Les Ottomans (Muallim Naci Caddesi 68, Kuruçeşme / +90 212 359 1533 / lesottomans.com). Les Ottomans is like no other hotel on earth. Its creamy, ivory exterior—which was rebuilt to match the original structure—gives no clue to what guests will encounter inside: an exotic, lavish fantasy that could be a stage set, except it isn't. It's like a cross between *A Thousand and One Nights* and the poshest, hippest club you've ever seen. The original eighteenth-century waterside *yalı* was the home of a powerful politician, Muhsinzade Mehmet Pasha, and like other Ottoman-era palaces, it was abandoned and in decline before it was demolished in 1933. The land was then used for coal storage. New owner Ahu Aysal reportedly rebuilt the former mansion for the equivalent of sixty-five million dollars. It's more than a hotel for her—she lives upstairs, and in an interview with *The New York Times*, she said, "This is my baby and it is my home, not just a business. I think people feel safe here and are comfortable because the owner is always here checking that everything is okay and that things are running as they should. We have the sense of being a family here. If I left responsibilities to a general manager and lived elsewhere, I think you would feel the difference."

Aysal is a modern-day "Sultan of the Bosphorus," and she hired local interior designer Zeynep Fadılloğlu to furnish Les Ottomans in true Sultan style: handmade Turkish furnishings are paired with Venetian, Indian, and South African decorative touches to create a look that is wildly imaginative while being simultaneously Ottoman and contemporary. (Les Ottomans is the first and, apparently, only hotel in Turkey designed according to the principles of feng shui.) The public rooms on the ground floor include a great bar area and sitting room and the indoor restaurant, Yali Hatun, which serves Ottoman and international dishes. The red-paneled ceiling was inspired by a box in the Topkapı Palace collection, and the chandelier in the restaurant is in the shape of tree branches. In warm weather, dining and drinking moves outside on the terrace at the Suyani Restaurant and Bar; the pool is here, too, as well as the hotel's beautiful wooden yacht (seating twelve), exclusively for the use of hotel guests.

There are only ten suites in this hotel, each completely different from the other and each quite spacious; a few are split-level rooms with spiral stairways. Just as in the public areas, suites feature modern conveniences such as flat-screen TVs that can be raised or lowered with the press of a button, fax machines, and computers, as well as richly upholstered furniture, antiques, and flowing velvet curtains with swags and tassels. Each suite, named after a gemstone, is unique: one has a view of both the Bosphorus and the pool; two have full Bosphorus views; one has a partial view of the Bosphorus; and six have garden views. A "garden view" here, though, is the only disappointing feature of the hotel, as the garden is not particularly beautiful or large, and does not hide the coast road just on the other side of it. As nightly rates range from 800 to 3,500 euros, I would advise requesting one of the four rooms with partial or full water views—pricey as they are, these rooms represent a better value than those facing the garden (unless the garden grows significantly or if the rate for the garden rooms is lowered). One of the best ways to take full advantage of Les Ottomans is to plan a once-in-a-lifetime reunion of family or friends and reserve all ten suites! (In fact, the hotel's press officer told me that is precisely what some guests, including Kevin Costner, do.)

As remarkable as the guest rooms are, the Caudalie Vinotherapie Spa may top everything in the hotel. *Vraiment*, it is extraordinary. The facilities are incredible, and the treatments offered are too numerous to list here but include private sessions, sauvignon and vigneron massages, sport and Swedish massages, Bordeaux stone massage, Turkish *hamam* massage, facial treatments, wooden barrel baths, mud treatments, liquid sound pool, oxygen therapy, solarium, and on and on. But here's the wonderful thing of it: Les Ottomans welcomes outside guests to the spa for the day for the cost of just one treatment. Yes, you may stay all day in paradise for what is really a very reasonable fee. There is no question that Istanbul can be exhausting, but you can rejuvenate your body and your senses by heading up the Bosphorus for some major pampering. Daily spa fees are 130TL for weekdays and 150TL for weekends; but if you've booked a massage or other treatment, the daily fee is voided and you pay only for the treatment(s) of your choice.

It's difficult to accurately describe Les Ottomans, so be sure to visit the Web site (the music's great, too!) to see for yourself. The hotel isn't for everyone—it's incredibly swish, and over-the-top for some. But it definitely raised the hotel bar in Istanbul and it won the top prize at the World Travel Awards in 2007 (World's Leading All Suite Hotel and Spa). As Aysal says, "I lived in Belgium for twenty-five years and whenever I came back here, I thought to myself that I wanted to show my friends the Ottoman way, Turkish people, and Turkish style. There were always lots of very trendy places but nowhere that I really thought was right. So I said to my daughters, 'One day I will go back and build one of the best boutique hotels

in the world.' . . . I am really happy and proud of myself
that Les Ottomans is now so well known and loved."

A few other hotels that have been highly recommended to me
and are worthy of your consideration are:

• Bebek Hotel (Cevdetpaşa Caddesi 34, Bebek / +90 212
358 2000 / bebekhotel.com.tr). An especially excellent
choice if you prefer to stay on the water and outside of
Istanbul proper, as many believe the Bay of Bebek is the
prettiest harbor of the Bosphorus. I visited here and loved
the smart, dark wood interior and the outside patio. I
wished, wished, *wished* I'd made a reservation! (With only
forty-two rooms one really needs to book in advance.)
Nine rooms have sea views and private balconies, twelve
overlook the main street of Bebek, and the twenty-one
deluxe junior suites are spread across four guest floors. The
hotel was founded in the 1950s; by the 1980s, its Les
Ambassadeurs restaurant was quite renowned, and the
Bebek Bar was included in the Best 50 Bars of the World
in 1985. A great waterside restaurant, Bebek Balikçi
(Cevdetpaşa Caddesi 26A / bebekbalikci.net), is steps away,
as well as some terrific shops and beautiful private residences.

• Hotel Empress Zoe (Akbıyık Caddesi 4/1, at Adliye
Sokak, Sultanahmet / +90 212 518 2504 / emzoe.com).
Named after the wife of Emperor Constantine IX, Hotel
Empress Zoe receives raves even from travelers who can
well afford to spend much more on a hotel room, no doubt
because of its intimacy, fine attention to detail, and tasteful
décor. The hotel's most unique feature is that it overlooks a
fifteenth-century *hamam*, but some might say its stone
courtyard (where breakfast is served in warm weather)
steals the show. The lobby makes you feel like you're in a

museum, with antiquities of all sorts, and guest rooms feature Ottoman and Asian textiles, dark wood, and antique
Turkish canopies above some of the beds. Rates are from
approximately from 75 to 240 euros.

• Hotel Hippodrome (Mimar Mehmet Ağa Caddesi 38, Sultanahmet / +90 212 517 6889 / hippodromehotel.com).
My husband and I stayed here on our first visit to Istanbul,
in 1990, and I'm happy that it's not only still around but
that I can recommend it just as much today as I would have
then. It was formerly an Ottoman house and is now a
modest inn, with a rooftop terrace and views of the Sea of
Marmara and the Blue Mosque. And the location is excellent.

• Misafir Suites (Gazeteci Erol Dernek Sokak 1, Beyoğlu /
+90 212 249 8930 / misafirsuites.com). I haven't yet seen
the Misafir but so many people have mentioned it that I
feel I already know it. "Best small hotel in the world" was
how one friend described it, and the service, guest rooms,
and value are all reportedly unmatched. Misafir, which has
only six suites, is owned by Joost Roojmans, who lives at
the hotel. Suites are quite spacious, decorated in a modern
Scandinavian style, and breakfast is included in the very
reasonable price.

• Mublis Bey Otel (Cankurtaran Mahallesi, Tevkifhane
Sokak 12, Sultanahmet / +90 212 518 0030 / hotelmuhlis
bey.com). Previously known as the Hotel Alibaba, the
hotel was renovated and renamed in 2007 and now has
nine rooms, three of them suites. Mublis Bey is owned by
the same family that owns one of my favorite Grand Bazaar
shops, Muhlis Günbatti (see Grand Bazaar, page 526).
Guest rooms here feature pretty rugs on hardwood floors
and are tastefully decorated and appointed with all mod

cons. The hotel is across the street from the Four Seasons, and its outdoor terrace, which has both covered and uncovered areas, has a sweeping view of the Bosphorus and the Princes' Islands. Great value—this is one of those places I always wish I'd find in the States, but never do.

• Sofa (Teşvikiye Caddesi 41–41A, Nişantaşi / +90 212 291 9117 / thesofahotel.com). Though the use of the word "sofa" is appropriate for a hotel (it refers to the central room in traditionally built Ottoman houses of the eighteenth and nineteenth centuries), the Sofa has virtually nothing in common with a *sofa*: it's one of the sleekest, hippest hotels in all of Istanbul. I didn't find the lobby very welcoming, but the front desk staff was exceptionally helpful (I was looking for a Nişantaşı address, and one young man gave me a map and nearly escorted me to my destination). Guest rooms (there are eighty-two) are as stark as the lobby but definitely warmer and highly designed. Café Sofa seems comfy, with its books and couches; the restaurant, Tuus, has round, podlike booths and serves contemporary Mediterranean dishes (there's also an outside terrace). The hotel has proven popular with business travelers as the ICEC convention center is nearby, and the Sofa has five highly equipped meeting rooms of its own.

When asked to share her most memorable moments in Istanbul, my mother-in-law, Sheila, immediately came up with four, all at the Çırağan Palace: "the infinity pool, which melts into the Bosphorus; the magnificent iced tea that was served that day—never in my long life has it been equaled, not even close; the wedding guests arriving by boat at the hotel dock dressed better than at any glitzy New York society wedding; and dinner with a view of the Bosphorus and being shown a gorgeous, whole turbot before it was served in a mouthwatering dish."

A la Turca

Turkish style is what the singular shop A la Turca has in spades. Owner Erkal Aksoy, who has been described as the self-appointed mayor of the newly hip Çukurcama neighborhood, moved his lovely shop here from Ortaköy and in so doing he single-handedly transformed what was a rather seedy neighborhood (a number of his friends followed). There are now approximately sixty antiques stores here, as well as other neat shops, though none are as atmospheric or beautiful as A la Turca. Even if you have not come to Istanbul looking for antiques or interesting *objets*, browsing the four floors here is like walking around someone's private home, except that nearly everything is for sale. Aksoy warmly welcomes every visitor, and you feel like a special guest while in his company. In addition to carpets and *kilims*, Aksoy displays what I can refer to only as treasures, unusual things that are difficult to describe except to say that you may want all of them. You may also want to move in so you may learn the stories about all these decorative treasures and be surrounded by such Turkishness. A la Turca is open by appointment only; one day in advance is usually sufficient (Faikpaşa Yokuşu 4, Çukurcuma / +90 212 245 2933 / alaturcahouse.com). Aksoy happily arranges mail orders and ships worldwide.

Alexander the Great

Beginning in Anatolia a mere nine years after being named King of Macedon, Alexander (known as *Iskender* in Turkish) conquered the Persian empire and beyond—all the way to India. He never set foot in Byzantium, and his empire didn't last beyond his death in 323 BC, but remnants of his time in Anatolia (and on three continents) are numerous. These can be found most notably at three different sites in Turkey. At the Archaeology Museum in Istanbul: a statue and bust excavated from the site of Pergamum and, in Room 3, the marble Alexander Sarcophagus, which is one of the most accomplished of all classical artworks, so named because it depicts Alexander on horseback battling the Persians, even though it was actually sculpted for King Abdalonymos of Sidon. At Ephesus: the Ephesians were already building a temple when Alexander arrived in 334 BC; he offered to pay for the cost of it in exchange for the temple being named after him, but the Ephesians declined by saying it was not fitting for one god to dedicate a temple to another god. And at the temple of Priene, which Alexander *did* pay for, in Ionian Turkey.

Michael Wood says of Alexander's journey that it "was by common consent one of the greatest events in the history of the world, opening up West and East for the first time; an extraordinary tale of bravery and cruelty, endurance and excess, chivalry and greed." Here are some great books to read about this remarkable moment in history:

- *Alexander's Path*, by Freya Stark (Overlook, 1988; originally published by John Murray, 1958).

- *Alexander the Great: Man of Action, Man of Spirit* (Discoveries series, Harry Abrams).

- *Alexander the Great: Son of the Gods*, by Alan Fildes and Joann Fletcher (Duncan Baird/J. Paul Getty Museum, 2002).

- *Alexander the Great: The Hunt for a New Past*, by Paul Cartledge (Overlook, 2004; Vintage, 2005).

- *In the Footsteps of Alexander the Great: A Journey from Greece to Asia*, by Michael Wood (University of California, 2001).

- *I Wish I'd Been There, Book 2: European History*, edited by Byron Hollinshead and Theodore K. Rabb (Doubleday, 2008), a neat, unusual book in which "twenty superb historians invoke dramatic turning points in the history of Europe and the West." One chapter, "At the Deathbed of Alexander the Great," takes readers back to "the last days of the greatest conqueror in history." The author, Josiah Ober, also recommends Paul Cartledge's book, as well as *Conquest and Empire: The Reign of Alexander the Great*, by A. B. Bosworth (Cambridge, 1998), and *Alexander of Macedon, 356–323 B.C.: A Historical Biography*, by Peter Green (University of California, 1991).

- *The Nature of Alexander*, by Mary Renault (Pantheon, 1975).

Readers wishing to retrace Alexander's steps in Anatolia themselves will want to know about a fantastic tour, In the Footsteps of Alexander, offered by a wonderful UK-based company, Peter Sommer Travels (+44 1 600 888 220 / petersommer.com). In 1994, Peter walked two thousand miles across Turkey retracing Alexander's route. He received the Explorers Club of America Young Expeditioners' Award for the journey, and he also became a sincere spokesman for Turkey: "The myriad ancient cities I had seen were embedded in my memory, but what remains foremost in my mind is the sincere friendship of the Turkish people, extended constantly to a weary traveler far from home. Every single day I was welcomed into their homes and showered with kindness and hospitality. Though just a brief affair, it was passionate in the extreme, and left me madly in love with the land that is Turkey."

Allahaısmarladık!

"Good-bye," or literally, "May God keep you."

Arasta Bazaar

The word *arasta* refers to a parade of shops or a covered market associated with a mosque. Istanbul's Arasta Bazaar (Sipahi Çarşısı) is adjacent to Aya Sofya and the Blue Mosque and is the last standing example of an open bazaar in Istanbul, dating back three hundred years. During the Ottoman Empire, it was known as the Sipahiler ("cavalrymen") Bazaar because mostly cavalry items were sold there. With more than seventy shops, the Arasta Bazaar is also a terrific place to shop—it may lack the exoticism of the Grand Bazaar, but it's quieter, less frenetic, and outdoors. My friend and Arasta vendor Ömer Eymen, owner of Eymen Halıcılık, at no. 107, is the official representative of the bazaar. He moved his former shop, next to the Cağaloğlu Hamam, to the Arasta Bazaar because it's a much better place to do business—both for the vendors and for tourists.

Lest readers think I am shamelessly promoting a rug merchant for no other reason than that he's my friend, allow me to explain how I met Ömer. When my husband I were first in Istanbul, we met another American couple, Sam and Debbie, who were there on their honeymoon. The four of us decided to go to the Cağaloğlu Hamam, but when we arrived at the entrance, we realized we didn't have quite enough money. The baths were closing in an hour and a half, not enough time for us to retrieve more money and come back (there were far fewer cash machines then, and only the central branches of big banks had them). We hadn't noticed that, the entire time we were discussing what to do, a man was standing on a nearby stairwell, and he'd heard every word of our conversation. He introduced himself as Ömer Eymen, proprietor of the rug shop behind him, and said that if we needed money he would lend it to us. We were shocked that a complete stranger would do this, but he said he was serious, so we borrowed the money and went to the *hamam*. Afterward, we repaid him, and because we really were interested in Turkish weavings, we asked Ömer to tell us about the beautiful things in his shop. Over the course of several days, we made repeated visits, for hours at a time, and we learned an awful lot. We felt ready to

buy something with confidence.
But Ömer said we should do
one more thing: visit the Turkish
and Islamic Arts Museum, where
we would see how Anatolian
weavings were a part of daily life
among village and nomadic
families of Turkey. My husband
opted out—he went to see the
Church of Saint Stephen of the
Bulgars, which has the distinction of having been constructed
entirely of cast iron, in Vienna,
and shipped in sections down
the Danube and across the Black

Sea—so I went on my own. Ömer was right. It was as if everything he'd told us had ten times more significance. We ended up
not purchasing anything from Ömer then—as our belongings
were in storage, we didn't have a mailing address, and we didn't
want to cart around a rug—but armed with our newfound
knowledge, we did buy some *kilim* weavings in Kaymaklı that we
later had made into pillows and a wall hanging. I knew Ömer
would have been proud of our selections.

Over the years, we've stayed in touch with Ömer, sharing cards
and photographs. With his two shops in Arasta he has much more
room to showcase his weavings. He specializes in antique textiles
and nomadic and tribal art, and when we met him, he dealt
almost exclusively with Anatolian weavings. However, the
nomadic tradition is dying out in Turkey, and basically what was
once a flood of items being sold by families is now a trickle, so
Ömer now carries many weavings from Central Asia, Iran, and
beyond. He has rugs, of course, but to me the really interesting
items in his shops are the camel bags, hanging cradles, wall hang-

ings, salt bags, etc., and his prices for both rugs and trappings are affordable. Naturally, I recommend a visit to Ömer's shop, but if my recommendation isn't enough, I'm happy to note that in a piece called "Istanbul: The Kilim Connection," which appeared in the December 2002 issue of *Travel + Leisure*, writer Carol Southern (who was Martha Stewart's first editor), included Eymen Halıcılık in a short roundup of recommended dealers. Ömer can be reached at +90 212 516 0733 and his Web site is Eymen.com.tr. Two Web sites for the Arasta Bazaar are Arastabazaar.net and Arastabazaar.com.

Here are a few other great merchants I especially like in the Arasta Bazaar:

• Cocoon, at no. 93, was established in 1996 by Seref Ozen and Mustafa Gokhan Demir, and they have an outstanding selection of textiles, ikats, flatweaves, trappings, and rugs from Anatolia, Syria, the Caucasus, Persia, the Yemen, and Central Asia. Ozen is one of the world's foremost authorities on Central Asian textiles, and he is held in high regard among collectors. He's written for *Hali: Carpet, Textile and Islamic Art* (and represents the magazine in Istanbul) and regularly exhibits at all the major tribal art shows internationally. Cocoon also has an appealing line of its own woolfelt items. The Arasta Bazaar shop primarily features hats. These were influenced by hats worn during the Ottoman Empire at Topkapı, the different styles representing the different ranks of the courtiers. But at the Cocoon shop in the Grand Bazaar (see page 526) the full array of felt items— necklaces, pins, headbands, handbags, etc.—are displayed. The Cocoon Web site, Cocoontr.com, features an excellent lexicon of rug and textile terms that weaving enthusiasts should consult, as well as a thorough list of dealers and resources.

- Iznik Classics, at no. 67, offers authentic Iznik ceramic reproductions (see Iznik entry, page 544).

- Troy Rug Store, at no. 39, was recommended by a friend of a friend who's been visiting owner Mustafa Cesur, and buying from him, for many years. True to Corinna's word, Mustafa is an incredibly kind man who does not believe in being pushy. Here in the Arasta Bazaar for four years, Mustafa began his business in Cappadocia in 1982. He and his handsome assistant, Nedim, will happily roll out their stock for as long as you want to see everything. Troy carries a broad array of weavings from Anatolia, Iran, and Turkmenistan though there are no antique pieces. Mustafa's favorites are the tribal and Kurdish weavings. Prices range from approximately $200 to $300 for a three-by-five-foot rug to $3,000 for a six-by-nine-foot carpet.

Aşure

Aşure, as Fergus Garrett notes in his piece on Turkish roses (see page 65), is a sweet pudding, or stew, traditionally served on the tenth day of the month of Muharram. Irfan Orga, in *Portrait of a Turkish Family*, writes, "In Turkey in the old days there used to be a month called *Aşure Ayi*. *Aşure* is a sweet cooked with wheat, sultanas, figs, dates, dried beans, what you will, the whole being boiled for several hours until the result looks a little like aspic jelly. The legend of *aşure* is that when Noah in the Ark found himself running short of supplies, he ordered all the remaining foods to be cooked together for one last gigantic meal. This was *aşure*—or so we were told. During the days of the Ottoman Empire a month used to be set aside each year for the making of *aşure* in all the houses of the rich, who afterwards distributed it to the poor."

Neşet Eren, in *The Art of Turkish Cooking*, relates her memoir of the *aşure* festival, which she said topped all:

Three days before the festival the tripods in the fireplace were removed to make space for the huge cauldron that was moved from the pantry to the kitchen. How we loved to watch the cook weigh the twenty different ingredients that went into the cauldron for the Noah's Pudding. We jostled each other eagerly waiting for the opportunity to light the fire. There would be a big scramble among us for pushing the torch under the cauldron and we would all rush out of the kitchen crying, "I did it," "I did it." The fire would burn for a whole day and a whole night, somebody keeping watch constantly stirring the pudding with a wooden spoon with a long handle. . . . And then the morning of the festival, Grandfather would descend from upstairs to make his yearly entry into the kitchen. Everybody would stand apart with his hands folded before him and his head bowed, which we children would imitate. Grandfather would speak a prayer, take the spoon, and serve the pudding into a bowl extended by the cook. Thereafter the poor of the village would come and each would get his bowl filled.

My friend Maha refers to *aşure* as Noah's Sludge, which makes it sound like something horrible. Paula Wolfert, in *The Cooking of the Eastern Mediterranean*, initially thought it was: "Before I even tasted this dish, I was sure I would hate it. I couldn't imagine a dessert made of white beans, chickpeas, husked wheat berries, and every conceivable type of dried fruit all mixed together and scented with rose water. And when I saw it, I was sure that I was right, because it was so unattractive. I was wrong."

For the record, I made the recipe in Elif Shafak's *The Bastard of Istanbul*, though it was May and pomegranates were not in season so I omitted the seeds. It was deliciously comforting, and unlike anything else I'd ever eaten.

B

Baklava

There are a number of confections in Turkish cuisine, but none are as celebrated as baklava. According to the Turkish Culture portal (turkishculture.org), the ancestor of baklava may have been a dish the Assyrians made with dried fruit sandwiched between two layers of pastry and baked in an oven. The earliest record of baklava as we know it today is in Damascus, from where it moved to Gaziantep, Turkey, before spreading throughout the country and the world. (Baklava is prevalent in Greece, Albania, Macedonia, India, Afghanistan, Armenia, North Africa, the Turkic republics of Central Asia, and the Arabian peninsula.) We know that by the seventeenth century, baklava was being baked in the Topkapı kitchens and that the Janissaries carried trays of it out of the palace in the Baklava Procession. In the first printed Turkish cookbook, Mehmet Kâmil includes five recipes for baklava: ordinary, with clotted cream, decorative with clotted cream, with melon, and one with rice.

Apparently it is the thinness of the pastry layers that distinguishes Turkish baklava from all others. Sheets of pastry are rolled out so thinly that, when held up, you can see the person's face as if through a net curtain! Though I am an accomplished baker and have made many savory dishes with phyllo dough, I admit to being rather intimidated to tackle baklava. So when I was hosting a Turkish feast recently, I decided to see if the restaurant Hamdi, in Istanbul, would send me a box of its unparalleled baklava. Unfortunately, Hamdi does not fill mail orders, and in any event I was told that the package might not make it through U.S. customs. An Internet search revealed that the famous Istanbul baklava shop Güllüoğlu had a shop in Brooklyn, so my problem was solved, and splendidly. Güllü Çelebi began baking his baklava in Gaziantep in 1871, and five generations and 138 years later, the company is the largest baklava producer in the world. In addition to standard baklava, Güllüoğlu makes more than fifty-five different kinds, as well as *kadayıf* and *fıstıklı*, other popular Turkish pastries. To become a master phyllo roller, Güllüoğlu requires a seven-year apprenticeship. For the Brooklyn café, Güllüoğlu products are sent directly from the factory in Istanbul frozen and vacuum sealed, and a trained baker bakes everything in custommade ovens. I still swoon over Hamdi's baklava, but Güllüoğlu's is outstanding. The original Istanbul shop is at Mumhane Caddesi 171, Karaköy / +90 212 249 9680 / gulluoglu.com.tr, and the Brooklyn outpost is at 1985 Coney Island Avenue / 718 645 6723 / gulluoglubaklava.com.

Bargaining

Bargaining, for goods and services, is an accepted way of doing business in Turkey, though it is becoming less so. Unfortunately, bargaining makes many North American visitors uncomfortable, because, I've found, they don't take the time to understand and appreciate the art of bargaining, and hence have some of the most backward and wrong opinions about it, usually stemming from the idea that they're surely being taken to the cleaners. Bargaining is fun, interesting, and revealing of national character. It isn't something you do in a hurry (don't be surprised if you spend several hours in one shop), and it's not an antagonistic game of Stratego—it does incorporate strategy, but it isn't battleships being sunk; it's goods or services on offer that you do or do not have to purchase.

I caution against placing too much emphasis on the deal itself. There are few absolutes in the art of bargaining—each merchant is different, the particulars of each transaction are different, and you will not be awarded a medal at the end of your visit for driving hard bargains, especially if you accumulate things you don't really want. More important than any of my tips that follow is that you do not lose sight of the fact that what you want is something that appeals to you in some special way that you bargained for in the accepted manner. Does it really matter, at the end of the day, that you might have obtained it for twenty or fifty Turkish lira less? If you end up with a purchase that you love and every time you look at it or wear it you have a warm feeling about your trip to Istanbul, it definitely does not matter what you paid for it. There is a difference between savvy bargaining and obsessive bargaining. I don't know about you, but when I'm on vacation, obsessing about mercantile matters is the equivalent of postponing joy.

Here are some well-practiced and worthwhile tips that have worked well for me in Turkey, Morocco, Egypt, southern France, and Asia:

- Educate yourself on the items you're interested in. If you've been able to learn how much these items sell for here in North America before you leave home, this is also useful information as you'll know how much (or how little) savings are being offered.

- Walk around the market or the Grand Bazaar first and survey the scene—don't purchase anything immediately. If you've skipped my advice just above, this is the next best thing you can do to educate yourself. It doesn't take very long to see that a lot of vendors sell identical merchandise, much of it kitschy and probably of interest only as gifts for children and wacky friends. Look for distinctive items, and identify those vendors you want to revisit.

- If prices are not marked, ask what they are for the items you're interested in, but don't linger and explain that you're just looking. What you're trying to do is ascertain the average going rate for certain items, because if you don't have any idea what the general price range is, you won't have any idea if you're paying a fair price or too much.

• If you do spy an item you're particularly interested in, don't reveal your interest; act as nonchalant as you possibly can, and remember to be ready to start walking away.

• It's considered rude to begin serious bargaining if you're not interested in making a purchase. This doesn't mean you should refrain from asking the price on an item, but to then begin naming numbers is an indication to the seller that you're a serious customer and that a sale will likely be made.

• Politeness goes a long way in bargaining. Vendors appreciate being treated with respect, and they don't at all mind answering questions from interested browsers. Strike up a conversation while you're looking at the wares: ask about the vendor's family, share picture of yours, or ask for a recommendation of a good local restaurant. Establishing a rapport also shows that you are reasonable and that you are willing to make a purchase at the right (reasonable) price.

• If you don't want to be hassled by vendors as you walk around, make sure any previous purchase you may have made remains hidden from view. To a vendor, anyone who walks through is a potential customer, but someone who has already spent money is even better. From a vendor's perspective, customers who have already parted with their money are interested in parting with more, if only they are shown something else they like. If you have purchased a rug and you decline an offer to look at some more by another merchant by saying you've already bought one, you may think you're saying, "No, thank you, I've already bought a rug and don't need another," but the vendor doesn't translate it the same way. He will (probably correctly) assume that you like rugs and will definitely be interested in purchasing another if he has an opportunity to show you some. A rug is hard to hide, but I always carry a tote bag for whatever else I've accumulated. A lot of items fit easily in the bag, and no one but me knows they're there.

• Occasionally, I feign interest in one particular item when it's a different item I *really* want. The tactic here is to begin the bargaining process and let the vendor think I'm about to make a deal. Then I pretend to get cold feet and indicate that the price is just too much for me. The vendor thinks all is lost, and at that moment I point to the item I've wanted all along, sigh, and say, "I'll take that one," naming the lowest price from my previous negotiation. Usually, the vendor will immediately agree to it, as it means a done deal.

• Other times I will plead poverty and say to the vendor that I had so wanted to bring back a gift for my mother from "your beautiful country—won't you please reconsider?" This, too, usually results in a price reduction.

• If you're traveling with a companion, you can work together: one of you plays the role of the designated "bad guy," scoffing at each price quoted, while the other plays the role of the demure friend or spouse who hopes to make a purchase but really must have the approval of the "bad guy."

• You'll always get the best price if you pay with cash, and in fact some vendors accept only cash. I prepare an assortment of paper bills and coins in advance so I can always pull them out and indicate that it's all I have. It doesn't seem right to bargain hard for something that's a hundred Turkish lira and pay for it with a five-hundred-lira note.

• Remember that a deal is supposed to end with both parties satisfied. If, after much back and forth, you encounter a vendor who won't budge below a certain price, it's likely that it's not posturing but a way of letting you know that anything lower will no longer be advantageous to him or her. If you feel you are stuck and have reached an impasse, try asking the vendor once more, "Is this your very best price?" If he or she has spent a considerable amount of time with you, this is the moment when it would be advantageous to compromise, or all that time will have been wasted.

• Pay attention when a merchant wraps up your purchase—dishonest vendors may try to switch the merchandise. Though this has never happened to me, I read a lot of letters from people who didn't know they were had until they got home.

• If you're a real shopaholic and plan to ship large items home, remember that rates are based on cubic measurement, not weight. Make sure the savings you receive at the market are truly significant to justify the shipping home.

• If you're interested in buying antiques—or making a large purchase of any kind—it's worthwhile to read "Know Before You Go," a brochure from the U.S. Customs Service. You can view it online (cbp.gov/xp/cgov/travel/vacation/kbyg) and download it, or simply go to Cbp.gov and click on Travel). Dull as it may sound, this document is actually very useful, especially the details on what you must declare, duty-free exemptions, sending items back to the United States, freight shipments, etc.

Bayram

The Turkish word that refers to a holiday or festival. In addition to Ramadan (*Ramazan* in Turkish), the two other major Muslim holidays observed in Turkey are Eid al-Fitr, or Festival of the Breaking of the Fast (*Şeker Bayramı* in Turkish), which is a three-day festival when sweets are eaten and distributed to celebrate the end of the Ramadan fast; and Eid al-Adha, or Feast of the Sacrifice (*Kurban Bayramı* in Turkish), which is celebrated over the course of four days during which sacrificial sheep are slaughtered and the meat is distributed to the poor. As the Islamic calendar is lunar, Seker Bayramı is celebrated in 2009 on September 20–22 and in 2010 on September 9–11. Kurban Bayramı will be celebrated in 2009 on November 27–30 and in 2010 on November 16–19.

The three holy nights of the year are Laylat al-Qadr, or Night of Power (traditionally thought to be the twenty-seventh night of Ramadan), which is the night on which the Koran was brought down to the first heaven before being revealed to Muhammad; Laylat al-Bara'ah, or Night of Record (which falls on the fifteenth night of Shabaan, the month before Ramadan), when God registers the actions that all mankind is to perform in the coming year and all the births and deaths that will occur that year are recorded; and Laylat al-Mi'raj, or Night of Ascension, which commemorates Muhammad's ascent to heaven. Though there are other days that are observed in the Muslim world—notably the birthday of Muhammad, which is frowned upon by more orthodox Muslims—the two Eids (*bayrams*) and the three holy nights are considered to be the great festivals of Islam and are the only ones universally observed by all Muslims.

Bey

The equivalent of Mr., but used after a man's first name, as in Mehmet Bey (Mr. Mehmet).

Bookstores

General bookstores are great, but specialty booksellers are even better. Specialty booksellers understand that the most committed of travelers are interested in books about art, cuisine, and history, as well as biographies, walking guides, novels, maps, phrase books, and memoirs. So they offer all of these in one place, and more. Sadly, some of my favorite bookstores are no longer around, but here are a few that still are and that I highly recommend. All do a brisk mail–order business:

- American Book Exchange, also known as Abe Books (abebooks.com), is a great source for out–of–print books.

- The Complete Traveller (199 Madison Avenue, New York / 212 685 9007 / ctrarebooks.com). About ten years ago, the longtime owners of this wonderful store decided to stop selling current travel guides and fill its shelves with out–of–print and rare travel editions instead. Original Baedeker's guides and the beautifully illustrated A&C Black travel books—originally known as the *Twenty Shillings* series—can usually be found here, as well as volumes for under a hundred dollars and some that are worth thousands.

- Idlewild (12 West 19th Street, New York / 212 414 8888 / idlewildbooks.com) is a relatively new store named after the original name for New York's John F. Kennedy International Airport. Owner David Del Vecchio, previously a press officer for a United Nations humanitarian agency, likes to say that "idle and wild are nicely associated with travel." When I last checked, the Turkey section included a few cookbooks, an Atatürk biography, novels by Orhan Pamuk, a history of the Blue Mosque, maps, and a full range of guidebooks.

- Kitchen Arts & Letters (1435 Lexington Avenue, New York / 212 876 5550 / kitchenartsandletters.com) is one of North America's premier stores devoted exclusively to food and wine. I found many of the Turkish cookbooks I recommend here—especially those published overseas—but the store also sells titles that are travel- and food-related.

- Longitude (115 West 30th Street, Suite 1206, New York / 800 342 2164 / longitudebooks.com) is first and foremost a mail-order company, though visitors are welcome at its storefront. Visit the Web site to request its very good catalog and to see the staff's essential reading recommendations for your destination.

Boza

An ancient beverage—the earliest documented evidence dates from the fourth century BC in Anatolia—boza is a thick, bubbly, nonalcoholic drink made from fermented and crushed millet. It's available and drunk only in Turkey and the Turkic Republics and is strictly a wintertime libation. Years ago, boza sellers would appear on the streets of Istanbul at the first sign of winter, advertising their wares with the cry, "Bozaaaa! Haydi Bozaaaa!" The peddlers wore very colorful clothing and poured the boza out from wooden kegs slung over their shoulders. Nowadays they are a rare sight, and boza is mostly sold at boza shops and some supermarkets, delicatessens, and pastry shops.

Without exception, everyone agrees that the best brand is Vefa. The Vefa bozacı shop, established by Albanian immigrant Hacı Sadık Abey in 1876, is still in the same family, and the décor and recipe for the drink have remained unchanged since it opened—even the glass that Atatürk drank from when he visited in 1937 is still there. Vefa Bozacı is in Aksaray (Katip Çelebi Caddesi 104/1, Vefa), and the shop is so famous that the entire neighborhood is known by that name. The shop is quite attractive; it also sells quality lemon and pomegranate sauces and vinegars. There is also a Vefa stand in Sultanahmet, on Ramazan Sokak. I've been told *boza* may be an acquired taste, but I like it. It's been described as one of the most unique flavors of Turkey, if not the world, and may also be made with barley, maize, wheat, or oats. Whatever grain is used, it's boiled until incredibly thick, like dough; then it's put through a sieve, and sugar and yeast are added. It's left in barrels to ferment, and when air bubbles form on the surface, the *boza* is ready, but only lasts for four to five days. It's usually served topped with cinnamon and roasted chickpeas.

C

Calligraphy

Though calligraphy reached its artistic pinnacle in Istanbul, calligraphy is not of Turkish origin. In the tenth century, when the Turks migrated westward, they adopted Islam as well as the Arabic script, which replaced the old Uyghur alphabet, a Turkic language that is still spoken by about ten million speakers today. Calligraphy was already a significant art by the time the Turks joined the Islamic world; only a few centuries after the Hegira, in 622, the Arabic characters were known to every Muslim. "Arabic" calligraphy over time became more accurately described as "Islamic" calligraphy.

David Roxburgh, in *Writing the Word of God: Calligraphy and the Qur'an* (published in conjunction with an exhibit of the same name at the Museum of Fine Arts, Houston, 2007), relates that when Muhammad was in his fortieth year and went to a mountain cave called Hira outside Mecca, for devotional purposes, the angel Gabriel came to him when he was asleep and said, "Recite!" Gabriel repeated the word two more times before Muhammad finally answered, "What then shall I recite?" Gabriel then recited the first five verses of what would become sura 96 of the Koran: "Read in the name of your Lord who created / Created man from an embryo / Read, for your Lord is most beneficent / Who taught by the pen / Taught man what he did not know." The pen, and by extension all of the implements for writing and the making of books—including papermaking, gilding, illuminating, miniature painting, and bookbinding—held an especially exalted place in Islamic arts, and as Roxburgh and Mary McWilliams note in *Traces of the Calligrapher* (also a Museum of Fine Arts, Houston exhibit, 2007), "Although no other book matched the Qur'an in holiness—as God's eternal, uncreated word—all books and the art of writing partook of its importance."

In its earliest form, consisting of very simple shapes, the script offered no clue that it would one day be held in such high regard. Over time, however, works of Islamic calligraphy became quite detailed and gorgeous; their creators were no doubt inspired by lofty sayings such as "Whoever writes 'In the name of God, the Compassionate, the Merciful' in beautiful writing will enter paradise without account" (attributed to the Prophet Muhammad's son-in-law, fourth caliph and first Shiite imam Ali ibn Abi Talib). In an article in *Saudi Aramco World*, writer Kamel Al-Baba notes that calligraphy is an art "with a history, a gallery of great masters and hallowed traditions. It is an art of grace and elegance which inspires wonderment for its appearance alone. What distinguishes calligraphy from ordinary handwriting is, quite simply, beauty." In fact, *calligraphy* means "beautiful writing."

The Ottoman Turks perfected calligraphy, and in Istanbul the finest and most mature works were produced. A phrase widely

quoted throughout the Islamic world is "The Qur'an was revealed in Mecca, read in Egypt, and written in Istanbul." As the Turkish Culture Web site (turkishculture.org) points out, the literal meaning of the Turkish word for calligraphy, *hat*, is "line" or "way." Husn-i Hat comprises beautiful lines inscribed with reed pens on paper using ink made from soot. Turkish calligraphists have always made the paper, pens, and ink they used. Pens were made of reeds or wood, and ends were cut into an angled nib, which must be recut regularly as it wears. The slightest deviation in the width of the nib alters the appearance of the writing, sometimes creating a serious artistic flaw.

In the thirteenth century, calligraphist Yakut al-Musta'sim made a breakthrough in calligraphy by using nibs of various widths and sizes in one composition. Sheik Hamdullah, an especially talented calligraphist from the period of Sultan Mehmet the Conqueror, was to elevate the art still higher: Sultan Beyazit gave Hamdullah his own collection of calligraphy, including all the examples he had of Yakut's work, and asked him if he could create a new, individual calligraphic script. After examining the six different types of script used by Yakut, Sheikh Hamdullah succeeded in creating a new, original script of his own. He is considered the founder of the art of Ottoman calligraphy.

The Museum of Fine Arts exhibits referenced above also traveled to the Asia Society in New York under the name of Calligraphy: Writing the Word of God (October 7, 2008–February 9, 2009), and I was fortunate to see it as it was one of the best museum shows I've ever seen. The show highlighted some of the chief developments that took place in the art and practice of copying Islam's sacred text from the seventh to the fifteenth centuries, and the objects displayed—scissors, reed pens, inkwells, penknives, paper burnishers, sand shakers, book pen boxes, folios, certificates, and *maktas* (*makta* is Arabic for "place to cut," and describes the small rectangular slab on which to lay the pen; *maktas* allow for making a precise cut, and some in this show were

crafted of walrus tusk, elephant ivory, and steel overlaid in gold)—
are truly beautiful, sumptuous even, "worthy of the book they
honor" as Holland Cotter noted in his review in *The New York
Times* (October 10, 2008).

Calligraphers were the most revered of all artisans, and perhaps
the most wonderful part of the Asia Society show was a film by
American-born master calligrapher Mohamed Zakariya. Not
only was it utterly fascinating to watch Zakariya at work, his life
story is equally so. As Esin Atıl (introduced on page 46) relates in
Mohamed Zakariya, Islamic Calligrapher (published on the occasion
of an exhibit of the same name at the Bellevue Arts Museum,
Washington) tells it, she first met Zakariya in 1972, when she was
working as a curator at the Freer Gallery of Islamic Art. He
showed up without an appointment and asked to look at some of
the most precious holdings of the Freer Gallery. Zakariya was
then a "quiet, slender young man with shoulder-length blond
hair, attired like a Californian flower child of the 1960s," and Atıl
was intrigued that he'd scribbled down a few accession numbers
obtained from the Freer's file cards, so she felt obliged to show
him a few works. Upon showing him the first folio, she was
immediately impressed with the way his eyes lit up: "Not even the
most ardent student of Islamic art had ever responded this way."
She then proceeded to show him everything on his list. Eight
years later, Atıl's assistant announced a visitor, and in walked a
clean-shaven young man wearing a three-piece suit carrying a
portfolio under his arm. Only after Zakariya reminded her of
their previous meeting did she recognize him. In the intervening
years, Zakariya converted to Islam and began teaching himself
Arabic. During a trip to Morocco he met his first teacher, an
Egyptian calligrapher, and a few years later, after Esin Atıl sent
samples of his work to the Research Center for Islamic History,
Art and Culture in Istanbul, he began a correspondence course,
studying under master calligrapher Hasan Çelebi. In 1979,
Zakariya's *The Calligraphy of Islam* was published (Center for

Contemporary Arab Studies, Georgetown University), and it is regarded as the first contemporary book by an Islamic calligrapher about his work in a language other than Arabic. In "The World of Mohamed Zakariya" (*Saudi Aramco World*, 1992), Heath W. Lowry (introduced on page 440) was quoted as saying it was inevitable that Zakariya's work "would begin pointing him more and more in the direction of Istanbul. The role of the Turks as the last great calligraphers is and continues to be recognized throughout the Islamic world." On May 23, 1988, Zakariya was the first American to receive an *icazet* (diploma) from the Research Center in Istanbul, a tradition that dates back to the fifteenth century.

In the Topkapı Palace collection there is a calligraphic album by Sheikh Hamdullah as well as a beautifully written copy of the Koran. Other places to see gorgeous calligraphy in Istanbul are at the Calligraphy Museum (Hat Sanatları Müzesi, Beyazit Square), which displays Korans, writing materials, bookbinding samples, imperial seals, diplomas, holy relics, and miniatures from the Ottoman and Seljuk periods; the Sakıp Sabancı Museum (Istinye Caddesi 22, Emirgan), which holds a wide range of examples spanning five hundred years, including rare handwritten copies of the Koran, framed inscriptions, *hilyes* (descriptions of the Prophet), *fermans* (imperial decrees), and *berats* (imperial appointments); and the Sadberk Hanım Museum (Büyükdere Piyasa Caddesi 27–29, Sarıyer), which has a very small but stunning selection.

Lastly, you must stop by and visit Nick Merdenyan in the Grand Bazaar. Nick embroiders beautiful Islamic, Jewish, and Christian calligraphic designs on dried leaves. He is not a trained calligraphist but the enthusiasm of people around the world for the leaves has been contagious. Nick patiently dries the leaves in his house, changing the places where they lie at least twice a week. "It's really great to share the tolerance and common cultures of three great religions with my customers," he says. My favorite design is Meeting Point, a perfect souvenir of Istanbul. Browse his collection at nickscalligraphy.com. Prices range from $500 to $1,200.

Cami

Cami (pronounced JAH-mee) is the Turkish word for "mosque." John Freely explains that when *cami* appears as *camii* it's because a noun is modified by a preceeding noun, so it's Sultan Ahmet Camii, but Yeni Cami (New Mosque).

Çay

Turkish tea (*çay*) could be said to be the national drink of Turkey. Visitors will literally have dozens, if not hundreds, of glasses while visiting. "Conversations without tea are like a night sky without the moon" goes the old Turkish folk saying. No matter where you are in Istanbul, glasses of tea will be offered and rapidly appear. Turks reportedly have one of the highest per-capita consumption rates of tea, averaging about a thousand cups per year. Turkey is the world's fifth-largest producer of tea, behind India, China, Kenya, and Sri Lanka. Tea bushes grow on the eastern Black Sea Coast from the Georgian border to the town of Rize—Turkey's tea capital—and stretching to Trabzon. Teahouses are much the equivalent of cafés in France, where people go to catch up on news and gossip and simply to socialize.

Though tea may sometimes be served in porcelain cups and mugs in Istanbul and Ankara, the classic tulip-shaped glasses are by far the preferred teacup, and are one of my favorite souvenirs. I actually bought two complete sets of tea glasses, one with plain glasses and those ubiquitous white saucers with the red thumbprints along the rim, and the other with etched glasses and stainless steel saucers. On my next trip, my challenge is to figure out how to get a Turkish double teapot into my luggage.

Cornucopia: The Magazine for Connoisseurs of Turkey

This outstanding magazine, which was launched in 1991 by Berrin Torolsan and John Scott, is an indispensable resource for anyone even remotely interested in Turkey and is simply essential for Turkey enthusiasts. I wish there were a magazine like this for all the destinations I highlight in my series. Berrin, who was born in Istanbul, and John, who arrived in Istanbul thirty years ago as a student, felt there was very little cultural information about Turkey in English at the time, so they view the magazine as having filled a gap. At first, the magazine was available only at upscale hotels; later it was sold at newsstands. Today the earliest issues have become collector's items (the very first issue, in fact, is completely sold out and unavailable).

The name derives from the Latin *cornu copiae*, or "horn of plenty," a horn overflowing with flowers, fruit, and corn, and a symbol of prosperity and abundance in the cities of Anatolia. The mix of articles in each issue is timely and unique, covering contemporary issues, history, and cuisine and including book reviews, restaurant reviews, and more, all accompanied by gorgeous photographs. When you subscribe to *Cornucopia*, you receive much more than a magazine: you are joining an entire community of people who share a love of Turkey, and your subscriber card entitles you to special offers and discounts on hotels, restaurants, apartment rentals, travel agencies, and shops (Iznik Classics and Şişko Osman Carpets & Kilims are just two of them). Additionally, some books not readily found in North America are available through the *Cornucopia* Web site, and its Arts Diary is an excellent source for Istanbul art galleries and international auctions for Ottoman and Turkish arts. I can't enthuse enough about this magazine, but I will borrow a phrase about it that appeared in *Departures* by Min Hogg, founding editor of *World of Interiors*: "It arrives and I drop everything." Very few items that arrive in my mailbox are so eagerly anticipated as *Cornucopia* (U.S. and Canada 971 244 8802 / cornucopia.net).

Crimea

The Crimean War, of 1853–1856, has been described as both a "largely forgotten conflict" and a "watershed in military history."

Yet few people today are likely to know the location of Crimea (the northern shores of the Black Sea), or be able to name the country it's a part of today (Ukraine) or explain the causes of the war (ostensibly to determine whether France or Russia would have authority over the Holy Land, but the larger issue was more important: whether France or Russia would dominate the Ottoman Empire). The war was between Russia and an alliance of France, the United Kingdom, the Kingdom of Sardinia, and the Ottoman Empire. When Napoléon III's ambassador to the Ottoman Empire urged the Ottomans to recognize France as the sovereign authority in the Holy Land, Russia disputed this newest change in authority. British statesmen used the Balance of Power argument, saying that Turkey couldn't possibly go it alone against Russia: the result would certainly be that the Russians would take the Dardanelles or possibly destroy Turkey altogether, and then "Russian ships would sail into the Mediterranean and cut British communications with India," as Norman Stone explains in "Crimea: A Brief History of an Unnecessary War," in *Cornucopia*. Thus, based on such real or imagined fears, Turkey declared war on Russia in 1853 and an Anglo–French fleet anchored in the Bosphorus.

The Crimean War is sometimes considered to be the first modern conflict. Military tactics that had been considered standard for two hundred years were abandoned in Crimea, and new techniques were introduced that then became the norm by 1914. Florence Nightingale's innovations in medical care created a new foundation for modern nursing. The subject of Tennyson's famous poem "The Charge of the Light Brigade" is a disastrous cavalry charge during the Battle of Balaklava in the Crimean War. And, due to the appearance of the electric telegraph, it was the first war to be covered regularly and rapidly, and public opinion in France and the UK was informed by newspaper reports as never before. Norman Stone notes that the 1860s were to be an extraordinary decade, "marked by wars of national unification—Italy and Germany in Europe, the great Civil War in America. At the time, there was tremendous energy and optimism, a belief in unstoppable progress, and there was even a sort of formula for achieving it. The Turks had already applied some of it with the Tanzimat (an Ottoman Turkish word meaning "reorganization" or "reformation"). But Stone concludes that the Crimean War "was blundered into, by men who did not really understand what they were doing. They have much to answer for."

Martin Randall Travel (martinrandall.com), an outstanding British tour operator, offered a Crimean War trip in 2007 that included Sebastopol, Alma, Balaklava, and Inkerman. "Perhaps no other group of battlefields survive so unaltered and so clearly elucidate the action. In most cases even the crops and vegetation remain the same. The sense of the past is hugely enhanced by the rarity of visitors and the absence of touristic paraphernalia. Until a few years ago the region was closed to foreigners and even most Soviet citizens because the battlefields are ranged around Sebastopol, for over two hundred years the base of the Russian Black Sea fleet." MRT offers a number of excellent trips to Turkey, some of which include Istanbul.

The Crimean Church in Istanbul, which John Freely has described as "one of the city's 100 most important buildings" and "by far the largest and most handsome of the western churches in the city," was conceived as a memorial to the Crimean War. According to an article by Geoffrey Tyack, "The Crimean Church, Istanbul," in *Cornucopia* 25, the foundation stone was laid on October 19, 1858, and stone from Malta was used for carved detailing, the tiles came from Marseilles, and the internal timberwork was from Trieste. The church itself, a fine example of Victorian Gothic, looks out of place in Istanbul, but it is very much a part of the community. It has had a topsy-turvy history since its completion, and it hadn't been used regularly for Sunday worship since the 1940s. It was formally deconsecrated in 1973 and then was neglected and vandalized. Thanks to the efforts of Father Ian Sherwood, in the 1990s, the Crimean Church was reconsecrated and restored. The church is on Serdarı Ekrem Sokak in Galata, and as Tyack notes, "With interest growing both in Victorian architecture and in the history of Istanbul's own highly diverse architectural heritage, the church deserves to be better known and its long-term future secured."

D

Dolma *and* Dolmuş

Dolma is the generic term for stuffed vegetables and derives from *doldurmak*, "to fill." According to Bade Jackson in *Turkish Cooking*, there are two types of *dolma*: one filled with ground meat and the other filled with a rice mixture. The rice *dolma* are cooked in olive oil and eaten at room temperature. Meat *dolma* is a main course, eaten with a yogurt sauce and is frequently prepared in an average household. *Dolmuş* is the Turkish word referring to a shared taxi—I love the association with a *dolma*: the driver doesn't depart until the taxi is "stuffed." (This is similar to a *matatu* in Kenya, which translates as "always room for three more.")

E

Ebru

Ebru is the Turkish word for marbled paper, made by floating paints on water and transferring them to the paper's surface. Robert Arndt, writing in *Saudi Aramco World* (May/June 1973), relates that as late as the 1920s, whole streets of Beyazit, Istanbul's printing and paper quarter, were lined with *ebrucus* workshops, and their production was used as the endpapers of books, as mats for decorative calligraphy, and as decorative panels on fine woodwork.

Ebru is also the name of a seven-year project that led to the publication of a book, in 2006, whose subtitle is *Reflections on Cultural Diversity in Turkey*. Attila Durak, a New York–trained photographer born in Turkey, and twenty-three other authors contributed to the book, which is said to be monumental not only in size (450 pages) but in its daring. The book highlights the huge Turkish ethnic mosaic and includes forty-four different ethnicities and sects. Durak traveled around Turkey, living with families and taking their portraits. In an interview with *The New York Times* in 2008, he said he compiled the book "to show that Turkey is a constantly changing kaleidoscope of different cultures, not a hard piece of marble monoculture as the Turkish state says, and that acknowledging those differences is an important step toward a healthier society." In the same article, Sabancı University anthropology professor Ayşe Gül Altınay pointed to *ebru*, the art form, as a metaphor for multiculturalism. "We're not a mosaic, different from one another and fixed in glass. *Ebru* is done using water. It is impossible to have clear lines or distinct borders."

The book is unfortunately available only in Turkish, but it apparently has hit a nerve all over Turkey, and its focus reminds me of a passage in Stephen Kinzer's *Crescent & Star*: "Turks are heir to every culture that ever exited in Anatolia. Their heritage is vigorous, cosmopolitan, diverse and unimaginably rich. They should embrace it wholeheartedly and become caretakers of all the glittering riches of Anatolian history."

Etiquette

A few of the more important gestures to understand in Turkey (and Greece as well) are those meaning yes and no. If you ask a bus driver if his route will take you where you want to go, and he makes a sharp *tsk* sound while throwing his head back and/or raising his eyebrows, this means no. If he responds with a nod of the head—usually a sideways downward nod, with his chin pointing to his chest—this means yes. If a shop merchant wants to show you something, and walks away from you while simultaneously moving his arm to and fro behind him and moving his fingers back and forth, this means "follow me" (in the States we would interpret this as "go away"). Turkish women will make a *tsk* sound when they see women who are scantily clad or wearing sleeveless tops. Lastly, it is considered extremely rude to show the soles of your feet and to sit with your legs crossed.

Europe

In response to seeing what he described as a "gloomy" Turk, British traveler Marmaduke Pickthall commented, "I think it is that you are trying to be something which you never can be, something which nobody with any sense would wish to be—a European." The road to possible membership in the European Union has been a long one for Turkey, and there are many Turks who would agree with Pickthall. In an interview with Hugh and Nicole Pope, authors of *Turkey Unveiled*, Orhan Pamuk opined that "Turkey is constantly moving towards Europe, becoming more Westernized. But a union will never be realized. Turkey's place is in continuous flux. This limbo is what Turkey is and will stay for ever. This is our way of life here."

It remains to be seen if Turkey will be accepted into the EU, but it's a subject that will dominate any discussion of Turkey at least for the foreseeable future. In *Crescent & Star*, Stephen Kinzer observes that for each of the more than a dozen countries that are waiting to join the European Union, the appeal of membership is political, social, and economic. "For Turkey it is also psychological. The central question facing Turks today is whether their country is ready for full democracy, but behind that question lies a more diffuse and puzzling one: who are we? The Ottomans knew they were servants of God and lords of a vast and uniquely diverse empire. The true heart of their empire, however, was not Anatolia but the Balkans. . . . But by caprice of history the founders of the Turkish Republic found themselves bereft of the Balkans and masters instead of Anatolia. To make matters worse, through a series of twentieth-century tragedies Anatolia lost most of the Armenians, Greeks and Jews who had given it some of the same richness that made the Balkans so uniquely appealing."

Eyüp

One of my favorite places in Istanbul is the Eyüp Mosque complex and the Pierre Loti Café, farther up the hillside, about halfway up the Golden Horn. The mosque and surrounding neighborhood are so named after Muhammad's companion and standard-bearer, Abu Ayyub al-Ansari (Eba Eyüp in Turkish), who also was one of the leaders in the first Arab siege of Constantinople, from 644 to 678. Eyüp was killed; in 1453, during the final Turkish siege of the city, Sultan Mehmet II and seventy attendants searched for seven days for Eyüp's grave. Though the story may be apocryphal, one of the attendants supposedly found the alleged spot, and to mark it, Mehmet built a *külliye* there. Thenceforth, John Freely tells us in *Istanbul: The Imperial City*, whenever a sultan came to the throne he was girded with the sword of Osman Gazi at Eyüp's tomb, a ceremony equivalent to coronation, which continued to the end of the Ottoman Empire. Ever since, Eyüp has been considered one of the holiest sites in Islam and is definitely the holiest shrine in Istanbul.

I like the mosque because few tourists visit it—perhaps because it takes some time to get here, or perhaps because the neighborhood is quite religiously observant—and because it's beautiful.

The atmosphere is very different from, say, the Blue Mosque, and it's much more solemn inside. Women are not admitted without their heads covered, and it's best if men wear long pants. After visiting the mosque and the tomb, walk up the stone walkway to the Pierre Loti Café. The walkway essentially runs right through the middle of a cemetery, so you have the opportunity to see hundreds of unusual tombstones (ones with turbans on top are for men, while floral designs are for women). When you reach the top of the hill, the simple café beckons, with its tables set up both outside and inside. The sweeping view of the Golden Horn is fantastic.

F

Franks

An Ottoman word that initially referred to the French, later it was the word used to refer to all Europeans. The Ottoman Empire sought to emulate France in its last century.

G

Galata Bridge

In *Stamboul Sketches*, John Freely writes that "nowhere else in town is the connection between the old Stamboul and the new more evident than on and around the Galata Bridge." This was more starkly so during the days of the sultans, as Lesley Blanch wrote in *The Wilder Shores of Love*: "Perhaps the gossip of the Paris salons reached the French Embassy at Pera. But no further. That last mile, across the caïques that bridged the Golden Horn, past the spices and serpent skins and perfumed roots piled along the Egyptian Bazaar, news from Europe faded, and was lost. It was said that ten thousand people crossed the bridge daily—but not one idea. This was the East, enclosed, remote. Time, like Western thought, flowed past the bubble-domed roofs of the Great Bazaar, past the minarets of the Süleimanye, on past the gates of the Seraglio. The East had its own rumors, its own dramas. No echoes of Paris reached so far."

When I first visited Istanbul, the old bridge—with the floating pontoons—was still in use. It had been built in the early 1900s, but nearing century's end it was no longer sufficient for the growing city. The new bridge is perfectly fine, but I am sentimental about the old one. The pontoon version allowed for the central section to be moved aside so that large ships could enter the Golden Horn. Every day, at four-thirty a.m., the central section was unlatched and pulled to the side by small motorboats. For thirty minutes ships sailed out, and for another half hour ships sailed in. At five-thirty a.m. the bridge was put back together. Underneath the bridge were dozens of fish restaurants, all basically alike, where you could bargain for the price you wanted to pay for your fish dinner. The new Galata Bridge is without a doubt not so quaint, but it is still colorful.

Leonardo da Vinci actually proposed building a bridge to join the two shores of the Golden Horn in 1502, in a letter he wrote to Sultan Beyazit II. It would have been the first bridge in history to have a parabolic arch, but the design was never executed and the first Galata Bridge was built in 1845. It's been rebuilt four times since then.

In early 2008, there was a terrific exhibit about the Galata Bridge at the Istanbul Modern. The curators emphasized that the location of the Galata Bridge leads to the usual East-West separation—Pera has always been more "Western" and the opposite side more "othered." Some historical texts state that Pera wasn't very loyal to the Ottoman Empire, and that the people of Pera sometimes sided with the enemies of Istanbul. "Starting from this departure point, it would not be wrong to assert that Galata Bridge is in the middle of an East-West dilemma. However, the recent notion of 'clash of civilizations' created and welcomed by Western thinkers is partially being nourished by this duality. While certain countries, religions, nations, geographies, lands are categorized under a particular pigeon hole, some others are preserved in much more privileged containers resting on a logic which can easily be conceived as racist." It was an incredibly thought-provoking exhibit, proving that Galata is much more than a means of getting from one place to another.

Germany

Turkey's ties to Germany date back to the late nineteenth century, when the Baghdad Railway was conceived. The Germans were dreaming of a Berlin-to-Baghdad route so they would have access to a port on the Persian Gulf, and the Ottoman Empire wanted to increase its influence in Egypt and on the Arabian Peninsula. As the Orient Express line was already constructed (the terminus being Istanbul's Sirkeci Station), a new line was planned to depart from Haydarpaşa Station, on the Asian side, and run through Turkey, Syria, and present-day Iraq, and all of it would be under German control. (Haydarpaşa was presented as a gift from Kaiser Wilhelm II to cement an alliance between Germany and the Ottoman Empire.) The railway became a source of international disputes before the outbreak of World War I and was never completed, but what sealed Turkey's fate with Germany happened at this same time. The Turks paid England for two battleships, and just before war broke out, Churchill decided not to send them, as it was not at all clear which side Turkey would support in the inevitable conflict to come. Shocked, the Turkish government had no choice but to now side with the Germans, and their relationship has continued—sometimes with difficulty—since then.

When Mary Lee Settle wrote *Turkish Reflections*, in 1991, many Turks were going to Germany as "guest workers." She notes, "in every place but Germany, where they are treated appallingly, their ability to work, their pride, their ease of life is honored. Only in Germany are there terrible street jokes. . . ." I was so sickened by one of these street jokes that I can't bring myself to share it here. Germany now has approximately three million Muslims, according to an article in *Spiegel Online International* ("Life in a Parallel Society," April 16, 2008), and the city of Berlin alone has about eighty mosques (there are about 180 mosques in the whole country). Not all in the Muslim communities are Turks, of course, but Turks are the majority. Since September 11, 2001, many Muslims feel increasingly excluded and rejected; therein lies one of the central challenges of Germany's integration policy.

Fatih Akın, a Turkish-German film director who was raised in Germany, has made several films in the last few years that explore the lives of Turks in Germany and how they reconcile living in a culture so different from their own. Among these are *Head-On*, which won the Golden Bear Award at the Berlin Film Festival, and *The Edge of Heaven*, which won the award for Best Screenplay at the Cannes Film Festival.

Giaor, giaour, *or* gavur

Variously spelled one of these three ways, *giaor* is the Turkish word referring to infidel, foreigner, or non-Muslim.

Golden Horn

According to Greek legend, the inlet of the Bosphorus known as the Golden Horn derives from Keroessa, the mother of Byzas, who named the waterway after her. Due to its deep water, the Horn was an obvious choice for the home of the Byzantine Empire's naval headquarters. To protect the city from naval attacks, a huge chain was pulled across the entrance and attached to the original Galata Tower (this was destroyed during the Fourth Crusade, but the Genoese rebuilt one in 1348). There have been only three moments in Istanbul's history when this chain was broken or circumvented: in the tenth century, the Kievan Rus' (a medieval state dominated by Kiev from about 880 to the twelfth century) took their longboats out of the water and dragged them around Galata and relaunched them in the Horn, only to have the Byzantines defeat them with their infamous Greek fire; in 1204, during the Fourth Crusade, Venetian ships broke the chain with a huge ram; and in 1453, Mehmet II imitated the Kievan Rus' after he unsuccessfully tried to break the chain with force, and had his boats taken across Galata and rolled down greased logs into the Horn. You can see sections of the chain in the Istanbul Archaeology Museum's excellent exhibit Istanbul Through the Ages—it's one of my favorite things to see in the city. The chain is displayed in front of a painting by Oya A. Sirinoz that is a view of the city walls and buildings together with the chain that closed the Horn in the fifteenth century. Sirinoz's work, done in 1994, is based on an engraving by Hartmann Schedel in 1493.

The waters of the Horn are cleaner now than they were several decades ago, when *Horizon* featured a Golden Horn photo essay by Ara Güler with this favored quote: "Istanbul—Constantinople—is a city without a center. But the Golden Horn is its heart, taking the place of plazas and avenues."

Grand Bazaar

Known as Kapalı Çarşı or Covered Market, the Grand Bazaar, one of the world's oldest shopping malls—and possibly the largest—dates back to the fifteenth century. John Freely, in *John Freely's Istanbul*, refers to the bazaar as a small city in itself. He reports that, according to a survey taken in 1976, there are more than three thousand shops of various kinds, along with storehouses, stalls, workshops—many in old Ottoman *hans*—as well as a restaurant, a teahouse, several lunch counters, a bank, and a public toilet, altogether employing more than twenty thousand people. Though it seems a veritable labyrinth, Freely says, "the bazaar is laid out on a fairly regular rectangular grid, at the center of which is the Old Bedesten, one of Fatih's original buildings, where the most expensive goods were securely kept. Shops selling the same kinds of goods tend to be concentrated in the same areas, and the streets are named after the various guilds that did business there in Ottoman times." An aerial view of the bazaar would reveal that the Inner Bedesten is covered by fifteen domes, and the New (or Sandal) Bedesten is covered by twenty.

A visit to the bazaar is much more than a shopping trip. Erin Cullen, in *Time Out Istanbul*, writes, "Entrance to the bazaar is an awe-inspiring experience regardless of how many times you cross the threshold. . . . Take some time to savor the history and the architecture of the bazaar which are spectacles in their own right." And Eric Lawlor, in *Looking for Osman*, says, "The bazaar made me a believer. Looking much as they did two centuries ago, its vaulted passageways weave back and forth like the splendid arabesques in Turkey's mosques. Brodsky called this place the heart, the mind, the soul of Istanbul. And one doesn't doubt it. Here, the city seems at its most uninhibited, seems most itself."

My words of advice about the Kapalı Çarşı, whether you are a first or repeat visitor, are: It will always take longer than you think (because it's interesting!) to walk around the market, so don't plan your schedule too tightly on the day(s) you plan to visit. The vendors in the *bedestens* generally have more interesting and unique stuff, so even if you see items you like in the lanes close to the entranceways, don't buy them right away—you can always come back. Adrenaline can run high in the bazaar: remember to pace your outing by taking a break for something to eat and drink (I'm a fan of the Fes Café and the Bedesten Café & Pâtisserie)—this is especially important if there is someone with you who really doesn't want to be in the bazaar (though it's hard for me to imagine that anyone wouldn't find a visit enjoyable). Remember that there is only one public bathroom, with an attendant you must pay; some stalls have regular flush toilets and others are Turkish toilets (see Turkish toilets entry, page 580). Have fun! Buying a souvenir at the bazaar, for you or someone else, and sharing a cup of tea with a vendor, is much more fun and memorable than buying something from a retail store.

Here are some vendors I particularly like that are selling items not readily found outside of Turkey:

- Abdulla (Halıcılar Caddesi 62 / +90 212 527 3684 / abdulla.com; second location at Ali Baba Türbesi Sokak 25/27, Nuruosmaniye / +90 212 526 3070). I would have stepped inside of Abdulla even if I hadn't read about it in advance. The entranceway is filled with a curtain of hanging beads, and it reminded me of when Greg Brady had hanging beads in *his* doorway when he turned Mike's study into a hip bedroom. But you don't have to be a fan of *The Brady Bunch* to love Abdulla, which specializes in natural-made home products such as towels, sheets, and *hamam* items: a *peştemal* (the cotton towel you wrap around yourself), soap (lots of appealing soap–on–a–rope varieties, and others packaged in a fez container), *kese* (a mitt made from hand–spun linen yarn indigenous to the Black Sea Kastamonu region), and metal bowls (for pouring water over your body). All the weavings are woven on hand looms and dyed with all-natural ingredients . . . and they're wonderful. All purchases are wrapped up in simple brown paper secured with twine and beads. I've found that the *peştemals* also work as tablecloths, and are great for the beach. Owner Metin Tosun (who owns Fes Café right next door) also stocks olive oil and beautiful, rare textiles from Anatolia that collectors especially like. Many are silk; Yeliz Altın, a very knowledgeable and kind associate at the shop, told me that many Turkish designers buy these fabrics by the meter and have them made into clothing. Yeliz also told me that though she isn't a member of the family who owns the business, she is made to feel like one. It's hard to leave here empty-handed. Tosun will fill mail orders but only with a wire transfer.

• Cocoon (Halıcılar Caddesi 38 / cocoontr.com). Cocoon's main outpost is in the Arasta Bazaar (see page 493) but its little shop in the Grand Bazaar actually caught my eye first. A few years ago, Cocoon owners Seref Ozen and Mustafa Gokhan Demir branched out into the world of design and fashion, and in this location is a bright, colorful collection of wool-felt items—headbands, pins, necklaces, bracelets, hats, handbags, and other accessories—that are hugely appealing. The original designs are terrific, and everything is hand-crafted. I bought oodles of things for my daughter and my nieces—though, make no mistake: Cocoon is not meant to be a store for kids. Happily, everything is lightweight and easy to fit into suitcases that are already jam-packed.

- CS Iznik Nicaea Ceramics (Takkeciler Caddesi 34–36 / +90 212 512 2872 / hakan_yaginli@hotmail.com). Hakan Yağınlı has a nice selection of good quality ceramics, many with fifteenth- and sixteenth-century Iznik designs. This is good to know about if true Iznik wares are beyond your reach. Hakan will pack up your selections for safe airplane travel.

- Deli Kızın Yeri (delikiz.com). Former New Yorker Linda Caldwell is the creative genius behind this upbeat shop, which offers inspired gifts and wearable items that reflect Turkish culture and design. The name of her shop translates to "the crazy lady's place," referring to the fact that Caldwell's friends have long called her crazy because she seems to follow the same road but is always trying to do the impossible. If "impossible" is defined as creating really cool and fun Turkish mementos and gifts, then I hope she stays crazy forever. Caldwell started Deli Kızın Yeri in 1998 after she and her husband retired to Istanbul. She'd fallen in love with Turkey and its traditional arts in 1973, when she first visited, and her goal is to create flat, packable items that travelers will have no trouble fitting into their bulging bags. She also tries to make them useful, so that they (hopefully) don't languish in someone's dresser drawer. I think she and her staff create must-have bookmarks, key chains, and cards—among other items—at reasonable prices. Caldwell believes she is the first foreign female to own a shop in the Grand Bazaar, an accomplishment worth celebrating. Caldwell used to fill mail orders, but does no longer, so her wares are only available right here.

• Derviş (Keseciler Sokak 33–35 / +90 212 514 4525 / dervis.com) is similar to Abdulla yet offers completely different spa- and *hamam*-related stuff. Owner Tayfun Malik Utkan promises visitors will be addicted to his shop after only one visit, and he's right. He's especially proud of his Anatolian silk items, which admittedly are beautiful, but I lusted after his *peştemals* in hand-spun organic cotton and extra-virgin olive oil soaps—which come in square, round, and large cube shapes—scented with rose, oregano, and other fragrances. Utkan also has a gorgeous collection of dowry cloths from all over Anatolia, most more than forty or fifty years old.

• Dhoku and EthniCon (Takkeciler Sokak 45/47, 49/51, and 58/60 / +90 212 527 6841 / dhoku.com and ethnicon .com). Dhoku (which means "texture") and EthniCon are sister companies, Dhoku specializing in wool *kilims* in modern designs by top designers and EthniCon specializing in reinvented and repurposed rugs—taking pieces from damaged antique carpets, nomad tent coverings, scraps, etc., and patching them together to make one-of-a-kind weavings. Both are quite hip, though EthniCon rugs have probably received more publicity as they are also sold in Conran stores in the UK and the States. "Arty modernist carpet collages" is how Seth Sherwood refers to EthniCon rugs in *The New York Times*, which I think is spot-on. My friend Amy bought one and put it in her bedroom. She wishes she'd bought a larger one.

• Erdün Collection (Şerif Ağa Sokak 34/39 / +90 212 526 7628 / erduncollection.com). Owner Bülent Vatandaş has been here for about thirty years and sells a fascinating collection of nineteenth- and early-twentieth-century Anatolian items used in daily life, such as coffee roasters, coffeepots, iron ladles for roasting coffee, lanterns, ladies'

soap boxes for the hammam, cowbells, water jugs and
pitchers, yogurt buckets, ink bottles, ceramic doorknobs,
wooden spice boxes, and—my favorite—lunch boxes,
which are the fanciest and most beautiful you'll ever see:
these are metal and they fold out into different sections,
meant to hold soup, meat, and vegetables. Most of these
items are family heirlooms, not antiques. Erdün also has a
fantastic selection of ceramic mosque balls—these are a bit
hard to describe, but they're beautiful. Besides these, Erdün
has hanging glass mosque lanterns, in varying sizes, which I
love. The small ones are approximately twenty-five dollars
and some have amber or glass beads "woven" into the
chain. I hang mine from my dining room chandelier and
they are so beautiful that, well, I should have bought thirty.

- Eski (Cevahir Bedesteni, directly across from Erdün). A
  family business since 1960, Eski is jam-packed with things
  like miniature paintings, silver Torah pointers, kiddush
  cups, narghiles, gorgeous ceramics, Russian samovars and

icons, daggers, cigarette holders, and paintings (which he will sell without the frame if desired) by both Turkish artists and Europeans who came to Turkey (these are more valuable). Prices vary, and Russian icons in good condition sell for approximately $500 to $10,000. With these items, "you have a chance to touch history," owner Eskici Irfan told me, and I realized that this is precisely what is appealing about nearly all of the merchants I recommend here.

- Koç (Kürkçüler 22–46 / +90 212 527 5553 / kocderi .com). I never had any intention to buy a coat in the Grand Bazaar. I only went to Koç because my friends and I needed a place to meet. They were serious about leather. I was serious about etchings. But when I met them at Koç, and Ilyas Koç buttoned me up in an olive green suede knee-length coat, I knew I wouldn't leave Istanbul without it. If you have even the tiniest desire for a leather jacket or coat, come to Koç and forget about all the other touts luring you into their shops. You will leave (or come back later, which is what I did) with an outer garment that you will have for the rest of your life, and with the knowledge that you paid much less for it than if you'd bought it at home.

- Muhlis Günbattı (Perdahçilar Caddesi 48 / +90 212 511 6562 / muhlisgunbatti.net). This is one of the most beautiful stores in the entire bazaar. Friendly and charming Günbattı deals in stunning antique Ottoman and Central Asian clothing and textiles (about 80 percent are Ottoman). Quite literally, some of these took my breath away. While the clothing items are undeniably gorgeous, I was really smitten with the embroidered bedcover weavings, which I envisioned covering my dining room table . . . and I could also picture a few others hung on a wall. Günbattı's wares are indeed the *crème de la crème* of fabrics, and in his fifty-three years in the Grand Bazaar he has built up an international clientele. He told me his best customers are Americans, but he also has a large following in Saudi Arabia, Kuwait, and Dubai. Even if you think you can't afford anything here, be sure to stop in: there are a number of items that are quite reasonably priced, and coming here first will help you be more discerning when looking at other weavings once you've seen the best.

- Şehrazat (Kalpakcılar Caddesi Sokak 4–6 / +90 212 526 1353 / aksuilyas@yahoo.com.tr). This tiny shop, managed by Mehmet—who has earned the title of "hajji" as he's made the pilgrimage to Mecca—*and he* looks like George Clooney—has a worthy selection of cashmere, silk, and pashmina shawls as well as hand-woven tablecloths and dowry pieces. Prices range from about ten to two thousand dollars, but even the most expensive shawls are quite reasonably priced, and I am kicking myself for only buying one scarf for my daughter here. The range of colors and patterns here is impressive.

- Serhat Geridönmez (Cevahir Bedesteni Şerif Sokak 69 / +90 212 519 8017 / serhatgeridonmez.com). Like other Grand Bazaar jewelers, Geridönmez began as an apprentice (in 1988), but unlike other jewelers, he is creating necklaces, earrings, bracelets, rings, and brooches that are unparalleled. Since 2002, he's been on his own, working with twenty-four-karat gold and semi-valuable coins and rare gemstones. Prices for his one-of-a-kind pieces range from $100 to $25,000, and Geridönmez is not inclined to bargain, or at least not in the traditional way. He doesn't have to, as demand for his work is high, and as some pieces are "onlies"—meaning that he will make only one—he knows he will sell them, at a price that reflects the value of his materials. I am still dreaming about a bracelet he made that had my name all over it, and of course no other bracelet I've seen since will do.

• Şişko Osman (Kapalıçarşı Zincirli Han 15 / +90 212 528 3548 / siskoosman.com). For top-quality rugs and *kilims*, old and new, you can't beat Şişko Osman. That's not to say there aren't other places to buy quality rugs in Istanbul, but Şişko has a fine reputation as one of the best dealers in the bazaar. The business has been in the family for five generations, since 1894, and even if you have no interest in buying a weaving, come to the shop anyway just to look and learn—and to see one of the bazaar's original *hans*.

And in the vicinity of the Grand Bazaar:

• Hereke Halı (Nuruosmaniye Caddesi 57 / +90 212 513 6474 / herekecarpet.com). This large shop is well known, reputable, and recommended for people who are looking for a quality piece but not necessarily a rare or very antique one. The word *hereke* refers to a highly prized carpet, especially one of pure silk. *Hereke* carpets were exclusively made for sultans, palaces, and mosques, and were often given as gifts from sultans to kings, emperors, and other rulers. The staff here consider the purchase of a rug to be an investment, and therefore they do not believe in rushing anyone into a decision. The main street-level room displays some very large carpets, and it's in the comfortable downstairs room that the staff rolls out their inventory of *kilims*, pile, wool, cotton, silk, and wool-on-cotton rugs, which also come in a huge range of sizes. Visitors are invited to schedule an appointment in advance of their arrival in Istanbul, and the staff will arrange for transportation to the store, free of charge (reservation@herekecarpet.com). And unlike the shops in the Grand Bazaar, which are closed on Sunday, *Hereke* is open seven days a week.

- Sevan Biçakçi (Gazi Sinanpaşa Sokak 16, Nuruosmaniye / +90 212 520 4516 / sevanbicakci.com). Though this thirty-something jewelry designer's baubles are inspired by Ottoman and Byzantine designs, Sevan's creations are far more elaborate. They're outrageous, actually, meant to make a statement. In an interview with a writer from *The Dallas Morning News*, Sevan said, "Where I am from, rings are the mirrors of the personality of the wearer. They tell all about the wearer." Though he no longer works alone, he creates only four hundred pieces a year. Each ring can take months, or longer, to complete, and some include tiny pieces of materials numbering in the hundreds and thousands. Such craftsmanship comes at a very steep price, but it doesn't cost anything to look. By appointment only. (A limited number of Sevan's designs are sold at Barneys New York stores / barneys.com.)

H

Hanım

The equivalent of Ms., but used after a woman's first name, as in Zeynep Hanım (Ms. Zeynep).

Harem

Lesley Blanch, in *The Wilder Shores of Love*, provides an easy-to-remember explanation of this useful word: "The word 'harem' derives from the Arabic *haram*, forbidden, unlawful. A certain area of land centered round the Holy Cities of Mecca and Medina was considered set apart, inviolate, and so described as *haram*. The word came to be applied, in its secular sense, to the women's quarters of a Moslem household—it was their *haram*, or sanctuary, territory apart, inviolate to all but the master of the household. The Selamlık, or men's quarters, derived from the word *selam*, a greeting, the Selamlık being the one part of the house where it is permitted to receive visitors." *Selamlık* also refers to the sultan's Friday procession to the mosque.

Hoş geldiniz!

Welcome!

Hürriyet

Hürriyet is the Turkish word for "freedom," and it appears often. A similar word, also seen everywhere, is *cumhuriyet*, the Turkish word for "republic." *Hürriyet* is also the name of a daily Turkish newspaper.

Hüzün

Hüzün is a Turkish word for "melancholy." In his book *Istanbul: Memories and the City*, Orhan Pamuk relates that when the word "appears in the Koran (as *huzn* in two verses and *hazen* in three others), it means much the same thing as the contemporary Turkish word. The Prophet Muhammad referred to the year in which he lost both his wife Hatice and his uncle, Ebu Talip, as *Senettul huzn*, the year of melancholy; this confirms that the word is meant to convey a feeling of deep spiritual loss. But if *hüzün* begins its life as a word for loss and the spiritual agony and grief attending it, my own readings indicate a small philosophical fault line developing over the next few centuries of Islamic history. With time, we see the emergence of two very different *hüzün*s, each evoking a distinct philosophical tradition." According to the first tradition, the word refers to moments when we may have come too comfortably close to worldly pleasures and material gain. The second meaning refers to *hüzün* "not as the melancholy of a solitary person but the black mood shared by millions of people together." *Hüzün* is an utterly Turkish word and state of being, and as Pamuk says, "It is one of Istanbul's great gifts to the human race."

I

Imaret

Imaret is a Turkish word that describes a building where meals are distributed free to the poor—a sort of soup kitchen—and usually part of a mosque complex (*külliye*).

International Istanbul Jazz Festival

The International Istanbul Jazz Festival, begun in 1994, is now one of the best-organized festivals in Europe. From the beginning, the festival was meant to go beyond jazz and include rock, pop, blues, reggae, New Age, etc. Among the artists who've performed over the years are Eric Clapton, Patti Smith, Wynton Marsalis, The Manhattan Transfer, Bryan Ferry, Sting, Lou Reed, and Suzanne Vega. The concerts are performed in different venues throughout the city, some taking place outdoors in parks and squares, and some at Nardis, one of the best jazz clubs in Istanbul. The festival is held in the summer, usually July, and tickets go on sale a few months in advance. Tickets may be purchased at the festival's main box office or from Biletix retail outlets or online (biletix.com). More details are found on the Web site of the Istanbul Foundation for Culture and Arts (iksv.org).

Islam

A basic understanding of Islam is essential for visiting Turkey. Though I am not an Islamic scholar, I have traveled to three Muslim countries and I have made a serious attempt to read a fair number of very good sources that were recommended to me by Muslim friends and a few others who actually are scholars. I remain grateful to them all, and I think you will be happy to have their recommendations, too.

The word "Islam" means "surrender" to the will of God, and the five pillars of Islam are *shahada* (professing that "there is no god but Allah and Muhammad is his prophet"); *sala* (praying five times daily); *zakah* (giving alms to the needy; welfare contribution); *sawm* (observing Ramadan, or *Ramazan* in Turkish); and *hadj* (making a pilgrimage to Mecca at least once in one's lifetime). It is helpful to know that Turkey is a Sunni Muslim nation and what that means (there are also some Shiite and Alevi Muslims in Turkey). The two great religious divisions of Islam are Sunnism and Shiism. Sunnis (or Sunnites) regard the first four caliphs as legitimate successors of Muhammad. The first four caliphs were Abu Bakr, Umar ibn al-Khattab, Uthman ibn Affan, and Ali ibn Abi Talib; they were friends and immediate successors of Muhammad. Shiis (or Shiites) regard Ali—the same Ali ibn Abi Talib, son-in-law of Muhammad—as the legitimate successor of Muhammad, and they disregard the first three caliphs who preceded him. Shiis take their name from Shiah i-Ali, or Partisans of Ali. (Ali was murdered in 661 by the Kharajites, who felt that the ruler of the Islamic community must be the most committed Muslim, not the most powerful.) Sunnis take their name from the word *sunnah*, meaning "custom" or, in the words of author Karen Armstrong, "the habits and religious practice of the Prophet Muhammed, which were recorded for posterity by his companions and family and are regarded as the ideal Islamic norm." Sunnis stress the importance of *sunnah* as a basis for law. The majority of Muslims in the world today are Sunni, and according to Armstrong, the difference between Shiites and Sunnis is now purely political.

Turkey, as a secular state, is a moderate Muslim nation. Tom Brosnahan notes on his Web site that he has found Turkey to be the *most* moderate and tolerant of all Muslim nations. Non-Muslims are welcome to visit all mosques in Turkey. He also notes that about 20 percent of Turkish Muslims feel they are Muslims first and citizens of Turkey second. The other 80 percent see themselves as citizens first.

If you've never read the Koran (more properly *Qur'an*), or haven't since your comparative religions class years ago, I encourage you to seize the day and pick up a copy. Becoming more familiar with this great spiritual (and literary) work is an enriching experience. The Koran is perfect companion reading for a trip to Turkey. According to David Roxburgh, in *Writing the Word of God: Calligraphy and the Qur'an* (Museum of Fine Arts, Houston, 2007), Muslims believe that the Koran is the "written record of a series of divinely inspired revelations, the actual word of God, mediated through the angel Gabriel to the Prophet Muhammad." Muhammad thus became God's messenger on earth, and as such he enjoys a place of centrality in Islam and is regarded as the "ideal" Muslim. Very strict Muslims hold that the Koran is untranslatable, which is why the art of translation is always an act of interpretation, and why a great number of translations are available. Roxburgh also notes that "there is evidence that the Prophet Muhammad started to make a physical copy of the revelations during his lifetime in Medina but that this project was incomplete at his death. Though the history of the editing of the Qur'an as a complete text is far from certain—how it was collected and arranged from a corpus of both written and oral sources, how it reached its final consonantal and vocalized form—the traditional belief is that it achieved full written form from a complete oral source during the Prophet Muhammad's lifetime or shortly thereafter through the agency of his most trusted companions."

One edition you may want to examine, which was recommended to me by two professors of Eastern religion (Bradley Clough and Jonathan Brockopp) is *The Koran Interpreted*, translated by H. A. Arberry (Macmillan, 1955), a standard edition in colleges and universities. Most scholars feel Arberry has struck a nice balance between a literal translation and one that captures the spirit of the text. Note the word "interpreted" in the title, the author's nod of respect for the Koran and an indication of the personal nature of translation. Another popular but controversial edition is *The Meaning of the Glorious Koran: An Explanatory Translation*, translated by Marmaduke Pickthall (Knopf, 1930; Everyman's Library, 1992). Pickthall was an Englishman who became Muslim and worked for the Muslim ruler of Hyderabad, the *nizam*. Many scholars today feel that Pickthall strays too far from the literal and that he is ultimately misleading, but however he may be perceived, it is his version of the Koran that I have in my home.

Some other excellent and related books that come highly recommended are *Islam*, by Fazlur Rahman (University of Chicago Press, 1979); *Muhammad*, by Michael Cook (Oxford, 1983); *Muslims: Their Religious Beliefs and Practices* in two volumes, by Andrew Rippin (Routledge, 1994); and *Textual Sources for the Study of Islam*, an anthology edited by Andrew Rippin and Jan Knappert (University of Chicago, 1986). Five of my own favorites are *The World of Islam: Faith, People, Culture*, by Bernard Lewis (Norton, 1992); *Cradle & Crucible: History and Faith in the Middle East*, introduced by Daniel Schorr and with contributions by David Fromkin, Sandra Mackey, Milton Viorst, Andrew Wheatcroft, Zahi Hawass, and Yossi Klein Halevi (National Geographic, 2002); and *Understanding Islam: An Introduction to the Muslim World*, by Thomas W. Lippman (Meridian, 1995).

Two more works by Karen Armstrong are *Islam: A Short History* (Modern Library, 2000) and *A History of God: The 4,000-Year Quest of Judaism, Christianity, and Islam* (Knopf, 1993). Armstrong's books explore a number of themes central to Islam that I feel are essential, though I'm not sure my scholar friends would consider them so. But as a parting thought, I would like to share one of them. Fundamentalism is not unique to Islam, and fundamentalists come in nearly every religious stripe—the word was first used by American Protestants, in fact—and it is a false stereotype to believe that Muslims are filled with hatred of the West. (It isn't difficult, however, to understand why some Muslims might be.) Muslims worldwide admire the efficiency and technology of the West, as well as some of our democratic ideals. In fact, what many Muslims dream of is a balance between modernism and Islamic traditions. In her book *Islam*, Armstrong writes, "The West has not been wholly responsible for the extreme forms of Islam, which have cultivated a violence that violates the most sacred canons of religion. But the West has certainly contributed to this development and, to assuage the fear and despair that lies at the root of all fundamentalist vision, should cultivate a more accurate appreciation of Islam in the third Christian millennium."

Istanbul Modern

The first modern art museum of its kind in all of Turkey, the Istanbul Modern (Meclis-i Mebusan Caddesi, Liman İşletmeleri Sahası, Antrepo 4, Karaköy / +90 212 334 7300 / istanbulmodern.org) is a terrific showcase for Turkish and international contemporary art. The museum was converted into a sleek, ultramodern building from a nineteenth-century former customs house for the Turkish Maritime Organization. Indeed, the museum's exterior doesn't look like much more than a spruced-up warehouse, but don't be fooled: the interior is attractive and filled with light. It's also completely wedded to the waters of the Sea of Marmara, which can be glimpsed periodically from large windows in the upstairs galleries. The museum opened in 2004 and I think it's not only a resounding success, but it adds an important imprimateur to Istanbul's commitment to modern art.

Istanbul Modern was mostly funded by the Eczacıbaşı family, noted arts patrons and pharmaceutical entrepreneurs. (Süleyman Ferit was the first Turkish pharmacist in Izmir, and with the introduction of surnames in 1934, the family decided upon Eczacıbaşı, meaning "chief pharmacist" in Turkish.) The permanent collection, housed on the first floor, features Modern Experiences and From Ottoman Empire to Turkish Republic, which I highly recommend. Among my favorite works on this floor are *Han Coffeehouse*, by Bedri Rahmi Eyüboğlu; *The Door*, by Burhan Uygur; and *On the Road to Revolution*, by Zeki Faik İzer. I also love *Stairway to Hell*, the sculpture of chain and bullet-shattered glass by Monica Bonvicini that connects the two floors (this was shown at the Istanbul Biennial in 2003 and donated to the museum by a local collector). The collection spans all styles of Turkish painting, which developed in the mid-nineteenth century and includes movements most visitors have never heard of: the 1914 Generation, Group D, Group Ten, the Black Pen Group, etc.

I asked the Modern's chief curator, Levent Çalıkoğlu, for a list of his top ten favorite works in the museum. I was happy that he also chose *Han Coffeehouse* as one of them, and his other nine favorites are *Forest Nymph*, by Hamit Görele (1940); *Abstract Landscape*, by İhsan Cemal Karaburçak (1964–65); *My Hell*, by Fahrelnissa Zeid (1951); *Death of the Poet*, by Cihat Burak (1967); *Abstract Composition*, by Nejad Melih Devrim (1947–49); *3 Men, 4 Women, Visitors*, by Ömer Uluç (1989); *Dog Walking Area*, by Özdemir Altan (1995); *Hallac-ı Mansur*, by Erol Akyavaş (1987); and *The Seaman*, by Mehmet Güleryüz (1988).

The Modern's gift shop stocks many appealing items, for yourself or as gifts, and the café (whose dominant color is red) is fantastic—one side completely faces the sea and the bar is hugely fun. The menu features *mezes* and light dishes, and every table is given great bread with a small bowl of olive oil filled with fennel seeds and red pepper flakes, a combination I immediately copied when I got home. The café is a destination in itself and I would recommend it as a dining option even if you don't visit the museum, though that would be a shame.

Istanbul 2010

Istanbul was designated by the European Union to be a European Capital of Culture in 2010. The designation lasts for a full year and is a huge opportunity for the city to showcase its cultural life and cultural development. (It is also the last time non-EU member counties are eligible for selection.) Among the goals of 2010 are improving the current conditions of structures of cultural and historical value, improving and increasing the diversity of the existing historical tourism destinations in the city, and promoting Turkey's cultural assets across Europe. The overall theme of the celebration is "The City of Four Elements," the elements being water, fire, air, and earth.

More information is available at istanbul2010.org.

İstiklâl

"My favorite word in Turkish is *istiklâl*," writes Stephen Kinzer in *Crescent & Star*. "The dictionary says it means 'independence,' and that alone is enough to win it a place of honor in any language. But the real reason I love to hear the word *istiklâl* is because it is the name of Turkey's most fascinating boulevard. Jammed with people all day and late into the night, lined with cafes, bookstores, cinemas and shops of every description, it is the pulsating heart not only of Istanbul but of the Turkish nation." İstiklâl Caddesi is indeed one of the most famous streets in Istanbul, and as it is a pedestrian zone, it's worth your time to stroll up or down it, if only to see a modern, cosmopolitan side of the city (there are chain stores and Starbucks mixed in with local businesses). During Ottoman times, the Grand Avenue (Caddes-i Kebir) was popular with intellectuals as well as European foreigners and local Italian and French Levantines, who referred to it as the Grande Rue de Péra. When nineteenth-century travelers referred to Constantinople as the "Paris of the East" they were referring to the Grande Rue de Péra.

In addition to its many shops, İstiklâl is also lined with some beautiful examples of nineteenth-century Turkish architecture, and there are a number of places to stop during a stroll for refreshment. One of my favorites is Café Markiz, formerly the Pâtisserie Lebon, with its pretty Art Nouveau interior.

Iznik

Iznik is both the name of a town, across the Sea of Marmara from Istanbul, and the legendary ceramic wares that were produced there. John Ash writes in *A Byzantine Journey* that the dominant motifs in Iznik ware are floral in intricate designs of "blue, turquoise, green, white and a startling tomato red. It was the addition of this lustrous red, which is unique to Iznik ware, that made the accurate depiction of so many flowers possible. As a result, any interior that is covered with Iznik tiles, be it a mosque, a palace or a tomb, becomes an image of paradise." By the early seventeenth century, Iznik wares deteriorated, and Ash notes, "The secret was lost, never to be recovered, and with the disappearance of the red, Iznik ceases to be of any significance in the affairs of the world." Over the years since then, master ceramicists have been trying hard to reproduce tiles and other objects of the same quality.

Though they may never reproduce Iznik exactly, at least one company has been successful at creating high-quality reproductions: Iznik Classics. The shop in Sultanahmet, near the Four Seasons hotel, is almost more of a museum than a store, except that, yes, everything is for sale. Be sure to walk both upstairs and downstairs to see everything—the downstairs rooms are truly impressive. Iznik ware is not by any measure inexpensive, but it is distinctive. Though I departed with two beautiful bowls, I am *still* thinking about a particular set of teal-and-brown tiles. Only after I returned home did I learn from a colleague that she had chosen a set of tiles and the store staff had them framed for her. What a great idea! I am making a beeline for the store on my next visit.

Iznik Classics has three shops in Istanbul: in the Grand Bazaar (Iç Bedesten Şerifağa Sokak 188 / +90 212 520 2568), in the Arasta Bazaar (nos. 67, 73, and 161 / +90 212 517 1705), and in Sultanahmet (Utangaç Sokak 17 / +90 212 516 8874).

Two essential Iznik reads are:

• *Iznik: The Artistry of Ottoman Ceramics,* by Walter Denny (Thames & Hudson, 2004). A gorgeous, oversize hardcover with beautiful color photographs, this is an authoritative volume on Iznik ceramics. Denny provides not only fine and fascinating details of Iznik pottery itself, but also an excellent overview of Ottoman artistic accomplishment. He reminds us that as the Ottoman Empire was an Islamic state, there were no large monuments of public sculpture or large paintings. As a result, what would be considered "minor" or "decorative" arts in the West were held in high regard in the Islamic world. "This distinction," writes Denny, "is a vital one for our Western understanding of Islamic art in general and Ottoman art in particular," and "had Vasari studied goldsmithing instead of painting, perhaps the history of Western art would have taken a different direction." Visitors to Turkey will not be left in any doubt that Iznik pottery is magnificent and worthy of the world's highest appreciation.

• *Iznik: The Pottery of Ottoman Turkey,* by Nurhan Atasoy and Julian Raby (Alexandria Press, in association with Thames & Hudson, 1994). When Walter Denny referred to this book as *the* essential work on Iznik, I knew I had to track it down. I couldn't see how anything could surpass Denny's own work, but I admit he was right: this is a stellar and lavish reference.

Atasoy relates that, according to archival sources, even during the sixteenth century, when the most beautiful Iznik wares of the highest quality were being made, the Ottoman elite much preferred Chinese porcelain, so that at Topkapı and in the homes of the privileged, Iznik pottery was used only as everyday ware. Registers from the palace treasury and kitchens state that not enough porcelain was kept in the palace to cater for the sumptuous banquets given during the celebrations for the circumcision of Prince Mehmet, son of Sultan Murad III, in 1582, festivities that lasted fifty-two days and nights. To make up for this shortage, 541 Iznik plates, dishes, and bowls were bought from the bazaar. The Chinese porcelains at Topkapı were very well protected because they were so highly valued, and the collection came to number more than 10,600 pieces, which have survived to our day. Iznik pottery wasn't kept in the same storerooms as the porcelain and no care was taken to protect it; as a result, there is no Iznik pottery in the palace collections. Chapters on the types and forms of Iznik, and how it's made, are quite detailed, and the color plates in the final section are gorgeous.

J

Jewish Community in Istanbul

In *A Travel Guide to Jewish Europe*, Ben G. Frank notes that "Istanbul was one of the most important Jewish centers of the world, replete with Jewish schools and scholars. It was even called the Jewish 'mother city.' " In an article in the travel section of *The New York Times* ("Where the Ram's Horn Sounded in the Land of the Sultans"), Joel Zack writes that once, "almost every Turkish town had a Jewish quarter, or Yahudi Mahallesi. But today, few Jews can be found. Most have emigrated, many to Israel. Communities that once numbered in the thousands now cannot raise the quorum of ten men needed for communal prayer." After Catholic monarchs Ferdinand and Isabella issued the edict of expulsion in 1492, Spanish Jews (or Sephardic Jews) fled to the Ottoman Empire, principally to Salonica. Leon Sciaky, in *Farewell to Salonica: Portrait of an Era*, notes that "Sultan Bayezit II, in a letter to his governors, ordered that they be received with kindness and that all possible assistance be extended to them in their resettlement. Oppression or ill-treatment to the newcomers was to be considered a major offense and severely punished. 'They say that Ferdinand is a wise monarch,' he exclaimed before his courtiers. 'How could he be one, he who impoverishes his country to enrich mine!' "

According to Ben Frank, by the sixteenth century, Istanbul, with 440,000 Jews, had the largest Jewish population in the world. Jews were one of the city's protected minorities, though this didn't mean they were exempt from special taxes or rules governing their dress and their housing. Turkey was the first Muslim nation to recognize Israel, in 1949. Since then, relations between the countries have had their ups and downs, but in 1993, Turkish foreign minister Hikmet Çetin was the very first foreign minister to visit Israel.

I bought a woven handbag (which I had made into a pillow) from a Sephardic vendor at the Grand Bazaar years ago, and he told me that, at that time, there were three daily newspapers published in Istanbul in Ladino, the dialect of Sephardic Jews. According to *The Cultural Guide to Jewish Europe*, "more often than not, Istanbul's Jews speak Turkish among themselves, even if most know French. Only the very elderly remember Ladino, their old language to which the Hebrew weekly *Shalom* (circulation of 3,500) still dedicates one or two pages in each issue." In all of Turkey today there are no more than 20,000 Jews.

We in North America are so accustomed to the customs and traditions of Ashkenazic Jews that it's easy to assume they are observed by Sephardic Jews, too. The sometimes vast differences between the two communities may be gleaned from an interesting book that accompanied an exhibit of the same name, *A Tale of Two Cities: Jewish Life in Frankfurt and Istanbul, 1750–1870*, by Vivian Mann (The Jewish Museum, New York, under the auspices of the Jewish Theological Seminary of America, 1982). The book is filled with illustrations of many ceremonial objects and prints that examine two different communities over a period of 120 years. Mann notes that at the beginning of Ottoman rule, the Jewish population of Istanbul was organized into congregations according to their members' places of origin. Even if one married and moved to a different neighborhood of the city, individuals still paid taxes according to their original congregations, such as Córdoba, Portugal, Sicily, Ohrid, and Salonika. In complete contrast to the ghettoized populations of European cities like Frankfurt, the Jews of Istanbul lived among Muslim and Christian neighbors in many quarters throughout the city and the suburbs.

I think a perfect visit to Istanbul includes seeing mosques, churches, and synagogues. Mosques and a church or two aren't problematic, but unfortunately one needs an appointment to visit a synagogue, so you need to plan in advance (either by sending a fax of a copy of the first page of your passport directly to the synagogue, or to a concierge or guide who will help you arrange the appointment). Of the sixteen synagogues still in existence—located on both the European and Asian sides of the city and on the Princes' Islands—only a few are active. There are two major synagogues in the city. One is Ahrida Synagogue (Kurtci Cesmi Sokak 15, Balat; contact the Balat Foundation at +90 212 523 7407 for visitor information), with a very pretty interior that was restored in 1992, in honor of the five hundredth anniversary of the Iberian Jews' arrival in Istanbul. The other is Neve Shalom (Büyük Hendek Caddesi 61, Karaköy / nevesalom.org), which has, sadly, been the object of three terrorist attacks: September 12, 1986, when more than twenty people were killed; November 15, 2003, when one of four car-bomb attacks killed fifty-seven people and wounded seven hundred (Al Qaeda claimed responsibility); and again on November 20, 2003, when two truck bombs exploded, killing thirty people and wounding forty. (On the same day, George W. Bush was visiting Tony Blair in London; the British consulate in Istanbul was also targeted.) The clock in the Neve Shalom lobby remains stuck at 9:17 a.m., the time of the 1986 explosion.

Two good resources for history and background information (and mentioned in this section) are *A Travel Guide to Jewish Europe*, by Ben G. Frank (Pelican, 2001), and *The Cultural Guide to Jewish Europe* (Chronicle, 2004). Joel Zack's New York–based Heritage Tours (800 378 4555 / heritagetoursonline.com) arranges highly regarded tours to Istanbul and other parts of Turkey (and Morocco, Spain, and South Africa as well) with an emphasis on exploring Jewish heritage.

K

Karagöz

Karagöz (meaning "black eye" in Turkish) is both the name of Turkish shadow theater and one of the central characters in this art, which dates back to the sixteenth century (and the nineteenth in Greece). Though the oldest Turkish shadow puppet still in existence today is only one hundred years old, we have an idea what the older puppets looked like from scenes depicted in Ottoman miniatures of the sixteenth, seventeenth, and eighteenth centuries. These often were of jesters and grotesque dancers.

Karagöz has been described as "a rich cross section of Turkish culture, namely, of poetry, miniature painting, music, folk customs, and oral tradition." Mary Lee Settle, in *Turkish Reflections*, describes the character Karagöz as a hunchback who was working on the Great Mosque in Bursa when it was built. "He was caught making fun of the sultan by using his hands to cast shadow figures on the wall. In a fury, the sultan had him executed. It was out of Karagöz's joking that the Turkish shadow puppets were born. The shadow puppets are still everywhere, as familiar as Punch and Judy."

Karagöz and Hacivat are the two lead characters, with Karagöz representing an illiterate but honest fellow and Hacivat belonging to the educated class. Shadow puppet plays have been especially associated with Ramadan, and years ago, it was one of the most popular forms of entertainment in Turkey. Today most of the stories (some of which were originally off-color or violent) have been adapted for their audience, mostly children.

The puppets themselves, usually made of camel skin and dyed, are simple but beautiful, and they make nice souvenirs. The best place to buy them in all of Turkey is in Bursa, at Karagöz Antikaci (Kapalı Çarşı, Eski Aynalı Çarşı Içir 12–13, Osman Gazi / +90 224 220 5350). Years ago, the original owner of the shop, Rafet Çelikkol, sent me some puppets by mail as I wanted to give them as a birthday gift to a friend. Today his son, Sinasi, is in charge of the store and is continuing to support the shadow puppet tradition.

Kebab

A kebab or *kebap* (or "kabob," as we pronounce it in the West) is a category of food that is typically Turkish, dating back to the times when the nomadic Turks learned to grill and roast their meat over fire. Bade Jackson explains in *Turkish Cooking*:

> Given the numerous types of kebaps, it helps to realize that you categorize them by the way the meat is cooked, as in *şiş kebap* and *doner kebap*. It is not that they are complicated or even particularly exotic, but their basic flavor and combination of simple ingredients has stood the test of time. The preparation of *doner kebap* always follows the traditional methods. First the boned leg

of lamb is marinated with herbs, yogurt, tomato, and onions for a few hours, then it is sliced thinly, and wrapped around a vertical spit and placed in front of a three-tiered broiler. As the spit revolves slowly, the outside layer of the lamb cooks. From this revolving action the dish takes it name *doner*, which means "to turn" in Turkish. *Şiş kebap* is another way of cooking meat. *Şiş* means "skewer" in Turkish. In Nomadic times the meat was cooked slowly over the campfires along with onions, peppers and herbs. It should be noted that the unique taste of kebaps is due more to the breeds of sheep and cattle which are raised in open pastures, than to their special marinades and the way of cooking.

Kilims *and* Carpets

Many visitors to Istanbul don't want to leave without a *kilim*, which is a flatwoven textile in Turkey (known as *palas* in the Caucasus, *gelim* in Iran, and *kelim* in Afghanistan) or a carpet, and I don't blame them—Istanbul's reputation as a carpet center is justified. The problem for tourists is that you will be bombarded with so many styles, colors, and kinds of weavings that it's difficult to make an informed decision. But it's not impossible, as my friend and dealer, Ömer Eymen (see Arasta Bazaar, page 493) helped me to understand. As Ömer recommended to me, I suggest that you make a visit early on in your trip to the Turkish and Islamic Arts Museum (even if you have no intention of buying a rug).

Reputable dealers will take the time to explain some important features about their *kilims* and rugs to you. Pay attention—take notes if you want—and if at any point you feel you are being pressured, walk out. There are plenty of quality rug dealers in Istanbul, so there is no need to rush into buying anything.

Kilims are generally less expensive than rugs, and many people prefer their brighter palette and more modern designs. *Kilims*

were traditionally used as floor coverings, door and window curtains, prayer rugs, and sometimes eating cloths. "They were also made," according to the author team of *Kilim: The Complete Guide*, "into every size of bag for storage and transportation, as well as serving as trappings to decorate the animals. Aside from domestic use, the flatweaves were made for donation to the mosque, and more recently for trade." They were used also as seat and banquette coverings, and larger ones were woven as walls for tents. Still more were used as mosque hangings—to separate the men from the women—and on the floor for praying.

Some characteristics that affect the price of both *kilims* and rugs are whether chemical or vegetable dyes were used (most of the time, chemical dyes are cheaper); age (most of the time, an older weaving will hold more value); and whether the weaving was made for a girl's dowry or for money (usually, if a weaving is made just for money it is inferior to one made for a dowry). In recent years, some disreputable dealers have been selling Chinese knockoffs, sometimes featuring traditional Anatolian designs, and not revealing this to the buyer (and the buyer is usually not educated enough about weavings to ask). Chinese copies are always cheaper, so always inquire about a rug's origins. This is not to say there aren't quality weavings made in China, but it the price is too cheap, there's a reason. It's best to do a good deal of looking first before you buy anything, and if you're buying an older piece that needs repairs, ask that they be included in the price, which should not be a problem. Remember that handmade weavings aren't perfect, and imperfections are part of their charm.

Happily, there are some good references to peruse before you arrive in Istanbul, and remember to measure floor or wall space or table size (to cover with camel bags or cradles) in advance if you're serious about making a purchase:

- *The Classical Tradition in Anatolian Carpets*, by Walter B. Denny, with contributions by Sumru Belger Krody (Scala in association with the Textile Museum, 2002). Accompanying an exhibit of the same name, this 128-page paperback is a great volume for readers who want to learn more about Anatolian weavings but don't want to delve into a huge tome. Denny and Krody note that George Hewitt Myers, founder of the Textile Museum, had collected 500 rugs by the time of his death in 1957, at age eighty-two; of these, 104 were Anatolian. They continue, noting that the knotted-pile carpets of Anatolia "constitute perhaps the oldest and richest carpet-weaving tradition, which survives in a significant number of examples today."

- *Kilim: The Complete Guide*, by Alastair Hull and Jose Luczyc-Wyhowska (Chronicle, 1993). Hull has traveled extensively in Afghanistan and Iran collecting and studying *kilims* while Luczyc-Wyhowska opened London's Kilim Warehouse in 1982 and specializes in the flatweaves of Anatolia. Together they have written what is likely the most authoritative book yet on *kilims*. The authors explain that Anatolia is also known as Anadolu, which derives from the Turkish *ana*, meaning "mother," and *dolu*, meaning "full," giving the overall sense of the "fertile mother" or "earth." *Anatolia* is used to mean "from, or of, the land or the countryside," and unlike the *kilim* culture in Central Asia, Iran, and North Africa, "where weaves are governed, restricted and inspired, more or less, within a tribal environment, that of Anatolia has been embellished by it rich folkloric tradition and diversity of foreign influence." After the enormous popularity of *kilims* in the Western world in the 1980s, the output of traditional forms of flatweave is waning, and the authors inform us that, in Anatolia, virtually no old indigenous examples remain. "The village weavers of today do not have the time or inclination to weave a quality *kilim*, for the faster the weaver can finish her work, the sooner she can sell it and buy a refrigerator or television set for her home. In one village, with no electricity supply, lived a weaver who had bought a refrigerator, proudly placed it in the living room and filled it with all her most precious possessions!"

• *Timbuktu to Tibet: Exotic Rugs and Textiles from New York Collectors*, by Jon Thompson, Thomas Farnham, and Daniel Shaffer (Hajji Baba Club, 2008). This catalog accompanied the exhibit Woven Splendor from Timbuktu to Tibet, shown at the New-York Historical Society in 2008 and at the Textile Museum from October 18, 2008 to March 8, 2009. The exhibit was organized to celebrate the seventy-fifth anniversary of the Hajji Baba Club, the oldest and most prestigious rug-collecting club in the U.S. (Note: this club is not the same as the International Hajji Baba Society.) According to the Hajji Baba Web site (hajjibaba.org), the rug craze began in the U.S. in the late eighteenth century; initially, all rugs, no matter their origin, were referred to as "Turkey carpitts." This exhibition catalog beautifully reproduces the approximately seventy-five rugs, costumes, and other textiles featured in the exhibit that currently belong to club members.

- *Turkey: The Rug Guide*, by Anthony Hazeldine, John Mills, John Carswell, Andrew Finkel, and John Scott (Hali, 2005). Though this little paperback (approximately 5½ × 8 inches) is not completely current, it's terrific, and I highly recommend it. Not only is the information about Turkish weavings— from all over the country—factual and interesting, the book also includes chapters on museums, hotels, and restaurants. The book is packed with color photographs and maps and is slim enough to fit in a handbag. It's not available in North America but can be ordered direct from *Hali* magazine or online retailers.

The world of Near and Far Eastern weavings is large. Here are just a few rug organizations and resources to know about:

- The Armenian Rugs Society (650 343 8585 / armenian rugssociety.com)

- The American Conference on Oriental Rugs (acor-rugs.org)

- *Hali: Carpet, Textile and Islamic Art* is the leading international periodical in its field. *Hali* is the modern Turkish word for "carpet" or "rug" and was written as *kālī* in Ottoman Turkish script until the late nineteenth century, as it was written in classical Persian and remains in modern Persian. The magazine has been described as "the glue that holds the international rug and textile art market together" and "the benchmark against which all other art publications measure their quality." It's a gorgeous, expensive magazine, published quarterly in London and not widely available in North America. I've seen copies only in museum shops and a few bookstores. Readers who are seriously interested in textiles should consider a subscription, but otherwise the magazine's Web site (hali.com) is extensive and is a resource on its own.

- International Conference on Oriental Carpets (icoc-orientalrugs.org)

- The International Hajji Baba Society (ihbs.org)

- The New England Rug Society (ne-rugsociety.org)

Konak

Konak is a Turkish word referring to the house of a dignitary or an otherwise notable person.

Külliye

Külliye refers to a building complex that forms a pious foundation (*vakıf*) surrounding a mosque. The buildings typically include a *medrese* (or madrassa, a religious school), a *türbe* (monumental tomb), *imaret* (see page 537), and possibly a hospital.

L

Lepanto

The Battle of Lepanto, in 1571, is a hugely significant conflict in Turkish (and European) history. Readers who have visited Vatican City may remember that in the impressive Galleria delle Carte Geografiche, the covered peristyle that connects the old Vatican

Palace to the Belvedere, there is an enormous wall painting of this battle. The site of this naval battle was outside the narrows in the Gulf of Patras, in Greece, overlooked by the castle of Lepanto (at the time, in fact, the gulf was known as the Gulf of Lepanto). The fleet that set out to fight the Turks was primarily Spanish and had strong papal and Venetian contingents. The Christians were victorious—the victory reasserted Spanish supremacy in the Mediterranean and was celebrated with much fanfare in Europe. However, Sir Charles Petrie, in his work *Philip II of Spain* (Eyre and Spottiswoode, 1963), notes:

> The battle of Lepanto did not break the back of Ottoman naval power, it did not recover Cyprus, and it did not lead to the policing of the Mediterranean by Spain. Though a tactical victory of the first order, because of the dissolution of the [Holy] League it strategically left the Sultan the victor. But morally it was decisive, for by lifting the pall of terror which had shrouded eastern and central Europe since 1453, it blazoned throughout Christendom the startling fact that the Turk was no longer invincible. Hence onward to the battle of Zenta, in 1697, when Eugene, Prince of Savoy, drove in rout the army of Sultan Mustafa II into the river Theiss, and thereby finally exorcised the Turkish threat to Europe. Though there were to be many ups and downs, never was the full prestige of Suleyman the Magnificent to be revived. His reign marks the summit of Turkish power, and it was the day of Lepanto which broke the charm upon which it rested.

More recently, historian Bernard Lewis, in *A Middle East Mosaic* (2000), notes that Lepanto made very little difference to the real balance of power in southeastern Europe and the Mediterranean. "The Turkish armies remained dominant on land; the Turkish fleets were swiftly rebuilt. When the sultan expressed concern about the cost, his grand vizier replied: 'The might of our empire is such that if we wished to equip the entire fleet with silver anchors, silken rigging and satin sails, we could do it.' "

Petrie also notes that "both Philip and Don John have been subject to criticism, chiefly civilian, for not having followed up the victory of Lepanto by an immediate attack upon Constantinople, which, according to the critics, would inevitably have been followed by the overthrow of the Ottoman Empire. The blame is usually placed upon the shoulders of the king either on the grounds of his habitual procrastination or of his jealousy of his brother." Godfrey Goodwin, in *Life's Episodes*, reveals a forgotten footnote about the beautiful Italian city of Vicenza, which he says "has two footholds in Ottoman history. It was here after the capture of Constantinople that Fatih's Akıncılar (mounted scouts) reached before turning back in front of the barred gates. It is here also that the palace of the governor was never completed because the money was needed to build two galleys to join the fleet of Don John of Austria at the Battle of Lepanto." Both the Museo de la Santa Cruz in Toledo, Spain, and Venice's Museo Storico Navale feature magnificent (and well-preserved) Lepanto banners, which would have flown from the sailing ships' mastheads. Also, Venice's Church of San Martino houses a wooden crucifix, known as the Lepanto Cross, as it was carried on a Venetian galley during the battle.

Two excellent accounts of Lepanto are found in volume I of *Decisive Battles of the Western World and Their Influence Upon History*, by J. F. C. Fuller (Eyre & Spottiswoode, 1956), and in "Victory at Sea, 1571: Lepanto," by Oliver Warner, in *Horizon*, July 1963.

Lokum

Lokum is the Turkish word for "Turkish delight." You will see boxes and boxes of *lokum* everywhere in Istanbul, but the only brand you should buy is Hacı Bekir. Why? Because it is, simply, the best. And if you are wondering how there can possibly be much difference between brands of Turkish delight, you're wise to wonder—but all I can say is that there *is* a difference. I was fortunate to meet the general manager of Hacı Bekir, one of the few employees of the company who isn't a family member, and he told me, "If you try two or three different brands, side by side, you will be able to tell the difference immediately." The company's story begins in 1777, when Bekir Effendi moved from Kastamonu, a Black Sea coastal community, to Istanbul. He opened a small shop in the Old City, selling *lokum* and *akide*, another boiled sweet. Upon fulfilling his religious obligation to journey to Mecca, Bekir became known as Hacı Bekir, a title of respect granted to all those who have completed the hajj, or pilgrimage.

Confectionery in Istanbul dates back to the sixteenth century, when honey and molasses were used as sweeteners and water and flour were the binding agents. Sugar produced in refineries in Europe appeared in Turkey at the end of the eighteenth century, and was called *kelle şekeri* and was sold in cone-shaped blocks. Hacı Bekir preferred this sugar, and when a German scientist discovered starch in 1811, he began using *kelle şekeri* with starch. This new combination led to the production of the choicest *lokum*, but it alone is not the reason for its high quality. Hacı Bekir uses only top-quality fresh fruits and spices—the company even owns some of the fruit orchards, so it has complete control over when the fruit is harvested—and uses no additives. As a result, shelf life is very short, one week at most (though if you buy a box to take home it will last a little longer). The color of the *lokum* will change if sits for too long. Additionally, Hacı Bekir sticks to tradition: after the ingredients are boiled,

lokum must rest for at least two days before being sold. Other companies sell *lokum* much earlier and also use vanilla to mask less-than-fresh fruit flavors. Hacı Bekir makes only three batches a week, and among its twenty-eight flavors are cream, hazelnut, pistachio, coffee, apple, orange, cherry, apricot, ginger, cinnamon, clove, and *mastica*. (*Mastica* is made from the Mediterranean plant of the same name, grown principally on the Greek island of Chios; one product made from *mastica* is a hard granule that turns into a gum when chewed—it reportedly was used as a breath freshener in the Topkapı harem. Interestingly, Chios was self-ruled during the Ottoman Empire, enjoying special privileges only because of its *mastica*. Mastihashop in New York [145 Orchard Street / 212 253 0895 / mastihashopny.com] is the official shop of the Chios Mastiha Growers Association and carries some nifty products such as lotions, soaps, confections, cookies, olive oil, and toothpaste, all made with *mastica*.) The most popular flavors at Hacı Bekir are hazelnut and pistachio (my own favorites).

Hacı Bekir also made almond pastes, and when he was awarded the Nişan-ı Ali Osman—a first-degree medal of honor granted by the sultan—he was also named Chief Confectioner to Topkapı Palace. This honorary title remained within the family as Hacı Bekir's son and grandson (Ali Muhiddin) took over the business. Today the company is a fifth-generation family business, and is known to be the oldest company in Turkey operating out of its original premises (the original store, near the Spice Market, has been open for 237 years). Some of the boxes of *lokum* feature a painting on the lid—this is actually reproduced from a watercolor painting that now hangs in the Louvre, which depicts Hacı Bekir working in his shop. It's by a Maltese artist, Count Amadeo Preziosi (1816–1882), a renowned Orientalist painter, and there is a lithographic print of the image in Topkapı. Hacı Bekir doesn't fill mail orders, but Krinos Foods distributes the *lokum* in the U.S., so all is not lost if you return home and discover you must have more.

M

Manzikert

Manzikert (or Malazgirt), north of Lake Van in eastern Anatolia, was the scene of "a tipping point in world history—and a disaster for Constantinople" according to Roger Crowley in *1453*. "Without Manzikert," says John Ash in *A Byzantine Journey*, "Anatolia might now be, for better or worse, part of a Greek state. The Ottoman Empire would never have come into being, and there would be no Muslims in Bosnia for Serbs and Croats to slaughter." The stage for the Battle of Manzikert, in 1071, was set years before when Turkish tribes continued to move westward until the Islamic world, from Central Asia to Egypt, was ruled by Turks. In Egypt the Turks were Shiite, while the Turkish Seljuks were Sunni. The Seljuks in Baghdad were troubled by unruly nomadic tribesmen, the Turkmen, who had a nasty reputation for plunder. The Seljuks convinced the Turkmen to set their sights on Byzantium, instead of on Islamic towns and villages within its realm. The Turkmen began raiding Christian Anatolia so frequently that there was no other choice for Emperor Romanus IV Diogenes but to personally travel east to repair the situation. When he arrived in Manzikert, he met a Seljuk army under the command of Sultan Alp Arslan, "the heroic lion." What happened next is "a curious affair": Arslan didn't want to fight—his objective was to destroy the Shiites in Egypt—so he proposed a truce. Romanus refused, and the ensuing battle was a shattering Muslim victory. Romanus then reportedly knelt down and kissed the ground in front of Arslan, who put his foot on his bent neck in a symbolic show of triumph and submission.

For the Byzantines, Manzikert was the "Terrible Day," and again according to Crowley, "a defeat of seismic proportions that was to haunt their future. The effects were catastrophic, though not immediately understood in Constantinople itself." The Turkmen poured into Anatolia, and after the deserts of Iran and Iraq, the Anatolian landscape was rather like paradise. Within twenty years they reached the Mediterranean coasts, and met with little resistance from the Christian population. Before long, the Christians were invited to assist in the civil wars that were regularly occurring and were weakening Byzantium. "The conquest of Asia Minor happened so easily and with so little resistance that by the time another Byzantine army was defeated in 1176, the possibility of driving back the incomers had gone forever," notes Crowley.

The battle is still commemorated every year at the site of the battlefield as one of the turning points in Turkish history.

Marmaray Project

In Istanbul's excellent Archaeology Museum, there is a temporary exhibit on the Marmaray Project, which will provide yet one more way for people to traverse Istanbul from the European side to the Asian. The name comes from combining Marmara with *ray*, the Turkish word for "rail." The system will allow for uninterrupted transportation for nearly one million people over a seventy-eight-kilometer-long commuter rail system between Gebze and Halkalı. If it's completed, the percentage of trips made in Istanbul by rail transport is expected to be the third highest in the world after Tokyo and New York.

This massive project includes a 13.6-kilometer Bosphorus crossing and an upgrade of suburban train lines. The Bosphorus will be crossed by a 1.4-kilometer earthquake-proof immersed tube, and sections of the tube will be placed fifty-six meters below sea level. New underground stations will be built at Sirkeci, Yenikapı, and Üsküdar, and there will be forty stations in total.

The project was begun in 2004 and was due to be finished in 2012, but it's currently two years behind schedule due to the excavation of a Byzantine archaeological find on the site of the European tunnel terminal. This find is equally noteworthy: it's the "greatest nautical archeological site ever discovered" and has revealed "the first Byzantine naval craft ever brought to light" (Richard Covington, *Saudi Aramco World*, January/February 2009).

Maşallah!

Also written as *Mash'Allah*, this phrase translates as "Gift of God" or "God has willed it" and is used as a blessing or an exclamation of joy when in the presence of something beautiful. (See also *Nazar boncuğu*, page 566.)

Midnight Express

The film that won screenwriter Oliver Stone an Oscar in 1979 may have single handedly damaged Turkey's reputation more than any political, religious, or cultural conflagration. The meaning of the expression is little known and interesting, as Tom Brosnahan relates in *Bright Sun, Strong Tea*: "After the collapse of the Ottoman Empire, when the new border was drawn between Greece and Turkey, the old railway line ended up partly in Turkey and partly in Greece. Until the 1970s when a new line was built entirely on the Turkish side of the border, a slow train departed Istanbul each evening at 10:10 p.m. bound for Uzunköprü, near the Greco-Turkish frontier. After leaving Uzunköprü it headed north toward Edirne, crossing the frontier into Greece at Phthion (Pithio). It stopped there to take on Greek border guards who rode the train until it crossed back into Turkey, reaching Edirne at 8:01 a.m." As this was a Turkish train—there were no official stops in Greece—it was entirely a domestic run, and therefore no passport was needed to travel on it.

Though drug smugglers named it the Midnight Express, it was very much a local train. Brosnahan continues, "If you had a good reason to get off in Greece, you could work up the courage to jump. After a convict jumped off the Midnight Express he'd call the American consulate in Thessaloniki, claim that he had lost his passport, apply for and receive a new one, and be on his way. If the border guards saw him jump, they'd jail him for a night, consult with the U.S. consulate, get him a new passport, and send him on his way." The employment of the Midnight Express train allowed for Turkish officials to release convicted drug smugglers pending appeal. This cut down on incarceration expenses, and as the convicts were being released, they would be told there was a slow train that made its way from Istanbul to Edirne through Greece.

In 2004, when Oliver Stone visited Turkey, he officially apologized for offenses to the Turkish people, stating, "It's true, I overdramatized the script." Billy Hayes, the American subject of the story, has also publicly stated that the movie differed from the book in several key ways and that some of the violence portrayed in the film did not happen to him while he was imprisoned. I sincerely hope that anyone who saw the movie, and anyone who sees it in the future, will understand that it's risky to dabble with illegal drugs in Turkey (as is the case in any other country, too), but by no means should one individual's experience in prison be an indictment of the entire Turkish population.

Music

The *Rough Guide to Turkey* features a very good twenty-six-page overview of the various types of Turkish music (there are likely far more than you thought!), including a guide to Turkish instruments and a selected discography. A few discs I bought in Istanbul that I particularly like and recommend include the following: *Istanbul 360*, from the popular restaurant of the same name, mixed and compiled by DJ Tekin (Yeni Dünya Müzik), and *Lucca Style:*

Satsuma, also from a popular club of the same name, in Bebek, compiled by Burak Öcal (A. K. Müzi, 2007)—both of these are great for cocktail or dinner parties. *East 2 West/Istanbul Strait Up,* by Mercan Dede (Doublemoon, 2005), and *East 2 West/Ethno-Electronic Tales from Istanbul,* by Mercan Dede, Burhan Öcal, and Ilhan Ersahin (Rh Pozitif), are lively, and there are other editions available.

Sultan Portreleri: Bosphorus by Moonlight (Kalan, 2004), which features Emre Aracı and the Prague Symphony Chamber Orchestra, is beautiful. Out of pure curiosity, I bought *Ottoman Music,* by Zeki Doğan (Çağri), which is historical Ottoman Janissary music. It's not exactly toe-tapping, but it's interesting . . . for a few minutes. "Uzun İnce Bir Yoldayım," by Aşık Veysel, a legendary Turkish folk poet, is one of the best examples of this type of music, and is very haunting.

The very best compilation of Turkish music is featured on a video documentary, *Crossing the Bridge: The Sound of Istanbul,* by Fatih Akın. *Crossing the Bridge,* produced by Strand Releasing, is just fantastic. It includes contemporary musicians in styles ranging from modern electronic, rock, and hip-hop to classical Arabesk (or Arabesque). (According to the *Rough Guide,* Arabesk refers to the dominant Turkish music during the 1980s and '90s and is a "working-class and, to an extent, outsiders' sound which addressed the everyday realities and problems of the *gariban,* the poor and oppressed.") As stated in *Time Out Istanbul,* "If you see the film after your visit to Istanbul, you'll recognize many places and sounds; see it before your trip and you'll be aware of some of the undercurrents that run through modern city life." The cinematography is also very enticing!

Two good music stores that will allow you to listen to (most) discs before you buy are Sel Kasetçilik (İstiklâl Caddesi 317 / +90 212 244 7188) and Mephisto (İstiklâl Caddesi 125 / +90 212 249 0696).

N

Nazar Boncuğu

This is Turkish for "evil eye," and nearly everywhere visitors look in Turkey they will see plenty of the blue glass evil-eye beads. Belief in the evil eye is not unique to Turkey—it's prevalent through the Near East, South Asia, and the Mediterranean. The blue glass amulet is hung from rearview mirrors on cars, on doors at home and at offices, on desk drawers, in windows, on walls, on the reins of horses—just about *everywhere*—and the amulet is meant as protection, to ward off the evil eye. Though there are some cultural differences, generally the evil eye refers to a belief that misfortune may result from the envy of someone else's good luck, and this envy could be of material possessions, health or beauty, or offspring. It is believed that some people can bestow a curse on others by the malevolent gaze of their eye, even if innocently.

Among Muslims, it is customary to say "Maşallah" ("God has willed it") when expressing any kind of appreciation (see page 563). I still have a newspaper clipping, now nearly twenty years old, in which a Fenerbahçe soccer goalkeeper, Yaşar, was quoted as saying, "I was afflicted by the evil eye. I let six goals through," when he was recounting a match (the champion Fenerbahçe team lost 6–1 to Aydinspor). As ubiquitous as the blue glass eyes are in Turkey, I remain fond of them, and I don't feel a trip has been complete unless I leave with a few in my suitcase.

Nettleberry

Nettleberry (nettleberry.com) is a South Dakota–based distributor of high-quality Turkish language and Turkish subject books that would otherwise be unavailable in the U.S. The Web site has an extensive selection of books for adults as well as children, from age two up to about thirteen or fourteen. Nettleberry is a great source for books about Turkey that you may be unable to find in general bookstores.

Nightlife

If I had been writing this book fifteen years ago, nightlife wouldn't even have been an entry in this Miscellany. But, as Seth Sherwood noted in *The New York Times* ("Party Destination of the Year: Istanbul," December 10, 2006), "Fueled by increasing affluence, greater links with the West, and a sizable under-thirty population, this sprawling city of domes and minarets is emerging as one of the world's most exciting nightlife centers." Pick up copies of *Time Out Istanbul*, *The Guide: Istanbul* (published bimonthly), and *Istanbul: Beyond Your Expectations* for club and entertainment listings (and more).

O

Orient Express

The Orient Express is the long-distance passenger train operated by the Compagnie Internationale des Wagons-Lits whose end points were Paris and Istanbul. Early routes forced passengers to disembark and take sections of the journey by boat, and the first train to make the entire journey arrived at Istanbul's Sirkeci Station on August 12, 1888. Sirkeci remained the easternmost stop until the final run, on May 19, 1977. In the 1930s the rail line acquired its reputation for luxury and exclusivity. In later years, due to border closings between countries, the Iron Curtain, and Communist nations replacing the original Wagon-Lits cars with their own carriages, the line simply couldn't continue as it once had. Today the service runs only from Strasbourg to Vienna, and in 1982, the Venice-Simplon Orient Express was established as a private venture, running from London to Venice, and it's quite expensive.

After the original Orient Express was created, the Compagnie des Wagons-Lits also built the Pera Palas hotel. Train travelers were transferred directly from Sirkeci to the Pera Palas, built in 1892. The hotel is in an architecturally distinctive building and I feel fortunate to have visited its lobby before it closed for what was universally regarded as an overdue renovation (it's due to reopen in late 2009). Its list of illustrious visitors is long, and it remains the "oldest European hotel of Turkey."

Sirkeci Station is beautiful and should definitely be a part of an Istanbul itinerary. It was designed by Prussian architect August Jachmund, and he included medieval rose windows, Mughal-inspired touches, and a Parisian domed roof in the structure. Though the restaurant is not known for stellar food, a meal there would be enjoyable. At night, the pink exterior is lit up and is quite magical. Istanbul's other train station, Haydarpaşa, is on the Asian side, and as a writer for *Time Out Istanbul* recently noted, "Although the days of twentieth-century intrigue are long gone, passing Istanbul's Asian train terminal on a foggy night is all the experience necessary to recapture the gloom and magic of old Stamboul." Most unfortunately, the future of both stations is yet to be decided: due to the Marmaray Project (see page 562), developers have presented plans to convert them into shopping centers or hotels and to build skyscrapers around them. Stay tuned—and visit the stations and take pictures.

P

Pierre Loti

Born Louis Marie-Julien Viaud in Rochefort, France, Pierre Loti is far more associated with Turkey—there is a famous painting by Henri Rousseau in the collection of the Kunsthaus in Zurich of Loti sporting a fez, and in the Istanbul neighborhood of Eyüp there is the Café Pierre Loti, mentioned earlier. Loti was a sailor and writer, and his pseudonym is said to derive from his extreme shyness in his early life, when friends called him *Le Loti*, after an Indian flower that loves to blush unseen. In 1876, he wrote *Aziyadé*, a novel that, like many of his other works, is part autobiographical (he was known to have had a Turkish mistress). In 1891, he was inducted into the Académie Française. As Barbara Hodgson says in *Trading in Memories: Travels Through a Scavenger's Favorite Places*, Loti lived until 1923, but "he remained firmly locked in the nineteenth century." Loti's home, preserved as a museum in Rochefort, apparently includes a Chinese pavilion, a Japanese pagoda, and a Turkish salon . . . all in all a true Orientalist fantasy. Contemporary fans may join La Societé des amis de Pierre Loti (pierreloti.org). New York–area readers are lucky to now have the Pierre Loti Wine Bar (53 Irving Place / 212 777 5684 / pierreloti winebar.com), which opened in early 2008 and is far more lush than the Istanbul café, which serves only nonalcoholic drinks.

Pomegranates

"Along with figs and olives," notes cookbook author Ayla Algar, "the pomegranate is mentioned in the Qur'an as an indication of divine abundance and provision for man and as one of the fruits of paradise." The pomegranate was one of the foods scouts sent out by Moses brought back from Canaan, proof that the Promised Land was fertile. It's also considered a fertility symbol due to its many seeds, and some Jewish scholars claim a pomegranate has 613 seeds, sealing its identity with the 613 commandments Jews are supposed to observe. Simply put, pomegranates are symbols of love and plenty, and visitors to Turkey will encounter them often.

In the winter months, when pomegranates are in season in the Northeast, I often mix pomegranate seeds in with mixed greens for a salad. Sometimes I buy a bag full of them and put them in a bowl, just because they look beautiful. And I drink a lot of pomegranate juice—POM brand is good, but recently my local grocery store started carrying a Turkish brand that I like even better (and it's less expensive).

In *The Bastard of Istanbul*, there is a revealing dialogue in the chapter entitled "Pomegranate Seeds":

> Hovhannes Stamboulian remained quiet for a while, chewing the ends of his mustache. Then he muttered slowly but surely, "We need to work together, Jews and Christians and Muslims. Centuries and centuries under the same imperial roof. We have been living together all this time, albeit on unequal ground. Now we can make it fair and just for all, transform this empire together." It was then that Kirkor Hagopian uttered those gloomy words, his face already closing up: "My friend, wake up, there is no together anymore. Once a pomegranate breaks and all its seeds scatter in different directions, you cannot put it back together.

Pukka Living

Pukka Living (pukkaliving.com) is a Web site about life in Istanbul. It's very up-to-the-minute and features "unique stuff only known to the locals with a zest in life." I've found out about some great people, hip happenings, and unique products and services by subscribing to Pukka Living's weekly e-mail. It's never boring.

Q

As with the letter x, there is no letter q in Turkish. But unlike for x, I haven't been able to find a single word having anything to do with Istanbul or Turkey beginning with q.

R

Rakı

Stephen Kinzer, in *Crescent & Star*, related that "the first friends I made in Turkey told me that if I really wanted to understand their

country, I would have to drink a lot of *rakı*. These were wise people, so I took their advice. Every year the annual level of *rakı* consumption in Turkey rises by slightly more than one million liters,
and my contribution to the increase has not been inconsiderable."
Pronounced RAH-kuh (not RAH-kee), *rakı* is one of several
anise-flavored Mediterranean alcoholic beverages. Like its counterparts in Greece (ouzo) and France (pastis), *rakı* is served in a
glass, usually with ice and a pitcher of water alongside, allowing
the imbiber to add as much or as little water as he or she likes.
When water is added, just as with ouzo and pastis, the clear liquid
turns cloudy. (Sambuca, on the other hand, is an Italian after-
dinner drink made from anise, but it is not served with water or
over ice.) Evliya Çelebi wrote that some taverns of his day sold
rakı made from bananas, mustard, cinnamon, cloves, and pomegranate.

Lonely Planet's *World Food: Turkey* guide states that the Turkish
name for *rakı* derives from the Arabic *arak*, which means "sweat"
or "sweating." "But according to knowledgeable sources, it first
came from East India where they'd produce it by distilling sugar-
cane sap mixed with rice yeast. The same sources say that dried
grapes and dates were used to produce it in Iran. In Turkey it was
originally made from barley and corn. There, the name evolved
over time from 'arak' to aroka, ariki, araki, arakı, and ırakı—until
it was finally shortened to rakı."

Rakı's true home is at a *meyhane*. White cheese, tomatoes,
cucumber, and seafood are favorite *rakı* accompaniments, all staples at a *meyhane*, a casual, family-style place historically owned
and operated by Greeks. I've noticed that outside of a *meyhane*,
even at the simplest places, *rakı* always comes with a small plate of
sliced cucumbers, salted almonds, or—my favorite—roasted chickpeas, or *leblebi*, which my husband calls "pressed dust" (try them
before you knock them!). Kinzer again notes that "the *meyhane*
culture tells a great deal about Turkey. Like the country, it offers
almost infinite possibilities because it blends the heritage of so

many different peoples. At a *meyhane*, the world can either be invited in or shut out. Turks have not yet decided which is the wisest path."

Ramazan

Ramazan is the Turkish word for the Arabic Ramadan, observed in the ninth month of the Muslim lunar Hijri calendar. I love the description of Ramazan in Irfan Orga's *Portrait of a Turkish Family*: "In those days during Ramazan there were no lessons in the schools and we were allowed home on leave. Twenty-seven years ago the streets at Ramazan were crowded as they have not been since and perhaps never will be again. Not only the Muslims who were keeping the fast were in the streets but the British, French and American soldiers were there too to watch the ceremonies. And on the last night of Ramazan, in the year of which I write, Bayazit Square and its Mosque were places not to be forgotten by those who saw them." Today in Istanbul, Ramazan may not be celebrated with quite the same fanfare, but it is still an exciting time to visit. Unlike in more observant Muslim countries, in Istanbul there are plenty of places to eat that remain open during Ramazan, so visitors shouldn't shy away from planning a trip that overlaps with the holiday.

S

Şadırvan

A *şadırvan* is a fountain in the vicinity of a mosque used for performing ritual ablutions before prayers. Two other interesting and related words are *sebil*, an Ottoman-era fountain from which water was distributed free to all passersby, and *çeşme*, simply a Turkish fountain. In *Stamboul Sketches*, John Freely notes that fountains and *sebils* are to be found by the hundreds in all parts of Istanbul, and Evliya Çelebi made reference to "scores of the most important street fountains and *sebil* of his day, and nearly all of them are still in existence." Kenizé Mourad, in *Living in Istanbul*, notes that building fountains was considered an act of charity by the philanthropic rich: it was a way of helping the poor and simultaneously vaunting their wealth. None of the *sebils* in Istanbul are now functioning, but almost all of the fountains are still in use. In fact, the *çeşmes* were for centuries the only water source for the common people of the city, and Freely estimates that they have probably been of more real service to the people of Istanbul than all the other pious foundations taken together. As readers who've been to Rome know, that city is famous for its fountains, too; but as Freely states, the fountains of Istanbul are totally different: "Here there are no dramatic sculptured figures, no allegorical river gods and spouting cherubs, no elaborate cascades and pools. The fountains of Istanbul are simple and utilitarian, but nonetheless they are often quite beautiful."

Seated Scribe *(1479–80)*

I am completely infatuated with this little painting, attributed to the Venetian artist Gentile Bellini and in the permanent collection of the Isabella Stewart Gardner Museum in Boston. "Such an adorable and exquisite thing. . . . It is joy and rapture," is how Mrs. Gardner described it to Bernard Berenson in 1907. Susan Spinale tells us that the folds of the scribe's turban hold in place a ribbed, red *taj*—headgear worn in the court of Sultan Mehmet II, who "nurtured a passionate interest in portraiture and particularly in Western traditions of the genre." An added inscription in Persian records the image as "the work of Ibn Muezzin, who was a famous painter among the Franks." Scholars have never doubted that the painting was produced by a European or "Frankish" artist, but it could have been Bellini, who was a guest of Mehmet II in Istanbul in 1479, or Costanzo da Ferrara, a court artist at Naples who also spent time at the Porte. *Seated Scribe* is reproduced in many books about Istanbul, and if you go to the Gardner and see the real thing, you will know immediately why it is so appealing.

Şerbet

When I first encountered the word *şerbet* (or *sherbet*), I thought it was Turkish for "sorbet." But in fact it refers to a uniquely Turkish drink, which is very sweet and is meant to be diluted with ice-cold water. One tablespoon of *şerbet* is enough for one small glass. Among the excellent ethnographic displays at the Sadberk Hanım Museum is one on childbed customs, as the periods immediately before and after childbirth have a place of special importance in the customs of the Turks. After a birth, pitchers of a specially prepared *şerbet* would be sent out to relatives, close family friends, and neighbors to announce the good news. If the baby was a boy, the neck of the pitcher would be tied with a red ribbon; if it was a girl, the mouth of the pitcher was tied with red–dyed cotton gauze. In the days that followed, guests coming to offer their congratulations would be served *şerbet* in cups set in silver holders. On the seventh day after a birth, the childbed—typically a hanging cradle—would be dismantled, and the Mevlud (a poem celebrating Muhammad's birth) or passages from the Koran would be recited and *şerbet* would be passed around to the guests. The closest equivalent to *şerbet* I can think of are the Italian-style syrups (like Torani), which come in a wide range of flavors, that you mix with cold water and serve over ice.

Soccer

The Turks are nuts for Turkish football (soccer), and most follow one of the three Istanbul clubs, Beşiktaş, Galatasary, or Fenerbahçe. I found out how intense the rivalry can be when my friend Maha and I tried to buy a soccer jersey for her brother. A merchant we befriended in the Grand Bazaar asked one of his assistants to take us to a shop just outside of the bazaar where we would find a full array of all the teams' jerseys. We didn't really care about the team as much as the style of the shirt, but when our friend's associate found out we might not buy a shirt from the team *he* supported, it was clear we had made a blunder. In fact, he told us in no uncertain terms that he could not stand in the shop with us if we didn't buy a jersey representing the Galatasaray team. He then brought out his cell phone and showed us a video he'd taken when the team had recently arrived at the airport. The scene was one I'd describe as mayhem, with people screaming as at Beatles concerts, and Maha asked, "Is that a fire there in the corner?" and he proudly said it was, a celebratory fire to be exact. So we looked at all the Galatasaray shirts, since it was clear we couldn't purchase any other kind, and as it turned out none of the styles were quite right for Maha's brother so we left empty-handed. But our new friend had a big smile on his face.

London-based writer Emma Levine—author *Frommer's Istanbul Day by Day* and *A Game of Polo with a Headless Goat: And Other Bizarre Sports Discovered Across Asia* (André Deutsch, 2000)—has been avidly following Turkish soccer since 1999, when she lived in Istanbul. She told me that the most sought-after tickets are for local derbies (those between the Istanbul clubs), which might not be the best introduction to the game as the atmosphere can be pretty frenetic. For other matches, tickets usually go on sale several days in advance. The best place to get them is any outlet of Biletix, Turkey's ticketing system. Ask in your hotel for the nearest one. City center outlets include İstiklâl Kitabevi 79–81 and İstiklâl Caddesi, Beyoğlu. Ticket prices for matches vary according to popularity, but usually range from 30TL–60TL (about $25–$50).

Sokak

The Turkish word for "street," *sokak* is sometimes abbreviated as *Sk.*

T

Tanzimat

Tanzimat is an Ottoman Turkish word meaning "reorganization" or "reformation," referring to the Ottoman Empire. It refers to a period between 1839 and 1876 that was characterized by attempts to modernize. One of the most notable reforms was to integrate non-Muslims and non-Turks into society by granting them more rights. Some of the men who were responsible for this reorganization included Sultans Mahmud II and Abdülmecid, Ahmed Cevdet Pasha, Ali Pasha, and Midhat Pasha. Among the proposed reforms were to guarantee Ottoman subjects perfect security for their lives, honor, and property; introduce the first Ottoman paper banknotes; adopt an Ottoman national anthem and Ottoman national flag; reorganize the finance system according to the French model; establish the first modern university and academies; establish railroads; allow non-Muslims to become soldiers; and establish the first stock exchange.

Tulumba

Tulumba (866 885 8622 / tulumba.com) is the largest Turkish online megastore in the U.S., so if you arrive back home and can't wait for a return visit to satisfy a yen for *simit*, black Turkish tea, Turkish music, or evil-eye jewelry, Tulumba is at your service.

Tuğra

A *tuğra* was the monogram of the sultan used to authenticate imperial documents. The Metropolitan Museum of Art has in its fine Islamic collection the famous *tuğra* of Sultan Süleyman the Magnificent, dating from the mid-sixteenth century and acquired in 1938. According to Annemarie Schimmel, writing in the museum's journal on Islamic calligraphy (1992), the *tuğra* was originally used as a king's emblem, as well as a specific design at the beginning of a document drawn up by a senior official, but in Ottoman Turkey, the *tuğra* became an elaborate, highly sophisticated motif. All *tuğra*, however, consisted of "three high shafts and two ovals protruding to the left, with the names of the ruler and his ancestors in the lower center. This arrangement has been explained as representing the three middle fingers and the thumb (the prints of which formerly may have been used for signatures). However, another interpretation is that the design derives from the three standards decorated with yak tails carried by central Asian Turkish rulers in battle or in processions. Whatever the true origin, drawing and embellishing a *tuğra* was an important duty in the imperial chancelleries."

Tulips

Who knew tulips could be so fascinating? Tulips are not native to the Netherlands, as many people assume. According to historian Mike Dash, in his thoroughly engaging book *Tulipomania: The Story of the World's Most Coveted Flower and the Extraordinary Passions It Aroused* (Crown, 1999), the tulip "is a flower of the East, a child of the unimaginable vastness of central Asia." The tulip didn't reach Holland until 1570, and taxonomists believe that the world's first tulips were thriving in one of the world's least hospitable environments on earth, at a point in the mountains where China and Tibet meet Russia and Afghanistan. Dash says nearly half of the 120 known species of tulips grow wild in this forbidding terrain. Nomadic Turks encountered tulips as they moved westward, across the central Asian plateau, and by about the year 1050, tulips were held in high regard in Persia. As the garden was and remains central to the Muslim vision of paradise, after the ban on images of living things was relaxed, late in the fifteenth century, tulips were depicted often in various art forms and even graced the sultans' robes. "Of all the blooms in a Muslim garden,"

Dash writes, "the tulip was regarded as the holiest, and the Turkish passion for this flower went far beyond mere appreciation of its beauty. For the Ottomans as for the Persians, it had a tremendous symbolic importance and was literally regarded as the flower of God because in Arabic script, the letters that make up *lale*, the Turkish word for 'tulip,' are the same as those that form *Allah*."

Ottoman gardeners considered only the rose, narcissus, carnation, and hyacinth to be the equal of a tulip, and all other blooms were considered "wildflowers," cultivated only occasionally. Eventually there were as many as fifteen hundred varieties of Istanbul tulips, and the first gardeners to devote themselves wholly to tulips lived during the reign of Süleyman. (By the time of Süleyman's death, in 1566, the tulip had come to Europe's notice as many European travelers had by then visited Turkey and commented on the impressively beautiful tulips.)

Sultan Ahmed III, in the eighteenth century, "was the greatest tulip maniac known to history," according to Dash. Ahmed was bursting with enthusiasm for the flower—he'd spent the first twenty-nine years of his life locked in the cage of Topkapı, only able to *look* at tulips in the gorgeous private gardens from his window—and the tulip became the most prominent feature of his long reign. Turkish historian Ahmed Refik refers to this period as the *Lâle Devri*, the Tulip Period. Tulip mania raged on for almost three decades, and after Ahmed, the tulip began its decline. "In the end it was so complete that the whole gorgeous panoply of Istanbul tulips—all thirteen hundred varieties and more—slowly vanished from the gardens of the empire and the memories of men. Today not a single specimen survives."

Tünel

In Istanbul, *Tünel* refers to two main things: the square at the end of İstiklâl Caddesi and the neighborhood around it, which is now very trendy, and Europe's first—and shortest, at only one minute long—underground system. Godfrey Goodwin, in *Life's Episodes*, refers to Tünel as "that romantic cable car that saved one from climbing the hill up from Galata Bridge." The system was built by French engineer Henry Gavan in the late nineteenth century at the request of Sultan Abdülaziz. The wooden cars were initially used to transport animals, but then were employed to carry European diplomats and businessmen from their offices in Karaköy to their residences in Pera. The wooden cars are no longer, having been replaced by metal ones, but, as Goodwin says, they still get you up that hill if you don't want to walk.

Türbe

Türbe is the Turkish word for "tomb" or "mausoleum."

Turkish Airlines

I always recommend that travelers first look into flying the airline of their destination—it's simply another way to immerse oneself in the journey. Turkish Airlines (800 874 8875 / thy.com) celebrated its seventy-fifth anniversary in 2008, and it's a very reliable airline with friendly, helpful, and unfussy flight crews. The airline was founded in 1933 with its first international flight, Ankara-Istanbul-Athens, made in 1947. Direct flights between Istanbul and New York began in 1994, and in 2003 the airline was noted for its low number of missing bags. I've found fares on Turkish Airlines to be competitive throughout the year, so it pays to check directly with the airline when you're researching your flight options.

In April 2008, Turkish Airlines joined the Star Alliance network, allowing the airline to expand its offerings in terms of network coverage, frequent flyer benefits, etc. The Turkish Airlines Web site is particularly helpful and thorough, and one of its best features is the Flex Pricer Module. This allows online visitors to precisely define the parameters of their trips, choosing exact days of travel, cabin class, and services. With the module, passengers can quickly see how the fare changes depending on the day of the week they select. Travelers may also want to consider Turkish Airlines for destinations other than Turkey, as the airline serves nine cities in Africa, thirty-four in Europe, twenty-eight in Asia, Montreal in Canada, and twenty-two U.S. cities.

Turkish Toilets

Never set out each day without stuffing some toilet paper or tissues in your pockets or your bag, as public toilets often do not have toilet paper. Nine times out of ten, the toilets you will encounter when you're out and about are of the squat variety, sometimes referred to as Turkish toilets. Though this topic is not the most pleasant of entries in this book, it is, in my opinion, one of the most important. Most guidebooks I've read over the years have provided few details on toilet etiquette and what to expect, so I am going to offer you some tips that I wish had been offered to me.

First of all, there is no reason to be intimidated by squat toilets; in fact, I've read that relieving oneself in this fashion is actually healthier than our fashion of sitting on a toilet seat. However, handicapped visitors or anyone of any age who has difficulty squatting and standing up again will positively not be able to navigate a Turkish toilet, as there is nothing to hold on to. As I noted above, it is often likely that you will not find toilet paper inside individual stalls of squat toilets. (And by the way, this is not unique to Turkey: even when I'm in Paris, a city with quite a number of Turkish toilets, I always have tissues in my bag.) At some establishments, you will enter the washroom and there will be a few rolls of toilet paper on a stool outside of the individual stalls. You may take from these rolls, but it's better to use the paper you've remembered to bring along in your pocket, in case you need more than what you've taken from the roll.

Inside other stalls, there will be a small faucet coming out of the wall, and sometimes there will be a small plastic bucket on the floor. The bucket is for toilet paper — *do not put toilet paper in the toilet itself* due to the country's weak plumbing facilities—and the faucet is for water with which to wash your left hand. This is actually a best-case scenario. In some cases, there is no bucket for the toilet paper, and you are faced with the dilemma of what to do with the paper. I have absolutely no idea what other people do with the paper, but I simply manage to neatly and cleanly fold the paper up, put it in my pocket, and then remove it and deposit it in the washroom's trash basket. (There usually is one, and for those times there isn't, I just throw it out the next time I see one.) This seems to work reasonably well.

The next hurdle to overcome is that, though there is a sink in most washrooms, most of the time with running water, there is rarely a towel of any kind with which to dry your hands. This is why I always carry those packaged towelettes, which are also handy in general. (And you'll also have your tissues, of course.) If there is a bathroom attendant, he or she will leave you in privacy and there will be a small dish set aside for you to place a few coins. When you walk out, the attendant will quickly reappear to clean the stall and collect the coins.

You may also encounter a type of squat toilet that flushes. Typically you pull down on a cord or chain, but remember not to flush your toilet paper down the drain. Some of these flushing varieties produce quite a wave, with the water coming up over the basin (and your feet). Guard against this possibility by not flushing until you're ready to step away; then flush as you simultaneously open the door of the stall and step out.

A final note to female readers: if you can avoid scheduling your trip during the time you're menstruating, you will be infinitely more comfortable and you will thank me, as negotiating squat toilets while you have your period is a whole other ball of wax.

U

Üsküdar

Üsküdar is an Istanbul neighborhood in Asia, directly opposite the mouth of the Golden Horn. It was founded in the seventh century BC by Greeks from Megara and was known as Chrysopolis, City of Gold. For centuries it played second fiddle to its greater neighbor Chalcedon (Kadıköy, which today has "virtually no historical monuments of any great importance" according to John Freely), and was referred to by the Delphic Oracle as "the land of the blind" for its founders' inability to see the superior merits of the site of Byzantium (both Chrysopolis and Chalcedon had poor defenses and were often occupied and destroyed by invading armies while Constantinople remained impregnable). By the twelfth century, Chrysopolis was called Scutari, taken from Constantine's Scutarion Palace that was built there (neither this nor any other Byzantine building remains today).

Mahmud I built barracks on the outskirts of Üsküdar in the eighteenth century and, as more were added over the year, it became one of the main military centers of Istanbul. The large barracks on this spot today, Selimiye (named after Selim III, who tried to get rid of the Janissaries but was deposed and killed in the early 1800s) date from 1853, and they are among the most enormous barracks ever constructed. They were converted into a British military hospital in 1854 during the Crimean War, and it was here that Florence Nightingale, with thirty-eight nurses, introduced new standards of hygiene. John Freely, in the *Blue Guide*, informs us that during the first months of the war, "conditions there were so bad that the death toll reached the appalling rate of more than 20 percent of the patients admitted. . . . Before she left Istanbul, in the summer of 1856, shortly after the end of hostilities, the death rate at the two hospitals under her charge in the city [she also ministered to patients at the Kuleli military hospital] had dropped to two percent, an enormous saving in lives."

South of the Selimiye barracks is the Crimean War Cemetery, well tended and kept up by mostly British contributions. Though it is kept locked and isn't signed, a caretaker usually emerges to unlock the gate. Again to quote Freely, the principal funerary monument here "is an obelisk of grey Aberdeen granite, with an inscription in several languages by Queen Victoria paying tribute to the brave men and women who lie here, so far from home." There is also a plaque dedicated by Queen Elizabeth II, dedicated to Florence Nightingale and her staff.

V

Vakıf

Vakıf is the Turkish word referring to a religious foundation (*waqf* in Arabic) that finances the construction of a mosque or an entire *külliye* and its upkeep through the administration of shops or rented accommodation.

Vienna

Twice, in 1529 and 1683, the Turks marched into central Europe, where they were stopped at the gates of Vienna. According to Simon Millar, author of *Vienna 1683* (Osprey, 2008), Vienna was seen as a major strategic aspiration for the Ottoman Empire, "desperate for the control that city exercised over the Danube and the overland trade routes between southern and northern Europe." To Europeans, Vienna became the city where the line was drawn in the sand, so to speak—as symbolic as Poitiers, where the Moors were stopped in AD 732 by Charles Martel—so the Ottoman army set up camp outside Vienna. In *A Fez of the Heart*, Jeremy Seal notes that the encampment set down a fabulous image that has at once haunted and enthralled Christendom ever since. The camp was pitched in front of the city in the form of a huge half-moon Islamic crescent, the thirty thousand tents visibly overshadowed by those of the sultan and his grand vizier, which were covered in hangings of richest tissue, colored green and striped with gold. Gold too, great knobs of solid gold, were the pinnacles above their tents, while carpets, cushions, and divans within were studded with jewels. Deep inside was a sanctuary housing the sacred standard of the Prophet as well as baths, fountains, flower gardens, and menageries. At the entrance, five hundred archers of the royal guard kept watch while thousands of turbaned infantrymen and black eunuchs passed among the field harems and their concubines, the Ottoman military kitchens filled with bejeweled silverware, the Turkish baths and bedrooms filled with priceless satins and velvets.

Needless to say, it was quite different on the other side of the walls. After the final, fifteen-hour battle, the Viennese were victorious. Philippa Scott, in *Turkish Delights*, tells us that the magnificent Ottoman tented city was captured and distributed after the siege ended.

Villages

Some cities around the world, such as New York, have been described as cities of individual neighborhoods. Istanbul, according to Anthony Weller in *Gourmet* (December 1988), was originally all villages. He explains that each village had a mosque, and some villages had baths, fountains, markets, and schools. Most were defined simply by families who shared common trade, origin, or religion. In 1871 in the old city, there were 321 such districts: 284 were Muslim, the rest Greek, Armenian, and Jewish. Today in Istanbul, these village outlines remain. "They make evident the central paradox of Istanbul: Although it has been one of the world's great cities since ancient times, its people are rural by nature, not urban. They live in cloistered neighborhoods and covet the Anatolian country life of their grandfathers. Relentlessly each street, each block, each corner becomes a village with no center but itself, so that life is lived in a European city in the style of nomadic Asia. The Bosporus runs through their souls."

W

Walls

I don't remember when I became consciously aware that I loved stone walls, but I know I have admired them for a long time. Actually, I love stone in general—whether smooth or rough; whether a building, walkway, tower, stairway, archway, bridge, aqueduct (and Istanbul has a stunning one, the Valens Aqueduct, built by Emperor Valens in AD 368, which carried water for fifteen centuries—up until the late nineteenth century—to a central cistern near Beyazit Square), whatever.

Readers who've been to Dubrovnik know that it is one of the world's supreme stone cities. The evening *passeggiata* there, on marble that has known so many footsteps and has been worn so smooth, is an impressive ritual. When my husband and I were there, we met another American, Dave, who was actually earning a master's degree studying the history of medieval stone walls. I was a bit jealous—it had never occurred to me I could study such a subject—but I quickly realized our good fortune in meeting him. I sure do wish he'd joined us in Istanbul, where the walls aren't quite as well preserved, but are still awe-inspiring. Istanbul's walls "form one of the most impressive monuments of the city, extending in a great arc, seven kilometers long, from the Sea of Marmara to the Golden Horn," notes Jane Taylor in *Imperial Istanbul*.

It's not difficult to understand, then, why many people would want to restore the walls. But the current restoration work has been cause for alarm among many of those same people. In an article entitled "Istanbul in Peril," which appeared in *Cornucopia*, John Julius Norwich describes the restoration as by turns "grotesque," "a tragedy," and "devastation." He refers to the walls as "the most majestic urban rampart in the world," and he refers to the restoration by saying, "Instead of leaving them to tell their epic story as they did so movingly in the past, the authorities have cheapened them, prettified them, and turned them into something little better than a Hollywood film set."

You may judge for yourself when you see the walls, but I don't mind allowing Norwich to have the last word. In *A Short History of Byzantium*, he reminds us that the Byzantines were human like the rest of us, deserving of praise and of blame much as we are ourselves:

> Much should surely be forgiven for the beauty they left behind them and the heroism with which they and their last brave Emperor met their end, in one of those glorious epics of world history that has passed into legend and is remembered with equal pride by victors and vanquished alike. That is why five and a half centuries later, throughout the Greek world, Tuesday is still believed to be the unluckiest day of the week; why the Turkish flag still depicts not a crescent but a waning moon, reminding us that the moon was in its last quarter when Constantinople finally fell; and why, excepting only the Great Church of St. Sophia itself, it is the Land Walls—broken, battered, but still marching from sea to sea—that stand as the city's grandest and most tragic monument.

Whirling Dervishes

The Mevlana Sufi order is a leading mystical brotherhood of Islam founded by Rumi, whose full name—Mevlana Jalaluddin Rumi—means "love and ecstatic flight into the infinite." Rumi was born in 1207 in present-day Afghanistan (then a part of Persia) to a family of theologians. The family fled the Mongol invasion and eventually settled in Konya, which was at that time part of the Seljuk Empire. By the time Rumi was twenty-four years old, he was already an accomplished religious scholar. He wrote a six-volume masterwork called the *Masnavi*, which is a mix of fables, scenes from daily life, Koranic verses, and metaphysics. Rumi believed in the use of music, poetry, and dancing as a path to God, and for him, music helped followers to focus their whole being on the divine; he believed in doing this so intensely that the soul was both destroyed and resurrected. From this passionate belief the practice of whirling dervishes developed into a ritual form. *Mevlevi* refers to the whirling dervishes and the *sema* is the dervishes' sacred "turning" dance. See my Web site for much more background on the dervishes, and note that there are several different Mevlevi groups that whirl on different days in Istanbul. Tom Brosnahan's Web site (turkeytravelplanner.com) details them and includes information on how to buy tickets.

Wine

Jancis Robinson, in *The Oxford Companion to Wine*, notes that archaeological finds support the theory that wine was produced near Mount Ararat—part of the region most closely identified with the origins of viticulture—at least six thousand years ago. Today Turkey is one of the world's top growers of grapes (though most are destined for table grapes or raisins) and the country has the fourth-largest vineyard area in the world. Atatürk founded the country's first winery in seven centuries in 1925 as part of his modernizing program, and in recent years Turkish producers have been focusing on higher-quality wines. I am a big believer in "what grows together, goes together," and I wouldn't dream of drinking anything but Turkish wine when I'm in Turkey. Three of the biggest names you'll see on store shelves and on restaurant menus are Tekel (the state-owned company), Kavaklıdere, and Doluca. I have tried them all, plus many others, and they are unequivocally terrific partners with Turkish food (and a few are perfectly great aperitifs all by themselves).

A great and atmospheric place to try some Turkish wines is Viktor Levi, a wine bar (*şarap evi*) that dates from 1914 (Hamalbasi Caddesi 8A, Galatasaray / +90 212 249 6085 / viktorlevisarapevi .com. In 1999 the bar was restored to its former glory. Viktor Levi pours special Turkish wines, a few imports, and some of its own label (I am partial to No. 59, but I also like Viktor Levi Red and Viktor Levi White); there are good hot and cold *mezes*, plus non-alcoholic drinks. There aren't many more pleasant places to stop for a break than this.

X

The letter *x* does not exist in Turkish, though it does in Greek. I could find no reference to a single historic site, still standing or completely destroyed, in Istanbul beginning with the letter *x*, though John Freely, in the *Blue Guide: Istanbul*, briefly mentions Xenophon and the survivors of the Ten Thousand, who arrived in Byzantium on the last stage of their memorable march back from the heart of Persia in 401 BC. "Xenophon and his men were treated so inhospitably by the Byzantines that they took control of the town and threatened to sack it, leaving only after they had exacted a large bribe from the city council." Xenophon recounted the journey in his famous work, *Anabasis*.

Y

Yok

According to Eric Lawlor, in *Travels with Osman*, *yok* is much more than a word. "While intended to discourage, the extent of that discouragement depends entirely on the way it is uttered. A *yok* can be nothing more than a demurral, albeit a firm one. Or it can be a door slammed in your face. A *yok* can mean 'I'm sorry,' and it can also mean 'drop dead.' You can't appeal a *yok*. A *yok* is final. Categorical. Unambiguous." And Jan Morris, in her *Rolling Stone* essay "City of Yok," relates that "the favorite epithet of Istanbul seems to be *yok*. I don't speak Turkish, but *yok* appears to be a sort of general-purpose discouragement, to imply that (for instance) it can't be done, she isn't home, the shop's shut, the train's left, take it or leave it, you can't come this way or there's no good making a fuss about it, that's the way it is."

Z

Zeytin

Zeytin is the Turkish word for olive, and *zeytinyağlı yemekler* refers to an entire class of *mezes*, olive oil dishes typically served cold. According to an article by Tom Mueller in *The New Yorker* ("Slip-

pery Business," August 13, 2007), a lot of olive oil produced in Turkey is shipped to Italy and later sold as Italian oil. Mueller relates how, between 1998 and 2004, an olive oil company called Casa Olearia "evaded more than twenty-two million euros (about thirty million dollars) in E.U. duties by illegally importing seventeen thousand tons of Turkish and Tunisian olive oil, apparently with the cooperation of Italian customs officials."

There are olive groves all over Turkey, even in the far eastern part of the country where, according to Lonely Planet's *World Food:Turkey*, "olives are not a favourite food and lard has prevailed as a cooking fat, the fields are dotted with these dusty-looking scraggly trees." With so many groves, you might think there would be an abundance of shops selling all kinds of olive oil–based products. They are surprisingly few, but among the best (and my favorite) is Laleli, a family-owned company with an attractive boutique in Bebek (Cevdetpaşa Caddesi 46D / +90 212 265 6617 / lalelioliveoil.com). The family's groves are around the Edremit Bay region in the Aegean, across from the island of Lesvos. "Turkish olives, Turkish oil, and a Turkish name," is how Laleli was described to me by one of the shop's friendly associates. The distinctive shop—with a bright white exterior and a beautiful chandelier of little glass bottles of olive oil inside—offers the full range of Laleli oils, which include extra virgin, early harvest, oil for cooking, classic olive oil, flavored oils, and Antik, my favorite—it's made from the oil of very old trees and comes in a bottle shaped like an amphora. Wonderful soaps, a few vinegars, and olives are available—the olives come in jars or in vaccumsealed packages—as well as attractive olive motif items. Tastings are encouraged, and Laleli has been honored with numerous awards, including a gold medal at the Los Angeles International Extra Virgin Olive Oil 2008 Competition. Mail orders are happily filled.

ACKNOWLEDGEMENTS

A book of any type requires the efforts of a staggering number of people, but an anthology requires even more. The likelihood is great, therefore, that I am forgetting the names of some people who helped create this finished book, and I can only hope that they will understand and forgive me. Enormous thanks most assuredly must go to Vintage publisher Anne Messitte, who was an early champion of *The Collected Traveler* sixteen years ago and who is *almost* single-handedly responsible for the series landing at Vintage Books. "Almost" because the support of Editor-in-Chief LuAnn Walther has been incalculable, not only because she embraced the books, but also because she turned this manuscript over to Diana Secker Tesdell, a gifted editor who is, serendipitously, a fellow Turkey enthusiast. In all my dreams I could not have conceived of a more perfect editor. Other talented colleagues in the extended Vintage family who diligently helped shape this book include Kathy Hourigan, Florence Lui, Roz Parr, Russell Perreault, Andrea Robinson, Irena Vukov-Kendes, Lisa Weinert, and freelance designer Jo Anne Metsch.

Teşekkür ederim to Tom Brosnahan, Gamze Artaman, Berrin Torolsan, John Scott, Ömer Eymen, Susan Ginsburg, Nabi Israfil, Mahir at the Turkish Tourist Office, and Cem Ongen and Marietta Mancuso at Turkish Airlines. Sincere thanks to each of the individual writers, agents, and permissions representatives for various publishers and periodicals without whose cooperation and generosity there would be nothing to publish. Extra special thanks to traveling companions and friends Maha Khalil, Arlene Lasagna, Amy Myer, and photographer Peggy Harrison, with whom I've come a long way since first working for WXAM-FM and WHSV-TV in Virginia. I am deeply grateful to Chip Gibson, my wonderful boss and mentor, who has graciously given me great latitude to work on this book. And finally, thanks to my husband, Jeff, and our daughter, Alyssa, who was recently told by a fortune-teller that she would live abroad and travel the world.

PERMISSIONS ACKNOWLEDGMENTS

ABOUT THE AUTHOR

Barrie Kerper is an avid traveler and reader who has lived abroad. She has over a thousand books in her home library—and an even greater number of file clippings—and has filled up three passports.